MISSION
OF
THE JEWS

Translated from French
MISSION DES JUIFS
Triomphe d'Israel
(1884)

High Antiquity of Judeo-Christian Tradition

"One of the main purposes of this book is to prove that Judeo-Christian intellectual and social esoterism is rightly the continuation, the fulfillment, of the whole antique theosophical tradition, of which the two Testaments have made us inheritors".

A. Saint-Yves d'Alveydre

This volume **Mission of the Jews** is a translation of a book published in 1884 by Alexandre Saint-Yves d'Alveydre (1842-1909) under the title **Mission des Juifs**. The translators have only added a short foreword and a chronological synopsis. To our knowledge this is the first translation from French into English. It is presented as written, without any commentaries or notes, thus reproducing precisely the original work of Saint-Yves d'Alveydre.

The same exact translation of the original book has been published with abundant notes and contextualizing commentaries under the title **The Golden Thread of World History**. That volume is underlining the universal scope of the book regarding Ancient Advanced Worldwide Civilizations of which modern Religions, Sciences and Societies are inheritors. That version aims at presenting the modern reader with new data not accessible at the time of the first publishing (1884).

MISSION
OF
THE JEWS

ALEXANDRE SAINT-YVES D'ALVEYDRE
Mission des Juifs – Triomphe d'Israel

translation and commentaries by
SIMHA SERAYA & ALBERT HALDANE

Manakael ●
MasterWorks

MISSION OF THE JEWS
TRANSLATED FROM FRENCH MISSION DES JUIFS
BY SIMHA SERAYA AND ALBERT HALDANE
FOREWORD AND CHRONOLOGICAL SYNOPSIS
BY SIMHA SERAYA AND ALBERT HALDANE

For information contact Publishing Management:
MANAKAEL MASTERWORKS INC
E-mail: archangel7997@gmail.com

Categories: Keywords
World History – Archeology -Anthropology – Political Science
Linguistics, Universal Language.
Philosophy, Religion, Spirituality, Mythology.
Hebrew Bible -Urantia Book.
Judeo-Christianity.
Old Testament, New Testament, Exodus, Genesis.
Celestial visitors, Annu Naki, Elohim.
History of Humanity, Egypt, Mesopotamia, Israel, Judea, India, China, Japan, Americas
Ram, Rama, Adam, Eve, Fo Hi, Christna, Zoroaster, Abram, Abraham, Melchizedek,
Moses, Orpheus, Jesus.

First Edition

ISBN: 978-0-9837102-7-1

Printed in the United States of America

Cover design by BUZBOOKS

Shekel Coin on page IV: Picture by Albert Haldane

This book lifts many of the veils which have long prevented a better understanding of the depth of Human History. And the author, in this tome, as well as in all others he produced, always remains faithful to the noble goal of uncovering and sharing Truth.

During his life in France (1842-1909), which he entirely dedicated to the propagation of his scientific, historical, linguistical and theological relentless research, Saint-Yves has inspired and encouraged countless authentic truth seekers.

Unfortunately, but not unexpectedly, amid the social turmoil and wars erupting in Europe at the beginning of the 20th Century, the meaning of his words has been distorted, his ideas grotesquely biased by ignorant politicized pseudo intellectuals for blatant self-serving purposes. The traces of those distortions can still be found, here and there, like persisting stains on a white cloth. The reader is warned.

FOREWORD

Alexandre Saint Yves, Marquis d'Alveydre (1842-1909) published this book under the title *Mission des Juifs* in 1884. The original French opus has since been reprinted several times in France, but, to our knowledge, was never translated into English until now, 2018 AD.

Our Providential encounter with the book in Paris

This book fell into our hands early in our life, while browsing in a bookstore in the Quartier Latin in Paris, a year before earning our post graduate degrees at the Sorbonne University.

The first reading has been informative, instructive, clarifying, illuminative, and yes, enlightening! We read it at different times of our intellectual journey, and the resulting illumination never diminished. Furthermore, while translating the French opus, assiduously seeking the finest English words to reproduce Saint-Yves' exact thoughts, our enlightenment even increased.

Your Providential encounter with this book.

As it has done for us, Providence placed this book in your hands, and we have no doubt you will experience a similar, possibly higher, degree of enlightenment.

World History

In this book the spotlight is deliberately directed by the author on post diluvian civilizations, meaning the successive dominant civilizations rebuilt and developed by the descendants of survivors of the latest destructive flood on Earth, locally resorbed 10,500 years ago.

Although the author alludes to even more ancient prediluvian nations, his narrative proper describes the major civilizing

Cycles starting 8,750 years before our time (2018 BC), on all continents on Earth, from East to West, from one Pole to the other.

The Golden Thread.

Thanks to his vast erudition, Saint-Yves is pointing at multiple monuments, artifacts, documents, leading us to perceive the lively thread linking the successive major civilizations and their heroic founders: Ram (or Rama), Abram, Moses, Orpheus, etc.

Simultaneously Saint-Yves teaches us how to discern the fundamental Celestial Spiritual Principles and Cosmic Laws, which positively sustain all terrestrial manifestations, material and societal.

All along his book Saint-Yves provides the reader with precious and precise information in regard with Sciences, Applied Arts, Educational methods and eternal Principles necessary for sustaining harmonious Social organizations, as well as the "Integral Science" passed on by ancient civilizations, worldwide, since millennia.

He tirelessly encourages us to share his intellectual efforts at perceiving the profound and essential Truths often concealed since centuries.

Cyclical Crises

Classicist investigator and impeccable teacher Saint-Yves illumes all the founding Principles of Harmonious Civilizations. He also reveals the Fundamental roots and causes of their cyclical disruption and turmoil, thus allowing the readers to recognize the striking similitudes with the no less destructive forces at play today everywhere.

Endowed with such knowledge and awareness modern citizens can confidently conceive effective crises resolutions to heal the contemporary forms of divisiveness and disharmony affecting their personal life, their intellectual, moral, spiritual standing, their social transactions, their nation, and planet Earth itself.

III

Conclusion

Now, ourselves, we do not hesitate to make a prediction: with each reading, veils will dissolve before the eyes of your conscience; a thread, until then invisible, will emerge from darkness, reveal its light, and transmute into a Golden Thread.

Then, seeing more clearly into the faraway Past, you will better Understand your Present Time, and will be well equipped, mentally and morally, to trace a path into the Future of humankind.

SIMHA SERAYA & ALBERT HALDANE
December 2018, South Florida

MISSION
OF
THE JEWS

First Published in 1884 AD
by Alexandre Saint-Yves d'Alveydre

In French as:

Mission des Juifs
Triomphe D'Israel

The 13 Chapter Titles, as well as the entire Text, have been faithfully translated from the original French opus.

All the Subtitles inside each chapter, have been created by the translators, most often using the author's own words.

Foreword and Synopsis have been added by the Translators.

Picture on page IV:
Shekel Coin of modern Israel displaying symbols of Ram's trinitarian governance.

VI

MISSION OF THE JEWS
CONTENTS

CHAPTER I
MODERN SCIENCE AND THE OLD TESTAMENT

AGE OF THE UNIVERSE – AGE OF EARTH

It cannot be denied: a profound, irremediable antagonism exists between the discoveries of modern science and the fundamental concepts of theology, between modern scientific findings and the chronology of Genesis as ascribed to Moses in the common translations of his testimonies: Vulgate, Septuagint, Targums, Samaritan Version.

The age of the Universe, or even the age of our planet Earth, may not be misconstrued at will; and, when confronted by science, religious education has the duty to urgently make great and indispensable intellectual efforts to decently tackle the topic of Creation.

Modern science, and by this word I mean, the totality of the physical and natural sciences, has rather unintentionally, given back to Earth and to the World, to Humankind and to God, their true magnitude, by breaking "the bed of Procust" where the notion of Cosmos and His Creator was curbed by prudence on one hand, and on the other hand by the dogmatic ignorance of the interpreters of Moses.

Natural sciences, Astronomy and Geology, credit to Earth alone an almost incalculable old age.

Today's (1884 AD) Human Sciences, Archeology, Philology, Anthropology, applying their investigations to History, claim the birth of terrestrial Humanity to be more than ten times beyond the 6,000 years assigned to the age of the entire Universe by the interpreters of Moses.

THE ORIGINS OF HUMANS

Moreover, all these sciences, or at least all their factual findings, disprove the paradisiac point of origin of physical Humanity on this Earth as being the unique and perfect origin imparted by these same interpreters to the advent of the corporeal humans on our Planet.

On the contrary, these sciences relate the material birth of humans on the various Continents as extremely gloomy and drowned, so to speak, constrained by the rigorous paths of its Fate-Destiny.

They show us these humans existing in the most rudimentary state of a latent Principle, stifled in a patent germ, and evolving only under the reaction of the physical environment in accordance with the laws of Time and Space.

They assert that these proto-humans, barely emerging from an earlier Animality, bearing its mark, as do, to this day, the anthropophagi in the physical order, and, as do today the "flesh-eaters" of the social order, meaning our current governments, on which the Beast continues to imprint this tendency to devour each other, like the worst animal species.

So that these modern scientific data are highly evocative of Sankoniathon's ancient teachings and of the first degrees of the Ionian Mysteries of Sidon, Tyr, and Ephesus.

These modern and ancient Ionian sciences both assert that elementary Nature, created nature, evolves according to an ascending progression, - which contradicts the current religious dogma of the Fall – both asserting that Nature processes only by creating sporadically corporeal individuals, thus progressing from Physical Diversity to intelligible Unity, and not from Unity to Diversity.

According to modern science, from a purely rational viewpoint, the humanity of flesh and bones, without taking into account its adjunct intelligible universal, cosmogonic Principle, appeared on several successive Continents, not perfect but as imperfect as possible, wild, naked, almost mute, cannibalistic, almost an animal in the devouring cycle of Animality, and having, on this terrible Earth, no other visible allies than giant dogs and colossal elephants.

And yet, even primeval, painfully emerging under rigorous intransigent laws of "created Nature", Humankind was, in principle, what it is today: in full development, perfectible, able to achieve Perfection itself, but, starting from the most rudimentary stage of Perfectibility.

Yet it was already coming out of Animality, directed by its specific natural forms, the signs and symbols of its adjunct cosmogonic Principle, encompassing its ontological faculties.

Such are the indestructible data that natural sciences and human sciences have developed since the rationalist impetus of Francis Bacon and the methodical regulation of Descartes.

Such were the teachings on the subject of our natural origins by the *religious scholars of antiquity*, by *Orpheus* and the Eumolpids, in the Mysteries of Delphi and Eleusis, by *Sankoniathon* in the Mysteries of Tyr, and finally by the whole school of the sanctuaries stamped with the feminine mark, passed on to us by the Yonijas of India.

MODERN SCIENCE VS BIBLE TESTIMONY

That body of knowledge is, apparently, in complete antagonism with the Genesis narrative the common vulgar translations lend to the ten cosmogonic chapters of Moses.

I do not wish to amplify the formidable doubt generated by this contradiction, though it is one of the main impediments to the coherence of the contemporary human spirit and of science itself, or, if you will, to the synthesis of sciences.

I found myself facing this daunting antagonism, which places our religious Tradition in opposition with observation and sensorial experience, tearing apart the traditional Teaching Authority, striking all divine sciences out of individual intelligences which only armed with weak, insufficient translations-interpretations of Moses' books, are powerless, unable to defend themselves adequately.

The terrible precision weapons the various physical and natural sciences employ, require in the other camp- the religious- the *same exactness, the same intellectual and moral conscience*, in order to reconnect itself to the general Education network, thus recovering its Authority on this Earth.

THE BATTLE OF FAITH VS SCIENCE

Basically, against the Church, against the Synagogue, against the Mosque, the scientific and academic forces are fighting with powerful artillery, to which the theologians continue to oppose tubes of glass and projectiles of papier mâché.

"Do not investigate, say the directors of consciences, *lest you lose your faith by examination!"*

-Not solid, then, this faith!

-What faith? and what is Faith?

To this, the most orthodox thinkers respond with St. Thomas Aquinas:

"Faith is the Courage of the Spirit, who rushes resolutely forward, sure to find the Truth."

Let us, therefore, courageously dive into the great battle of ideas, confident that our faith will lead us to Certitude, if we know how to heed accurately the teachings of the divine Founders of our Religion and our Society.

Now it is up to the lay people to have the courage to enter the battle, as long as the priesthood, sound asleep and helpless, for various reasons, do not know how to lift the veil which robs them of the marvels of Shem's tabernacles, that is to say the colossal Universal Science, embedded within the 50 chapters of Moses' Sepher and its social significance, which Jesus has restored to the entire Human Race.

The troubled conscience of the multitudes watches attentively the struggle of the two factions of Education, or at least its apparent consequences, which are the political antagonism of the naturalistic militants facing the religious activists, some pushing for the nominal Republic, the others for the Monarchy, all leading to arbitrary governance: Caesarism.

THE GRAVEST PROBLEM OF OUR TIME

As the strength of the facts and large battalions of followers seem to grow indefinitely in the camp of science, as new discoveries fill the arsenals of applied science, the popular flock is confusedly moving towards those whom it believes to be the strongest, and Naturalistic philosophy tends more and more to predominate and promote its antisocial policy from top to bottom, in a day-to-day sectarianism, and in the perpetual self-interest masquerading as beneficial opportunism.

This is the gravest problem of our time, and it is from the

depths of this Dyarchy of the human spirit that all anarchies derive.

But let no one assume that such a divisiveness can be solved in an arbitrary way.

The resolution may be attained only through the *intellectual Authority of the Total and Integral Truth,* in which all truths can be reconciled; this requires a functional hierarchy and a harmonious synthesis, in both dimensions, sensorial and intelligible.

It is by no means my intention to diminish, in any way, all the irrefutable truths modern sciences have accumulated, nor to equal those sciences with the sectarian inferences which natural philosophers have thought possible to draw and which are by no means as logical deductions as they pretend them to be.

Indeed, it is a patient, methodical, loyal investigative work, free from any ulterior motive of political domination, which has been achieved by the modern scholars in perceiving the underlying laws of Nature.

But the half-baked philosophical scribes drew and continue to draw inferences from those scientific discoveries, with the intent to elaborate an anti-religious doctrine challenging all religions. Those rationalist dogmatic philosophers are doing a work unhealthier, more arbitrary, than any Talmudist or sectarian Christian theologian have ever done to true religious knowledge.

RELIGIOUS INTELLECTUAL DESERTION

This deceitful insufficient criticism is shattering the wholeness of the Heavenly Human Higher Intelligence, the wholeness of all Universal Principles, the Universal Ideas, and generous cosmic Ideals.

It is this unhealthy disintegrating purpose which, once again, inspires the Politics of short-sighted Expediency, from the top down, and gives way to the Instinct of the Beast which presides over all the anarchies, dragging us to final ruin.

Oh! If the ideologue sophists and politicians, statesmen or demagogues, had respectfully studied the Social dynamics, as deeply as the scientists in their Institutes study and respect the dust we are trampling on, the air we breathe, the drop of water, its little world of infusoria, and the microbes, all would be well.

Then Moses and Jesus would appear in their true light, and their fulfilled Promise would shine through the whole spiritual Body of Humanity liberated from false politics, thus reorganized under three distinctive social authorities functioning in harmonious interactive Unity.

THE SCIENCE OF THE SPIRIT

On the other hand, if, since the sixteenth century, with the same intensity as their naturalists challengers, the theologians had endeavored to use St. Thomas Aquinas' beautiful definition of Faith, if *researching within the Scriptures the text unadulterated by the translators*, they had, in both Testaments, sought, pursued, lovingly embraced, *the other side of Reality*, the Creative Nature, the Science of Spirit, meaning the religious Truth, or in other terms, the Religious Synthesis, then, the Unity of the Universal Knowledge and Teaching, the Highest Authority, would have reemerged, tiara on the forehead, sole shepherd of a unified flock.

But on this issue of the Science of the Spirit, as in many others, singular deviations occurred in the teaching institutions.

While the *priesthoods slumbered on the literal translations of the sacred texts*, they abandoned the core true teaching, without following it through with enlightened Higher Thoughts and Intelligent mediation; therefore, all over Christendom, the public mind is opened wide, not to the descending Higher Light but only to the light from below, to the bold facts and laws defining only Created Nature.

Now, these gleams and sparkles of natural science will blind the entire Social Order with an infernal red glow, devouring everything on its path as long as the sacred Luminous Synthetic Tradition does not come back to us from above.

Though, this synthesis is far from easy, and it requires, from the Judeo-Christian ministries, a singular openness, not only of intelligence and inclusiveness, but above all of open-heartedness and tolerance.

It is very difficult today to maintain the ancient distinction of the middle ages between the *clerics*, those who received the light, the *clergy*, the enlightening agency, *the lay people*, plebeians of the spirit, the *laity*, the plebe of Knowledge.

Galileo, Newton, Pascal, Lavoisier, Cuvier, all the Fathers of modern science, all the legions of their disciples alive or dead, can scarcely be considered as mere *laymen* in the old sense of the word; for Religion means Synthesis, and *all scientific truth has its rightful place in the Integral Truth*, and must have this place de facto in any religion synthesis aiming at a positive social efficacy.

JUDEO-CHRISTIAN HIGHER SCIENCE

Either Moses, then Jesus, have or have not sufficiently armed the synagogues and churches they have raised up for the momentous upcoming ideological battle, leading to the great peace of the Holy Ghost and Truth.

If they have, it is necessary to remove the veil which, in the Jerusalem Temple, was torn at the death of Christ, and, resolutely*, proceed to the deep examination of the ancient Mysteries*, and that is what I do in this book.

In the second case, if they have not, it is urgent to raise up our arms to Heaven, and to pray the Invisible Powers to send a revelation which completes those of Moses and Jesus.

In any event, we must discern and respect, in them as well as in us, the integral cosmic Truth, and dare recognize its immense worth. We must interconnect Humankind's intellectual mindal and moral good with the Real Plan of The Universe, as it is revealed, and the Social Ideal Order, as it is willed to occur.

Now, in writing my *Missions*, fulfilling my duty as a religious and social missionary, I do not pretend to operate as innovator, but as the humblest disciple of both Jesus and Moses.

I am confident the facts and Truth revealed to Humankind by Moses and Jesus, supreme authorities of the Judeo-Christian Social Order, must have in themselves the hidden intrinsic force of the Ultimate Truth, and of Living Spirit, for without it our Society would have already collapsed, to be completely transformed and reorganized around another form of religion.

They are making a profound error those who, in the name of philosophical doubt, saw only the rational, mechanical side of the social issues, ignoring their organic facets; and, following Montesquieu, they have regarded Judeo-Christianity as powerless to intellectually define and virtually organize its Promise of a relatively ideal Social Order. From this source of superficial thoughts, the encyclopedic School has produced a torrent and the French Revolution a deluge, attempting to do away with the implementation of the two Testaments in Science and in Social Life.

CHILDISH TRANSLATIONS OF THE SACRED VERB

After the vain war against the childish translations of the sacred Verb, and against the most superficial exoteric aspects of Judeo-Christianity, they thought they had wrecked the architectural plan of the Kingdom of God, and demolished everything, hoping to rebuild on a clean slate, only by way of sensory experimentalism and instinctive naturalism.

The *French Revolution* has only been useful at unclogging and liquidating the social congestion; however, it has produced in the intellectual order a new sectarianism, much more crude, despotic and depressing than the old.

This official administrative machine, called University, built for producing mediocrity, has become the new Bastille of this new dominant sectarianism, which itself, as was the old system, is lacking a new vibrant Synthesis.

However, in vain will we search for that Synthesis outside the *esoteric* Tradition of the two Testaments.

Let us examine why the French Revolution has erred in regard to fundamental principles, and we shall see later, in the course of this book, how Christianity alone, sustained by Moses' teachings, has sufficient authority and quality to intellectually give birth and bring to completion a new profound Revolution, this time by renewing the Social fabric, all over the world.

UNBALANCED SOCIAL ORDER

Here is how the secular Encyclopedists, the French Revolutionists and all their resulting naturalistic doctrines are fundamentally and radically self-deceived, not regarding the Civil Order and its common law, but concerning the foundation of a new Principled Social Order and the establishment of a constitution associating three distinctive concordant powers.

To fight with any serious chance of winning against the Social Spirit of Moses and Jesus, the sophists philosophers and the politicians should have, at the least, sought in naturalism itself, their own coherent principles, their neo-religious connection, their social specification.

From their point of view, which is that of an overthrown Catholicism, they could not see that their secular Revolution was to be, bottom line, only a transitory upshot of Judeo-Christianity unfolding around itself.

Admittedly, this Revolution has its dignity, its usefulness in many aspects; it is generating for the nation of France essential organic benefits, and in a continuance sui generis within the European collectivities which have not experienced, like France, the brutal dissolving, the more or less efficient eroding of the political powers based on arbitrary principles.

But in the logic of naturalistic philosophies, of sensory rationalism, of Voltairean sectarianism, the revolutionists could only find some measure of equilibrium based on a principle from below, for they had overthrown the social pyramid, condemning the nation to walk on its head and hands. To their new cult the revolutionaries kept from the old Theogony only:

1- the terrestrial face of the Truth, Created Nature, they named Goddess Reason, "Deesse Raison".

2- the Supreme Being, an adjunct presented as a Celestial Essence, cosmologic Supreme Power, though entirely Intelligible to the human mind. This Supreme Being was de facto subjugated by the Goddess Reason which was invoked and celebrated at the altar of the material physical order.

For, in fine, they had summoned vengeful thunderbolts, a travesty of Moses' Jehovah, who decrees only a list of the rights, but not of the duties of Humankind, contrary to the genuine Jehovah who wanted and wants the integral execution of the Promise of His Kingdom as illuminated in the two Testaments, by Israel and by Christianity, united for the same purpose.

Therefore, it's not within the Higher Intelligible Essence, but within the sensorial Substance of beings that they found a safeguard for the rights of Humans, so placing their newly concocted Decalogue under the authority of a naturalist Ionian genesis.

It had become necessary, at the risk of being mistaken, to push the intellectual and moral conscience of this sectarianism to the end of its logic, and it was not to the Father, it was to the Mother, it was not to God, but to Created Nature, to Cybele, to Mother Earth, that the revolutionary agents erected new temples and altars.

SOCIAL BALANCE IN DANGER

But then, from top to bottom of the national organism, Priesthood, Sovereignty, Authority, Power, sword and hand of Justice, family and social powers, it would have been necessary to change everything radically, putting everywhere the man in the background, the woman in front, as it was at the origin of the Keltic Race and Druidic worship.

Now, if it has not come to pass, if, at such a solemn and tragic moment of history, in a revolutionary storm so massive its convulsions equaled it to a new civil genesis; if then a woman did not receive the inspiration necessary to run to Notre Dame, to go up to the altar, and to proclaim this radical change of worship, of principle and of social direction, it is because the Son of Mary, the Galilean, is the Master to all, our true theocrat, leading us from above towards the realization of the Promise, as I have myself sufficiently proved in *the Mission of the Sovereigns* and in *the Workers' Mission.*

SOCIAL HARMONY IS OF DIVINE ESSENCE

Likewise, Moses cannot be seen to be an ignorant or imposter, for Death does not give birth to Life; and that's what this book will prove superabundantly, I hope.

To summarize, *there is therefore a whole other aspect of Truth, of Science, of Life,* of the Way open to individuals or collectivities, an aspect inversely proportional, but absolutely *concordant* with the purely natural, physical, rational, sensory, of this same Truth, of this same Science, of this same Life, and of this same Universal Way.

The Judeo-Christian tradition, revisited in its scientific, esoteric spirit, responds precisely and entirely to this immense desideratum. Before bringing it to consciousness and conquering the intelligent consensus of the reader, I will take as the crow flies, a synoptic view of current knowledge.

From this height, one can glimpse from below the unbelievable altitude of *Science and Wisdom that the inspiration of Moses had reached in the temples of Egypt and Ethiopia.*

His book of Principles (7 days of Genesis) and ensuing forty chapters, which are commonly taken for a physical creation, are in fact erecting the intellectual pyramid, whose *true hierophant came to us as Jesus Christ.*

∞

CHAPTER II
ESSENCE AND SUBSTANCE OF THE UNIVERSE

LIMITATIONS OF MODERN SCIENCE

Essence corresponds to the *Intelligible* Realm, and *Substance* corresponds to the *Sensorial* world; together they sum up the *integral parallelism of the two aspects of Science.*

In the present state of knowledge, the whole essential and living side of the Universe and its Beings is patently ignored, while the substance of reality is studied with a precision that depicts, in details, the material levers of the Cosmos; conversely, the Soul and the Spirit are ignored, while, from top to bottom, they incessantly self-animate, preserve and transform the Cosmos, in a perpetual action, multiple in form, one as to the Principle.

Whatever may have been said on this subject, analysis always precedes the synthesis in the intellectual categorizations of Societies; only later synthesis is made, once the cloak of the sacred texts is lifted, showing clearly the universal goal toward which the Providence was secretly leading the peoples, until the time when, by exercising their supreme free will, they manifest their conscious intelligent adhesion to the Way.

In its powerful advance, the positivism of the human mind has not a single path, as some schools believe, it has three main ones.

The lowest path *juxtaposes,* without correlating them, the observed facts, the developed experiences, the approximated laws, all of which often keep a rather arbitrary relation between the observer-experimenter and the observed-experienced reality. We are, at present, still at this primary level of secondary sciences education. (1880 AD)

Physics, Chemistry, Physiology, Anatomy, Astronomy, Geology, etc., etc., all the current nomenclatures of scientific particular facts remain to be coordinated with each other, so that, from the study of their mutual relations, their reciprocal convertibility, the real Science can be born. At this step Science will be attaining the secondary degree, which deserves the name of *comparative science.*

But this comparative step, once attained, leads itself to a third, that in turn deserves the name of *superlative* or superior, which leaning on the whole classed and judged sensorial Order, defines *the other side of realities and beings,* the Earth, the Universe, the Intelligible.

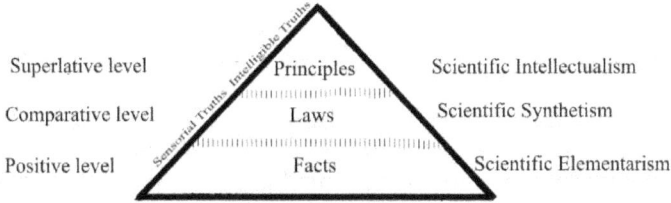

Superlative level	Principles	Scientific Intellectualism
Comparative level	Laws	Scientific Synthetism
Positive level	Facts	Scientific Elementarism

Physical life, in which the rational faculty alone can only lock us up, without allowing us to assess its core value, *is a form a delusion* as much as a relative reality, which do not carry its own authority or its own elucidation.

To all the mystics of the Rational mind, materialists or spiritualists, life is a dream; and one can only escape when reaching the plane of pure Intelligence.

THE SCIENCE OF THE SOUL

But Higher Intelligence can only free its total and specific energy if, being in control of the physical order, armed with its specific sciences and methodologies, it consciously takes charge of the Universal Truth, which is always entirely accessible to it.

Upon reaching this depth of Science, Intelligence is becoming Religion, for it achieves full scientific synthesis, and, through worshipping and rites, it can authorize, enlighten, absolutely vivify the social organization in its entirety.

The human sensory perceptions and the ensuing reasonings, are not direct in their progress; they are all reflexes, inverted.

Mental reflection alone, inner act of the psychological energy and intellectual light, is in perpetual need to straighten out and dominate perceptions and their exoteric causality; furthermore, it needs to constantly create new perceptions in order to continually surpass the limits imposed by our physical organs to the unlimited radiation of our will.

For example: we do not feel the diurnal gravitation of the Earth, let alone its two other movements, one annual, the other cyclical. Our reflexive material senses feel neither the dash of the Globe, which exceeds 100,000 kilometers per hour, nor its jolts, or, if you will, its irregular oscillations.

In our ordinary physical state, we do not sense whether steel is magnetized or not, nor do we feel the intimate relation that makes terrestrial magnetism, heat, electricity, which manifest as atmospheric agents of this living force and which the ancients called *Aether*, Soul of the world, *Jesus* called *Spirit of God*, *Moses* called *Rouah Ælohim*, the *Brahmans* to this day call *Akasa*.

Unless related to this essential force, no one can through sensory organs, differentiate a wire in which is running an intense galvanic current from an ordinary wire: nor can one perceive the magnetic action of a thermo-electric device, even less the special aura of every mineral, every metal, every plant, every animal. For a person of flesh and blood, at least for its sensory organs, the specific nature of Life and its inherent forces, be they physical or biological, are indeed pure occultism, or, if you will, occlusion.

To understand these realities in their essence, the *superior faculty of the Soul,* so aptly named Intelligence, at certain ancient epochs, with the assistance of the Divine Will, has created means of observation and experience, methods of investigation and control, devised more precise senses than human's own sensory organs. In our actual present time, instruments for chemical and physics research, are but a limited number of the much larger array *obtained and operated by our remote ancestors.*

RATIO MATTER-SPIRIT IN OUR SOLAR SYSTEM

This chapter is expressly aimed at exploring the relation and the proportion existing in the Universe between intelligible

Life and its sensory supports, between the Essence and its substantialized forms of beings and things.

It is possible to form a clear idea of these relations, at least as far as our Solar System is concerned, in the same manner other beings would in their own solar system.

To comprehend that, one can do what follows: Calculating the average distance between the Sun and the most proximate fixed Stars, we will obtain the radius and diameter defining the extent of the biological action of the Solar Light.

Once this diameter is known, the capacity of this organic Sphere in the Cosmos will be easy to determine. So much for the Space and volume of our Solar System. It remains for us to calculate how much space the condensed substance, improperly called Matter, occupies in our Solar System.

Between Substance and Matter there is this enormous difference: Matter is properly speaking a caput mortuum, worthless remains, temporary inter-cyclic, inter-organic, resulting from a previous biological work.

As soon as Life, the Essence of things, reintegrates this matter in its cyclical operations, it organizes it, transmuting it into substance.

It is therefore rightly that all the ancient scholars of the sacerdotal tradition said that Matter does not exist, that it is a pure illusion of the senses, a Maya destined to never be, destined to be constantly transformed, perpetually submitted to new intelligible forms, in which prevails this *Universal Essence, which we call Life.*

But, back to our calculations. The attraction of the Planets between themselves as well as the attraction of the Sun vis-à-vis the Planets give the means to calculate their total weight.

We can therefore determine, with a rather rigorous precision, the relationship that exists between the sphere of freedom, the life of our solar system and the substance that constitutes necessity, mutability, apparent support.

From this calculation, which everyone can control, it

follows that a cubic meter of solar living Space, corresponds to the thousandth part of a milligram of substance vivified or not.

This amounts to saying that condensed ponderable substance, is equivalent in the World to a sub-multiple of weight so imperceptible to our most precise scales that, atmospheric air, and even absolutely dry and pure hydrogen, are extremely heavy bodies in comparison.

What is true for our Tourbillon is also true, in the whole Universe, for all Solar Systems which expand in the Infinite Space, like swarming molecules designing their total orbit around a common center, which the ancient Sages placed in the Constellation of Aries. Substance properly so called, including Matter, is not even a physical Unit in the Universe, but hardly an infinitesimal sub-multiple.

Life - invisible to the eyes of flesh - with all its Divine Mystery which is *accessible only to pure Intelligence*, fills alone the unlimited Space, which is itself enveloped and vivified by an impenetrable and ineffable Absolute.

SCIENTIFIC STUDY OF INTELLIGENCE AND SOUL

The foregoing data result from my long and careful study of our present knowledge, interpreted in the light of an absolute Religious ideal, meaning ignited by a true spirit transcendentally scientific, eternally alive, the like with which *Moses* wrote his first 50 chapters of Genesis, in hermetic Egyptian, in ideographic hierograms.

If the *hierarchy of sensory forces* - wrongly named physical - from terrestrial magnetism to solar light, is sustained by such a minuscule divisible substance, what is to prevent us from thinking that this already admirable reverse is hiding a more magnificent face.

Who and what could prevent us from acknowledging that, *above, below, beyond, within*, there is *another cognizant hierarchy of animating Powers*, giving to all beings and things, the Essence, the Force, the Substance, the Faculties of manifestation?

We may as well posit that above this hierarchy there is yet

another third, that of the Principles, Forms, Faculties, not of the created beings, but of *the Being of beings*, of the intelligible Universe, of the Sovereign of all kingdoms, and finally of that what the ancients *called Creating Nature, Isis, Urania, eternal Wisdom, the Verb*, etc. ...?

What could prevent us from acknowledging that this third hierarchy, pure Intelligence, this Superior Nature, is *Providence*, the living confidante of the Living God, with whom every religion establishes more or less exactly, more or less saintly, more or less truly, the concordance of Societies, the communion of Intelligences and of human Souls?

Finally, what could prevent us to acknowledge that, radiating from the center of this triple sphere, containing the universe without being limited by it, *the Ineffable Supreme Being and Form*, live in Eternity and Infinity, in an inaccessible Creative Union, even more absolute than Unity?

MOSES: AN EGYPTIAN SCIENTIST

This hierarchical quaternary, each level with its exact principles, may be revealed by deciphering the 50 hermetic chapters of *Moses' Sepher Torah*.

This divine man, in addition to his direct inspiration, had received the supreme initiation in the temples of Egypt and Ethiopia, where he had communication of the ancient scientific traditions, which the oldest civilizations of this globe have bequeathed, from cycle to cycle, from priesthood to priesthood.

This *quadruple hierarchy of Truths*, of realities, and consequently of sciences, is positively signified within the name of four letters which *Moses* gives to the unchanging aspect of Divinity, to the Divine Structure of the whole Universe, *mysterious tetragrammaton* whose keys have not been totally delivered in writing.

Here is how, in the sanctuaries of Thebes, secretly behind closed doors, it was answered, to that algebraic eternal X:

What is Truth?

X

The answer was: **I, E, V, E,** and the initiator was explaining geometrically the answer as follows:

I God   Theogonic Sciences
E Universe   Cosmogonic Sciences
V Mankind   Androgenic Sciences
E Earth   Physiological Sciences

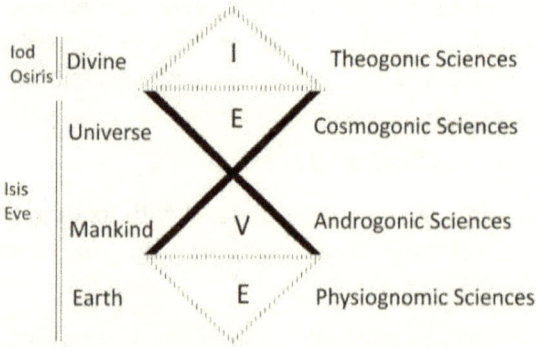

Iod Osiris	Divine	I	Theogonic Sciences
	Universe	E	Cosmogonic Sciences
Isis Eve	Mankind	V	Androgonic Sciences
	Earth	E	Physiognomic Sciences

It is this Mystery that *Jesus* evokes, in His profound prayer, when he says, "*Be your Name sanctified!*", including the Social Order, the collective and individual humankind.

On this Name, on this Hierogrammatic Schema, there would still be many things to say, but I must here confine myself to the ancient Synthesis of Sciences.

VITAL ALLIANCE OF SCIENCE AND RELIGION

In summary, starting from the physical sciences of our time, we have indicated that, in the Universe, the Earth, the plastic substance, divisible, accessible to our sensory perceptions, was infinitesimal, almost nil, with respect to the living space that encloses it.

We have suggested that above the forces currently studied in our universities, there may be others, as real, though inaccessible to the senses alone, but that, *in a very remote antiquity, Sciences* have exactly discerned, cultivated, ranked according to their essence.

We have affirmed and presently affirm, that *Jesus Christ* possessed this ineffable, integral Science, the same that *Moses* had received from learned priesthood combined with divine personal inspiration.

Moreover, we showed that *Moses* entrusted the Principles of this complete Science in the text of his cosmogony hermetically encrypted in the Egyptian way.

The above-mentioned data in this chapter should suffice to entice two feebly scientific mysticisms of our time - the vague materialism and the vague spiritualism - to combine in a genuine synthesis. However, this Synthesis, in human Intelligence and in the Essence of things may take place only when animated by the Universal Life, which is also the true Way of the Spirit.

The preceding notions do not detract from the strength of our current scientific state; on the contrary, they confirm it, they authorize it in all its present and future developments.

But let us return for a moment to the fact that in every renascent civilization, as in ours since Francis Bacon, human intelligence proceeds from analysis to synthesis, from the positive or elementary degree, to the comparative.

The children learn words before expressing ideas, classify the sensorial forms which surround them, before dominating these symbols through intelligence, and positioning each of them at their exact place in the set of things they know of.

In brief, in our times, as in all the ages of Humanity, the Knowledge of visible things is the pedestal of that of the invisible, the Science of the perceivable elements is the precise foundation on which rises that of the Intelligible Universals.

That is why modern scholars are raising, without knowing it, to the Religion of Moses and Jesus the only pedestal that becomes it. On this pedestal renewed Religion will appear in its true height, in its true light.

Without the physical, chemical, natural, mathematical sciences, without the requirements that their methods and their exact concepts give to the intellectual and moral conscience of the secular world, from one end of the Earth to the other, neither the Talmud, nor Christian theology, could ever lift the sacred veils, the shrouds which still envelop the dazzling Truth, the Divinity of Universal and Social Life.

It is therefore from the very heart of modern science that one must come to the aid of ancient Science - true Osiris asleep in the Amenti - and it is up to the lay Intelligence, addressing the sacerdotal Intelligence, to liberate the true Spirit enclosed in the sacred texts, to proclaim piously, but strongly: *Lazarus! Lazarus! stand up!*

Conversely, even when fully conscious of the presence of the Living Spirit revealed by the antique trinitarian synthesis, modern science and its body of savants unaided by the sacerdotal corps, cannot achieve the noble goal they must pursue: trinitarian hierarchy of knowledges, trinitarian concordance of realities, encompassing together *the integral Truth*, the *revelation of the Divine within Humankind's Social Order*.

This mutual connection, without amalgamation, this reciprocal animation of secular and religious teachings is indispensable to the very existence of the entire Judeo-Christian Society.

This mutual connection founded on Moses' Cosmogony and Christ's Social Promise – once instated firmly thanks to the first High Council, which I have named Council of Education - will allow the re-establishment of the Social Authority definitely separated from political power proper.

SEPARATION OF AUTHORITY FROM POWER

I ask the reader to refer to the chapter on definitions, which I have put in the first pages of the book Mission of the Sovereigns.

The capital difference between the *Authority* and the *Power* is for the first time clearly posited. At the present time the Authority, though feeble, though not clearly instituted, resides in whosoever teaches anyone anything useful, the first of the scholars and the last of the mothers, in the first of the religious or lay doctors and in the last of the humble priests, pastors, popes, rabbis or village pedagogues.

It is this vague feeling of rightful authority, even imperfectly formulated in the conscience of the sincere revolutionist, that makes him/her stand up, for the honor of the whole Human race, against the arbitrary Powers which attempt to trample upon the genuine natural Authority.

Having sufficiently proved that I was not a savage revolutionary, I feel I have the right to rise against the Arbitrariness which subjugates Authentic Authority, by masquerading it as administrative officialdom and governmental Powers.

To reconcile all the teachings in one and the same Council of Education and Public Education is to restore the Authority on its eternal bases, consequently restoring to the Political Power the Arbitral control and the authorization which it lacks.

The Muslims, through Muhammad, have rather received the legendary tradition of Talmud than the tight chain of initiations that has come to us from the temples of Kaldea and Egypt, through the Abramids, Moses and Jesus Christ.

UNDERSTANDING THE ANCIENT SACRED SCRIPTURES

For our two communions, Israel and Christendom, the peace fostered by the diverse Teaching Institutions, their reformation in the same Council, in the same Social Power, would be the cornerstone of the grand edification, contained in principle in the two Testaments and in their same Promise of a Reign as perfect as possible.

That is why I have, in the two previous missions, indicated the necessity of conforming to the religious Tradition, by reconstituting the three great Social Orders, of which I have just recalled the first, and whose *organic concordance* constitutes this form of free and synthetic government, which I have called Synarchy.

I hope I have shown in this chapter, by placing in the reader's hand the infinitely small weight of the material universe, that it is not in this infinitesimal sub-manifold that the "Principles of Life" of the beings must be sought, individual or collective.

I hope I have proved *that ancient scholars have had very serious reasons to consider Science in a more complete way than we do today.*

The sacred books of this long ago past still in our hands are - if and when we know how to read them - an irrefutable testimony of this ancient Science. Among us Judeo-Christians, the Kaldeo-Egyptian Cosmogony of *Moses* is the keystone of the total rebuilding of the Truth; this cornerstone supports the Decalogue, the Prophets, the Gospel, the Promise, as well the Talmud and the Al-Coran.

Furthermore, on this same cornerstone, lean back all the truths and all Truth of the social cycles and civilizations prior to Moses and the Abramids.

Lifting from above the first veils covering Moses' Cosmogony, will illuminate at once the Intelligence of the entire terrestrial Social Order, and, reviving the antique Unity, bringing back the Great Peace to the World.

Light calms fire, Intelligence soothes the passions and the devouring instincts.

If, in the name of Moses and God, we maintain the cloak of ignorance, the intellectual night on the Universe, on Judeo-Christendom, and through it, on the whole Earth, it amounts to authorize everywhere the mutual dissociation of all political fanaticisms; it equals to let rule the nocturnal animals, the personal governments or popular tyrannies; then will supervene the worst instincts, the worst passions, all the international wars, all the civil wars.

So, *sursum corda! Hearts up!* in the name of *Moses*, in the name of *Jesus*, in the name of the Living Spirit who alone fills the Universe, and, sure of victory, let us leap into the fray, with the olive branch in hand.

CHAPTER III
ESSENCE AND SUBSTANCE OF BEINGS
AND OF TERRESTRIAL ELEMENTS

INSTABILITY OF DENSE BODIES ON EARTH

After having shown the infinitely small proportion of the ponderable substance in relation to the Life that fills the Space in the Universe, I wish to lead the reader to understand how *unstable* are the apparently *"densest bodies"* on Earth, and, moreover I want to bring to light the *double aspect of Science and Truth*.

Physical, chemical, electrical fires transform the solid and cohesive state of the hardest metals. Molten solid gold emits subtle vapors that can gild a piece of silver; and yet, after twenty-four hours of melting in a graphite crucible, gold will have lost none of its weight. But bring to a few thousand degrees the physical heat or its equivalents: there is no molecular constitution, subject to gravity, that will not reduce to imponderable atoms, not only gold, but platinum, chromium, rhodium, iridium, etc.

All deep underground plutonian rocks were once imponderable, then gaseous, then liquid, before serving as a solid base for minerals and underwater Neptunian terrain, from the Cambrian to the Alluvial era. The most resistant bodies, the most static, so to speak, are also the least dynamic: a small quantity of powder of fulminate, of fulmicotton, of dynamite, blows up a block of basalt rock.

HIGHER BEINGS INHABIT OUR SOLAR SYSTEM

The Sun, which, by the radiant breath of its light, by the propulsion of its biological energy, hunts, rotates and attracts all the Planets, vivifies and defines the qualities of all that they contain, is relatively less ponderous than phosphorus.

The *Higher Beings* who inhabit the central Star of our Tourbillon are certainly almost without weight, however their intellectual, animistic, instinctive senses, are all the more direct and highly more puissant than those human organs are endowed with.

TEMPLES WERE SUPERIOR UNIVERSITIES

In the ancient temples, the studies on the divisible Substance, which we improperly call Matter, had been advanced to a point barely imaginable today.

Long before the Roman republic, Moskoush, whom we call Moscus, taught at Tyr the doctrine of atomicity, as in the other sanctuaries long before him.

Moreover, the old erudite bodies, who then were the priesthoods and the lay Initiates, had made such a thorough study of the *Forces, Powers, Essences, and Cosmogonic Principles*, that it would require, not a chapter or a book, but an entire library to expound upon.

In the next chapter I will solely indicate the most ordinary, the most exoteric points of the following subject: *Sciences in Antiquity*.

It was all these sciences which, from degree to degree, had led the priesthoods to the notion of this indivisible Substance and this pure Spirit, which we *call Creative Nature and God*.

If beyond simple and inorganic elements we consider the organized beings we see with our eyes, it will be easier for us to make the reader grasp the double object of Science.

It is common knowledge today, that within the visible terrestrial substance of plants and animals only ten elements remain stable after incineration, while ninety vaporize. It all comes down to a very small number of elements occupying a very small place in the molecular hierarchy.

Among gaseous substances: oxygen, hydrogen, carbon, nitrogen. Among solid substances: phosphorus, sulfur, silicon, sodium, potassium, calcium combined with a little fluorine.

Such are all the typical molecules - so far ascertained - the Earth delivers to and takes back from the individuals of the two so-called organic Regnum, *more truly defined as organized from above*.

NATURE AND HYPERNATURE

From the chemical viewpoint, if we ignore the *Intelligible Order,* that is to say, the specific, invisible universal Powers of Life and the combinations they produce according to the environmental circumstances, it is impossible not only to distinguish the vegetal individual from the animal individual, but even to perceive something other than metalloids or metals.

Yet these individuals are certainly something else; for they manifest essences, forms, faculties, cosmogonic concordances, distinctly specified by biological Powers I deem *acting from above,* through reproduction and visible germs, while their Universal Principles remain imperceptible to human senses.

Manifesting within the physical life of living beings, whence does the force of specification come from?

Natural sciences give answers in their own domain; but they can only reach and reveal the sensorial beginnings, certainly not the *intelligible Principles,* in short, the *true origin* of the existing individual, the germ, the medium of incubation.

But these germs and these milieus will never deliver to the analysis of chemists anything they did not themselves borrow from the physical Earth, that is to say those same simple elements, animated, and combined by Universal Puissances existing beyond the flesh and bone of humans, imperceptible to the common senses.

The real origin of primordial germs therefore remains a latent truth, and, for research, a question which belongs only to pure Intelligence.

These primordial germs, whose Principles reside elsewhere than on Earth alone, here below are present in a state of divisions and submultiples, manifestations of an intelligible Unity, an animating Power, invisible, belonging not to Earth, but to our Solar System and, through it, to the whole Kosmos.

These germs, composed of the same chemical elements, are reproducing, through the plastic faculty of maternal milieus, a hundred thousand types of plants, two hundred thousand distinct types of animals.

Whence is the Force coming, which, through the biological cycles of the life of this Globe, has specified, and specifies these seeds, transient receptacles of a permanent Force, passing on divisional varieties of the Higher invisible, indivisible, Unique Species, which manifests into individual visible multiple discrete identities?

Vainly would we attempt to find this specifying force in the Sexes of the individual bodies or in the whole Ancestry up to the first individuals, or in the total Plastic Substance up to the first Plasma which manifested in the Oceans and on the Earth as soon as the temperature and all the other vital conditions of the Planet have allowed for it.

ANCIENT SCIENCES SUPERIOR TO MODERN SCIENCES

Thus, we understand we can only discern the virtual division of Life, the temporal transmission of the Higher Force and the cosmogonic Powers which constituted, and still constitute, the physical scale of beings; in other terms we clearly discern only the biological low point of our planet.

Yes, *the essences, the types of all beings, reside elsewhere than in the mortal individuals, who refract them* here below in their multiplicity of forms, or, in other words, in their divisional form.

This ontological and cosmogonic issue in itself only would require the complete reconstitution of several sciences in order to illuminate intellectually, from top to bottom, and to bring back to their true meaning, to their real ideography, botany, zoology, anthropology and all related topics.

In vain would we expect to receive the synthetic Truth and intrinsic reality on these issues, while questioning only the physical, chemical, natural sciences.

Anatomy will tell us the apparent forms of these beings, physiology will tell their patent functions, their most grossly obvious organic faculties, chemistry will tell what the Earth has lent to these beings, and how they have transformed it by assimilating it under the influence of unknown forces: all this data is a great deal for barbarians to grasp, I admit, but is little for real civilized peoples.

None of these purely nomenclated sciences will reveal to us the *Intelligence, the Divine Essence which reside in us*, neither the living essential Idea, the occult faculties, the probable benefits, nor the actual relationships expressed by these corporeal appearances, signatures of some Thing behind, and even more of some One beyond.

THE GREAT BOOK OF THE DEAD

In vain shall we ask dead bodies to expose what living bodies themselves cannot reveal to our physical eyes; in vain shall we question the material Globe, leafing through earth strata, like through the heavy pages of the grand Book of Life; each page has taken millions of years to open up to the Sun, to the Moon, to the Stars, to the entire Kosmos, leaving afterward their physical traces, skeletal hieroglyphs of the ancient beings.

The mammoths, the ten-meter-tall behemoths, the five-meter-long Brazilian lion, the twenty eight meter-tall felis smilodon, the diornis bird as big as an elephant, the ornitichnithès, a still more colossal bird, judging by its strides of three meters, all those beings who have returned to the invisible are but signatures of their indestructible celestial Species, the symbols of the biological and purely intelligible Powers of the Cosmos.

The horse is there, on this terrestrial leaflet, lying nearby the gigantic dog; and humans lived there too, as witnessed by the traces of burning fires in these hills, and by those colossal bones in caves still known today to some Asian archeologists.

Let's open this dark leaflet of the great Book of the dead. Here are six-meter-long turtles, twenty-five-foot crocodiles, swan-necked iguanodons, forty-meter long lizards, plesiosaurs, and pterodactyl dragons, of which Apollonius of Thyane still saw the last degenerate representatives in the Caucasus.

Noteworthy: the monkey is there, witnessed by that skeleton found in the London-Clay of Suffolk, at 52 ° north latitude; therefore, humankind was not far away.

Here are whales, thirty feet below the soil of Antwerp; and here again in Norway, three hundred feet above sea level.

MINUSCULE MASONS OF THE EARTH

Let us go down to the bottom of the issue, cross the coal strata, go to the primitive pages, to the oldest sedimentary rocks, discard palms, giant bamboos, gigantic reeds, colossal ferns, reach the simplest beings, those who have bloomed within the first breath, the first kiss given from Earth to Heaven, after each deluge.

Here, in the palm of my hand, is a little carbonate lime, a little siliceous earth. This represents the work, the effort of a thousand million humble little creatures, their mortal remains, the result of their energy, their heavenly motto, signifying the task they accomplished here below.

As numerous as the Stars of Heaven, they were the masons of the Earth; they, the tiny ones, worked in the mountains; peaceful atoms of the sea, they were the associates of the terrible subterranean fire, in the construction of the Alps, the Cordilleras, the Himalayas, the Caucasus.

They surrounded the bareness of the Plutonian Earth with a belt of rocks and massive terrains; they made a garb for the Giant, stocking it for millions of years, with heaps of their microscopic cuirasses.

They built the basements that support us, the stones of the cities that shelter us, the plaster that binds them, the lime that coalesces them.

Humble symbols of Peace and Labor, they did more to build the foundation of the Land of the Living than all the carnivorous barons of the seas, of the rivers or forests, more than sharks, gavials and roaring monsters.

Dead, they dazzle the eyes through the microscope by the beauty and the infinite variety of their geometrical forms, they challenge calculation by their innumerable multitude.

Living, their vital power and resilience are still a more magical wonder.

ONLY PURE INTELLIGENCE CAN FATHOM LIFE

How were they born? How are they born? No natural history can say it.

For the naturalist, whether he examines the infusoria or recomposes the leopard of the plaster of Montmartre or the human skeleton of Ventimiglia, the issue of Life is unfathomable, insoluble.

The origin of the ephemeral insect is as mysterious as that of the eagle; and the fly has not more revealed the Occult, of which it testifies, than the condor or the ciron (mite) more than the fifteen-foot lion, which was jumping in Brazil, thirty or forty thousand years ago.

The life of myriads of indomitable beings, teeming in a cubic millimeter, in a grain of oceanic protoplasm, or in a drop of storm rain, is a miracle no more explicable to the sensory observation than the incalculable masses of mammoths found in the frigid regions of the North Pole or Siberia.

Life is no more understandable, with our current methods, than the heaps of enormous carnivores, hastening, confused in the same madness of terror, pell-mell with the leaping herbivores, throngs of souls and terrorized flesh, under the universal hallalis of hunters' waves; terrified beings rushing under the whip of lightnings, winds, rains, creeping foams, far from the forests, far from the plains; dashing assault on the mountains among the thousand times reverberated echoes of thunderbolts and abysses, and vainly rushing toward the caves, where the destructive mass of the seas came, thundering upon them.

Generation may be effected by sexes, or by buds, or by split, the ancestry be double male and female, or the individual split in two, or a right side joined to a left side, a left side to weld to a right side, one must agree again, *the transmitted vital force remains occult*, as well as the Powers it represents.

Only pure Intelligence, correlating methodically sensible phenomena, may-under the aspect of universal ideas-distinguish immaterial forms, the biological Puissances at play, and give them the names of Kingdoms, Genera, Species, etc.

As for the transformism theory, useful as a clock and calendar of transformation of vegetables and animals, and as a geo-anatomical chronometer, it proves only one thing, but it certainly proves it: the visible repercussion of Life on our Planet has been ascending toward humankind.

But transformism does not invalidate, on the contrary, that the percussion of the plastic Earth by the *Celestial Puissances* was made, invisibly for any eye of flesh, and according to a descending process, going from the Universe to the Earth, from the Universal to the particular.

These two contrasting motions, ascendance and descendance, can only be *concordant*.

It is a childish argumentation to claim the primitive cell, the monad, the monere, the organic matter had, in the beginning, the faculty of spontaneously producing Organicity, without any other intervention.

In the realm of chemistry, there is no organic substance, there are only bodies, organized under the influence of an operation which emanates from transmitted internal forces, or from external forces as first creative and sustaining cause.

Whence came the force which vivified the first cell, the first monad, and through it the primitive sarcode/protoplasm?

Whether it is inside or outside the plasma, *the reproductive Puissance is*, and that's all that can be said.

DESCENDING PUISSANCE AND ASCENDING EMERGENCE

But without resorting to other proofs, it is absurd to admit that the Earth, an integral part of a Solar System, can engender anything without the help of the Life of that system.

So, there is a cosmogonic Truth and necessarily a science corresponding to this Truth.

In brief, whether that Science applies to the hierarchical chain of existences, an ascending chain from its terrestrial origins, Flora and Fauna up to Humankind, whether it applies to the chain descending from its celestial Principles, its solar Puissances, its intelligible Kingdoms, until occurs the emergence of those same sentient creatures, *Science again, has two faces, two aspects inversely proportional and necessarily concordant.*

One must turn to Ontology, a branch of Cosmogony, in order to acquire the knowledge of all transmitted life.

It is Cosmogony that must be questioned about the celestial transmission of Life operated by the Universe on any given Solar system or Planet.

Mechanical cosmography will never suffice to affirm the association of the human Spirit with its living source, which is *Life, Intelligence, universal Spirit.*

Alone Physical chemistry and anatomy, even decorated with the name of physiology, will not help the Sage and the Savant to reflect, understand and master their possible empire over the perfectible essence of Beings and things; nor will physiology help them acquire the *psychurgic and theurgic operative power*, that the ancient priests and the ancient Initiates possessed, *by association with the Higher Hierarchies of the Universe.*

LIFE PRODUCES ONLY LIFE, NOT DEATH

It remains for me to bring to awareness, that death is only apparent, whether it devours successively the divisible substance of individuals, whether it attacks them collectively, such as during cataclysms by Water, Atmospheric, Volcanic disasters, or attacks on the entire Globe.

If, at the present time, and this is more than probable, a Planet similar to ours, at the same rank in any solar System, crosses the ages we have traversed before the last 6 deluges, it is necessarily the theater of the same celestial actions, the same terrestrial phenomena, which manifested themselves on our Globe and at the same period of their existence.

So, it is clear, the Reigns are immortal, and therefore so is their entire Intellectual Constitution, up to and including the Essence of the Individual.

This is what the savant priesthood of the civilized world was teaching more than 10,000 years ago.

ESOTERIC COSMOLOGY: MOSES, ORPHEUS, PYTHAGORAS

Pythagoras, who drew his doctrine from the sanctuaries of Africa and Asia, depositories of these traditions, thus expresses himself, according to the ancient Science called Thaot: *"You will know, if Providence wills it, that Nature is everywhere similar."*

Before *Pythagoras, Moses* and *Orpheus* received the same information in the same centers of knowledge.

SCIENCE AND RELIGION: NECESSARY ALLIANCE

I have yet something to say regarding the age that modern science assigns to the Earth, while comparing the chronology presented in the commonly translated Bible, with the chronology of the geologists; as loyally, I intend to demonstrate to scientists the truth of the esoteric Cosmogony present in the Scriptures, strong foundation of the religious tradition, so justifying the *necessity of an alliance between Science and Religion.*

According to the geologists, the solidification of the first plutonian underground layers of the Globe would have begun 300 million years ago, at the Poles, where the seas still agglomerate today as mountains of ice.

This cooling would have lasted for thousands of centuries, the solid polar layers collapsing while sailing on the ocean of fire toward the equator, and deep currents rolling their flames towards the Poles. The future mass of solid and liquid substances, Neptunian islands, and seas, was entirely comprised in the fully dilated atmosphere. Each one can do, if interested, the calculation of this dilation.

One has only to take a table of equivalents, calculate the ratio of the volume of a molecule of water to that of a molecule of vapor, and continue the mathematical analogy up to rhodium and iridium.

These *principles, known to all antiquity*, have nowhere been better described than by *Moses*, in his *ideographic text*, hermetically written by him, in the Kaldeo-Egyptian manner.

The construction of the Neptunian layers took several tens of millions of years, perhaps 100 million: Cambrian, Silurian, Devonian, calcareous, coal, Permian, Triassic, Liassic, Jurassic, etc. up to the molasse group, the diluvian and alluvial terrain.

If we only consider the coal formation, the calculations give enormous figures.

Since the fine series of works inaugurated by Chevandier, Cotta, Dechen, etc., we conclude that the formation of every meter of coal took an average of 20 thousand years and estimate more than 10 million years elapsed since the formation of coal. This real antiquity of the Earth was *well known to the learned savants long before Moses*, from Etruria and Egypt to India and to the ancient Continents now partly gone.

The sacerdotal Etruscan savants measured the great cosmic and terrestrial revolutions in six immense periods, according to the ancient Egyptian data.

It is to calculate exactly these Periods in the past and in the future, that the *scientists of India, inheritors of the science of the Rutas* (Atlanteans of the Egyptians and the Reds of America), had astronomically regulated the Kalpa to 4,320,000,000 years, and the Maha-Youg 4,320,000 Earth years.

The *Chinese* also base their *genethliac science* on the Cycles they received from Hindu, Tibetan, Kaldean, Egyptian sanctuaries; but they reduced them, as a decimal submultiple, to the so-called Kaldean Cycle: 432,000 Earth years.

The Egyptians started from those same bases, whose unity was a Revolution of the fixed Stars, which they calculated to be 36,000 terrestrial years. Considering the following numbers,

36,000
432,000
4,320,000
4,320,000,000

it will be easily noticed that they *come only from the same set of calculations and therefore from the same sources*.

In fact, the Egyptian cyclic Revolution of the fixed Stars is exactly the twelfth part of that of the Kaldeans and the Chinese, $36,000 \times 12 = 432,000$, and the one hundred and twentieth part of the Maha-Youg of the Hindus.

This Revolution of the Fixed Stars represented an hour or a month, either of the Universe, or of a single solar Tourbillon.

This hour of 36,000 years, multiplied by 12, gave its first cycle of 432,000 terrestrial years:

The Maha-Youg was the decade of this cosmogonic day or cosmogonic year, namely:

432,000 x 10 = 4,320,000

The Kalpa represented 1,000 divine decades, or 4,320,000,000 terrestrial years, therefore 10,000 hours, 10,000 days or 10,000 years *of the Universal Being*, according to the cosmogonic object of observation.

As far as the Earth is concerned, the same proportional measure was applied in the Maha-Youg to the various Manous, to the various inter-diluvian Cycles and to the cosmic Reigns that preside over them. Having ignored these data, *common translators entirely misrepresented the time periods* of the Yougs of the Brahmans, the Sares of the Kaldeans, the Sethics of the Egyptians, the Shandas, and the Yemei of Moses, etc.

THE SAVANT TEMPLES OF HIGH ANTIQUITY

Being a reflection of the Universe, the ancient temples possessed scientific doctrines, other information than the stupidities now credited to them.

As for the Science of which I speak at this moment, without revealing it entirely, it was a state secret, in Europe, in Africa, in Asia, in the former Southern Hemisphere of which America is a debris, as it is still to this day in some countries of the Far East.

It is to honor this Science that the observatory towers were raised not far from the altars, the crypts, and subterranean passages; it *was upon this Science the worship was regulated,* during the public festivals of the cities and the countryside, through the rites of the domestic hearths.

This science, like all others of a certain order, was transmitted only to the wise.

Hermes, Porphyry, Origen, Jamblicus, Diodorus, Plutarch, Livy, Aulu Gelle, Damis, Philostratus, and many others are unanimous on this subject.

As for the modern authors who laughed at this ancient

Genethliac science, either they did not know of it, or they judged it from the foolishness of the Middle Ages, as if one wanted to understand chemistry and astrology of the ancients by reading simplistic stories like the "Cassette of the little peasant" and consulting the hyperboles of false occultism such as the "Petit Albert" and the "Red man of the Tuileries".

On the subject of the four *Times or Seasons* which succeed each other on Earth, from one deluge to another, in this organic Cycle which Hindu Science called Manu, here is, in its purity, the ancient Tradition, different from the current interpretation of the Brahmans who misrepresent it and reverse their chronological order. The *worst Season is the first*, the one that *immediately follows each deluge*. It is the Satya-Youg, the era of Seth of the Egyptians, Saturn of the Etruscans and Greeks, the age of stone, lead and iron, the era of Shiva.

Then comes the *second Season*, the Tetra-Youg, the age of Brahma, Horus, Iao, IEVE, Jupiter, Times of the renaissance of Social Life: religious initiation, taming of animal species, appropriation of habitable lands, reinvention of Sciences and applied technical Arts; it is the age of bronze.

Then *the third Season*, the Douapar-Youg, brings a regularization, a systematic extension of the previous period; it is the time of great planetary works, the containment of rivers, the boring of isthmuses, the construction of highways, aqueducts, etc.; it is the age of feminine initiation, of the natural sciences, of applied technical arts advanced to the extreme, of Saravasti, Isis, Ceres, the silver age.

Finally, *the last age,* the golden age, opening now for humankind, is the Kali-Youg, season of great spiritual harvest, great crops of all social goods, Vishnu, Osiris, the time of fulfillment of all the Sacred Promises, of the Total Science, of the Constitution of a Universal Alliance among all the Cults and all the Societies of the Earth. The Hindu savants called *"Manu"*, the *intelligent heavenly Puissance*, who, *from one deluge to another*, presided over the evolution of the four ages of this Cycle.

They ascertained the total duration of terrestrial Humanity

should be 14 Manus, that is 168,000 years, a Period equaling to 4 fixed star Revolutions plus 2 Manus, according to their calculations and those of the Egyptians.

According to them, we have reached the Seventh Manu of the fourth Age, Kali Yuga, the Golden Age, which would give terrestrial Humanity an antiquity of 80,000 years, through 6 past deluges.

MORAL CAUSES OF RECURRENT DELUGES

The *Cause* that ancient priests assigned to deluges was *astronomical and geological*, both *correlated to universal moral* Causes.

The temples' savants had asserted that the physical law at the origin of deluges was the shift of Earth's magnetic axis, the successive rise and lowering of each Pole, causing a sudden rupture of equilibrium in the underground fire, the seas and the atmosphere. In this regard, unexpected discoveries would be made by digging the underground of some lands such as the Sahara, Greater Tartary, and, above all, what remains of the Austral Continent.

There is a great deal of attention to be paid to certain islands of Oceania, which must, though inhabited by regressed savage population, contain *antediluvian buildings*, monuments of grand architecture, built prior to the latest polar shift.

Moreover, we can hardly explain otherwise than by this *alternation of domination of the Poles*, the European fossils themselves, some of which denote a very hot climate, while others, more southerly, indicate an extremely cold climate.

Do I need to say that *Moses knew all these traditions*, as well as the highest-ranking priests of Egypt, the most learned in Science and Wisdom?

The reader has already thought about it.

REBIRTH OF THE DIVINE SCIENCES

The immense benefits and legacy of contemporary physical and natural sciences open the path for a possible rebirth of the divine sciences. Consequently, they lead to the glorification of Moses as well as of Jesus Christ. Thus making it impossible for us to continue to offend, not only these divine Founders of Social Orders, but, through them, God, Nature, the Universe, by attributing to the colossal scholar of Sinai, to the superhuman thinker of Golgotha, such a simplistic genesis, chronology, ideology, which would shame the humble assistants of our laboratories, the students of our faculties, the guardians of our museums.

Two formidable questions are now before us:

1-Principles and Origins of Life in the Universe and on the Earth,

2-Origins, Principles, Purpose of the Hominal Reign, with its Social Order, established on the three other planetary Reigns.

Those "how and whys", are the real and noble purpose of the search for Truth; to answer with the grave and sanctimonious voice of the modern Fathers of knowledge, only carry these immense questions higher and deeper, to the core of Science itself. But, on the other hand, *in vain can one continue answering those questions with theological routine, that is to say only with the primitive translations of the fifty chapters of Moses.*

In vain should we continue to abet the concept of a terrifying Unfathomable being, which one should name only trembling to the marrow, for fear of offending Him by an error; and to continue to accept the answer that the God of the gods, suddenly emerging from an eternal inactivity, set himself, 6,000 years ago, to work hastily, and to make, in 6 days, this Universe, then subsequently repent.

Certainly, if the divine Founders of the Societies had not adhered more strongly to the eternal Truth than their ignorant translators, it would be like having sealed all the religions under the same tombstone of absurdity at once, in the pale sepulcher of Pharisaism, of the Quietism, and especially the modern creed of nothingness.

IGNORANCE SEEDS ATHEISM WHICH SEEDS ANARCHY

Without the help of antique Tradition, without the help of *esoteric Science,* enclosed in the Old Testament, without comparative Theology and Theodoxy - so frightening to the sectarian scientists - humankind will never come out of its slumber, out of its intellectual, and consequently, moral and social impotence.

We are no longer in the Middle Ages, and the darkness of winter is replaced, today, by the Renewal of Spring, after the breakup of the ice.

To persist in presenting the Creation of the World under its crudest veils, is to remove from Moses' hieroglyphs, and consequently from Jesus, the Intelligence of the Savant, the Consciousness of the Wise; it is to inspire atheism to the semi-savants and half-literates; it is to raise the hatred against the priests and the priesthoods, to order the disuse of every religious Principle and, consequently, of all social synthesis, to encourage the righteous passions and logical instincts of the ignorant and implacably attentive childish crowds.

The mainstream person, the workman, the soldier, the peasant, even with what little natural knowledge they possess, through the newspapers or books they read or listen to, seek, anyway they can, food for their moral and intellectual life.

The best ones know too much already not to think for themselves: there is a God, but He is not, He does not act as they say.

The others, led by the troop of half-literates and semi-savants, who seek power through social anarchy, mock the members of the sacerdotal body before shooting them dead, and pursue them, even in their death, as they have them buried without religious rituals.

Everything may be justified by "sufficient reason", as Leibnitz claimed; although it is time all these reasons of dissociation be challenged and disqualified, in the name of that Supreme Reason which is called Science and Social Life.

MOSES AND JESUS: FOUNDATION OF SOCIAL HARMONY

In the two preceding Missions I wrote, I have glorified, History in hand, the Divine Mission of Jesus Christ; I have demonstrated it scientifically by its very action on our Social

Order, of which He is the Founder and the Pontiff King; and I proved that it was for not having complied with His spirit that the General Government of Europe fell into armed anarchy. I insisted on proving, in an almost geometric way, that, despite its rulers, Christendom is animated by His Founder with such vital and social energy that it is irresistibly committed to a healthy, free, peaceful Constitution, through the restoration of His Trinitarian and social Powers.

That testimony, from the layman I am, is all the more sincerely religious that it is spontaneous, foreign to all sectarianism, independent of any personal interest.

In this book I persist therefore in the accomplishment of my hard task with the same courage, with the same conscience, with the same love of Truth. The *source of the veiled Intellectuality of Jesus Christ's moral movement,* and its total social significance, *is enclosed in the Sepher of Moses,* and chiefly in the first ten chapters, which constitute his Cosmogony.

And now, after the last eighteen centuries of individual preparation and purification, the veil must fall in front of the teaching Corps; it has become essential that the whole Judeo-Christian Truth appears scientifically to the eyes of scholars as well as the eyes of theologians.

For in his Book *Moses* himself covered his thoughts with a triple hermetic veil only to be later lifted by Initiation.

And in the parables of His Testament, *Jesus Christ* promised the Kingdom of the Holy Spirit, *where all truth will be demonstrated and known.* This is why the philosophical school, which speculates on natural truths, although without reaching their core meaning, has rendered, and still renders, but unknowingly, a great service to the profound Science, enclosed in the Spirit of the two Testaments.

CONSEQUENCES OF CHILDISH BIBLE READING

From Voltaire to Byron, from Shelley to Mgr. Colenso, Anglican bishop of Cape Town, the superficial criticism has been unleashed unbridled.

This criticism, however, did not refine its argumentation as strongly as did the great exegetes of the Church itself, from St. Jerome, St. Augustine, Origen, Marcion, and the rest, up to the Father of the Oratory, Richard Simon.

Less profound than the old, modern criticism has become more popular, and the least educated of the schoolchildren often summarize it in jokes of dubious taste:

"No, God did not come down here with hands to sculpt in clay a human mock, he did not use a mouth to blow into the nose of a man made of clay, with a chisel to pull the seventh rib from this man and extract a good woman of the same kind, with a rope to park them in an English garden under two trees unknown to all botanists, finally bringing with him a rattlesnake, a talking reptile, to poison the existence of this honest and primitive household." Jokes of this kind abound in Byron's humorous writings. The same feeling pushed to a grandiose desolation is found in Queen Mab, which Shelley wrote while still being a student at the university. But all this literary mockery is genuine and deserves a different answer than a theological anathema.

However, one can only precisely answer with reference to the antic Tradition, specially to its esoteric message, and by demonstrating that, under these common fables about genesis, *under these thrice veiled hieroglyphs, is concealed the Scientific Truth*, awe inspiring by its elevation and profundity, permanently *open to wide-ranging scrutiny and calling always for the most daring decryption of its Mystery.* What they take for the total thought of Moses is only the crudest interpretation of it.

They fight against ghosts, against the veil of Isis; but the goddess is behind, smiling, and loving them so.

Their struggle against what they believe to be a mistake is sincere; but, under the letter, *the Living Spirit* can reassure them and guarantee them the possible access to the strong *formidable reserves of Judeo-Christian esotericism.*

SAVANT SYMBOLISM FROM THE PAST

At the beginning of the Isis Mysteries, the recipient was given a small box of hard stone, looking like a humble symbolic animal, a small insect, a beetle.

Ugh! a modern skeptic would have said.

But upon opening this modest hieroglyph one found an egg of pure gold within, containing, sculpted in precious stones, the Caribes, the *revealing Gods*, and *their twelve sacred Mansions*.

Such was the exquisite method according to which ancient wisdom contained piously in the Word and in the Heart the Knowledge of the Truth; and this veiled symbolism, this hermeticism with its triple seal became deeper and deeper, more and more learned, as the degree of Science drew nearer to the Divine Mystery of Universal Life.

Now, no one has better handled this ideological hermetism than Moses in his 50 chapters.

FUTILE MOCKERIES

For want of knowing these things, Voltaire and his whole school look like lowly educated and misinformed children when they speak of the stupid origin their loosened mind inflicts on religions.

Let us listen for a moment to Voltaire, so called the king of wit, who would have invented vaudeville, but who preferred to apply the vaudevillian tricks to exegesis. *"It is thundering: who makes thunder? It is undoubtedly some snake of the neighborhood.*

"Let's run and worship this serpent: hence the religious cults."

The serpent himself would not have mocked the "Zaire" play better; but what, in fact, does this mockery aim at? At the core of the Hierographic Authority of Moses? At the core of the sacerdotal authority of Jesus Christ? Not at all.

Isn't it targeting only the political powers which, from Constantine to Frederick the Great, wished to make the clergy and the Church the instrument of personal government?

But Voltaire was only the devoted courtier of these Powers of Anarchy from above.

This mockery really only reveals the ignorance of the common interpreters of Moses and Jesus and the semi-knowledge of those who believe they strike these two intellectual and moral giants, by annoying their translators.

But, peace to all, peace to all the dead especially, peace to the ghost of Voltaire! He has had here his relative usefulness. Let him sleep quietly within his award, the apotheosis which the universal mediocrity has rewarded him with; mediocrity which today struggles with itself within anarchy from above and below.

WORSHIP, TRUTH AND CONSCIENCE

Religion, Worship itself, and the whole Judeo-Christian edifice remain, with their immense organic reserves, the only recourse which can allow Israel as well as Christianity to constitute itself definitively into a Social State as perfect as possible.

No, Religion is no more born of ignorance than Worship originates from fear.

To pretend that is to insult Humanity, even more so than to insult the inaccessible Divinity.

Humans are born brave, and given their physical weakness, remain far more valiant than the lion and the elephant.

Consider this: the roaring of the lion salutes the stars, at dawn the elephant turns towards the Sun, and glorifies it by raising and lowering its trunk, so we can and must expect from mankind a Hosanna worthy of itself and of the living God.

Once again, neither constraint nor fear push humans on their knees to worship, it is *Beauty, it is Goodness, it is Truth*, it is enthusiasm and loving admiration. To the apparent disorders of physical Nature, the human-child presents his two clenched fists.

Through the voice of the Kelts, our forefathers, the nascent Societies cry out to the rain of meteors thundering in the atmosphere:

Heaven, you can crush our heads,
You will not crush our spirit!

Humans, indignant, through Job's ulcerated lips, speak

vehemently against God himself who shows him Fate instead of Providence, the head of Medusa instead of the divine face of Pallas; And he said to the Eternal,

Lord, I see my evils: show me your justice!

Humans, in their most divine expression, through the heavenly mouth of Christ, and that of the Orphic Prometheus, say: *Truth belongs to souls without fear; Heaven belongs to fierce spirits!*

Yes, if Religion had not been born from the free assent of two colossal forces - *Thought and Conscience* - *binding themselves to the moral and intellectual Forces of the Universe*, if man at last was not of the race of the gods and from God, never would have a prayer ascended the invisible, shaking, touching, through the hierarchy of all the Higher Beings, that great Soul of the Universe which animates us all, and which illuminates from the top of Heaven an ineffable Intelligence.

Yes, if at the core of reality, the Essence of beings was not One, if their substance was not homogeneous, no communion of the visible with the invisible would have been possible, and never an altar would have risen on the face of Earth.

In summary, in this chapter, I hope I have made it clear that, if the legitimate field of study for natural sciences is the sensorial substance of earthly beings and things, their *indispensable complement* is found in the *divine sciences* which, alone, have for object the other side of the same Truth: the intelligible Essence of these same beings and these same things, whose source is the Living Universe, total manifestation of the Living God and his Creative Faculty, the *Living Creative Nature*.

In the next chapter, I will take the readers by the hand, and they will touch, like St. Thomas, in the very depths of antiquity, the scientific Truth. In order not to shatter too quickly their mental constructs, I will only make their thoughts touch the most exoteric part of the ancient Science synthesized under the name of Religion.

However, it will undoubtedly be seen that, even from the physical and natural point of view, this incontrovertible ancient

Science had been advanced as far and farther than did sciences in western countries for the last 200 years.

Then, gently attracted to the tabernacles of Shem, every attentive and sincere mind will be able to follow us into the depths of ancient sanctuaries and civilizations, of which the two Testaments have made us heirs by the Order of the Abramids, of Moses, and of Jesus Christ.

∞

CHAPTER IV
SCIENCE IN ANTIQUITY

COLLEGES AND SAVANT TEMPLES 5,200 YEARS AGO

I have indicated in the preceding chapters that all degrees of Knowledge of the scientific Truth had been accessed by human minds in high antiquity, and it is still partly known today by some Asian and European Sages.

I have affirmed that the scientific notion of the Oneness of the Living God had been the supreme reward of this series of intellectual and psychurgical efforts.

It remains to be proved here with documents that, in spite of the decadence of the pre-moisiac Social Structure, a decadence which began more than 3,000 years before our era, the forces that we have known and used, as best as we could, for the past 100 years (1750 AD-1880 AD), were still handled at the beginning of Christianity with sufficient precision, by the priesthoods or Greco-Italian scholarly institutions.

Yet for 3,200 years before our era, these polytheistic Colleges were only fragments of dismembered temples of science, diminished factions issued from the former intellectual and social Unity which had been called IEVE, and I will prove this elsewhere.

However, the authors I will quote do not disclose in any way the formulas used by the Etruscan or Egyptian priests, Keltics or Greeks, for none of those secret formulas was ever allowed to be divulged entirely outside the sanctuaries, and no ancient writer would have revealed the ancient mathematical equivalents, had he known them. Most of the writers never knew them.

USE OF ELECTRIC POWER FOR PEACE AND FOR WAR

Let's start going back in time to the beginning of our era.

Affiliated with the ancient scholarly or priestly institutions like all his colleagues of antiquity, the architect of Saint Sophia of Constantinople, Anthème de Tralle, used electricity with powerful effects of which degree we do not as of yet know.

In Agathias, (living in 555 AD) *de rebus Justin,* Book V, Ch. 4, one can see Justin projecting lightnings and thunderbolts on Zeno's house, and using steam as a force to move an entire roof.

In *The Ecclesiastical History* by Sozomen, Book IX, Ch. 6, one can still see the sacerdotal corporation of the Etruscans defending successfully with thunderbolts the city of Narnia against Alaric's warriors.

Moreover, these same savant-priests offered the Christians of Rome to come and save their capital city; but the very ignorant Christian priests, already assuming this science to be of the devil, refused, and Rome was sacked.

In *Titus Livius,* Book I, Ch. 33, in Pliny, Historia Naturalis., Book II, Ch. 53, Book XXVIII, Ch. 4, we can, through much earlier annals, trace Etruscan science, as far as electricity is concerned.

Lars Porsenna, (circa 508 BC), operates, on the territory of Volsinium, the fulmination - lightning strike - of an animal belonging to one of the species extinct today. The ignoramus Roman barbarian Tullus Hostilius, rummaging through a manuscript of the royal priest Numa, finds some fragments of electro-dynamic formulas. He undertook hastily to apply them; but, for lack of knowledge, he departed from the sacred rite: thunder broke forth in the Heavens, and Tullus Hostilius died thunderstruck in his sweltering palace.

In Ovid, and Denys of Halicarnassus, we are told that Sylvius Alladas, (circa 800 BC), eleventh king of Alba since Aeneas, also throws lightning and thunder, but skipping a rite, does not shield himself, does not prevent the shock in return, and perishes.

In all the temples dedicated to Jupiter, to IEVE, to Iou-Evohe, were *developed scientifically the electric force,* as well as the *moral Faculties,* and the *intellectual Principle,* all *correlated in the Life of the Cosmos.* Hence this saying of Stobeus, speaking of the priests of Zeus: Eliciunt te, Jovem, electumque vocant. *They attract you, O Jove, and they call you the Attracted one.*

Such were the science and art which were sheltered behind the altars of the Keraunos of the Greeks, the ancient Keron of the Kelts and Phoenicians, the Turanians and proto-medes Aryas, named Keraniou in current Breton and Gaelic languages.

That is why Servius, Book II, tells us: *The ancients did not light a fire on the altars, their sacred formulas caused the "fire of Heaven" to appear.*

And if I wanted to quote only the poets who, until the time of Jesus Christ remained interpreters of the Oral Tradition, I would need a volume to quote the Greek Aedes, the Latin Vates, the Keltic Bards, the Scandinavian Keltic Scaldes or Varaighes, etc., etc. In Wales country, any blazing glow is still known today as the Druids' fire.

A whole lost system of lightning conductors armed the temples of Juno in Italy, Hera in Greece and Ionia: see the Roman or Greek medals.

From the physical viewpoint, not to mention the other point of view, it was in these temples that meteorology was studied, as was cytology in the temples of Cybele.

The *temple of Jerusalem*, built by the priestly architects of Tyr and Memphis, following an Egyptian and Kaldean design, also had a metallic armor with gold cusps: that is twenty-four lightning rods linked to wells. Josephus in War of the Jews, Book V, Ch. 14, records that fact, and there is no indication that the temple has ever been struck by lightning for 1,000 years.

Khondemir, Dion Chrysostom, St. Clement of Alexandria, Suidas, Amnien Marcellin, attribute the same knowledge to successive Zoroasters, to the Magi, to the Kaldeans.

Zend avesta quote: *"Evoke and understand the heavenly fire."* One may find the same evidence in Phleton's commentary on the rituals of the Magi, in Psellus' observations on the Kaldeans' liturgy.

This thread of ancient science is found in the Yadjour-Veda, although the books of the Aryas contain mainly long past memories recounted by the local bards rather than the recollections of the metropolitan priesthoods.

In India, the proofs are innumerable, and I will come back to it, when I will be presenting the *esoteric sciences* which this sacred old country has preserved until today.

Oupnek Hat quotes: *"Knowing the real nature of fire, sunlight, lunar magnetism, atmospheric and terrestrial electricity, is the third quarter of sacred Science."*

Note the mention of a third quarter, which proves once more that *Integral Science was divided into four hierarchies.*

At the time of Ktesias, the Brahmans still knew of the lightning rods.

Here is an extremely significant quote of Phléton: *"If you multiply your calls, you will see me envelop you, you will see the lightning, the mobile fire which fills and floods the Ethereal Space of the Heavens."*

This fragment of the ritual of the Magi is to be compared to the terms used by Pliny, according to the ancient Etruscan records:

Impetrare Fulmen, cogere Fulmen. The first phrase entails the power to invoke the manifestation of Electricity, we would say today, from the physical viewpoint alone, the *action of extracting electricity.*

The second phrase expresses the act by *which this force was projected as an explosion, a* fulmination.

According to Suidas, one of the Zoroasters chose to be consumed alive by lightning, in order to close his mission on Earth and be reborn among the Higher Gods.

In Eusthatius, we can see Salmoneus build an altar to Zeus-Kataïbatès in the city of Olympia and *attract the celestial fire* down to the altar.

That fact confirms Servius, cited above.

EGYPT CENTER OF INTEGRAL SCIENCE SINCE 4,000 BC

During the 4,000 years before our era, from the whole of southern Europe to the northern Tauris lands, *Egypt* stood as the sacred Metropolis, the *great University*, the seat of *complete Science.*

Each rank of the priesthood, from the lowest to the Highest Pontificate, represented one degree of integral Science and

Wisdom, open through Initiation to the elite of the lay people, which constituted a second Magisterial Power; the third one, everywhere, was the local Assembly of family fathers and mothers. It is within this great *Egyptian School*, itself *interdependent with other Tibetan and Indian centers*, of which I shall speak later, that all the priestly institutions of the Mediterranean coast were formed.

Before the last flood, other metropolitan centers had existed in other vanished continents. In its primitive purity, in its period of functional efficacy, Polytheism, which lasted about 3,400 years before Christ, was not the vain anthropomorphism, the vain degenerate theology such as it has been vulgarized.

Behind Polytheism, in the temples, at work was an often-perfect synthesis of all the sciences, including a *complete multi realms Cosmogony*. Through the practice and exercise of that harmonious Synthesis the priests and the Initiates revered, in full knowledge as well as in full consciousness, the *Great Union and Great Unity*. Later in time, when the polytheistic temples grew in number, they came to represent for the Sage and for the Savant only the various faculties of the universal Teaching - the cult of the diversity of cosmogonic Principles - although all was secretly reintegrated to the antique Unity.

ENLIGHTENED WORLD CIVILIZATIONS BEFORE MOSES

Thus, *enlightened Theocracy*, which, many thousands of years before Moses, reigned over all Earth, still continued, from the depths of its principal sanctuaries, *to protect the Sciences and the applied technical Arts* against political anarchy, against social decadence, the causes of which will be mentioned elsewhere in this book.

It was from these temples, refuges of the ancient civilizing intellectuality, that was surging all the traditional light, at which source the seekers, at will, were drinking all the lessons their intellect and their conscience could wish and ask for, commensurate to the mental and moral strength they personally guaranteed.

Elementary Education and Instruction were, next to *Calli-*

pedia, provided by the Family. The latter was regulated religiously, in the home, according to the rites of the ancient cult of the Ancestors and Sexes, in addition to many other sciences which I will not name here.

Professional Education and Instruction was provided by what the ancient Italians called the *gens* and the Chinese the *jin*, meaning *by the tribe*, in the ancient and little-known sense of this term. More complete studies, analogous to our Secondary Instruction, reserved for the adult, were the task of the temples, and were named *Lesser Mysteries*.

Those who had, after numerous years, acquired the natural and human knowledge of the *Lesser Mysteries* earned the title of *Son of the Woman, of Heroe, Son of Man*, and were granted certain Social Powers, such as all branches of Therapeutics, or the Mediation between the governing leaders, or the Arbitral Justice, etc., etc.

The *Greater Mysteries* completed these teachings by another higher hierarchy of Sciences and associated technical Arts, whose attainment gave the Initiate the title of *Son of the Gods*, or *Son of God*, according to the temple's rank, rural or metropolitan, in addition to certain social Powers called sacerdotal and royal.

There is no example that any Initiate to the Greater Mysteries has ever betrayed the secrets, apart from what Providence has allowed for the mitigation of public ills, brought about by schisms and arbitrary politics and which, since the time of the Nimrod Empire, has seized the General Government of the Societies.

The myths of Prometheus and Tantalus are a symbol of the dangers and punishments awaiting the imprudent, if he spoke or acted before the time signaled by the Divinity.

I indicated in the preceding chapter that astronomy had advanced to an incredible high level, as had all the sciences and all the technical arts which were connected with it in the minds of the ancient Sages.

I also hinted that the temples possessed a wonderful knowledge in chemical science.

That will be easy for me to establish by citing the industrial applications which bear witness to this science, which, as an applied art, had reached a singular practical perfection, even in the hands of the workmen.

APPLIED TECHNICAL ARTS KNOWN AND LOST

In his manuscript, Panselenus, a monk of mount Athos, citing some Ionian authors, reveals the *application of chemistry to photography*. This fact has been brought to light during the trial of Niepce and Daguerre (mid-19th Century).

Although in any everyday spoken language, the scholarly terms come from a dead language, one could however easily find in the manuscript of Panselenus the description of the dark room, the optical apparatus, the sensitization of the metal plates, but it was more difficult to determine the nature of the chemical agents used, the words pointing at them probably coming from a scholarly ancient language similar to Egyptian.

All the following industrial arts, whose notions were given by the temples to the masters of the crafts, suppose an inorganic and organic chemical science, complete, both from the *theoretical and practical* point of view:

Mineralogy, exploration and exploitation of quarries and mines, treatment of ores, reduction of oxides, metallurgy reduced to its maximum simplicity, ceramics, artificial reproduction of precious stones, glassworks with all our known glasses including the flexible glass, (that we have not yet found as of 1880 AD), manufacture of colors and dyeing of fabrics.

Some chronology will be useful here.

In their collections the numismatists of China have coins which go back to the time of Yao; some even date from before the foundation of the Chinese Empire. Among those, some coins from India, bearing the stamp of an Aries, symbol of the rule of Ram. It was on the orders of Emperor Kang-Hi that the collections were assembled.

Now, the first astronomical recordings made in the Celestial Empire, referring to nearly 3,000 years before our era, as well as the collected Hindu coins alone, reveal a whole previous civilization.

Moreover, in Egypt, the use of iron was observed, thanks to a metal rod found in the masonry of the Great Pyramid of Giseh.

Neither the granite of the Hamma-maat quarries nor the basalt of Upper Egypt could be carved, not only without iron, but also without an excellent steel containing a certain quantity of stainless metal.

There is much to be said about the issue of steel manufacturing among the ancients, and the word for it, "adamantinos (unbending)" reveals a great deal about it.

Consider that 4,135 years before our era the founder of the fourth Memphite dynasty, Khou-Wou, mentioned by Herodotus as Cheops, ordered the construction of his pyramid as well as the reconstruction of the temple of Denderah.

The mines of Sinai, Ethiopia, Syria, the Caucasus, Greece, Taurida, Italy, Spain, etc., had been in full activity for thousands of years.

Egyptian civilization, according to Diodorus, was 180 centuries, 18,000 years older than Menes. And Menes reigned around the year 5,000 BC.

Although modern in comparison with such an antique epoch, which had passed through a series of rebirths and decadences, as asserted by archaeologists today, Job's hermetic poem lends a poetic flair to this *ancient metallurgy*.

Here it is without change, verses to verses:

Silver surges from the mine;
Gold refined; the rock
Melts, and delivers liquid
Copper; from ore
Iron flows.
From darkness
Human extracts the abysses
Here death lies in the stones.
He digs, far from the living
Roads that no one treads.

Far from the homes of the living
He dangles in the void.
The soil from which wheat grows,
Its bones by flame gnawed,
Hides easily its sapphires
And its gold veins:
No bird can glide in,
No hawk watches,
No wild beast's foot thumps,
No lion's claw scratches there.
Man alone extends his hand
And the granite is torn,
And the mountain, jumping,
Cuts itself into galleries
And reveals its treasures.
The man drains the underground water
And drags everything in broad daylight.

This curious document, borrowed from the ancient Ethiopians, shows what was, from time immemorial, *the work of the mines, the use of powder to blast the rocks, the digging of the galleries around a central well, the sealing of the waters' infiltration, mineral processing.*

But everything is linked within human activity; and the numberless architectural works, such as the Sphinx, the temple of Aarmachis in Egypt, the caves of Ellora and Maha-Bali-Puram in Asia, built prior to the time of Menes, 8,000 years before the present century (1880 AD), attest the existence of all crafts, the application of all the technical arts and sciences *within a colossal civilization,* and a *well-established society, since many centuries already.*

WARFARE ARMAMENT TECHNOLOGY OF THE PAST

However, to accustom the reader to the true spirit of this past, let us continue to find some vestiges similar to our modern discoveries.

It is easy to see that pyrotechnics was perfectly known in the most ancient temples. We find it again in Byzantium.

Porphyry, in his book on the Administration of the Empire, describes the artillery of Constantine Porphyrogenetus (circa 950 AD). The artillery of prince Leo the Philosopher (circa 850 AD) as well as its musketry is described in the book Military Institutions, Book II, p. 137.

Ammien Marcellin (circa 400 AD), Book XXIII, Ch. 6, Pliny, i. II, Ch. 104, indicate quite clearly that the Persians long time ago used firearms. Valerianus, in his book "Life of Alexander", describes the bronze canons of the army of India.

In Ctesias we find the famous Greek fire, a mixture of saltpeter, sulfur and a hydrocarbon, used well before Ninus, in Kaldea, in Iran, in India, under the name of Bharawa fire.

This name, which alludes to the priesthood of the Red race, the first legislator of the Blacks of India, denotes by itself an immense antiquity.

PROHIBITION OF WEAPONS OF MASS DESTRUCTION

There is a law in the *Code of Gentoo* prohibiting the use of weapons of mass destruction based on lightnings or fire, killing more than a hundred men at a time.

About 4,000 years before Christ, following great troubles first in schools, then extending to civil riots, Science, previously accessible to many became closed to the public, therefore the pyrotechnics were used solely for the defense of the temples and their domains consecrated by the ancient Universal Alliance.

When strangers attacked the cities of Persia, says Philostratus, the Magi from the top of the walls stroke the assailants with flames and thunder. By similar means the priests of Delphi defended their territory against the Gallics and the Persians themselves.

In their reports, Herodotus, Justin, Pausanias, describe actual explosions of mines engulfing Persians or Gallics under rains of stones and projectiles mixed with flames.

On the other hand, Plutarch, who was a high priest, and knew what to expect, tells us that from Delphi to Thermopylae, all the Greeks were Dorians, affiliated with the Mysteries of their temple.

Servius, Valerius Flaccus, Jules the African, Marcus Graecus, describe the powder in the terms of ancient traditions, and the latter, populist Marcus Graecus, keeping no secret, discloses the exact proportions as they are known today.

Claudian describes fireworks, spinning suns, ancient amusements of Egypt, China and the rest of Asia. Nowadays, firearms are in the hands of all governments based on personal interest and power, used to their mutual destruction.

In earlier times, initiated in the temple, the sovereigns would have been mercilessly deposed by the priesthood and the whole college of Initiates, if they had arrogated to themselves the right to dispose of such devices of death, of whose Theocracy, in agreement with public mores, prevented disclosure and limited their use.

One can say the scientific spirit of the ancient religion had been removed from the sanctuaries, enslaved to the Arbitrary Policy, if the pathetic Caligula could, as Dion Cassius mentions, buy from a Kaldean the secret of handling explosive powder, the art of summoning lightnings and thunder.

After *electricity, steam and pyrotechnics*, it is easy to identify that the ancients had practical data on *terrestrial magnetism* which necessarily *implied a scientific theory*.

Suidas shows us the statue of Serapis *levitating* inside the vault of a temple at Alexandria; Cassidore shows us the statue of Cupidon *hovering in the air* in a temple of Diana.

APPLIED TECHNICAL ARTS IN ANCIENT CIVILIZATIONS

In the Odyssey, Book VIII, IV. VII, Book XIII, Homer, clearly points at a sort of compass, a secret intelligence which, without the help of the Stars, guides the Pheacian ships.

These Pheacians were affiliated with the learned circle of the Cyclops, who themselves were attached to the sanctuaries of Lycia, the Olens, the Zamolxis and the Abaris and to the temples of Hoeinus, Balkan and Kaukayon.

We will see later in Isaiah that the Phoenician pilots of Sidon and Tyr were Sages affiliated with the Mysteries.

Like Abaris, Pythagoras, a pupil of Egyptian priests, knew the compass: Jamblic, Life of Pythagoras, Ch. 27; Herodotus, Book XV, § 36; Diodorus of Sicily, Book III, Ch. 2; Suidas, etc.

Among the Finns, as among the Chinese and the Hindus, the compass was known.

The natural magnet was called *Indi*an stone, lapis *Indi*cus.

In Plutarch, Life of Alexander, Ch. 29, in Herodotus, Book VII, Ch. 74, in Seneca, Natural Matters, Book III, Ch. 25, in Quinte Curce, Book X, last chapter; in Pliny, Historia Naturalis, Book XXX, Ch. 16; in Pausanias, Arcad., Ch. 23, we can find our acids, our bases, our salts, the alcohol, the ether, thus signaling an organic and inorganic chemistry, of which these authors had no longer knowledge or would not deliver the key.

Pliny speaks thus of the dyeing on fabrics, practiced by the Egyptian industry: Once the subject is drawn on the bleached fabric, each part of the pattern is coated with varied gummy compositions, in order to absorb different colors.

After processing in the boiler, the intended colors reveal themselves as indestructible, for the craftsman is fixing them in such a perfect manner that time does not alter them, and even concentrated detergents cannot attack them. Their fresco painting was equally unalterable.

In Egypt, Industry and applied Arts drew their data from the Science possessed by the Priesthood; and an example reported by Pliny is showing a problem of very complicated chemistry which had been then perfectly solved.

Democritus, the first exoteric secular experimentalist, lived for many years in Egypt; he brought back his extensive knowledge of the mineral and vegetal kingdoms, his powerful physical and chemical experiments, his fine works on the reverberatory furnace used to *artificially recompose precious stones*, and many other secrets it would take too long to list.

Optics, acoustics, the study of the laws of light and sound, have been so deeply developed that our current sciences are far behind. (year 1880 AD)

Theories of colors and sounds phenomena had been condensed into their true musical laws, into their real arithmetic and geometric progressions.

With regard to optics, the learned masters knew of and used all our instruments, mirrors, concave and convex lenses, conic prisms, dark room, catoptric apparatus, microscopes, telescopes. A glimpse of these facts can be found in the writings of Cicero, Seneca, Aulu-Gelle, Jamblique, as well as in recent archeological discoveries.

Acoustics were geometrically applied on earth and underground, in temples, theaters, hypogea, with great precision and prodigious power. As for Music, it would be impossible for me, without writing a special volume, to show how far it had been carried, not only as an art, but as an absolute science of method, of analogy, of universal key.

What remains today of their Astronomy and Architecture suffice to demonstrate the mathematical and mechanical deep knowledge of the priests, who were the initiating masters of Pythagoras, Archimedes, Ktesibius, Heron, Architac, etc.

But the exoteric marvels of these geniuses cannot give an even faint idea of the miracles of Science and applied Art contained in the sanctuaries.

Even the *railways* have been used whenever necessary. Rails have been found, not only at Eleusis and in Egypt, but a whole system of locomotion similar to ours is also described in old Chinese books, which deal with certain sciences, before and until the time of the construction of the great wall.

I would also have many things to say about *antique telegraphy*, which was prodigious, though as natural as our telephony; but I cannot go beyond the limits imposed on me by the topic of this chapter.

SCIENCE MERGED AND IMMERSED IN DIVINE TRUTH

Anthropology, which has existed here in France for barely twenty years (in 1884), was well known in the temples of

Europe, and particularly in those of Asia and Africa.

The sanctuaries of Asia have five more superimpositions of Neptunian layers than on our continent, and skeletons of giant humans have been found there. Lucretia, echoing the Ionian temples knowledge, mentions anthropology, in four verses, De Natura Rerum, v. 1282-1285:

Hands, nails, teeth: this was the first arsenal.
Then came the stone, and the tree also provides its branches
Then humans seize metals: iron, brass.
Iron, however, was known only after the bronze.

I wish I could speak here of the other human sciences, from anatomy and physiology to psychurgy, and the *divine sciences*, from ontology to cosmogony and theogony!

But I must take into account the average knowledge level of the Western readers and their mental environment; and if I was rushing the readers too fast towards unknown intellectual orbs, their mind would at first find itself so estranged, it would *refuse to admit that Science can be completely merged with Divine Truth and with Universal Life.*

I therefore completely limit myself in regard with the disclosure of the esoteric side of the ancient Synthesis, at least the side corresponding to the full exercise of intellectual, moral and organic faculties, which are as yet atrophied or dormant among my contemporaries.

HIGHER CIVILIZATION AS FAR AS 30,000 YEARS AGO

Now, to what depth of antiquity can we go back historically, to find a complete civilization, armed with the ensemble of Sciences and related technical Arts, such as I have suggested? Obviously, it is not from the modern theologians we can obtain answers to this question, for not only did they constantly fail to recognize the qualitative significance of the Science of Numbers, as embedded by Moses in Genesis, but they made every effort to attack his true thought by defending the feeble tales they themselves had created.

Moreover, the ignorant demagogy of the first Christian

Councils, joined to the imperial arbitrariness, having imposed the mediocrity of the vulgar on the Fathers of the Church, even on the most educated, stamped upon the entire dogma an absolutely crude character, which renders the Judeo-Christian truth very difficult to identify and to reconcile with the antique Universality of human and divine realities.

The Jewish priesthood, especially since the exile of Babylon, and even before the captivity, ever since the institution of royalty (King Saul circa 1030 BC), had fallen into the same wanderings; but, at least, the body of the lay Initiates and the Nazarenes, from whence emerged the Prophets, still preserved, more or less clearly, the *Oral Tradition*.

Disdainful Jewish and Christian priesthoods, far from having recourse to this Authority (sustained by lay Initiates and Nazarenes), contributed to its annihilation. Therefore, the apparent indifference of present-day science to theological scholasticism is the most healthy and serious point of support which can restore the true esoteric spirit of the Testaments.

NECESSARY RENEWAL OF JUDEO-CHRISTIAN LEGACY

Faced with the above described quandary, my current so singular intellectual and moral position is difficult to defend without departing from the absolute Truth; I pray the reader to keep in mind that the more I profess respect for Moses and veneration for Jesus Christ, the more deeply I recognize the validity of their sacerdotal heirs' mission, provided its true spirit is restored; also the more I feel I have the duty to wash away from opinion and public conscience all obfuscations which prevent the true thought of the two Testators to appear in its true light, and avert it to bear all its divine intellectual and social fruits.

The quibbles, pettiness, prejudices, of Talmudists or Christian theologians, prove nothing against the *absolute Truth of the Mission of Moses and Jesus Christ,* nor against the writings or the authentic words of these divine Missionaries, nor against their religion, nor against their cults, nor against their priests.

All these errors are human things and ignorance makes them excusable and forgivable.

But, as all the sciences, of which the secular world is today equipped, make it possible to restore the total field of truths, the official theologians, like the Talmudists, cannot henceforth sin by ignorance, but only by laziness, snootiness and bad will.

But let the people not forget that the priest at the altar is only the symbolic representative of the consent of the Social State to its Founding Principles, and that if, turning towards the crowd, it is up to him to say: *May the Lord be with you!* it is also up to secular society to be the guardian of the Holy Spirit, and to answer to the priest: *May the Lord be with your spirit!*

Everything is true in the organism of religions, if we know how to understand it, and remember it in time.

NECESSARY INTELLECTUAL REVIVAL OF PRIESTHOODS

The present circumstance of the Judeo-Christian world is extremely dire, and may lead the priesthood toward two paths:

-If they persevere in their errancies, they will tread the path to blasphemy against the Holy Spirit who is the very Truth and Wisdom of Science,

-If they make the *intellectual and moral effort that Providence expects from them*, they will return to all the sanctity of their august role. They will recover the power of social authority which Moses and Jesus Christ, - sustained by the intellect and awareness of their Lay Societies - can bring back to their priests along with the Holy Spirit, who is also the Social Spirit.

I will therefore be forced to address persuasively the theologians, in order to strike and break their false mental categories.

But, to the sectarian camp of irreligious criticism I say "make no mistake": it is not as an enemy of religion but as a therapist of the Intelligence; it is not to kill, but to vivify, that I will use the weapons of the Eternal Verb.

I will do my duty entirely and without fear other than that of God; but once it is done, the ecclesiastical world of all Christendom will have to fulfill its own duty, on pain of defaulting on their most serious obligations towards Christ and the divine Constitution of the Universe, of which Moses bequeathed us the Sacred History.

The famous *non-possumus* - *we cannot* - has its reason d'etre, only as long as the entire secular Christendom, failing to reconstruct its intellectual and social synthesis in the real light of Moses and Jesus Christ, does not at once respond to all its clergy: *Scimus, sumus, possumus, volumus. We know, we are, we can, we will.* But, once this answer is made religiously and scientifically, then it is up to those who hold the keys of the Church to open their sacred cupboards, and lock in it the wine of the grand harvest, the bread of the grand crop, in order to offer them formally to God,

I have analyzed enough, in the two preceding missions, all the causes of *"we cannot"*, not only of the old papacy, but of all the Christian priests, not only of a political Christian church, but of all the political churches, not only of the priestly Order regularly and apostolically constituted, but also of all the secular disorder, dissociated intellectually and practically; and it is from within evil itself, and its causes, that I have pointed out the possible emergence of the good and its principles.

SYNARCHIC CIVILIZATION UNDER ATTACK

In this book, all my statements are documented. *The Kingdom of God, the Trinitarian Synarchy and its Universal Alliance are not only the Promise of Judeo Christianity, but they existed as true foundation of the social organism, in a worldwide civilization* preceding the institution of the arbitrary Empire, characterized by the name of Nimrod.

Let's go back to the antiquity of this Civilization. There are everywhere honorable exceptions; but, generally, the conduct of the Christian theologians with regard to all the religious societies, of all the theocratic monuments, apparently foreign to Moses and Jesus, has been as sectarian, as barbarous as possible.

Had it been in their power, they would have *annihilated all these testimonies of previous civilizations.*

This fury of destruction is by no means religious, as has been commonly taught, but the exact opposite is true: it was done in the very spirit of ignorance and its corollary, arbitrary politics. This spirit of sectarian domination has inspired almost all new peoples, since the new Babylonian empire, symbolized by the name of Nimrod, the Tiger.

SYSTEMATIC DESTRUCTION OF ANCIENT DOCUMENTS

Rome, the last offshoot of this arbitrary empire, spent its time obliterating the religious and social history of previous nations. In 51 BC, the Bruckion library of Alexandria, which contained 700,000 volumes, most of them written in Egyptian, was torched.

It was this same spirit of Nimrod, and by no means Christianity, that inspired the destruction of Gnostic encyclopedias.

It was this same mania of ignorant and brutal domination that armed with torches the monks in Ireland, who burned 10,000 manuscripts in runic characters carved on birch bark, containing the recorded traditions and annals of the Keltic race, native of our European Continent.

In Spain, in France, in Germany, in Italy, by cartloads, Arabic and Hebrew manuscripts were brought to the stake.

A bishop even claimed, in one of the councils of Toledo, that the Vulgate of St. Jerome was to be considered as Jesus Christ in person between the two thieves: the Septuagint version and the Hebrew text of Moses.

At the end of the last century (18th century), the same fury of burning everything reached a whole hieroglyphic library, possibly containing august *testimonials of the ancient Egyptian Science and the old Universal Alliance.*

In the small Egyptian port of Ouardan, the Reverend Father Sicard made an autodafe with piles of ancient papyri, under the pretext that, as long as he did not understand them, they were, obviously, books of witchery inspired by the devil.

Historian Savary reports the fact in his Letters on Egypt; but let's quote Reverend Father Sicard himself:

"I was informed there was in this village a dovecote full of papyri covered with magical characters, bought from some religious heretic monks. Without qualm I made the use I had to make of them and planted in their place a cross of Jerusalem the Coptes revered with great devotion."

This confession of the Reverend by himself is found in the Edifying Letters, Lettres édifiantes, p. 53.

I could multiply indefinitely examples of this nature; but I am too disgusted, and others than me have taken care of or will take care of this saddening chore.

CYCLIC MARKERS

What of the sacred *books of the Hindus?*

Our Christian pagans think themselves piously obliged to disfigure the venerable antiquity of these documents, to smear them with childish subterfuges, to escape from this past which alone could restore to Moses his scientific grandeur, and to both Moses and Jesus, the universal goals of their Mission.

What of Egypt? Plato, initiated into the Egyptian temples Mysteries, tells us that, 10,000 years before Menes, there existed a complete civilization, of which he had had the proofs before his eyes.

Herodotus emphasizes the same fact, while adding that oaths are sealing his lips, and that he trembles at the idea of revealing anything pertaining to Osiris, God of the antique Synthesis and Universal Alliance.

Diodorus certifies he learned from priests of Egypt, that they had proof of a complete social structure established well before the time of Menes and having lasted 18,000 years until Horus. Manetho, an Egyptian priest, reveals a meticulously recorded chronology, originating at the time of Menes, taking us back to 6,883 years before the present year 1883 AD. (= 5,000 years BC)

Moreover, Manetho records that even before king Menes, Viceroy of India in Egypt, several immense cycles of civilization had succeeded each other on Earth and in Egypt itself.

All these impressive testimonies, to which we can add

those of Berose and all the libraries of India, Tibet and China, are considered null and void by the deplorable spirit of sectarianism and obscurantism, concealed behind the mask of theology.

Torrents of ink, bile, blood, have been spent to insure the triumph of that erroneous sinister pedagogy. Violent tyrannies have been imposed, so darkness could extinguish all light on the past, and therefore on the present and future.

Now, the secular University has maintained these methods, without modifying them; and it is still, from one end of Europe to the other, the chronology of the Septuagint, of Jerome and Usserius, which serves as a basis for the primary and secondary Education.

What are we to do? Ignore all the books of Higher Education? The Vedas, the Pouranas, the Y-Kings, the Papyri, the Steles, the Greek books? Annihilate all the works of philology, archeology, anthropology?

At this idea the very enlightened average churchmen and lay civilians will protest with just indignation.

However, one must reach a just solution to this quandary; and this book has no other purpose than to prove that we can and must do so.

We can no longer teach that the Universe is 6,000 years old, we can no longer burden the legacy of Moses with this primitive childishness, while at the same time we learn from the sacred books of India that the Seventh Manu, seventh inter-diluvian Cycle, which began 4,000 years ago is now at the present time completing its cycle.

Two manus ago, 8,000 years ago, the last Black Sovereign of India, the Rawhon Daçaratha, the Indian Emperor, whose Pha-Rawhons of Egypt, Persia, Phenicia, and Tauris, were only the vice- kings, Daçaratha, I say, was dethroned by Rama, the chief of the Keltic immigration from Western Europe. Daçaratha was the fifty-fifth solar monarch since Ikshaukou, who had been the first Red Race colonizer of India.

At that time, one finds this sovereign at the head of an immense civilization dating back nearly 600 centuries (60,000 years) before the supposedly biblical date of Creation; and in that same book we learn about the crowned heads of the two Social Orders, installed 8,500 years back from the actual time I am writing these lines (1880 AD); they rule in colossal cities: Ayodia, metropolis of the solar dynasty, whose diameter was 60 kilometers, and Pratishtana, seat of the lunar dynasty, built on the same scale.

Certainly, in that Cycle of civilization, the Unity of Humankind in the Universe, the Unity of the Universe in God, the Unity of God in Himself, were taught not as a primitive obscure and obscurantist superstition, but as the luminous, dazzling crown of a quadruple hierarchy of Sciences, animating an organic cult, of which Sabahism was the form.

ISHWARA-EL, ISRA-EL

The name of the supreme God of this Cycle, *Ishwara*, Husband of Living Wisdom, *Pracriti*, the Creative Nature, is the same that Moses will reveal 5,000 years later, receiving it from the Kaldean Tradition of the Abramids and the sanctuaries of Thebes, to make it the cyclic symbol of its movement: *Ishwara-El*, or, by contraction, *Israel*, meaning *Intelligence or Royal Spirit of God*. The sparks of the great center of the old Universities' Alliance, the ancient civilization before Abraham and Moses, still subsist, like fire beneath the ashes. In time it has been more or less obliterated in the thought process of the priests, Brahmans, Tibetans, and Buddhists, as in the minds of the Guebres, Chinese scholars, Japanese priests, Tatar shamans, etc. However, through Higher Education, all this intellectuality, along with its sacred testimonials, is *now inserted in the intellection of Christendom*, and must necessarily be integrated there.

This integration should not be realized solely through chronological necrography, decorated with the name of History, but also through *comparative Theology*, and, thus, attain universal *Theodoxy* and universal Sociology.

Either Christianity is able to support and synthesize scientifically this deluge of ancient intellectuality, or, Christianity will inevitably sink in that flood of intellectual chaos.

ASIAN INTELLECT COMPARED TO WESTERN CREEDS

This book has no other purpose than to prove that *Judeo-Christian* intellectual and social *esoterism* is rightly the continuation, *the fulfillment, of the whole antique theosophical tradition*, of which the two Testaments have made us inheritors.

A time will come when new Judeo-Christian missionaries will reestablish a perfect communion of Science and Love with all the other religious centers of the Earth.

But until now, our civilization, far from connecting with the Intelligence and Soul of its older sisters, has perpetually darkened and desolated them, without understanding their profound piety for the ancient Human Cycle, for the ancient Kingdom of God, whose reconstitution they are still awaiting.

Better informed than the Europeans about the science of divine and human things, less ignorant of the real history of the World, *the Asian sages, who are more or less consciously attached to the old Cycle*, will never admit our Judeo-Christian exotericism, as presented to them by our missionaries; neither will they admit, among other things, its false chronology, that Jesus would have destroyed with a smile, Moses with a frown, the Abramids with a shrug.

On the other hand, will Asian initiators and initiates more easily admit our scientific spirit, which they perceive to be in diametrical opposition to our religious "ignorantism"?

They will not admit it more if, from the stage of analysis, we do not proceed to the stage of a fair and scientifically valid synthesis, in other words a precise religion and science Synthesis. For the High Initiates, of whom I speak, and who inspire now and will inspire more and more those Societies differing from ours, and whose peoples comprise nearly one billion soul, to those peoples, to *know means to pray, and be connected through love and wisdom to Universal Life*.

But our present scientific mind appears to them as marked with a bestial character, barely human, and least of all, divine.

Yes, it is the Beast that they see in it, blaspheming, dissolving with hatred and madness the whole of Humanity, using and destroying, at pleasure, all the energies of the peoples, all the forces of the Planet.

It is the fiercest Fate, not the Providence, which they see on the throne of our sovereignty, under the honorific palms of our official scholars, under the costumes of our diplomacy, behind the sword of our men of war, behind the counter of our financiers, in the papers of our state loans, behind the industrial Moloch attended by our subservient engineers.

By its diplomatic-military constitution not only does Europe expose, that it is armed for its own destruction and for theirs, but also all its social organization hurls to the entire planet the symbols of its potential universal annihilation.

The respectable Sages, the religious men, deeply instructed, not only in their ancient sciences, but in those of our own Universities, the initiators and initiates of whom I speak, do not confine themselves to seeing these things, or to discuss them among themselves; but they write about them, in a form as moderate as it is determined, to the attention of these Europeans whom they know to deserve their confidence.

For my part, not having asked them and not owing them any form of initiation, I feel free to address them one day in the fraternal spirit which animates me towards them.

Many things can be said in regard with the forms and appearances of our Judeo-Christianism and its social expression, Judeo-Christianity.

FUTURE ALLIANCE OF WEST AND EAST

But in the sanctuaries of Asia one should be aware that our European world is at work for the benefit of all Earth, and that the conclusion of this work, in spite of appearances will and is in Principle, *embedded within the Esotericism of our religious Tradition, and is aiming at the renewal of the ancient Cycle and the ancient universal Alliance.*

Do not overlook that all the prophecies of the world proclaim to all peoples that their national resurrection, their social salvation, the reconstitution of the ancient Covenant and the ancient Universal Peace, will emerge from the European West, from the Varaha, the ancient land of the Kelts Varaighes, Motherland of the first Kelt peoples, a Mother still in the midst of a painful labor.

All will occur through the triumph of the Judeo-Christian Tradition, rid of its veils, fulfilling for the entire Humankind its Divine Promise, reconstituting the three Social Powers, which I define by the name of Synarchy.

This is the *providential purpose*, which, in a rigorously positive way, orients our Judeo-Christianity, in spite of the apparent contradictions and the momentary impotence of its only real Authorities, who are the Teaching institutions, religious and civilian. The political weight, or, if you will, the balance of these mental contradictions, indeed resides, in the West, both in the civil and economic order.

The resulting present social landscape, I know, exhibits more and more the stamp of Anarchy, along with all the ruins it brings about.

RENEWED UNION OF SCIENCE AND CONSCIOUSNES

This anarchy persists only as long as the exotericism of the two Testaments stifles their organic reserves; the reality will change singularly its appearance the day when, in the full light of modern Science and modern Consciousness, *the Intellectuality of Moses and Jesus*, as well as the very positive social goal they have proposed, will be finally defined and be addressed directly.

This book, I hope, will be the Ultimatum Organum, the Masterwork, through which any thinker and any believer worthy of the name will reach the same conclusions regarding Universal Synthesis and Synarchy.

For the moment, I wish to indicate *that ancient Wisdom, the ancient Science of divine and human realities, existed in the very ancient Cycles of Civilization.* Moses and Jesus restored to us its purest intellectual and social light. Also, at present time, venerable human Communities still retain from this enlightened past a rather respectable sum of esoteric and positive traditions.

It is in Asia, and particularly in India, in Tibet, and in China, that the Spirit of ancient Science is confronting the Europeans' ignorant disdainful "scientiform" rationalism, vaguely marked with a superficial Judeo-Christianism.

Although I am free to go to the bottom of some data, I want to stay on the middle path and deliver the information that any curious mind can acquire, if it so wishes.

Thus, I will give the floor to the group of personalities living in the Himalayas, who, under their name of Initiate, Koot Hoomi Lal Sing, half Tibetan, half Hindu, have allowed some of their English correspondents, Mr. Sinnett among others, to publish the part of their letters they would deem appropriate to publicize.

Sinnett, Occult World, p. 85-95. London, Trubner and C. 1883 AD.

Dear Sir, Availing of the first moments of leisure to formally answer your letter of the 17th ultimo, I will now report the result of my conference with our chiefs upon the proposition therein contained; trying at the same time to answer all your questions.

I am first to thank you on behalf of the whole section of our fraternity that is especially interested in the welfare of India for an offer of help whose importance and sincerity no one can doubt.

Tracing our lineage through the vicissitudes of Indian civilization to a remote past, we have a love for our motherland so deep and passionate, that it has survived even the broadening and cosmopolitanizing (pardon me if this is not an English word) effect of our studies in the hidden laws of nature.

And so I and every other Indian patriot feel the strongest gratitude for every kind word or deed that is given in her behalf.

Imagine then, that since we are convinced that the degradation of India is largely due to the suffocation of her ancient spirituality; and that, whatever helps restore that higher standard of thought and morals must be a regenerating national force; every one of us would naturally and without urging be disposed to push forward a Society whose proposed formation is under debate; especially if it really is meant to become a society untainted by selfish motive, and whose object is the revival of ancient science and tendency to rehabilitate our country in the world's estimation.

Take this for granted, without further asseverations.

But you know, as any man who has read history, that patriots may burst their hearts in vain if circumstances are against them. Sometimes, it has happened that no human power, not even the fury and force of the loftiest patriotism, has been able to bend an iron destiny aside from its fixed course, and nations have gone out like torches dropped into water in the engulfing blackness of ruin.

Thus, we who have the sense of our country's fall though not the power to lift her up at once, can not do as we would either as to general affairs or this particular one. And with the readiness but not the right to meet your advances more than half way we are forced to say that the idea entertained by Mr. Sinnett and yourself is impracticable in part.

It is in a word impossible for myself or any Brother or even an advanced neophyte, to be specially assigned and set apart as the guiding Spirit or Chief of the Anglo-Indian Branch.

We know it would be a good thing to have you and a few of your selected colleagues regularly instructed and shown the phenomena and their rationale.

For though none but you few would be convinced, still it would be a decided gain to have even a few Englishmen of first-class ability enlisted as students of Asiatic Psychology.

We are aware of all this and much more; hence we do not refuse to correspond with and otherwise help you in various ways.

But what we do refuse is to take any other responsibility upon ourselves than this periodical correspondence and assistance with our advice; and, as occasion favours, such tangible, possibly visible proofs as would satisfy you of our presence and interest.

To "guide" you we will not consent. However much we may be able to do, yet we can promise only to give you the full measure of your deserts.

Deserve much and we will prove honest debtors; little and you need only expect a compensating return.

This is not a mere text taken from a school boy's copybook, though it sounds so, but only the clumsy statement of the law of our order; and we can not transcend it.

Utterly unacquainted with Western, especially English modes of thought and action, were we to meddle in an organization of such a kind you would find all your fixed habits and traditions incessantly clashing, if not with the new aspirations themselves, at least with their modes of realisation as suggested by us.

You could not get unanimous consent to go even the length you might yourself. I have asked Mr. Sinnett to draft a plan embodying your joint ideas for submission to our chiefs, this seeming the shortest way to a mutual agreement.

Under our "guidance" your Branch could not live, you not being men to be guided at all in that sense. Hence the Society would be a premature birth and a failure, looking as incongruous as a Paris Daumont drawn by a team of Indian yaks or camels.

You ask us to teach you true Science, the occult aspect of the known side of nature: and this you think can be as easily done as asked.

You do not seem to realize the tremendous difficulties in the way of imparting even the rudiments of our Science to those who have been trained in the familiar methods of yours.

You do not see that the more you have of the one the less capable you are of intuitively comprehending the other, for a man can only think in his worn grooves, and unless he has the courage to fill up these and make new ones for himself, he must perforce travel on the old lines.

Allow me a few instances.

In conformity with exact modern Science you would define but one cosmic energy, and see no difference between the energy expended by the traveller who pushes aside the bush that obstructs his path, and the scientific experimenter who expends an equal amount of energy in setting a pendulum in motion!

We do. For we know there is a world of difference between the two.

The one uselessly dissipates or scatters force, the other concentrates and stores it. And here please understand that I do not refer to the relative utility of the two as one might imagine; but only to the fact, that in the one case, there is but brute force flung out without any transmutation of that brute energy into the higher potential form of spiritual dynamics, and, in the other there is just that.

Please do not consider me vaguely metaphysical.

The idea I wish to convey is, that the result of the highest intellection in the scientifically occupied brain is the evolution of a sublimated form of spiritual energy, which, in the cosmic action, is productive of illimitable results, while the automatically acting brain holds or stores up in itself only a certain quantum of brute force that is unfruitful of benefit for the individual or humanity. The human brain is an exhaustless generator of the most refined quality of cosmic force, out of the low, brute energy of nature; and the complete adept has made himself a centre from which irradiate potentialities that beget correlations upon correlations through Aeons to come.

This is the key to the mystery of his being able to project into and materialise in the visible world the forms that his imagination has constructed out of inert cosmic matter in the invisible world. The adept does not create anything new, but only utilises and manipulates materials which nature has in store around him; a material which throughout eternities has passed through all the forms; he has but to choose the one he wants and recall it into objective existence. Would not this sound to one of your "learned" biologists like a madman's dream?

You say there are few branches of science with which you do not possess more or less acquaintance, and that you believe you are doing a certain amount of good, having acquired the position to do this by long years of study. Doubtless you do. But will you permit me to sketch for you still more clearly the difference between the modes of — physical called exact — often out of mere politeness — and metaphysical sciences? The latter, as you know, being incapable of verification before mixed audiences, is classed by Mr. Tyndall with the fictions of poetry. The realistic science of fact, on the other hand, is utterly prosaic. Now for us poor and unknown philanthropists, no fact of either of these sciences is interesting except in the degree of its potentiality of moral results, and in the ratio of its usefulness to mankind. And what, in its proud isolation, can be more utterly indifferent to every one and everything, or more bound to nothing, but the selfish requisites for its advancement than this materialistic and realistic science of fact? May I not ask then without being taxed with a vain "display of science" what have the laws of Faraday, Tyndall, or others to do with philanthropy in their abstract relations with humanity viewed as an integral whole?

What care they for MAN as an isolated atom of this great and harmonious Whole, even though they may sometimes be of practical use to him? Cosmic energy is something eternal and incessant, matter is indestructible, and there stand the scientific facts. Doubt them and you are an ignoramus; deny them, a dangerous lunatic, a bigot; pretend to improve upon the theories — an impertinent charlatan. And yet even these scientific facts never suggested any proof to the world of experimenters, that nature consciously prefers that matter should be indestructible under organic rather than under inorganic forms; and that she works slowly but incessantly towards the realisation of this object — the evolution of conscious life out of inert material. Hence their ignorance about the scattering and concretion of cosmic energy in its metaphysical aspects; their division about Darwin's theories; their uncertainty about the degree of conscious life in separate elements; and, as a necessity, the scornful rejection of every phenomenon outside their own stated conditions and the very idea of worlds of semi-intelligent if not intellectual forces at work in hidden corners of nature. To give you another practical illustration.

We see a vast difference between the qualities of two equal amounts of energy expended by two men, of whom one, let us suppose, is on his way to his daily quiet work, and another on his way to denounce a fellow creature at the police station, while the men of science see none. And we — not they — see a specific difference between the energy in the motion of the wind and that of a revolving wheel. And why? Because every thought of man upon being evolved passes into the inner world and becomes an active entity by associating itself — coalescing, we might term it — with an elemental; that is to say with one of the semi-intelligent forces of the kingdoms. It survives as an active intelligence, a creature of the mind's begetting, for a longer or shorter period proportionate with the original intensity of the cerebral action which generated it. Thus, a good thought is perpetuated as an active beneficent power; an evil one as a maleficent demon.

And so man is continually peopling his current in space with a world of his own, crowded with the offsprings of his fancies, desires, impulses, and passions, a current which reacts upon any sensitive or and nervous organisation which comes in contact with it in proportion to its dynamic intensity. The Buddhist calls this his "Skandha," the Hindu gives it the name of "Karma"; the Adept evolves these shapes consciously, other men throw them off unconsciously.

The adept to be successful and preserve his power must dwell in solitude and more or less within his own soul. Still less does exact science perceive that while the building ant, the busy bee, the nidifacient bird accumulate, each in their own humble way as much cosmic energy in its potential form as a Haydn, a Plato, or a ploughman turning his furrow, in theirs; the hunter who kills game for his pleasure or profit, or the positivist who applies his intellect to proving that $+ x + = -$, *are wasting and scattering energy no less than the tiger which springs upon its prey. They all rob nature instead of enriching her, and will all in the degree of their intelligence find themselves accountable.*

Exact experimental Science has nothing to do with morality, virtue, philanthropy, therefore can make no claim upon our help, until it blends itself with the metaphysics. Being but a cold classification of facts outside man, and existing before and after him, her domain of usefulness ceases for us at the outer boundary of these facts; and whatever the inferences and results for humanity from the materials acquired by her methods, she little cares. Therefore as our sphere lies entirely outside hers — as far as the path of Uranus is outside the earth's — we distinctly refuse to be broken on any wheel of her construction. Heat is but a mode of motion to her, and motion developes heat; but why the mechanical motion of the revolving wheel should be metaphysically of a higher value than the heat into which it is gradually transformed — she has yet to discover.

The philosophical but transcendental (hence absurd?) notion of the mediaeval theosophists that the final progress of human labour aided by the incessant discoveries of man, must one day culminate in a process, which in imitation of the sun's energy — in its capacity of a direct motor — shall result in the evolution of nutritious food out of inorganic matter — is unthinkable for men of science. Were the sun, the great nourishing father of our planetary System, to hatch granite chickens out of a boulder "under test conditions" tomorrow, they (the men of Science) would accept it as a scientific fact, without wasting a regret that the fowls were not alive so as to feed the hungry and the starving. But let a Shaberon cross the Himalayas in a time of famine, and multiply sacks of rice for the perishing multitudes — as he could — and your magistrates and collectors would probably lodge him in jail, to make him confess what granary he had robbed. This is exact science and your realistic world.

And though as you say you are impressed by the vast extent of the world's ignorance on every subject, which you pertinently designate as "a few palpable facts collected and roughly generalized and a technical jargon invented to hide man's ignorance of all that lies behind these facts"; and though you speak of your faith in the infinite possibilities of nature — yet you are content to spend your life in a work which aids only that same exact science. You cause a waste of cosmic energy by tons, to accumulate hardly a few ounces in your volumes — to speak figuratively. And despite your intuitive perceptions of the boundless reaches of nature, you take up the position that unless a proficient in arcane knowledge will waste upon your embryonic Society an energy which without moving from his place he can usefully distribute among millions, you, with your great natural powers will refuse to give a helping hand to humanity by beginning the work single handed, and trusting to time and the great Law to reward your labour.

Of your several questions we will first discuss, if you please, the one relating to the presumed failure of the "Fraternity" to "leave any mark upon the history of the world." They ought, you think, to have been able with their extraordinary advantages to have "gathered into their schools a considerable portion of the more enlightened minds of every race." How do you know they have made no such mark?

Are you acquainted with their efforts, successes, and failures? Have you any dock upon which to arraign them? How could your world collect proofs of the doings of men who have sedulously kept closed every possible door of approach by which the inquisitive could spy upon them. The prime condition of their success was, that they should never be supervised or obstructed. What they have done they know; all those outside their circle could perceive was results, the causes of which were masked from view.

To account for these results, men have in different ages invented theories of the interposition of "Gods," Special providences, fates, and the benign or hostile influences of the stars. There never was a time within or before the so-called historical period when our predecessors were not moulding events and "making history," the facts of which were subsequently and invariably distorted by "historians" to suit contemporary prejudices. Are you quite sure that the visible heroic figures in the successive dramas were not often but their puppets?

We never pretended to be able to draw nations in the mass to this or that crisis in spite of the general drift of the world's cosmic relations. The cycles must run their rounds. Periods of mental and moral light and darkness succeed each other, as day does night. The major and minor yugas must be accomplished according to the established order of things. And we, borne along on the mighty tide, can only modify and direct some of its minor currents. If we had the powers of the imaginary Personal God, and the universal and immutable laws were but toys to play with, then indeed might we have created conditions that would have turned this earth into an

Arcadia for lofty souls. But having to deal with an immutable Law, being ourselves its creatures, we have had to do what we could and rest thankful.

There have been times when "a considerable portion of enlightened minds" were taught in our schools. Such times there were in India, Persia, Egypt, Greece and Rome. But, as I remarked in a letter to Mr. Sinnett, the adept is the efflorescence of his age, and comparatively few ever appear in a single century. Earth is the battle ground of moral no less than of physical forces; and the boisterousness of animal passions under the stimulus of the rude energies of the lower group of etheric agents, always tends to quench spirituality.

What else could one expect of men so nearly related to the lower kingdom from which they evolved? True also, our numbers are just now diminishing but this is because, as I have said, we are of the human race, subject to its cyclic impulse and powerless to turn that back upon itself. Can you turn the Gunga or the Brahmaputra, back to its sources; can you even dam it so that its piled up waters will not overflow the banks? No, but you may draw the stream partly into canals and utilize its hydraulic power for the good of mankind.

So we, who can not stop the world from going in its destined direction, are yet able to divert some part of its energy into useful channels. Think of us as demi-gods and my explanation will not satisfy you; view us as simple men — perhaps a little wiser as the result of special study — and it ought to answer your objection.

"What good," say you, "is to be attained for my fellows and myself (the two are inseparable) by these occult sciences?" When the natives see that an interest is taken by the English and even by some high officials in India in their ancestral science and philosophies, they will themselves take openly to their study. And when they come to realise that the old "divine" phenomena were not miracles, but scientific effects, superstition will abate.

Thus the greatest evil that now oppresses and retards the revival of Indian civilisation will in time disappear. The present tendency of education is to make them materialistic and root out spirituality. With a proper understanding of what their ancestors meant by their writings and teachings, education would become a blessing whereas now it is often a curse. At present the non-educated as much as the learned natives regard the English as too prejudiced, because of their Christian religion and modern science, to care to understand them or their traditions. They mutually hate and mistrust each other.

This changed attitude toward the older philosophy would influence the native Princes and wealthy men to endow normal schools for the education of pundits; and old MSS. hitherto buried out of the reach of the Europeans would again come to light, and with them the key to much of that which was hidden for ages from the popular understanding; for which your skeptical Sanscritists do not care, which your religious missionaries do not dare, to understand. Science would gain much — humanity every thing.

Under the stimulus of the Anglo Indian Theosophical Society, we might in time see another golden age of Sanscrit literature. Such a movement would have the entire approbation of the Home Government as it would act as a preventive against discontent; and the sympathy of European Sanscritists who, in their divisions of opinion need the help of native pundits, now beyond their reach in the present state of mutual misunderstanding. They are even now bidding for such help. At this moment two educated Hindus of Bombay are assisting Max Muller; and a young Pundit of Guzerat a Fellow of the T.S. is aiding Prof. Monier Williams at Oxford and living in his house. The first two are materialists and do harm; the latter single handed can do little, because the man whom he is serving is a prejudiced Christian.

If we look to Ceylon we shall see the most scholarly priests combining under the lead of the Theos. Society in a new exegesis of Buddhistic philosophy and — at Galle on the 15th of September, a secular Theosophical school for the teaching of Singhalese youth opened, with an attendance of over 300 scholars: an example about to be imitated at three other points in that island. If the T.S. "as at present constituted," has indeed no "real vitality" and yet in its modest way has done so much of practical good, how much greater results might not be anticipated from a body organized upon the better plan you could suggest!

The same causes that are materialising the Hindu mind are equally affecting all Western thought. Education enthrones skepticism but imprisons spiritualism.

You can do immense good by helping to give the Western nations a secure basis upon which to reconstruct their crumbling faith. What they need is the evidence that Asiatic psychology alone supplies. Give this and you will confer happiness of mind on thousands.

The era of blind faith is gone; that of enquiry is here. Enquiry that only unmasks error, without discovering anything upon which the soul can build, will but make iconoclasts. Iconoclasm from its very destructiveness can give nothing, it can only raze. But man can not rest satisfied with bare negation. Agnosticism is but a temporary halt.

This is the moment to guide the recurrent impulse which must soon come, and which will push the age toward extreme atheism, or drag it back to extreme sacerdotalism, if it is not led to the primitive and soul-satisfying philosophy of the Aryans. He who observes what is going on today, on the one hand among the Catholics, who are breeding miracles as fast as the white ants do their young, on the other, among the free thinkers, who are converting by masses into agnostics — will see the drift of things. The age is revelling at a debauch of phenomena.

The same marvels that the spiritualists quote in opposition to the dogmas of eternal perdition and atonement, the catholics swarm to witness as the strongest proof of their faith in miracles. The skeptics make game of both. All are blind and there is no one to lead them! You and your colleagues may help furnish the materials for a needed universal religious philosophy; one impregnable to scientific assault because itself the finality of absolute science; and, a religion, that is indeed worthy of the name, since it includes the relations of man physical to man psychical, and of the two to all that is above and below them. Is not this worth a slight sacrifice?

And if after reflection you should decide to enter this new career, let it be known that your Society is no miracle-mongering or banqueting club, nor specially given to the study of phenomenalism. Its chief aim is to extirpate current superstitions and skepticism, and, from long sealed ancient fountains to draw the proof that man may shape his own future destiny, and know for a certainty that he can live hereafter, if he only wills; and that all "phenomena" are but manifestations of natural law, to try to comprehend which is the duty of every intelligent being. You have personally devoted many years to a labour benevolently conceived and conscientiously carried out. Give to your fellow creatures half the attention you have bestowed on your 'little birds," and you will round off a useful life with a grand and noble work.

Sincerely your friend.

Here is how I got my hands on this remarkable letter:

Today, January 3, 1884, I finish dictating, according to my notes, this chapter: *Science in Antiquity.*

Now, a few weeks ago, I was asked to become a correspondent in the Theosophical Society of Madras.

I declined this honor; the intellectual pennant I am bearing for more than twenty years, and which I have been raising publicly in the last two years, is forbidding me to engage its universality and its social significance in any particularism whatsoever.

Nevertheless, I was given several copies of an Anglo-Indian newspaper, or rather Indo-American, "The Theosophist", printed in Madras, which, although interesting in many respects, did not tell me anything new.

In addition, to these journals was added an English pamphlet, The Occult World by Sinnett, 1883, where I found the letter I have translated into French, the pure pearl of the East which I have just enshrined in this chapter.

Thousands of years ago, a living Initiate of the Ionian Mysteries would not have had better or more clearly spoken if, through time travel, he had witnessed the actual spectacle of the workings of that Eastern world.

The reader will see, I hope, in this profession of faith from one of the affiliates of the great Brotherhood of the Himalayas, a powerful and living confirmation of the rigorous accuracy of my information and conclusions.

For the moment, it is to this unknown brother, brilliant representative of the esoteric science of his order, it is to this Oriental so remarkable that I want to answer, from the bottom of our Occident, our Judeo-Christianity and our modern science, from the heart of this ancient Keltic land, called Varaha in Sanskrit, the motherland of the Kelts Varaighes, from which these same Aryas left, 8,600 years ago (1880 AD).

In my current book I am endeavoring to unveil the history and social tradition of these early peoples.

INTRODUCTION TO DIVINELY INSPIRED SOCIAL ORDER

As indicated in previous chapters the natural order was not the only object of study; antique science developed four fields of study. Three of them *concerned Creative Nature, Created Nature,* and *Human Nature*, which is their link, their hierogram being EVE, la VIE, Life.

Symbolized in Moses' tradition by the first letter of the name of I E V E, the fourth order corresponded to a completely different hierarchy of knowledge, marked by the number 10.

This number 10 was especially at the center of the Dorian initiations of India, Egypt, Kaldea, Persia, Israel, Greece, Etruria, etc., etc....

It is through this Dorian channel that the intellectual flow of esoteric science and exoteric testimonies were transmitted, thus tending to the complete reconstitution of the ancient "Cycle of the Lamb and the Ram", of the old Universal Alliance, the old terrestrial Public Peace, the Reign of God, finally accomplished in this world as in the Universe.

Such is the true significance of the Dorian program of the Abramids, Dorian priests of Kaldea, of Moses – Egyptian Dorian priest of Isis and Osiris -, of Jesus finally, who, reserving esotericism for future eras, impressed on the tradition of the Lamb a new vivid irresistible "psychurgical" impulse towards its social, universal fulfillment.

But it is not enough to express these things, we must prove them, and this book will, I hope, be an irrecusable demonstration. I wish this book gets in the hands of all the noble minds of the East, of all the patriots, whose religious thoughts are still nurtured by the *grandiose remnants of the old intellectual Universality,* of the ancient social Cycle! May it be for them a consolation, a hope, a certainty of the upcoming fulfillment of all their wishes, by means which Providence never fails to place at the service of good human will! A last word to these noble minds:

Do not hasten to make a final judgment on modern science or on the Judeo-Christian religion.

Brahma did not create the World in a day; and for human societies as for individuals, the birth and growth to the fullness of moral, intellectual, and, consequently, social life, requires necessarily its proper time cycle.

MOSES: HIGH PRIEST IN EGYPT

My works have only one goal, to prove that this time cycle has arrived, and to formulate, based on Christianity and modern science in present-day Europe, what the best minds of all cults, all schools, all races, have always thought and still think as to the Principles of general Government and Rules of particular Societies.

But let us return to the intellectual plow, which must be used into the European field of understanding, so that Judeo-Christianity can bear its final fruits of wisdom and love, intelligence and social happiness.

It is impossible to admit that Moses was not aware of the intellectuality of his time, nor of the scientific tradition of earlier times.

We know the names of his priestly masters, *Iah-Men-Iah, Mem-Bra, Jethro*, etc.

But to keep the modern reader at a comfortable plane of thought, let's explicit information only at the exoteric level.

Either Moses was instructed in the Egyptian sciences, or he ignored them.

However, Philo, St. Clement of Alexandria, the Acts of the Apostles, tell us that he was deeply versed in this knowledge.

Strabo learned from Egyptian priests that Moses belonged to their priesthood.

Manetho, an Egyptian priest, tells us Moses was a priest of Osiris or Ammon-Ra, gods and academic symbols of the Ram Tradition.

Therefore, *Moses could not say what his translators are making him say*.

Consequently, *all the scientific and chronological errors of Genesis are caused by translators and theologians, and not by Moses*, thank God!

The second book of Sepher Torah, *Veelle-Schemoth, Exodus*, Ch. XII, verse 40, informs us that the Hebrews had been in Egypt for 430 years.

It is therefore clear they spoke Egyptian, and *Moses wrote his books in this language and, especially, in the ideographic language* of the priests of Egypt.

Why in this language and not in Hebrew? because the Hebrew word, which means emigrant, alludes to a mixed crowd of expatriate peoples, not to a language, which each group must inevitably have lost. The Hebrew people, a group of men and women of different races instituted as one nation by Moses, later in time, lost in seventy years of captivity in Babylon its Egyptian-Phoenician language, and adopted Syriac-Aramaic, a Kaldaic dialect.

Therefore, knowing that they stayed in Egypt more than 400 years where no institution had united them in a national body, one cannot expect that this people, or rather this group of tribes, of White, Black and Red races, had not lost their original dialects, mixture of primitive Keltic language with ancient idioms.

ANCIENT LINGUISTICS

Though admitting the books of Moses were written in the language of the priests of Egypt, one may ask *how then the priests wrote their texts*, particularly how did they write those hieratic books which contained the Greater Mysteries and *their special sciences: Cosmogony, Theogony*, etc.

Apart from the esoteric Tradition, we must ask the ancient writers, who can enlighten us, especially those of whom we know to have been initiated to the Mysteries.

Apuleius, Book XI, and Cheremon, through Porphyry and Eusebius, will answer the following:

The priesthood had in Egypt several kinds of writings corresponding to the various degrees of the Mysteries; all these writings were hierographic, that is to say, *scientifically composed* according to positive principles, and being not understood totally by the vulgar, but only by the scholar.

The hieroglyphs, a kind of scriptural algebra, semi-ideographic, corresponded to the first part of the Mysteries, and their phonetic sense was alone completely accessible to the crowd.

At the second part of the Mysteries there were more secret writings.

Finally, at the third part, there *were ideo-logical characters, corresponding to a very ancient phonetic language*, and the latter with accents above and below.

This last language, the most secret of all, was devoted to the sciences of which I spoke, and absolutely *incomprehensible without a key*.

Thus, the first word of the Cosmogony of Moses, *Be-Reshith*, signifies:

Core Principle for the wise-savant,

Origin for the semi-savant,

Beginning as vernacular spoken word.

As the Egyptian priests had penetrated more deeply the genius and the essence of *the Verb* than our philologists suppose, we must find in this hierogram *Be-Resh-ith* itself its reason and its explanation.

It is in its *root* that one must look for its *radical meaning*.

This root is *Roesh*, which means the *head, the chief, the prince, the Principle*. This *root Roesh* is found *in almost all language: Rex, Richt, Right*, etc. I have defined in the Mission of the Sovereigns, page 249, what the ancients understood by Principle: *A Principle is a radical, a root, a starting point for a certain series of specific consequences belonging only to it*.

The *ancient morphology or qualitative geometry* taught in the temples, basis of hieroglyphics, symbolized the Principle idea by *a point in the center of a circle*. Moreover, it is the scientific Principle of the whole Universe.

Instead of Principle, read it as meaning origin or beginning, and the 50 chapters of which this word is the starting point, will take a purely natural, material, anthropomorphic, phantasmatic aspect, instead of an intellectual and rigorously scientific aspect. I could further pursue the analysis, up to the hierographic and geometrically precise meaning that Egyptian priests *attached to each letter* of their sacred alphabets; but it would be out of place here.

MOSES' "GENESIS" IS A BOOK OF SCIENCE

Moses' Cosmogony is a formidable book of science, and I wish only to give you some glimpses on this science, reserving more details for those who, in the future, will be in charge of its development and applications, in many fields of research, including societal organization.

When Geoffroy Saint-Hilaire, who was more than an ordinary naturalist, attempting to understand the first causation of *physical life*, he characterized it in a very remarkable way by these words: The *Attraction of Self by Self*.

In fact, *this natural* Principle seems to be the opposite of Moses' Principle, the one we have scrutinized above (Be-Roesh-It), and which expresses the *Universal Cyclic Attraction*.

But, be aware, the famous serpent of the so-called garden of delights does not mean anything else, in the Egyptian text of Moses than what Geoffroy Saint-Hilaire has just expressed: *Nahash*, the *natural original Attraction*, whose hieroglyph was a coiled serpent.

The word Harum, which in the text of the legislator of the Hebrews follows the preceding hierogram Nahash, is the famous Hariman of the first Zoroaster, and expresses the universal drive of *Created Nature*, caused by the preceding Principle (Nahash). As for the famous Satan, the so-called principle of Evil, it is nowhere mentioned in the text of our Cosmogony.

Not knowing how to decrypt it, the ordinary readers accused Moses' text of not having mentioned the *Soul, the ethereal Essence of the Human Being or all other beings*.

However, here is the name that Moses gives to this Essence, *Nephesch*, a contraction of three roots *(Ne-Phe-Scha)*.

This hierogram-*Nephesh* in no way expresses only the abstract soul of the theologians, but the *Living Soul*, the psychurchic and physiological Essence at the same time, triple and one, in the image of the Universe itself; the same Essence Plato and Pythagoras saw, observed, knew, experienced, in the same sanctuaries as Moses.

Now this word, like all those whom this Egyptian priest employs, has *three meanings*, when we read it phonetically, one *positive or proper*, the other *comparative or figurative*, the third finally *superlative or purely scientific*.

And if one wonders why Moses wrote in such a way, all

antiquity will answer that not only the Egyptian priesthood, but *all the learned schools of the world, did not write otherwise on scientific subjects of this importance.*

Let's move on to *Adam*'s hierogram.

It is enough to read the word by which the Samaritan writers translated it: meaning the *Universal, the Infinite.* It is easy to spot that *this hierogram Adam is not about an individual silt made man such as presented by the Septuagint and the Vulgate.*

Adam is thus the Universal Man, or the Universe itself comprehended as an animated Being.

It has also been said the word *Nature,* or the idea attached to it, did not appear anywhere in Moses' Cosmogony.

That's another mistake, because here it is: *Shadeh*; and its masculine: *Shaday,* meaning the *fecundity Principle,* of which the nature is the living receptive Faculty. It is true that the Septuagint and the Vulgate translators have reduced Shadeh into mere "agricultural field" in place of universal Nature.

Thus, the translators have transformed into many little men all the derivative Principles, themselves emerging from the Universal Principle, Adam.

This is how they transformed into geographical rivers all Cosmic Fluids. This is how they made a mere boat of the Thebah, instead of the Solar System whose Thebes of Egypt bore the name. In the same way they made a *dove* out of the word *Ionah,* issued from the Yonijas of India, the Ionians of Syria, Assyria and Greece, while in reality this word signifies *the feminine faculty,* plastic, universal, of which the dove is only one of a thousand symbols.

In the same way they made a simple raven of the Amenti, of the Erebus, which Orpheus learned about in the same Egyptian sanctuaries.

Now, the hierogram *Ionah* designates the *Cone of Light* which has the Sun as summit and its base on each Planet during the Day. As for the hierogram *Erebus* it designates the *Cone of Darkness* which covers every Planet at Night, with its summit residing on one or several Moons.

Those translators have also found a way to disguise into a person (Hanoch) the annual rotation of the Earth around the Sun in 365 days: Wa-îhîou khol îmeî *Hanôch* hamesh we-shishîm shanah we-shelosh mœôth shanah.

The totality of Hanoch's days was five and six decades and three hundred temporal revolutions (365 days).

UNIVERSAL SOCIAL STATE BEFORE THE FRACTURE

All the ancient religions, up to and including Christianity, came out of the ancient centers of initiation, and these centers were erudite institutions, the most important of which were organized into the four hierarchies of Sciences of which I spoke above.

The *multiplicity of religions* dates only from the year 3300 BC, and was, either the result of a great schism that took place at that time, or the local effort by the Initiates to repair everywhere, as much as they could, the political fractures, the multiplication of arbitrary unaccountable governments surging from the rupture of the former General Arbitral Government.

As a last summary, *up to 3,000 years before Christ, existed a Universal Social State,* coordinated within itself by a whole hierarchical series of arbitral institutions. The Religion of this Social State, from which all the different existing cults proceed, was *merged with Science* through 4 hierarchies of knowledge: *Physiological, Human, Cosmogonic, Theogonic.*

Temples and sanctuaries were the highest savant institutions; the lay Initiates were given all their light, according to their initiation degree, and constituted a second social Power, corresponding to our magistracy; the heads of families, men and women, formed everywhere in their local assemblies, the third Power.

Later in this book, I will demonstrate the positive existence of this ancient Ram's Synarchy, the causes that inclined it to ruination, and how to this Trinitarian social order succeeded the arbitrary policy with its two forms of government, Monarchy and Republic, defined in the first chapter of the Mission of the Sovereigns.

This Synarchic Social State was known in Europe, Asia, Africa, and even America, under the names of *The Universal Theocracy of the Lamb, Universal Arbitral Empire of Ram.*

When schisms, and their resulting pure politics, had dismembered this ancient Universal Alliance, when they had multiplied and opposed one to the other those fragmented dominions and religions, they became enslaved to the monarchical or republican politicians. Then the Initiates did what was in their power: They tried locally *to redress the religious universities, sectarianized and darkened by their official slavery to anarchic powers.*

When they could not, they relied on public mores to institute a moral culture, by means of a worship appropriate to the circumstances; and everywhere they combated arbitrariness.

The purest part of *the ancient encyclopedia of the Temples' knowledge was salvaged, in Kaldea by the Abramids Order, in Egypt by Moses, who selected a people to be the guardian of the letter, encrypted, and protected, within his five Genesic books.*

But it was necessary that this movement towards the re-establishment of the ancient Order of Things be directed towards the *whole of Humanity,* and it is what *Jesus Christ* did.

Such is the capital value of the sacred books which are the basis of Judeo-Christianity. Such is their relationship with ancient Science, with modern Science, with the Ancient and the New Cycle to come, of Lamb and Ram.

THE TRUE ORIGIN OF THE HEBREW PEOPLE

In the next chapter, we are going to find out *whence came the Hebrews,* who were *deemed worthy by Providence* to carry their sealed "marching order" through the centuries; and we will show that this noble people, who have never recognized any other legitimate Government than that of God, has in their veins the same Keltic blood as we, Europeans and Turanians.

CHAPTER V
REAL ORIGIN OF THE HEBREWS

SUCCESSIVE DOMINANT RACES

Each continent has seen its organic kingdoms completed and crowned by a special human race.

These creations have not been simultaneous; various continents have emerged from the seas at considerable intervals of time corresponding to the *inter-diluvian cycles* known to the ancient Indian priests.

With regard to the varieties of the physical Human Species, it is in Europe that we must look for the origin of the White Race, in Asia that of the Yellow Race, in Africa that of the Black Race, in the Austral Continent, engulfed by the last Great Flood, the original place of the primeval Red Race, of which the American Indians are but remnants refugees, troglodyte on the mountain tops.

As for the Hebrews, like all human Variations where the blood of the white race predominates, they are ancient Europeans who have become creoles and half-breeds, alternately Asian and or African.

I am aware that such data are not being respected by many current schools which, unknowingly, are still under the yoke of the *erroneous translations of Moses' Genesis*.

If we do not start from the fact that the primitive terrestrial human was wild, cannibalistic, rudimentary and elementary, we will never attain the truth about this simple matter of human origins.

Obviously if we blind ourselves to the fact our long-ago forefathers were cannibals, cousins of the monkey species, but instead convince ourselves that physical Humanity surged out of a single couple miraculously endowed with all the perfections, installed, 6,000 years ago, in an Eldorado situated to the East, between the Tigris and the Euphrates, then certainly all the branches of this singular human tree will have to come from this single Asiatic root.

But *Moses* never aimed at creating any muddling of the sciences of the *sensorial Realm* with those of the *intelligible Realm*; for he was in possession of data other than scholastic childishness, other information than fabulations, good enough at most for elementary education of children or childlike peoples.

Some schools reject the tale of Eden, the unique couple, the fall, as contrary to the ascending movement of the laws of physical Nature; nevertheless, they persevere in the theological rut, declaring the Asian plateaus the source of all the Races.

I think I have sufficiently demonstrated that the ancient priesthoods in general and the priests of Egypt especially, were in no way ignorant, and that *Humanity, 10,000 years ago, was not less scientifically informed than today.*

THE ADAM PRINCIPLE

Yet I reiterate here that the name *Adam* never defined a man of flesh and bones, but a *cosmogonic Principle.*

To release Moses, the Hebrew legislator, from the theological slanders he has been subjected to when he spoke of the Father of the Human Race, I am asking the reader to follow me behind the triple veil I have evoked previously

Being a reflection of IEVE, similarly male and female, the ADAM Principle conveys a much broader meaning, even vaster than the significance projected by the naturalist philosophers who impress on terrestrial corporeal humanity the magnifying title of *Human Regnum,* thus signaling - somewhat unwillingly- the existence of a specific cosmogonic Force. ADAM is the hierogram of this universal Principle; it represents the Intelligent Soul of the Universe itself, the universal Verb animating the totality of the Solar Systems, not only in the visible Order, but also and especially in the Invisible Order.

For when Moses speaks of the animating principle of our solar system, it is no longer Adam that he mentions, but *Noah.*

Shadow of IEVE, living thought and organic Law of the Ælohim, Adam is the celestial Essence from which emanate all past, present and future Humanities, not only here below, but through the immensity of the Heavens.

It is the Universal Soul of Life, Nephesh Haiah, Homogeneous Substance, which Moses calls *Adamah*, and which Plato calls the Higher Earth.

Now, I do not interpret, I literally express the cosmogonic thought of Moses; for such is the Adam of the sanctuaries of Thebes and of Bæreshith, the *great celestial Hominal* of all ancient temples, from Gaul to the depths of India.

As to the so-called *Eden*, here is what it means in the hermetic text of Moses, priest of Osiris: *Gan-Bi-Heden*, sojourn of Adam-Eve, represents *the Organism of the universal Sphere of Time*, the Organization of the Totality of what is temporal.

The famous rivers which are four in one, that is to say which form an *organic quaternary*, do not point at the Tigris and the Euphrates any more than the Tiber, the Seine or the Thames, because, once again, the *first ten chapters of Moses are a Cosmogony and not a geography*.

So these so-called rivers are in fact *universal fluids*. Starting from *Gan, the organic genetic Power* par excellence, these fluids engulf the *Temporal Sphere, Heden*, (Zoroaster's boundless Time), placed itself between two Eternities, the former one, *Kædem*, the other posterior, *Gholim*.

Moses calls these fluids *Phishon, Gihon, Hiddekel, Phrath*.

I will not express them here in English; but I will point out to the reader that Orpheus, a contemporary of Moses, initiated in the same sanctuaries as him, calls *Physis* what the Hebrew legislator characterizes under the name of *Phishon*, and that Gihon, Hiddekel, and Phrath have no less importance.

To this fluid, Phishon, the one who allows the *Principle Adam-Eve* to render its creations physical, Moses connects three homogeneous forces under three different states, which are *Hawilla, Beddolah, Shoham*. These three hierograms have singularly captivated, during the Middle Ages, those disciples of Hermes who wanted to decrypt them.

WANDERING HEBREWS

But after vindicating Moses about Adam and Eden, let's go back to the Hebrews.

Their ancestors like the Europeans' are named Ghiborim by the theocrat Moses.

This hierogram is found exactly, though contracted, in the name Ghèbres.

The main root *"Bor"*, extracted from Ghi*bor*im, refers to humans from our northern *bor*eal hemisphere.

Such, indeed, are the Ghiborim, the Ghiboreans, the Hyperboreans, to whom all the members of the White Race owe their life.

It is not irrelevant to notice that the same name is found in Gibraltar, Ghi*bor*-al-thar or thor.

Now, the peoples who most claim the Ghiborim ancestry as the primeval origin of the White Race, are certainly the Celts, or rather the Kelts. The root of their name is *Eld, Ald or Old*, which we will find later in the East in the words Kaldea, Aldea, the Indian commune, as in Portugal in Aldea the Portuguese rural commune, etc., etc. The Keltic word, *Ka-Eld*, therefore meant the *Assembly (ka) of Ancients (eld)*.

The name of *Scythes,* which the then domineering Blacks gave to the Whites out of contempt, meant what is violently separated, what is spit, the white spit itself, because of the Kelts' white skin color.

On the other hand, our rough Kelts ancestors called the Black peoples of a similarly unflattering name: *Pelaska*, meaning skins of the woods, burned skins.

It follows from the foregoing there is no mistaking, in seeing, like Moses, in the Hebrews, as in the Arabs, in the Bedouins and Berbers, the *Kelts Bodhones*, the wandering Scythes evoked by the ancient authors.

Moreover, all these peoples, have acquired in the South and West of Europe many original signs and symbols, as irrefutably testified by linguistics, anthropology and archeology.

As for the *idioms* so improperly called *Semitic*, they are today, in the view of all the scientists, the result of one of the *first mixtures made between the dialects of the White Race and those of the Black Race*, with predominance of the latter.

Emigrants, not conquerors, but followers of the male Principle, persecuted, hunted after bloody battles by the College of Druidesses, the Bodhnones Kelts followed two different routes, which both led them to the kingdoms, empires or the colonies of the *Black Race, then masters of the World and in full civilization bloom.*

Some, crossing Gibraltar, the southern boundary of the Ghiborians of Thor, -such as the Borysthenes was their limit to the East-, entered Africa, and were rallied by the Egyptian and Ethiopian Social State.

The others following, from Iberia and Osk-Tan, or Occitania, the coasts of southern Europe, have entered and stayed in either the Black colonies of Italy and Greece, or went further into the kingdoms of the Black race from the Caucasus, Crimea, ancient Persia, where they founded the *Hebyreh,* a small White Race kingdom, which preceded the conquest of Iran by the white race, as reported in the epic poem the Scha-Nameh.

Through Ethiopia and ancient Persia, a considerable part of those peoples also reached Arabia, the kingdoms of the Tigris and Euphrates, and finally the great Black Race Empire, called for this reason the *India.*

At that remote time when these exoduses were underway, *three Races were superimposed in Africa, in Asia, in the Caucasus,* and finally on *all the coasts of the Mediterranean,* forming a great civilization dwelling in colossal cities. One race, the *Yellow,* almost confined to Asia, was dominated, the other, the *Black race, was dominant* under the religious name of *Gian-ben-Gian,* the *Universal,* son-daughter of the Universe.

The oldest of all, the *Red race,* which had bequeathed its immense civilization to the Black peoples, existed only as a minority. One can still see it wandering today, not only in America, where it is weakened, but also on the banks of the Nile, among the almost pure Bisharis, among the Foulbs mixed with the Yellow race, in Central and Western Africa, among the Fulani, Pouls, Fellahs, Fellathas, south of Timbuktu, in the Sudan, in Nigritia, towards the Foutah, and even Senegal.

WHITE KELTS BLEND WITHIN THE BLACK RACE EMPIRE

When the *Kelts bodhones* dispersed in the Blacks' Societies, they found these peoples living in an incredible prosperity, with thousands of fortified cities, most often carved into the mountains; their formidable scale, impressive architecture, splendid aesthetics were beyond anything imagination could conceive.

The absorption of emigrants into Egypt, Libya, Ethiopia, Persia, India, Arabia, Syria, Crimea, was slow, without brutality, and imprinted deeply upon the ancestors of the Hebrews and the Arabs the stamp of Black Civilization, then sovereign.

However, due to *the social character* of their institutions, the White tribes, while mingling with the Black families, preserved their independence, their Keltic commune, their tribunal of the Ancients, and many customs, many other memories that never were entirely obliterated.

Everything *about Science, applied technical Arts and Crafts* was borrowed from the Black Gian-ben-Gian culture, and if the dialects, while admixed, kept many Keltic words and roots, the writing and its direction were entirely borrowed from local temple-universities of the Black Race.

This fact proves that besides the cult of the Ancestor in the home, the emigrants had no priesthood, apart from heads of families or leaders of tribes; here's why: at that time, *Science, applied Art, Religion were one and the same thing,* whose Principles of Unity had been clearly determined.

ORIENTATION OF ANCIENT SCRIPTS

Thus *Language,* whether written, carved, or spoken, *was conjointly a Science and a Religious Art.* The priest or the simple scholar of the Black Race followed in their manner of writing certain rules and rites they had inherited from the Red Race, before that race was engulfed while still at the top of their civilization, during the submersion of the Austral Continent.

The Nahash-Savant guiding his pen or his stylus, was turning his head towards the South Pole, and, in a form of homage, he was *conducting the scripted words towards the East,* the source of the Light, and of all the cosmogonic, psychurgic, and intellectual ideas he was connecting to it.

Thus, the *scripting proceeded from right to left*. Such was also the direction adopted by all the ancient Kelts who had for masters-teachers the ancient Red or Black priests.

This direction of writing persisted for a long time in Europe itself, in the Gian-ben-Gian colonies, which gave our barbarian ancestors their cursive writing, as indicated by the meaning of the word *Runes* (run).

Before these exoduses, the Mediterranean Sea was for a long time called the Black Sea, the sea of burned skins, Pelasks, and, later, Pelagos. Many centuries later the Mediterranean Sea received the name of Great Green, given by the European Kelts, once they became masters of Egypt.

In the North, on the contrary, the sea took the general name Sea of the Whites or White Sea.

More than a thousand years before these exoduses, the entire coastline of Southern and Western Europe had been covered with huge forts, gigantic Cyclopean walls, built by the colonists of the Black Race.

The Black Race, attracted by the rich mineral resources, had treated the White Race as the White Race has treated the Reds of America since Christopher Columbus.

This conquest and its purpose were imprinted in the minds of European barbarians as the idea of evil par excellence, which, for our Race, remains attached to the very evocation of the South Pole: Sat, Set, Seth, Sothis, Saturn, Sathan, South.

Hell, as imagined by the theologians was born in the bowels of our Continent, where, under the eye of the Black engineer or the Black foreman, the White man smashed the rocks, dug the galleries, searched the earth, extracted the ore, and carried it in the victor's furnaces.

But the European had an advantage: the shelter of the forests, the shield of extremely cold climate. There, able to retreat, he could still go on the attack.

Once the yoke was shaken, after centuries of colossal and

incessant struggles, the Druids, the priests of the Ghiborim, gradually changed the direction of the Runes, in Greece, Etruria, Gaul, Iberia, and, all the more so in Northern Europe.

Masters of their own intellectuality, awakened by the erudite teachers of the Black Race, *the Druids traced the written Word, orienting themselves toward the Boreal Pole* and directing their hand from West to East, *from left to right.*

Therefore all the writings in the rest of the world which follow that direction clearly reveal a European origin, affirm an armed conquest of the White Race, a victory of the Kelts of our Continent, whatever may be the demotic or priestly character, phonetic or ideographic signs, regardless of the blend that the conquering race was able to make between its own language and that of the invaded Civilization.

SPECIFIC PATH OF THE EARLY HEBREW MIGRATIONS

As for the migrations of the *Bodhones*, from which the *Hebrews* derive their origin, they will remain marked by the intellectual seal of the Black Race, both in the direction of writing and in the predominance of the Pelasgic dialects, both in ideographic genius and in the scientific spirit of their sacred monuments.

The cause is, once again, that these expatriations led these emigrants to voluntarily adopt the customs of the Social State where they sought refuge, not as masters or conquerors, but as hosts and disciples.

In turn, this infusion of Keltic blood will also affect to a certain extent even the Pelasgic dialects themselves: Basque, Etruscan, Egyptian, Ethiopian, Syriac, Kaldaic, Zend, Proto-Mede, Akkadian, etc.

Except Basque which is more closely related to the dialects of the ancient Red Race, all these languages, will allow the attentive linguist to easily perceive their relationship with the primitive Keltic, as we can still guess from what remains of the songs of the Edda, Gaelic books, Kymric and Keltic dialects, and finally, in all the Indo-European languages, where the roots plunge more or less deeply into the ancient Keltic.

The anthropological characters of the Bodhones have acquired their differential aspects only thanks to the change of milieus; still they remain marked by the stamp of the Europeans who had received before these exoduses the infusion of the blood of the Black Race, on the shores of the Atlantic or those of the Mediterranean.

The peoples who, long after this infusion, formed the Latin and the Greek groups, joining Armenians, Phrygians of the Caucasus, Tauridians, Afghans, Ghebres, Arameans, Phoenicians, Egyptians, etc.., will present undeniable anatomical, cranioscopic, physiognomonic analogies, as well as with the Hebrews and the Arabs.

The type of the hooked nose Bourbons dynasty is the weakened characteristic of this profile, found on old medals, where the large cheekbones of the Black peoples have bent the nose of the White people.

KELTS FIND REFUGE IN THE SOUTHERN BLACK EMPIRE

The peoples of the first exodus of which I speak were always grateful to the Black Race for having opened their arms to them.*Moses* himself will marry *Zipporah*, the *daughter of a Black High priest of Osiris* in the valley of Jethro.

The legislator of the Hebrews will make his wife of that dark virgin of Ethiopia after having been for a long time the disciple of her father, Black guardian of the most luminous traditions of the prediluvian civilization of the Red Race.

Chant of the Shulamite of the Bible *"I am black, but I am beautiful"*, thus will say in his songs more passionate than religious the Louis XIV of Judea, King Salomon.

Nearly 9,000 years ago, the Black Race opened its ancient treasures of Wisdom, Science, Love, to the poor Kelts Bodhones, still faithful to the male Principle, banished from Europe by the *white ferocious Druidesses*.

This name of Bodhone sounds like a melancholy melody; it means without *bed*, without shelter, and is found in the current word *Bed*ouin. It is the patronymic name of those who will be without a nation.

Job, whose hieroglyph was Keleb, *Canis Major* of Sirius, the dog star, which signals the exaltation of the soul in extreme joy or extreme pain, Job will become the unifying symbol of this wandering race, filled with incurable nostalgia while wandering on the whole Earth.

The words Jubilee and Jubilation are rooted in the name Job, and now are applied to the feelings of spiritual happiness.

TIMELESS WORLDWIDE MISSION OF THE HEBREWS

This cabalistic poem of Job will truly be the song of the Bodhones rejected from all the female sanctuaries, invoking everywhere the male God, asking him for the supreme Wisdom and Science, that even the male sanctuaries of Persia, India and Egypt will grant them only at the cost of thousands of tribulations.

Noble Race which, thus uprooted almost 9,000 years ago from its country of origin, was devoted since that time to have for homeland only the whole Earth!

One cannot see it without emotion, in the depths of this painful past, this Race fleeing the Keltide, the ringing forests, the dolmens and the bloody knives of the Druidesses.

Through the shores, seas, islands, mountains, deserts, from civilizations to civilizations, here they are forever wandering, in Southern Europe, in Africa, in Asia, crossing in Time and Space all human environments, all Societies, and retaining their intellectual echoes, like the infinite voices of the Ocean resonate in giant seashells.

It is thanks to these resilient wanderers that has come to us the most divine currents of ancient Science and Wisdom; it is through those stiff-necked men that no political power can ever submit, that has been transmitted the scientific and social marching orders of the great Dorian initiation, of the Abramids and of Moses, messages which Jesus Christ, the Galilean, has chosen to spread over all Humanity, like the steel wire conducts the message of the lightning.

Since those remote times, in the depths of the sanctuaries of Gaul, the prophetesses had already predicted that the Savior of the World would be born of a virgin; and the last ontological effort of the Bodhones Kelts will indeed, from the bottom of Galilee, in front of genuflecting Europeans, elevate Mary holding in her arms Jesus, radiant heart of Humanity.

What would have been these Bodhones if they had remained happily in the Keltide?

Provencals, Gascons, nothing less, but also nothing more in the great organic work of the human race.

But grander destinies awaited them, and still await them in the future, for their own happiness as well as for the benefit of all humankind. If the linguist and the anthropologist can easily recognize in Hebrew, as well as in Arabic, the traces of the language of the Keltic race, the more the archaeologist can recognize in the Bodhones the old habits of the Ghiborim.

Near Gonior (Israel), one can still see Druidic monuments like the stone heaps of Kairnac (Brittany).

In the Kahnat of Han (Kanaan), the raised rocks are called by Jacob *Dyal-Aad*, meaning *witness-clusters*, by Laban, *Idger-Si-Heduta*, meaning *monuments of testimony*.

Jacob in Egyptian idiom, Laban in Kaldaic, both record the same Keltic European traditions.

THE POWER OF BLACK CIVILIZATION

Noticeably, the Black Race which, *thousands of years before the exodus of the Bodhones*, had covered the Earth with grandiose cities carved in the rock, had no such Keltic habits of displaying raw stones.

The Black Race rulers employed hundreds of thousands of White and Yellow peoples, either to carve the Caucasus or the Himalayas, the rocks of the Nile Valley or those of Hindustan and Ceylon, or to cover the hills with gigantic square cities, surrounded by formidable walls colossal enough to sustain large buildings.

The Cyclopean ruins of El-Khan still give little idea of the power of the Pelaskas, the engineering resources of *Gian-ben-Gian*, and one can find these vestiges even in their ancient naval stations in the North-West of Europe.

The previous data explain why the Kelts have since hated the giant architectural stonework, a hatred the tradition changed into religious superstition.

Their only shelters were forests, where the military tactics of the Blacks, like their cavalry and their war machines, became powerless. For the Ghiborim, every wall, every organized big city was the affirmation of the Spirit of the South, the work of the enemy Power.

It was from those cities that came out, preceded by drummers and resonating fanfare, the armies of the Blacks covered with metal scales, copper, silver or gold helmets, infantry, cavalry, engineering, even artillery, floating in the wind their white silk pennants ornate with the yellow Rawhon, the Golden Dragon.

It was through these bronze gates and drawbridges that the priestly engineer came out with his dark squadrons, his blueprints covered with strange characters, his various tools, to seek the water sources, minerals and underground metals. (tools unknown as of today 1884 AD).

And the Black priest engineer, with his commander's staff, was sending to the quarries and the mines the White men with blue eyes, the tattooed giants, grumbling under harsh discipline, like lions, that until the time of Aristote and even that of the Niebelungen, still inhabited our wooded mountains.

It was in these accursed cities the beautiful White Women with their long luminous hair disappeared, sometimes carried off at a gallop by the dark cavalrymen, sometimes running toward them like Atalanta, of their own free will.

Thus the curse of the Druids and Druidesses, the imprecation of the Ovates and Eubages, the fury of the Herolls and the Khans, thundered against the Civilization, against the Black City, against the cut stone.

And, 7,000 years later, the voice of the last Odin, Frighe, son of Fridulf, native of Asgard, former lieutenant of defeated Mithridates, will gather from the Caucasus to the Atlantic all the ancient Keltide, and, through millions of white breasts, will roar the same imprecations against Rome, daughter of Babel, City of mixed blood, against her arbitrary empire, against the Empire of the Creoles.

THE LOVE OF KELTS FOR UNCUT NATURAL STONES

But these stones debased by the demons of the South, these granites, are nevertheless venerable bones of the old living Earth, of the old Mother, the great Bride of the Living Sky.

The Kelts endeavored to avenge the outrage imposed on these stone-bones by the Southern Dragon: they will be the sacred witnesses of the oaths and power of the Whites; they will rise and move of their own accord to their magical prayers; they will flow from the blood of the sacrifices to the Ancestors gathered in the clouds under the light of the Moon.

It is not because they are not able to carve them the Kelts will leave uncut these stone-bones, these fragments of Herta's skeleton; it is because they no longer want to do it, having done it too much, as military prisoners serving the Black Race.

They will play with these blocks like children with dice, they will raise them like pins in memory of their leaders, they will pile them up like ossicles in honor of the Genii and the Gods, they will know how to arrange them in a so wonderful balance, that with a little finger a child will make thrill, throb, murmur, masses of granite weighing thousands of kilograms.

The priests and the bards of both sexes will evoke from the bosom of the feverish atmosphere the diaphanous people of the Souls; in front of them, the heroes will renew the extreme oaths, and each tribe will raise its stone in testimony of a won battle, a victory to be gained, a memory to perpetuate.

KELTIC-DRUIDIC SOURCES OF THE HEBREWS

It is under this atavic impulse that we will see again in *Joshua, Chap. IV Verse 2-9,* the Hebrews arriving in the Khanate of Han, (Kanaan), plant, pile up, juxtapose huge rough stones, like their Arab brothers, like their forefathers the Ghèbres, like their ancestors the Kelts, sons of the ancient Ghibor (Ælohim-

Ghibor, Him, the Powers of the Boreal Pole).

Even today, the Kelts of Ireland, as in Ossian's day, swear by the Powers, which in the old days were invoked while standing beside the famous stone of Power.

Dying *Joshua* will gather in Shekhem his Kelts Bodhones, *mixed Black and Red races, which had become the Israelite tribes.* He will remind them that it was to introduce IEVE in the human organic societies, that Moses organized them into a nation, that it was to reflect IEVE on Earth as he is in Heaven, that they were extracted from Mitzraim (Egypt), and he asked them to swear loyalty to IEVE (Yahveh).

Then, in commemoration of this solemn oath, he will act like an ancient Druid, he will choose an enormous stone, and have it set up under the oak tree which is always standing near the sanctuary of the Eternal.

Instructed by *Moses*, priest of Osiris, on the real origin of the Bodhones Kelts, *Joshua*, himself an Egyptian initiate, will act, as did at the same time the priesthood of the European forests. Later Israel will behave like Judah.

On Mount Garizim, the El-Hara-Kah, place of the altar, there will later stand only 10 uncut massive rocks instead of the original 12, and the altar will be renamed El-Haker-Belathat,

Desolate Samaria will have seen two tribes renounce the Trinitarian Synarchy instituted by Moses, in favor of a political monarchy; and of the 12 zodiacal stones, the 12 testimonies bearing the name of Israel, there will remain only 10.

The Hara-Kah of Garizim and the altar built by Joshua are both Druidic monuments. The same Keltic signals will be found in Deuteronomy, Leviticus and Exodus.

"Do not make idols, do not tolerate carved images, do not tolerate figurative stones in your country"

"If you raise for me an altar of stones, do not cut them. To lift the chisel on them is to desecrate them."

Many thousands of years before Moses' time, the Bodhones Kelts in Spain, Italy, Greece, the Caucasus, Hebyreh, remained faithful to this ancient protestation of the White Race against the ancient Civilizations.

The representation of the cosmogonic Powers, their magnetic attraction followed by the anointing of oil, was made with stones, either celestial or terrestrial, definitely not carved.

The Ghebres of ancient Iran did not cut the stones of their altars, they raised and superimposed crude rocks, so reports the commentators of the Avesta.

From the Atlantic to the depths of the Tatara, the *Athorney*, the White law enforcer, although faithful to Thor, Bor, Oghas, was perceived as impure if he did any work on stone and iron, foundations of the colossal abhorred Cities.

Even today, to grasp the unity of the Keltic dispersed peoples, one may observe that an Irish peasant and a Tatar Uighur can understand each other, almost as easily as a Breton of Roscoff and a Keltic of Wales.

The ancient curse of the Druids against any political civilization resounds wherever the Bodhones wandered, and is signaled by the presence of uncut stones, not only in our Continents, but even in America, by the migrations of the Seafearers Bodhones, Kelts *Scandi-navian*, meaning *wanderers on ships*.

Through their deep and all scientific symbols, the Kelts who had become Egyptians, will recount that it is with an iron weapon that Seth, Smou, Bubon, Typhoon, the Southern Genie, struck to death Osiris, the living Unity, the social God of all the human kind.

They will thus only reminisce what the ancient black Race, 24,000 years before, had said and rehashed against the preceding Red Race rulers, until themselves succeeding it, they too produced admirable architects and wonderful sculptors.

With the Ghiborim this iron phobia will even enter the temples of Asia. It is true that the metalwork in Asia included iron and copper. Then, as nowadays, although in a different state of mind, sacred archaeologists will gather in the temples' museums the tools of the Ancestors, their instruments of flint and obsidian.

Certain surgical operations, a legacy of the sacred hygiene of the ancient Austral Red Race, will be practiced for a long time only with stone knives, as is still the case in the now regressed tribes of Oceania.

The same use of stone knives is reported in Joshua (Chap V verse 2, 3), with regard to the mass circumcision of the Israelites at the camp of Dyel-Dyel, after the crossing of the Jordan river.

In Algeria, digging the soil, one could find nowadays, Kelts' spherical tombs from a time anterior to the first exiles of the Bodhones, when the Kelts war prisoners of the Black armies, were buried with the primitive tools they had brought from Europe or cut during their captivity; however our modern military surgeons will detect traces of cranial trepanation their ancient colleagues, surgeons in the Black armies, may have performed only with steel instruments.

Same facts have been observed in tombs of ancient Europe.

The curse of iron will be carried by our ancestors to the south of Africa, where, among peoples once more barbarous, the corporation of blacksmiths will be labeled as evil Genie.

Thus, Ignorance has interpreted literally the chemical allegory of the learned disciples of Thoth: *Iron is the bone of Seth, its red oxide is the dried blood of Osiris.*

As signaled in the preceding sentence, let's be reminded that, in ancient chemistry, Oxygen was allegorically assigned to the hierarchy of male substances.

The hierogram by which Moses characterizes water, is always used in its dual form, which proves that he knew the chemical composition of water: Maiim (mayim), meaning the double waters. (H_2O).

I could extend this chapter a great deal; but I only wish, on this river of centuries past, to pile up enough solid documents, like a ford, so that the readers can assure their march and follow me safely.

HEBREWS ARE THE RESERVOIR OF SOCIAL WISDOM

I hope I have achieved this goal, and that the reader will now understand the Jews represent nowadays but the most vivacious of our ancient Gibhorean tribes; they are the best in keeping the memories of our past after 9,000 years, the best in keeping alive its social and intellectual organicity, under the terrible blows of Time, hostile peoples and Fatalities, like a hammered metal well shaped in the midst of fiery tribulations.

When these Bodhones left Europe, they certainly were unaware of the mission which Providence, from above, was planning for them.

Social, above all, like the Kelts, irreducible to all political mechanics, to any personal government, they carried with them the cult of the Ancestors, the Keltic commune (Aldea), the arbitral judiciary system.

And these institutions, however elementary they may have been, have preserved for 9,000 years their own physiognomy, and are still giving them their strength today.

It is thanks to those institutions and the social character which they have impressed upon these nomads that the Jews have survived all the political empires of Asia, and it is thanks to them that the Orthodox from Kaldea and Egypt, have selected and organized these ancient tribes into a national body, so they would carry, *like pure blood-horses,* through the centuries, their *encoded marching orders, the encrypted message of ancient Science and Religion, their memories and their social hopes.*

It is not insignificant to notice that the word *hebrew* is a Keltic word, which is found not only in the words Iberia, Abaris, Aborigine, Hebyreh, etc., but also in Hebrides.

This root was still present during the last century in Brittany, in the name of the maritime officer who delivered to the ship captains their official letters of departure, as this officer was called Hebruyn, meaning expeditor, or rather "expatriator", if you allow me this play of word.

RAMA THE KELT ENTERS THE WOLRDWIDE STAGE

At this point we will let go these expatriates and find them later wandering in Asia and Africa.

Crossing four centuries after these first exoduses, we will

witness the religious and military conquest of the entire Social State of the Black Race by a great part of the peoples of the White Race, under the leadership of a man of extraordinary genius. This *theocrat and conqueror is scarcely alive in the minds of Europeans*, although he is revered in all Asia, under various names, through written and carved memories, or directly engraved in the minds.

The few erudite scholars who dig up the literary fragments and other debris of Greece and Italy, are merely conjecturing the presence of this divine man rather than clearly knowing about him.

Nevertheless, since Anquetil-Duperron, Fabre d'Olivet, and the Indianist scholars of the Calcutta school, since Champollion and all the consecutive archaeologists, have opened before the European Mind the sacred history of all the peoples of the East, it is possible for every mind, for whom the past is anything but dust, to see clearly, under these ashes, the Living Soul, organizing Power of the intellectual and social Constitution, then revered in all the temples of the civilized World.

The man of whom I am talking about, *Ram*, was a western Keltic personality; *he led part of the White Race people into Asia, into Africa, and united all the kingdoms, all the European colonies of the Black rulers under the same intellectual Theocracy, under the same Trinitarian and arbitral Empire, which lasted more than 3,500 years*, until the revolution which, under the name of Nimrod, imposed onto the World Personal Government with its Arbitrary Politics. In the next chapter, we will see the rising of this Theocracy of the Lamb, this Empire of the Aries, which gave its name to the Aryas who were bearing the standard of the Aries, and of whose peoples we will find later the scientific and social Tradition embedded in the Dorian order of the Abramids, within the Dorian works of Moses, within the teachings of Jesus Christ.

Moreover, we will find it again embedded in the Second Testament; chiefly Saint John is giving us a glimpse of their esoteric doctrine.

CHAPTER VI
CYCLE OF RAM - UNIVERSAL EMPIRE OF THE
ARIES - UNIVERSAL THEOCRACY OF THE LAMB
TRINITARIAN SYNARCHY

MEETING OF NORTH AND SOUTHERN CIVILIZATIONS

8,600 years ago, the situation of the people of the Black Race (*Gian ben Gian*) and that of the White Race (*Kelt Gibhorim*), was respectively as follows:

Pushed back from almost all the coasts of Europe, where they had established settlements of mixed races, the *Black Gian-ben-Gian* remained entirely masters of Asia and Africa. Their principal colonies were Egypt, Asia Minor, ancient Taurida, China before Fo-Hi, Japan, Persia before Iran, Tibet, etc.

Their metropolitan center was Ethiopia, as long as the Red Race had lived and dominated the Earth with all the splendor of its civilization.

But since these Red populations had disappeared with their native austral land, due to the cataclysm which also engendered the current Continents of Northern Hemisphere, the race of *Black Koush* had made the major colony of the Red Race its metropolitan center, and given it its color name: *India*, country of dark *Indi*go. India then still bore other names expressing religious or social ideas: Bharat-Versh, meaning Tabernacle of Bharat, Bharat-Khant, meaning Government of Bharat.

Bharat, which means Creator, or Law of the Creator, was the ancient hierogram of the priesthood of the Red Race, which had given the Black race her first teachings and her first laws.

The Bharat-Versh then had two capitals: *Ayodhya, A-Yod-Hy-A*, meaning *Principle (A) – Male (Yod)– Being (Hy) – Principle (A)*, *Pratishtana, Prat-Ishtan-A*, meaning *Nature-divine-Principle.*

VITAL IMPORT OF THE NAMES OF PEOPLES AND PLACES

One cannot pay too much attention to the proper *names* of antiquity, because they are far from being the fruit of chance or banality, as they are erroneously construed to be since the downfall of the savant temples.

Cities were built, nations were organized by scholarly or priestly bodies, and the names given to them were composed according to the rules of an absolutely precise Art.

These *names expressed the essence* of a specific character and were given according to a precise *symbolic linguistic science*.

Above is an example of this science, when giving the religious significance of the Bharat-Versh, and the social meaning of the Bharat-Khant.

The names of the two ancient capitals of India also express their specific roles: *Ayodhya*, the *city of God*, was the seat of the Solar University and Dynasty

Pratishtana, the *city of Nature,* was the center of the Lunar University and Dynasty.

The name of *Jew, Youd,* that some Bodhones will one day take, will be composed of the same root as *A-yod-hya.*

This root belonging to the letter Iod, the first of the name of IEVE, will signify, in qualitative arithmetic the decade, in morphology or qualitative geometry the radius perpendicular to the equator, as a hierogram the male sign the Eternal Masculine, hence *Yod, Iud, Iehudim,* the masculine, the masculinist, the unitary theists, and finally Yodi, who, in Egyptian as well as in Hebrew, applied to India, the orthodox land par excellence.

In Persia, the two metropolitan cities of the Blacks were called Ishdankair, Center of God, and Bamiyan, Temple of the Dove.

The same word Ishdan, which we have just seen in Pratishtana (often in ancient languages d=t), is still found in the Hungarian, where it means God or Genie.

Under domination of the Blacks Asia Minor was called Plaksha, the Jurisdiction of Peace. Its capital was Salem, the Sphere of the Union.

Egypt was called Mitzra and Chemi; Mitzra was referring to the tight narrow shape of this country, Chemi to its Sun.

The capital of Egypt, then dug in the living rock, was called

Thebah, the Solar Ark, the City-Principle. *Thebah* is also the name Moses will give to the organic tourbillon of our solar system.

The Black Koushim named all of Africa *Libya*, meaning *heart*. This word proves that the form of this Continent had been *geodetically determined*, either by their engineers or by the savants of the Red race, and it is found in all our languages, to express all the physical or moral ideas that are attached to the word *heart*: *leb* in Hebrew, *lobe* in French, *love* in English, *liebe* in German, *lioubof* in Russian, *louba* in Slawon, *lubie* in Polish, *loubitsa* in Serbian, and even in the old French word *lubie*, caprice of the heart.

The name of Western Europe was Varaha, that of Eastern Europe Kourou. Varaha meant Earth surging out of the Ocean, the Continent of the West. This word is found in Vareh, as in Varaighes, as well as in Arabic Baraha, which still expresses the idea of vast Continent. We will soon find that name brought to Asia by the White Ghiborim, even to India, witnessing the presence of the Varvaras successors of the Dravidians, and attesting a migration from Western Europe.

This name will persist, in Europe, in a multitude of river designations, cities or countries; this name is also given to peoples who emigrated from the West to the East of our Continent: *Var, Varaighes, Warszawa, Warsaw, Varna*, etc.

The Keltic priests will make of the root *Varaha* the sign of what is pure blood, or core meaning, finally of *Verity*.

This root will also express conflict: *War*, the uprising of the *Varaha*.

Kourou, as understood in the Hebrew language or rather by Moses' Egyptian language, means the rule of the waters, that which stops the level or the course of the water; and the presence of salt mines in Poland sufficiently explains the accuracy of this expression, which corresponds to the time when our Continent slowly resorbed the waters from which it had emerged. These two words Varaha and Kourou are found in the most ancient traditions of India.

I interpret them by Moses's Egyptian and not by Sanskrit, because Sanscrit unfolded only subsequently to the conquest of the Aryas, therefore it did not exist at that time; *Moses' Egyptian was a non-spoken perfect hierographic scientific language* adopted from the temples of Egypt.

Varaha and Kourou, therefore, expressed the novelty of the northern continent, closing in on itself; and its recent release of waters had occurred 2,000 years back, that is to say, today, about 10,700 years ago.

It is worth noting that today's Sea of Varechs-Kelp or Sargasso Sea, lies in the former place of the Northern Hemisphere prior to the last pole shift.

If, as I am sure, Ancient Science has revealed in depth all the cyclical Mysteries of the Universe and, a fortiori, of our Solar System and our Globe, one *might predict Europe*, at the time of the writing of these lines, would have 1,300 years remaining before disappearing once again as a Continent under the seas, (except for its mountains becoming islands), due to the same *moral and physical causes* which made it emerge from the Ocean.

COLOSSAL ARCHITECTURAL WORKS

Around 8,600 years ago, the great labors of the sacred engineers, known under the names of *Brahmanic works*, of the expedition of Osiris, Bacchus, Hercules, etc., had just been projected. The Nile itself was not yet dammed, says Herodotus, and most of its waters rolling west from the first cataract were running along the current oases of El-Kharcen and El-Bahrié.

The architectural work of cutting slabs out of the quarries, or carving them in the mountains themselves, was performed with incredible power in India, Persia, Caucasus, and Egypt, where, as the time went on during long centuries, only the old works will be repaired.

Ancient symbol of the Red Race, the enormous Giseh Sphinx already existed, as well as the original Ipsambul temple.

Oriented to the East, as it is today, stood the *Sphinx. dyed in dark red* with a mouth two feet three inches in diameter and the rest to match. Flora and Fauna were then as powerful in

Egypt as in India. In Persia, the city of Bamiyan was entirely carved in the rock.

Two gigantic statues remain standing, still bearing witness of these remote times. One serves as cariatid guarding the entrance of a temple, where an entire army was able to stay with all its equipment and luggage. Ayodhya, on the south bank of the Sardjou river, a tributary of the Ganges, was as we have said, 60 miles long. According to the Pouranas this city was the *Metropolis of the Earth*.

If I wanted to make here a vain display of erudition, it would be easy for me to show the main fortresses of the Gian-ben-Gian, their organization in its details, their sanctuaries, their public mores. But we must confine ourselves to what is indispensable for the reader to see clearly this past, leaving to his intelligence the task of completing us.

The *Emperor of the Black Race*, the supreme Sovereign of the *Solar Dynasty*, bore the title of the former kings of the Red Race, *Rawhan* or *Rawhon*, Dragon, Supervisor General.

His viceroys of the Mitzra, Plakska, ancient Persia, had the title of *Pha-Rawhon*, meaning a *reflection of the Dragon*, Rawkh-Shasas, *Shasas* word meaning then *faithful* in the ancient Persia of the Blacks, as well as its equivalent in Egyptian language, *Shesus*.

8,600 years ago, the ruling Rawhan at Ayodhya was Daça-ratha, the fifty-fifth solar monarch since Ikshauku, as per the Brahmans.

His coat of arms embroidered on the banners, struck on the coins, was the Dragon, which is still much later found in the names *Darick, Darack, Dragme, Drack-Mon*, meaning Dragon of the Moon, Silver Dragon, the first currency the Southern Europeans received from the Black Rulers, and later replaced with coins stamped with the Aries or the Lamb, which will still be in use by the Abramids.

I do not need to recall here what memory the coat of arms of the Dragon impressed in the legends of our three Continents, from India to China, from the depths of Europe to the borders of Africa.

SOCIAL ORDER AND WORSHIP OF THE BLACK RACE

The *social state* of the *Gian-ben-Gian* was caste-free, as Buddhists prior to Sakya-Mouni often recalled; it was perfectly organized, with sex equality in the home and in the temple, organized in Communes where the electoral rights belonged to fathers and mothers; guilds of crafts and applied Arts were affiliated to the Priesthood, the Sovereign Assembly of the Teaching Corps.

The Divine Sciences proper were in the custody of the Sacerdotal University and the Solar Dynasty.

The triple levels of the natural sciences corresponding to the triple Nature as encrypted in the name of E V E was shared between the lunar Priesthood, lunar University and lunar Dynasty.

The intellectual and social constitution had been developed by religious Order of *the Reds* under the name of *Bharat*, 2,300 years back.

The *religious system*, or rather the *Scientific Synthesis*, went up to the unity of God, symbolized in the hierogram of *Wodha*. We will find this name everywhere, up to Scandinavia.

It is this same verbal symbol, altered in *Budh*, that will later eventually be carried by so many Indian reformers.

This great Unity was manifested by an Androgynous Dyad, *Iswara,* the Male Spirit, and *Pracriti*, the Feminine Intelligence.

As I have said, the Organicity of the Universe, the *Cosmogony,* and, all the more so, *Theogony,* were reserved for oral teaching, and formed with the double hierarchy of natural sciences and human sciences, the Quaternary figured in the Holy Name (IEVE).

The *visible signs of the Universe* were apprehended solely by the *spirit of worship,* only as far as they carried intelligible and living meanings. The ordinary people, as they do always, perceived these visible signs to be the Universal Intelligences themselves.

Thus, the further away from the metropolises, the more the vulgar willingly fell into the worship of the celestial Stars, the Earth, animals, plants, elements, while scholars and sages revered the Intellectual Reigns, the hierarchy of Intelligible Cosmogonic Puissances, of which all these aspects testify, each according to rank.

All possible manifestations of Life in all its categories were the object, not only of study, but of necessarily correlated worship; and in the spirit of the ancient world of which I speak, all the symbols of the divine and universal laws engraved in the human organism, were piously understood and revered.

All the Oriental lands preserve to this day the memory of this symbolism and organic cult, and the Europeans who, when visiting India, Japan or elsewhere, smirk at the sight of certain processions of natives gathered behind certain symbols, prove only their ignorance, the separation of their understanding from Life itself and its Spirit.

The public holidays were then grandiose. The theatrical performances, named Nataks, did not yet carry the Sanskrit names of Dramas and Tragedies, which signify celebrations of Aries. In these Nataks were staged the great allegories of the Universe and of Humanity.

The singing of the choruses, Ghana, meaning instrumental harmony, Vadhia, the astronomical march of the choral masses, were regulated by the priesthoods on six perfectly distinct musical modes, from the arithmological point of view as well as from the geometrical point of view; those modes by no means corresponded to the two European modes in several different tones, as is wrongly believed today.

These six modes, mathematical symbols of the great Celestial Year and the little terrestrial year were named Malava, Sriraga, Hindola, Dipaca, Megha, Bhairava.

We find this musical system of Bharat beneath all the old popular melodies of the Earth.

I regret here not to be in the opinion of the eminent Rajah Sourindro Mohun Tagore, when he thinks he can state that ancient India did not know the Science of Harmony.

In my hands I have irrefutable proofs to the contrary; and this science, because of its universal analogies, was, in India as well as everywhere, part of the most secret esoteric knowledge, though, as an art, it was in the hands of everybody.

Today, old European barbarism says, with the Paris Conservatoire and its organ, Mr. Fétis: Music is the art of forming pleasant sounds in the ear; and Descartes had said it before him. Antiquity saw in music something considerably more important; but let's move on.

In what precedes, I wanted only to let the reader *feel the high degree of culture reached by that highly ancient Social State*, where the Bodhones Kelts had taken refuge, 400 years before the time which we will explore soon.

Welcomed with kindness, the exiles had settled in the lands which had been conceded to them even as far as Arabia.

The most intelligent among the Bodhones had assimilated the Sciences and applied Arts of Gian-ben-Gian, the others engaged in agriculture or commerce; all were self-governed according to their Keltic customs, of which the strong institution of the kahal (gathering of all, "assembly" in Hebrew) was the principal organ.

The kahal is, strictly speaking, the commune known to our fathers, the arbitral legal power appointed by the heads of families, men and women. The delegates of the communes then formed the assembly of the Haqs.

Here was then the Social State of the White Race in Europe. Entirely based on the necessity of war, the original Keltic Society was necessarily turbulent.

Many revolutions had already shaken for centuries the tribes of Varaha and Kourou.

ORIGIN OF THE BATTLE OF THE SEXES

At the origin of all Races, *women* are the first to awaken to the knowledge and to the perception of *invisible things and beings*.

Among the Kelts, also, as everywhere else, *women* had been the first *interpreters of Divinity*, and men had worshiped them as such.

Religion, Life, Science and Love, had for a long time been the mediating organ of the College of *Druidesses*, with its divisions into different classes of *magicians, priests, seers, and therapists*.

But after having been beneficent initiators and truly enlightened from above, after having been the luminous mistresses of the intelligence, the soul and the heart of their Race, after having founded the Cult of the Ancestors and instituted the three Orders of the Priesthood, Military Jurisdiction and Municipal Administration by the Elders, the *Druidesses, under the impetus of some ambitious female politicians*, wished to maintain by Superstition and Power an Authority which the inspiration and creed alone gave them.

Instead of mediating Providence, they soon became the interpreters of the fiercest Fatality, and *men revolted against them.*

The same social phenomenon has been duplicated everywhere, even among the natives of Tierra del Fuego, who have since regressed to primitive state, and who yet offer to the traveler's observation certain strange celebrations in commemoration of the *rebellion of the Male Faculty against the Female Faculty.*

We will observe later the reversal of the same fact, brought about by an identical cause, specifically the *Female rebellion of the Amazons due to persistent political domination of Men.*

In the name of Thor, in the name of Friga, from the depths of the ancient sanctuaries where the Druidesses evoked the Souls of Heroes, the Spirits of the Ancestors, bloody decrees thundered over the male heads of Keltide; and it was against the best, those males who could claim the rulership, that was directed the tempest of the domineering female passions.

Born of the valor and the military courage of the Race itself, which up to then had been their safeguard, a terrible superstition decimated the elite of the males.

Everyone has in mind the horrible human sacrifices with which the Druidesses have bloodied, not only Europe, but Africa and Asia up to India.

At any moment, the bravest among the males were chosen

to be dispatched to the other side of Life, as messengers sent to the Ancestors, Bor, Thor, Oghas, Teutad, Heroll, Friga.

The decree was cast from the sanctuaries, and these valiant ones ran to the rocks of the sacrifice, full of faith, full of hope, smiling, stretching their throats to the knives. It was for them the supreme feat of courage, the bloody sunset of earthly life. From Spain to Great Britain, from Scandinavia to the depths of Kourou, the purest virile blood was running at the time of grand astrological epochs.

Every military leader suspected of attempting to shake off the yoke of feminine priestly Power was called by the lugubrious voices and was honored to be slain first.

The men-at-arms saw, continually, their generals, their herolls, their hermen, at every moment go to their death as soon as their influence began to grow.

These noble victims were struck here with the sword, crushed under rocks, drowned in gorges, elsewhere devoured by flames, sometimes buried alive.

As far as Sicily, as far as Africa, as far as Greece, the fumes of blood are rising, the cry of violent death tearing the air.

From Iceland itself, these atrocious customs will cross the waves, and penetrate into the heart of the new Red Race.

And, later, this ferocious custom, overturning, will precipitate the women themselves under the knife of the male sacrificer, in the waters, earth and pyres.

Then, a reformer appeared in the West.

THE RISING OF RAMA

Having meditated for a long time on public evils, having profoundly instructed himself in the Sciences and the technical Arts, -not only those of the Druids and Druidesses, but also those of Black Priests of the South-, Ram returned to his country, and attempted through wisdom and gentleness, to appease these raging passions.

Seeing the Kelts, trained for warfare since their origin, in the grip of the most terrible of civil wars, that is the *battle of the Sexes* for the priestly Authority, he used all the power of his genius to institute *equality of Man and Woman* at the altar, at home and throughout the Social Order.

In order to reconstruct the history of this extraordinary man, we must resort to consult the sacred books of the White peoples, those peoples he later led towards Asia and Africa.

Due to fanaticism and spirit of domination, both fruits of ignorance and dark passions, *we have nothing left of our ancient runic annals.*

The *Edda* is a recent work, if we compare it to the antiquity we are dealing with here; and without Moses, without the Puranas, without the Avesta, without the Y-Kings, and what the Greek authors have allowed us to glimpse at from the traditions of their sanctuaries, we have no historical means of reconstructing the real substance of this very important Cycle.

RAMA THE GREAT REFORMER

Writings of Indians, Aryas, Iranians, the poem of Job, all give to the *Keltic reformer* the name of the symbol figuring on his coat of arms: *Ram* or *Rama*, in original Keltic, *Aries.*

Elihou, one of Job's wise friends, emblemizing the Bodhones' goodness, will be spoken of as *descendant of Ram.* The Persians, because he reformed the zodiacal calendar, will also name this personage, *Ram*, Chief of the Stars' course.

Iran will bear its name: *I-Ram*; and the ancient Iranians will also call him *Gian-Shyd*, the winner over the Universals, the victorious *Cid* (chief) of the Black ruling.

This name will later be altered into Dyem-Schid.

The *Brahmans* will insert his name into theirs, which will signify the *paternal Power or Ram's Authority*; they will also call this religious hero *Deva Nahousha*, the *divine renovating Spirit*; and the Greeks will make him, according to India's writings, their *Dionysos.*

His name will be found in Ra-Hammon, in Egyptian, *Aries-Law*; and the temple of Hammon will indeed be the keeper of Science or the Law of Aries.

The same name will mean in all the languages of the East, that what is elevated, and the *Elevation* par excellence.

The word *Py-Ramid* will mean *Paternal Power of Ram*, and these gnomonic monuments will become the undeniable symbol of the incredible *Synthesis of Knowledge* brought back to Unity by this reformer.

In *Moses'* Egyptian language, the same name is found in the word *Rammamah*, meaning *thunder*, whose direct practical handling was, as I said, familiar to the ancient Priests.

After the expulsion of the schismatics, who we know as Hicksos or Pastors, the *Orthodox pharaohs* will use this name *Ramses* as a religious symbol.

The Orthodoxes of Kaldea will do the same, and that name will serve as a hierogram to the order of the *Ab-Ramids, or Abram*. At Tyr, the rulers will also boast of the name *Hi-Ram*.

We will see the Quirites replacing the name Valentia with *Rome*, for the same reason.

In Kanaan, several very ancient cities will be called *Rama*.

Several thousand years apart, various epics will come out of the sanctuaries to celebrate the same hero.

In Georgia, the Hero with the skin of a panther, holding the banner stamped with the Ram figure, will be celebrated in the Kartlistz hovreba wcrphoviz tkho sani, ancient book unfortunately burned in part by fanaticism.

In Greece, Nonnus will celebrate him according to the traditions of Eleusis; but the most gigantic poem in the world was consecrated to him by India, in the *Ramayana,* many centuries earlier.

Finally, the same glorious name, surviving after Mohammed in the memories of the Arabs, will continue in that of *Ramadan*, the judgment or the *great festival of Ram*.

It is from these traces, through these historical poems and memories, and especially from the sacred books of the East, that we can reconstitute in a positive way the history of this theocrat.

The Brahmans give him for fatherland Western Europe, the Varaha, for symbolic wife Sita, for race the White race that the Blacks called Scythian.

His emblematic brother, that is to say, the people he made his ally in Europe, is *Lack-man*, a Keltic name still found today in the name Polach, the Poles.

His principal lieutenant, generalissimo of all the foresters, is *Han-u-man*, a Keltic name, which can be transcribed in English as *Han of men, Chief of men*.

After having done in Western Europe prodigies of science and benevolence to carry out a peaceful reform, after having established the equality of the male and female priestly colleges, and established the *Noel* festival, *New Heyl*, *the new salvation*, the *new Renovation*, in order to perpetuate the memory of his Alliance, Ram was forced by the recrudescence of the domineering passions, either to civil war or to exile.

He had rallied to his coat of arms a multitude of men belonging for the most part to the caste of the workers; but at the same time, he had against him the military party and its leaders.

The clans most protective of their power and the weight of their sword, those clans of the Bull, the Crane, the Salians, etc., pushed for civil war, and there was an immense clamor of opposition when *Ram rose amid his faithful allies the standard of Aries*.

Ram had earned a high rank among the priests; but it was enough that he wanted to reform them, to have against him those who had an interest in maintaining the status quo.

A large segment of the priesthood stirred up the wrath of the men-at-arms.

"What! this preacher whom the effusion of blood frightens, this "giver of blessings" who wills to stop the bloody sending of our heroes-messengers to the Ancestors, this coward raises the standard of Aries! Him Aries! Him Ram! Come on! Ram the herd leader is a fierce fighting animal! It is Lamb that this preacher of peace must be named! Ram, never! Lam or Lamb, that's the right name!"

We will see later in what dazzling glory, in what divine light, Ram will wash these insults out.

Lam will *become the theocratic title* he will transmit to his successors, Sovereign Pontiffs of his Universal Empire.

And after 8,600 years one may count today nearly half a billion faithfuls to the *Lamas*.

Meanwhile hatred was arming itself in the Varaha, and the most violent force wanted to drown this innovative party in a sea of blood. Supported by the working caste, joined by the best men and women from the other social classes, the minority proclaimed *Ram Sovereign Pontiff*.

A death warrant was issued from the Seyn Island by the Druidesses, and it resounded throughout the Keltide.

Three options were open before Ram: either to fight his own people, or to accept a useless death, and the slaughter of his followers after him, or to exile himself, as had done the Bodhones 400 years earlier.

EXODUS OF RAMA AND HIS FOLLOWERS CIRCA 8,600 BC

Ram chose the exile, and all his partisans followed him. Telegraphic fires were lit on the mountains, the messages carried across the seas, and from the depths of the Varaha to the Kourou an *emigration of several millions of men and women began*.

The *first disciple* of Ram was proclaimed *Hanouman, Chief of the Army*; the reformer and his partisans crossed the whole of Europe, more as conquerors than exiles. Moreover, he carried new multitudes on his way, peoples *his Science healed*, his enthusiasm and his happiness exalted with irresistible ardor.

It is from him that dates the use of sacred *mistletoe*, extremely difficult to spot (on oak trees), and whose effectiveness against some terrible epidemics depends on the precise astronomical time it is being collected and prepared.

He taught the Kelts the preparation of fermented beverages, the selection and cultivation of plants that can produce wine, beer or alcohol.

The original Ramayana records the power of this great man, as *theurgic savant, miracle worker, therapist, organizing genius,* not only in war, but in peace which he safeguarded everywhere after his victories; and his immense goodness is revealed in all the words that Valmiki places in his mouth: *"To win is to forgive."*

- Always wait for the wounded enemy to get up. - Give to all, do not receive from anyone."

This divine breath, which does not falter a second, is reminiscent of the purest spirit of Christian chivalry.

But we will see that Christianity itself will be the resurrection of this sacred tradition.

Educated in all possible Sciences, Ram had previously planned his course towards what some authors would call today the *equator of contraction*, in a word, to *attain the regions of Asia analogous to Europe.*

After storming the fortresses of the Caucasus, he reached Tatarah and found strong allies there. They were tribes attached to the ancestor Oghas; and, as I have said above, the similarity of Oyghouri and Irish still bears witness to this ancient kinship. Allied with the Yellow peoples, those tribes followed Thor's European law, from astronomy to the last details of what the ancients called the Law.

Always fighting the Black Kushits, these Kelts, former prisoners of war, inhabited the region which, since the alliance of their standards, that of Taurus with the banner of Ram, the Aries, will from then on be called *Thor-Ram*, and become the *Turan*.

FOUNDATION OF A NEW WORLDWIDE CIVILIZATION

One can figure out the size and location of this empire, by spotting on a map the principalities or kingdoms of Khiva, Bokhara, Ivhokand, Tashkende, Hasrat-Sultan, Mainome, Ankhoy, and Herat.

These tribes recognized *Ram* for their supreme leader, and he *thoroughly reformed their intellectual and social state.*

He remained in Turan until his troops were fully armed, organized, disciplined, and supplied for the terribly difficult conquest that was about to take place.

The alliance of the Kelts of Europe, who will become the *Aryas* or people of *Aries*, with the Scythians of Asia who will become the *Turanians,* or people of *Thor* associated with Ram, will be broken definitively only towards the year 3,200 B.C.

Even today, these distant memories persist in the mores that certain hordes of Ta-tzi can no longer themselves explain, due to their decline and fall from a high state of civilization to one bordering on barbarism.

They still bear the black or white Lamb on their banners and celebrate festivals similar to those of our ancient Britons: the triumphal abduction of the Ram; almost all of them, still look with piety towards the land of the *Lamas, Sovereign Pontiffs of the ancient universal Empire.*

On the stepped valleys in the Caucasus, the ancient temples hanging over the mountains of Georgia, are full of sculpted stone Rams, *symbols of Ram's Law.*

The cult of the Ancestors, which Ram instituted at the foundation of his Theocracy, remained among these lively peoples as a feeling, *though absolutely obscured as a science.*

Once ready, Ram directed his march toward the kingdom of the Blacks to which he gave the name *Iran*; he defeated the Dragon's army in a pitched battle, laid siege to the capital Isdhan-Kair, and after breaking its square walls with his war machines, he prevailed.

The Bodhones of the Hebyreh rallied to him like the Turanians, and he drove the Dragon's army out of all their famous strongholds, notoriously impregnable, Balle, Merw, Mesched, etc.

The debris of the vanquished fell back to their other colonies: Armenia, Plaksha, Arabia; and the bulk of the army went to cover in India.

It was then that Ram received from his troops the title of Cid, meaning "Triumphant Winner", and *Gian-Shyd*, winner of the Universals, which will become *Djemschyd* through language transformation.

EMERGENCE OF SOCIAL SYNARCHY

At that time was established this wise and learned synarchical organization of Iran, this *pure Law, model and prototype* on which will be more or less regulated the Order of the lay Initiates symbolized under the patronymic name of Zoroastrians.

Zend Avesta, IX. HA: Zoroaster consulted Ormuzd, and said to him: *"O Ormuzd, infinite Perfection, divine Justice, World Arbitrator, who is the man who in the past has consulted you in these places as I do today?"*

Then Ormuzd replied, *"The pure Gian-Shyd, Leader of the peoples. I put in his hand a sword of light, a golden sword, and he conquered the East, then he marched towards the country of the South, which he found beautiful. "*

I will not elaborate here on the hidden meaning of the Avesta or the wonders it reveals about Ram, because the reader might not be willing to follow me that far.

Although this ancient book reached us only as fragments, abridged and altered by ignorance, after long centuries of decadence produced by arbitrary personal governments, if we wanted and knew how to read this ancient book in the spirit in which it was first written, it would reveal *extraordinary things*; but let's move on.

Let us confine ourselves here to some features of the *religious and social state* Ram gave to the Kelts in this part of the World.

If one remembers what I said about the polar and heliacal orientation of the scripts, one will understand why the Runic, Georgian, Armenian, Tibetan, Sanskrit, etc., *write from left to right*. On the present ruins of Istakar, several monuments bear inscriptions from left to right, and particularly the monument which the Persians call the throne of Gian-Shyd.

From the religious point of view, Ram kept unchanged the *quadruple scientific hierarchy of Gian-ben-Gian* or Jaïnas, crowned by the positive revelation of the *Divine Unity, Whod.*

He renewed the consecration of the ancient sacerdotal body by introducing his own priests; and the *Cosmogonic and Theogonic Sciences* remained the subjects of Higher Education.

As for the common people, to connect their souls by a link that was universally accessible to them, Ram instituted the cult of the Ancestors, but freed from the atrocities that Politics had admixed to that cult in Europe.

All the *Black Sages, all Savants of the Yellow Race, joined him*, and enthusiastically accepted this innovation which established the Social State on its true basis: *The Life of the Dead.*

STRUCTURE OF SOCIAL SYNARCHY

It is from this Cycle that the *Souls and their different hierarchies beyond the grave were scientifically known* and artistically revered in Asia, then in Africa, at home by a constant worship, in the Social State by splendid public festivals of day and night, which corresponded to the *living relations of these souls with the astronomical position* of the Earth.

In the home as in the Social State, Ram instituted the woman, not only the equal of the man, but her superior in the great intellectual, moral and physical *mystery of the Generation and the Incarnation.*

It is Ram who uttered this beautiful maxim the Zoroastrians will repeat after him:

"The field is worth more than the seed, the girl more than the boy; the virgin excels the lad, the woman the man; the mother equals ten thousand fathers."

He instituted the *differential Initiation of the Sexes*, and at the altar of the home the woman was a priestess just as the man was a priest.

Having thus based the Religion of Organic Life on the Authority of the Cosmic Life of the Souls, Ram organized Iran as follows:

In memory of the Varaha, his homeland, he raised the city of Var, a huge square city, enclosed in colossal walls, which in case of danger could shelter the rural populations and the herds against an offensive return of the rebellious Gians.

"Black giants, with white teeth, with elephant ears" says the Vendidad about these, alluding to their peculiar head covering, that of the ancient Reds, as seen nowadays on the Egyptian monuments.

The region of which Var was the metropolis was divided into sixteen governments, and was called Vara, in memory of Western Europe.

The social root unit was the Family, *Na-Mana*.

The family groups, fathers and mothers, constituted the first molecular unit, the Clan, *Viç*, which we will find in Italy in *vicus, vicinus*.

The clustering of families formed the Zantu, which we will find in France in the Centon or Canton.

The clustering of the Zantus constituted the Daghu, and the federation of all the Daghus was assembled in the Daghu-Çacti.

The governor of the clan or Vic was named Paiti, meaning father of the locality, and exercised the power only jointly with the family chiefs of Na-Manas, men and women.

The same Vic title was given to the dignitaries invested with the presidency of the other constituencies: Zantus, Daghus, Daghus-Çactis.

The latter also bore the title of Ivan of the Vara or Varkana.

Conversely, the arbitral power radiated from the Varkana to the last of the Paitis, through all the assemblies, to the level of all the Na-Manas.

MODELS OF EDUCATION AND WORSHIP

The priests instituted by Ram did not preach, and never spoke outside of Universities' Education.

Chosen preferably among the *Ghiborim* or *Kelts of Hebyreh*, they were divided into *scholars* and official *ritualists*.

The latter consecrated the hearths, the assemblies, the works of the fields and cities, the festivals of the material elements, vegetal and animal beings in the service of man; finally, they enacted an intelligent veneration, savant and genuine, to Earth and to Mankind, to the Atmosphere and to Heaven, to Birth, to Life, to Death, to the physiology of this Globe and its Solar System.

This silent fulfillment of the rites of Science and Integral Life testifies to the exceptional wisdom of the founder; and there, as in Egypt, this silence may have led some modern archaeologists to believe that there was no worship at that time.

The bards alone spoke and sang, nevertheless according to

the Law and without unlocking the symbols of their teachings and their poems.

Men and women who wanted *to access the Mysteries of the Pure Law* did so by retreating in one of the holy cities or in the consecrated places, as is still done today in Tibet, in India, in Japan, etc.

Under this *government led by Principles*, under this *Synarchy*, says Tradition, there were no sectarians, despots, beggars, intolerance, arbitrariness, no revolt in the Vara.

PUBLIC WORKS AND AGRICULTURE

The great public works were, everywhere under the direction of the savant bodies, executed by voluntary local workers: highways, canals, draining of marshes, inland seas filled, and new soils seeded.

As the physiology of the Earth was perfectly known, the forests, the waters, the vegetable seeds, the stallions, useful to humans, were by religious Law the object of a particular care.

Agriculture, viticulture, animal husbandry, and animal and plant breeding were admirably taught and practiced according to ancient principles, which were later found in Nabathean agronomy.

Not only the vine, but *asclepias acida* and other plants were cultivated for the purpose of extracting wine and alcohol: *keasoum*. In short:

1- the Sacerdotal teaching corps was the *depository of Science* and constituted the absolute Authority.

2- the lay Initiates assembled in the Daghu-Cacti constituted a *Royal Power of Justice*;

3- the assembly of families, Na-Manas, Zantus and Daghus constituted a third social power, devoted to *local Justice and local Economies*.

TERRITORIAL EXPANSION OF RAM'S SYNARCHY

Back to history: The *Gians* had again threatened the borders and, facing the risk of being crushed under the combined effort of the armies of the Rawhan of Bharat-Versh and the pharaohs of Plaksha, Armenia, Egypt, Ethiopia, Arabia, Akkadia, it was necessary for Ram to act, conquer or perish. The military work had been carried on with the enthusiastic vigor of a young people, driven forward by an all-powerful genius.

The beautiful organization of Iran and the Turan had risen up, giving to his chief, arms, armor, cavalry, infantry, engineers, corps of pontoniers, chariots armed with scythes and fire, colossal siege machines, provisions, ammunition, not to mention a whole fleet on the Caspian sea; this sea was much larger then than today, for not only was it attached to the Aral Sea, but it covered part of Central Asia and deserts, near the Oxus and Jaxartès, Syr and Amu-Daria.

The purpose of this fleet was to prevent the landing of the Blacks' army from ancient Taurida, and, after having destroyed the enemy sea squadron, it ensured the transport of troops between the Caucasus and the Caspian mountains, thus conquering Plaksa from the north, then marching down again toward Egypt.

Meanwhile, another army, following the Khaver Desert, crossed the Zenderud, drove back the Gians, and ascended the Tigris to join the other troops.

Converted to their cause by the Bodhones of Hebyreh, the *peoples of Arabia embraced the doctrine and the cause of Ram*, and made their connection with this second army, which Ram commanded in person.

All the peoples of this new Cycle, in their Sacred Tradition, concur to highlight the fierce heroism with which the Gians defended themselves. But the religious enthusiasm Ram inspired to his troops was irresistible, and successively all the strongholds of the South and North surrendered.

THE AMAZONS OF SALEM

The fortress that resisted in the most dreadful manner belonged to a people of *Keltic women militarily installed* for some time in a kingdom whose capital was *Salem*, which will one day become *Jerusalem*. The name of *Ha-mas-ohne*, meaning *"male-no"*, *without males*, and not, as often translated mistakenly *"teatless"*.

We find this radical *mas* in a multitude of languages; *mas* in Latin, *mâsle* in French, *maschio* in Italian, *moth* in Irish Keltic, *maz* in Polish. The Sanskrit books whichh have kept the memory of these women call their kingdom *Stri-Radjya*.

In Boun-Dehesh, the Zoroastrian writers cite *Salem as the metropolis of the Amazons.*

This all female people expatriated as a result of the civil wars in which the *two sexes of the White Race* had fought for religious power, had adopted a cult founded *on their hatred for men.* Governed by a Queen, just like the bees, they accepted men only as prisoners of war or slaves in their harems.

THE BODHONES RESISTANCE

The Bodhones, which we saw going into exile more than 400 years ago, had fallen into a contrary excess by a *reversal of the causes* of the persecution that had afflicted them in Europe.

We shall see those Bodhones roaming in desertic territories, isolated from the civilized centers, return to a state bordering on barbarism until the time of Mohammed, and preserve in Yemen these distant memories reduced to the state of abominable superstition.

They were foolishly *considering the women as impure*, and the Koran will have to forbid them to cry at the birth of the girls and especially forbid to bury them alive.

RAM ENTERS IN SALEM, KALDEA AND EGYPT

Upon entering Salem, Ram consecrated one of his lieutenants *King of Justice under God the Supreme*, Wodh-Iswara-Elion, with the title of *Milich-Shadai-Ka*, which we will find later in the famous Order of *Melchizedek*, king of Salem.

The conquest of Plaksa having been completed and organized, Ram marched south toward the Persian Gulf, and founded the first *Nineveh, Nin-Weh* meaning *child,* the *colonial son*, and also founded *Han,* meaning *sister of the Armenian city.* He made of this capital (Nineweh) the religious and social center of the country to which he gave the name of *Neo-Keltide*, or *Kaldéa: Ka-Eld, Ka-Ald,* the gathering of the Ancients.

He then conquered Egypt, to which he gave the religious and social constitution known by the name Ra-*Hammon*, *Law of Ram*, and the famous Zodiacal Aries enriched with precious stones, grand hieroglyph of the temple of Hammon, dates from that time.

His Synthesis of sciences, under the name *O-Sir-Is*, meaning *Lord of Intelligence*, remained intact until the year 3200 BC.

I will later describe the *arbitral organization of Egypt into three Councils or Social Powers.*

Since Osiris-Hammon, that is to say since Ram, whose festival was celebrated at Noel (New Heyl), up to the time of Pharao Menés, (circa 3150 BC) meaning *Envoy of the Council of the Gods* of the Hindus, there was no king in Egypt, but only a president of this same *Council of the Gods.*

This is why Manetho (circa 300 BC), Egyptian high priest, characterizes the time of Menes as being the *Reign of the Gods.*

Meanwhile, Hanouman (Ram's highest lieutenant) had advanced into India, where the capital of the Bharat-Kant offered him a formidable resistance.

The Black Rawhan, Daçaratha, after a desperate battle, had shut himself up with his innumerable troops in Ayodhya, the city 60 miles in diameter, where Ram's lieutenant had besieged him and starved him.

One can read in the *Ramayana* the story of these colossal wars, which have since been confounded in the Greeks' imagination with the *struggle of the gods and giants.*

Warned by his lieutenant, Ram returned to Iran for more troop's levies, and sailed into India by the route that all the conquerors have since followed.

Upon his arrival, the assault was given in his honor, and the immense metropolis was won under the acclamations of Gian-Shyd-Rama. Deçaratha managed to escape, and started a new war, which lasted another seven years, says Valmiki.

Cities, plains, forests, mountains, everywhere fights between giants were engaged, their solemn stake was, for both Races-Nations, the tiara and the scepter of the whole Globe, the Universal Priesthood and the Universal Empire.

In all these great works, the sacred writers show *Ram protected by the halo of a more than human power.*

Growing in pace with evolving circumstances, his genius found constantly renewed resources in the *ancient magical science and in his own inspiration*; he so reinforced *the Laws of Nature by activating the Laws of Creative Nature,* multiplied what the common people call miracles, attracting in his irresistible whirlwind, friends, enemies and even the animals themselves.

His kindness never faltered, nor his indomitable energy.

RAM ENVOY OF PROVIDENCE

When not combating, Ram instated everywhere leniency, mercy, peace, the famous *aman* of the East. His intellectual strength was directly derived from Providence, the living Intelligence of the Universe.

Through the still vivid admiration of the Orientals for this genius benevolent conqueror, one will not find any testimony depicting him as the sinister figure of a political hero, a brutal conqueror, an ill-fated man, such as History will see cyclically rise again and again, from the time of Ninus-Nimrod (circa 2,100 BC) to the present day, like a bloody Comet, creating a fiery trail of death and ruin. Ram was not one of these destroyers, he was a religious founder of Social State.

Nimrod, Alexander, Caesar, Attila, Charlemagne, Genghis, Timur-Lan, Charles V, Bonaparte, each operating in a fragment of Ram's past global Empire, appear merely like lost, aimless pale copies of his minor divisional lieutenants

They brought plagues, no God's benefits, no masterwork survived them; conversely, Asia and Europe, to this day, are still benefiting of all that the Cycle of Ram created in the Religious and Social Order.

Ram wears on his head a tiara of light, and every tiara that has been worn since, originates from his Sovereign Pontificate, every miter has been modeled on his headdress, imitating the horns of the ram.

Ram holds the sword while preparing his social master-work, but it is a golden sword, say the Zoroasters, it *strikes only to heal and reharmonize the entire Organism of Humanity.*

From this conquest, under the breath of this pure spirit, universal love of Humanity will emerge igniting the most powerful philosophy and poetry ever felt and expressed. Later on, decadence and ignorance will impersonate this spirit as the god of wine.

Now, if man is restless on this Earth, if his collective Soul serves, without his knowledge, as battlefield for the Powers of the Invisible Order, one can imagine the elation and holy joy surging in the heart of *Adam-Eve of Heaven*, at the sight of the grand spectacle produced by this brilliant choreographer, this glorious son of the Varaha.

His opponent, the *Black Rawhan*, whom Valmiki calls Daçaratha, and Nonnus names Deriades, *was not, either, an ordinary man*, nor was he willing to yield without combat the tiara and the 2,200 years old crown of his Race.

We can see in these two authors, Valmiki and Nonnus, so remote in time and space, how this leader of the Black peoples fought tooth and nail while retreating to the far South of his lost empire, how finally, putting the sea between him and the supreme defeat, he crossed the waters on *an immense bridge* of boats toward the island of Lanka, and found refuge there into antediluvian cities.

However. when forces of Providence arm the soul of a man with the purpose to regenerate the future of humankind, Destiny is powerless in assisting an adverse will and in preserving intact a past whose transformation has become necessary.

Even if that man, envoy of Providence or Pure Intelligence, appeared to be vanquished by Fate or domineering instincts, he would rise again like he did on the Golgotha.

But here, this genius of light had to win immediately in order to build his work completely and all at once.

A bridge of boats was thrown over the sea, and the Hindus

still revere today, under the name of *Ram's Bridge*, the rocks which served as its foundation. Thus the Keltic People of Aries, Hanouman in the lead, entered Ceylon. From Jaffnaptnam, the great army marched on Lanka-Pour, behind which walls Daçaratha had entrenched himself with his troops, his priests, his princes, and his family.

The other fortresses were easily conquered, as well as the great and magnificent antediluvian city Anoura-dhapourala.

The great Khan, the generalissimo of Ram, soon concentrated all his forces on Lanka-Pour, and when the siege work was finished, a rain of fire fell on the Rawhan's palace, and the assault was launched. Ram joined in the fray the Rawhan Daçaratha, who would not surrender, and who was killed in singular combat by the chief of the Kelts of Aries.

THE NEW KUSH EMPIRE

Then began the time for the establishment of the new religious and social organization in all India, and this old metropolis remained the center of the universal Empire, under a new name, that of *Kush, or Kansh*, replacing *Bharat-Versh and Bharat-Khant.*

This is the origin of this famous *country of Kush;* here is why later historians seem to situate it in so many various locations: the name *Kush expressed the Masculine, Arbitral Empire of the Holy-Fire*, of which the hieroglyph Aries was the central symbol.

As Moses will report, when, to the arbitral Empire of Kush will have succeeded the arbitrary fragmented empire of Nimrod, many countries distant from the center and far from each other, wishing to escape the pressure from neighboring petty suzerainties, will later declare themselves to *be a country of Empire*, or *country of Kush.*

That is why, from Arabia to Ethiopia, Syria, Crimea, Tauris of the Caucasus, so many "countries of Kush" are to be found.

Ram consecrated and established as Emperor the first *Kousha* of India, in the metropolis of the world, Ayodhya.

It is from this moment that all trace of the Lunar Dynasty disappeared in the chronology of the Brahmans, and is replaced by the mysterious name of *Youd, Yod,* or Wold-Ester or Istir, lieutenancy of the Masculine Principle.

This Kousha reigned as King of Kings of Justice, as the Arbitral Emperor of all the rulers of Arabia, Kaldea, Siam, Japan, proto China, Iran, Turan, Caucasus, Plaksa, Egypt, Ethiopia, Libya, and finally all the colonies of the Aries empire, in the islands and on the shores of the Mediterranean.

The name of *Bacchus,* which means the *return of Koush, Back-Kush,* expresses nothing but the recurrent movement of the imperial order of Aries, from the depths of India to Italy, Gaul, Spain and Portugal.

SOCIAL ORGANICITY OF THE EMPIRE OF KUSH

We have seen in Persia how Ram, the theocrat, had organized the *Union of the Sexes and the Family based on the Communion of Cosmic Souls,* the Ancestors or Assours, how he had constituted the local Commune with a Science and an Art that few legislators have reached and that no one ever exceeded.

The *Book of the Dead* of Ancient Egypt is one of the thousand fragments of his Scientific Religion.

Since Ram's aim was not domination or power, but the *establishment of the Authority of Truth in the Living Organism of Societies,* his work was so durable that, after 8,600 years its communal foundations are still alive and even more firm than those produced by our ephemeral political machines.

THE ENDURING ALDEA

Anyone who has observed India with any attention has been struck by the indissoluble nature of the *Aldea.*

I have already given the ancient etymology of this radical in the words Celtic or Kelt and Kaldea, Ka-Eld, Ka-Ald, meaning *gathering of the Ancients.*

The Aldea, Antique institution par excellence, is still active today as the Hindu commune, unchanged since its foundation by Ram; every educated Brahman, every Pundit agrees that this social molecule has hardly changed since its establishment, except since the English conquest which has altered it more even than the Muslims and the Mongols have.

Though momentarily weakened, the Aldea has survived intact, with its land boundaries, its cadaster, its own administrative system, its local jurisdiction, a small autonomous society, although subject to the central government.

The type of government on which the Aldea was organized was precisely that which *we will find in the books of Moses*, and to which I gave the name of Synarchy.

The assembly of fathers and mothers (*ka-ald-ry*) was appointing three special councils under the presidency also elected of a *thas-ild-ar*, father (thas) of the elders (ild) of Aries (ar).

These three councils corresponded to the intellectual, moral and economic life of the Aldea.

The first assembly was the guarantor and guardian of all the commitments, all the pacts made, on the one hand between the individuals as family members and the Aldea, on the other hand between the Aldea and the religious, juridical and social constitution of the Empire

This council was delegated to the *ra-ias-som*, meaning *Oversight, Respect of mores, Just government*. The second assembly was the keeper of the public peace, justice of peace and police, and its delegate was *ta-le-ari*, meaning *Jurisdiction - Directed - People of Aries*. The third assembly was in charge of the administration of Aldea's economic interests, its treasury, its revenues, its taxes, the control and exchange of securities, gold and silver currencies; and its administrative delegate was the *Schar-raff*, meaning *Overseer of Prosperity*.

These three Special Administrations were appointed at a general meeting or Kaaldry, at the request of the Thasildar.

We will find this assembly of the *Ancients in Israel*, almost under the same name, *Kahal, Kohelet*, local union of all.

At the request of the Thasildar, the Central Priesthood attached to the first assembly a Pundit priest, mathematician, naturalist and astronomer, a physician, a schoolmaster, a corps of musicians and devadassys, or bayaderes (sacred dancers).

The latter, analogous to the Vestals, vowed chastity.

Thus, the social organs represented by the Rajassom, by the Taleari, by the Scharaff, corresponded, the first to the *intellectual and moral life*, the second to *the civil and juridical* life, the third to the *material and economic life* of the Aldea.

DAY-TO-DAY LIFE IN ONE VILLAGE CIRCA 7100 BC

Let's visit one of the villages of this Cycle and see how this organization functions.

No agent of the Central Power torments the Aldea or distorts the *local liberties* of this small but integral society, as enlightened, as well organized, as happy as possible.

What of the *intellectual and moral life* of the Aldea?

The Synthesis of Religion, Sciences and applied Arts, is there at work, consecrating the institutions, the mores, the solemnity of the marriage, the birth and the death, the altar of the domestic hearths, the mutual home to home commitments, the agricultural labor enlightened by the great astronomical festivals.

Not only Humans, but Earth and Heaven, elements, animals and plants are religiously and scientifically fathomed.

The temple is open to the adult, the school to the child; to all Wisdom is offered, graduated according to the Age, according to the Sex, according to the Rank defined by the personal aptitudes.

However, Wisdom is not enough for the happiness of these peasants, these humble people: *the Truth* offers itself to them in the form of aesthetic and accurate Beauty; the Science of Life will appear charming to these modest ones, and it will cultivate their thoughts, their hearts, their manners with a wonderful art that will bring forth the Divine out of the Human weaving harmony and happiness into a delightful social tapestry, as recounted in the sacred books of the Aryas.

Living Art will be everywhere, at home, in all the relations between Humans and with Nature, in the public festivals that Greece will later take as models.

The language that the Pundit and the schoolmaster speak will eventually evolve into the most beautiful and poetic tongue in the world, and all that it teaches will be punctuated by the most dazzling lyricism that has ever emerged from fervor for Truth, from the vigorous concurrence of Intelligence and Soul with the Science of Life.

The Aldea schoolmaster was much more than the humble pedagogue of our villages. Struck in a mold other than the official and administrative mechanics provided by our bureaucratic Universities, this Aldea teacher was above all a *charmer of souls*, and able to *invigorate Life* more than automatic memorization.

He also was the *Rapsoada* (Rhapsodist) of the evening gatherings, and no decree was then needed to make the instruction obligatory, for it was given in such a way that receiving it was a pure pleasure, not only for the child, but also for parents and grandparents.

Listening to the wonders of the Pantcha-Tandra admirably recited between songs and beautiful dances, under the fairy radiance of Mâ, under the Hindu moon, sun of unparalleled nights, it was the reward of the schoolboy, encouragement more effective than punishments and slaps.

And so instead of our lifeless methods, the children's souls were filled with a superhuman poetry, the living communion of the Truth and the Just, expressed through symbols, legends, masterful allegories, beneficent fruits harvested from the tree of Knowledge grafted on the tree of Life.

Guided by the Pundit, this schoolmaster, this humble rhapsodist, often fakir and marvelous magician, was the well-styled interpreter of the great priestly culture, the rural coryphée of the most savant social aesthetics. That same rhapsodist will also organize the heliacal or lunar festivals, the games, the theater and the role-playing mysteries, Aldea's form of experimental psychology, interpreted according to the canons and the rites safeguarded in the temples.

It is he who will direct the drama, *Da-Rama*, the

representation of the *Law of Aries*, the tragedy or the heroic comedy that *Vyasa* will have composed, divine echo of what the Initiates will hear in the crypts of the underground temples, in the sanctuaries from India, Tibet, Persia, Egypt, and finally all the old world.

ARTISTIC EXPRESSION OF SACRED SCIENCE

Even today, although weakened by successive conquests, although exploited to the point of ruin, the rustic Aldea, sometimes still hears and sees the theatrical representations *Avany, Sarangua, Sacoun-Tala*, from the Hymalaya to the mouths of the Ganges, from Ramisseram to the peak of Woddha, renamed peak of Buddha since Sakya-Mouni, and renamed again peak of Adam since the Muslim invasion.

The execution of these masterpieces will almost always be so perfect, so artfully alive, so natural, so filled with the religious inspiration that created it, that the mechanical teaching of our dance Conservatories, the entrechats of our dancers, our absurd operas, *all devoid of intellectual or moral significance,* may appear singularly outclassed.

Alas, conquests and arbitrary political governments, brought ruination, eroding the "heart", the "head" and the "limbs" of this ancient society of the Aries.

For many centuries, the actors, men and women, remained religious, affiliated to specific Orders.

The masterpieces of Indian sculpture, prototypes of those of Greek art, were due to these wonderful actors, who will serve as a model for the sacred artist.

In the immense crypts of the temples, in the light of the lamps and fires of Bengal, the actors in those dramas, at first ecstatically dormant, then awakened in the *great Inner Light* by the priests, would seize there, *in the realm of Absolute*, the ideal scene, and impress it on their theatrical attitude and expression.

Thus, Art and Science have emerged entirely from sanctuaries; and many centuries before Phidias and Praxiteles, the divine prototypes of Humanity have presented themselves alive before the dazzled contemplation of the Daouthia, the Ramana, the Aryavosta.

It is thus finally that, projected into the remotest Aldea, the *celestial vision of Beauty* was offered to all *Padiahs*, by all the sacred mimes and sacerdotal bayadères.

We will find this enthusiasm wherever the Empire of Aries will carry its theocratic Constitution.

As far as Taurida, Thrace, Greece, Etruria, under a thousand different names, the *civilization of the Aries and the Lamb* will carry the *torch of the Divine Life*, the *Adveniat Regnum Tuum,* the *Fiat Volontas Tua, sicut in Coelo et in Terra.*

Such was the organic impulse that Ram's genius, enlightened by a tradition of more than 7,500 years, impressed upon human generations; such was the intellectual mold in which they were to be minted.

19TH CENTURY FRENCH VILLAGE VS ANTIQUE ALDEA

Let us now go up the ages, and examine, in present-day Europe, any village which bears in its social institutions the mark of Nimrod's political order, although the *esotericism* of its religious spirit leads the village inhabitants toward the transfiguration of the Synarchic Order of Ram.

Here is the church steeple, the temple of the Lamb, and here is the schoolhouse, and that's all. One can see a humble priest ministering Death, devoid of all knowledge of the relation linking Life and Death itself; we can also see an unfortunate schoolmaster, whose memory alone has been exercised and cultivated: that is all the State is giving to the European Aldea, in the name of Education and public instruction.

It would be almost enough, if the priest and the pedagogue knew or could learn what they do not know; if they were not jailed within a double State wall; if they were not weakened and stamped both with the seal of an inept bureaucracy; if, free in the Corporation of their respective peers, they found there the intellectual and moral atmosphere, the mastery, the Authority caring for their proper values, which alone can support the individual in his professional activity.

Now, what strikes us first of all in those villages is the absence of any social aesthetic, of any Art of Life, of any callipedia at home, as well as in public festivals.

At church, a desolate music accompanies uncultured voices, and the pedagogue-citizen molded at the university by an amorphous atheism no longer honors with his presence the church lectern.

The unfortunate priest can barely find an altar boy, a little rascal to reply *Et cum spiritu tuo. And may the spirit be with you.*

Yet the school teacher and the village priest are the only two representatives of the Educating Civilization; for I do not suppose we should admit to this title the firemen or the municipal council, who, more often than not, speak a patois of the Middle Ages, and sign their name like the ancient analphabet soldiers (with a cross).

Sometimes, there is also that odd gentleman who comes to spend a short season in the castle there; but ninety-nine times out of a hundred, he is but a fugitive of his social class disconnected from any living link with the rest of the village social fabric.

Let us return, then, to the priest and the schoolmaster, both instruments conscious or not of a double antagonistic policy, both agents of two jailing bastilles, the Clerical Church and the Anticlerical University, both engaged in a dogmatic and budgetary conflict; both are lost sentinels in a forgotten village, guards of a double spirit of domination, openly shooting at each other. For shorten the cassock, and you obtain the garb of an academic Jacobin, still a state employee, just more intolerant than the priest. Among the public servants, the worst kind is the one that infiltrates Education.

As I said in *Mission of the Workers*, the teacher as well as the priest should only and absolutely depend on free associations; in contrast, causing them to be dependent on any political power, devalues in them the only social Authority which deserves respect, debases the level of moral and intellectual values, of which they are the initiators.

I must insist: it is to *the Assembly representative of all the Teaching Bodies, Religious and Secular*, that the Social Authority belongs, and only that Assembly has the right to authorize and control the Power of Education.

In the absence of this type of authority and power, no organic society may harmoniously unfold, and therefore every society would necessarily lose its living organic form to become mechanical and dead.

Wherever pure Politics dominate, Power is deprived of Authority and represents only a transitory pact with iniquity, anarchy, the stupid spirit of brutal domination.

If grown human beings bend, then certainly they deserve these plagues; but at least children, source of human generations, should be safeguarded from this intellectual and moral poisoning.

And to that effect, one must not impress the wilt of Politics upon the Educators, not impose on them the spirit and the uniform of a corrupting and corrupted Power.

Whether he is leaving the religious seminary or the lay training school, *anyone who is honored with the mission of teaching young children, of instructing adolescence, must not be the employee of a State jailing bastille, the agent of an electoral prison, a creature of the political parties.*

So, animated by an opposing spirit, the priestly cassock and schoolteacher's coat, fighting each other in this village, have a common battlefield: childhood. In the home, the man and the woman, without culture, having had their baby born by chance, similarly let their child's brains grow by chance.

In a matter of a mere twenty years, physical, moral and intellectual renewal of all our rural populations could be carried out; but in the present state of things, their existence is more reminiscent of the Cave of the Troglodytes than the little light and warmth of our cities.

Is it from the church, is it from the school that this living ray of light could surge, in order to vivify the brains and heart of these unfortunate children? I strongly affirm that, today, it is from the church alone that emanates the weak spark of social life which still reaches them.

Yes, the unfortunate priest, whom the clerical discipline condemns to waste his time reading his meagre breviary, is a more complete human endowed with a Living Soul, compared to the academic schoolteacher trained like an automaton, who can only mechanically coerce the young brains.

In this child, in this social atom, resulting from a badly constructed family molecule, a communal molecule distorted by the political centralization of Powers, the priest of today can seed a consciousness, can elevate a thought like a blooming flower, creating a more accomplished social being thanks to his Gospel, his Decalogue, his rites stronger than his theology and dogma; *whereas the official bureaucrat of the anticlerical University will give the world only one more anarchist.*

The reader cannot accuse me of hard-core clericalism; on the contrary, I am precisely a theocrat, and in that capacity, I have made the vow to fight error where it is most dangerous for Societies, meaning in the Priesthood itself.

I have decried the ecclesial dogmatism *for having misunderstood Moses, ignored the Living Spirit of Jesus Christ and his social significance,* so that it is well established that no pact exists, nor will ever exist between my conscience and the domination of any political sect.

That said, I maintain that, despite everything, despite the straitjacket that politicized councils and governments have put on his mission, despite the handcuffs that the state binds him with as a civil servant, despite the primitive notion he has of the Universe, Earth and Humanity, this priest, by that alone that he is committed to a Higher Principle, although undefined, is able to sketch somehow the Soul of a human being; whereas the official pedagogue, the academic transformed into a governmental instrument, will awaken only the *radical egoism* of a merely anthropomorphic being.

The positivist philosophers themselves have very clearly

seen that the level of the human spirit is even less debased in convents and seminaries than it is in the official schools of the State.

The human spirit is less derelict and less disheartened by the psychological methods of the Priest than by the mnemonic programs of the lay schoolmaster; for, at least, the Priest preserves alive in his mind the height of a Principle of Universality, and, consequently, maintains an impregnable refuge open to his intellectual freedom, whether he actually benefits from it or not.

Remove from the villages the teaching of the priest, the orthodox minister or the pastor, erase the few of antique art contained in the little village chapel, its mysteries and unexplained sacraments, let the cottages become deprived of this theurgic, though very weak, ray of light, extinguish the holy lamp of the humble church and let shine only the meager lantern in front of the secular school, then come back soon to see the results.

The flail, the scythe, the fork in his hand, the peasant will fall on all that comes to him from the City, on all who bears an administrative uniform, and he will grind under his wooden shoes any constraint issued from the central political Power.

He will begin with the taxman, continue with the board of conscription, and end with the sub-prefect, after having dismissed the schoolmaster and knocked out the member of congress who, to be elected, has promised everything, and will have delivered nothing once nominated.

One must never be afraid to show evil, when its tendency is the indication of the necessity of good; and I am not afraid to assert here that, from one end of Europe to the other, as it has been instituted since 1648, there is a latent, but terrible outbreak of a rural civil war, compared to which all the Jacqueries of France, all the riots of Germany's peasants, all the massacres of the Fenians of Ireland, have only been a prelude.

The faults of the governmental or demagogic politicians, the weight of their foreign or national ambitions, their social misunderstandings, their economic wastage, fall on the peasant in the form of a tax of gold and blood.

And not being swayed, like the urban worker, by the activity in the City, he will become implacable, the day when the agricultural products of the New World will, in Europe, bring challenge and competition, and therefore impoverish him.

The city laborer absorbs, as best he can, some hazy bits of civilization; but the peasant hardly speaks the language of our capitals and does not partake in its spirit.

He barely touches the books of the peddler, while the legends of his evening pauses, which go straight to his heart, are unknown to the scholar and told only in local patois.

The city wants his money and his life, without giving him anything in return, and the official, who comes from the center of power, is to him the representative of a kind of foreign domination.

No happy escape looms beyond his hamlet; he instinctively hates the administrative machinery, the law that consumes his meager inheritance, the tax and the conscription which deprive him of what he loves, and he hardly distinguishes the verb to Love from the verb to have.

His children are his workers by right of birth; he recruits them to feed fowls and cattle; and if the mandatory schooling takes away from him his young helpers, without compensation, he finds this law iniquitous, and he may be right.

Once grown up, and when he begins to replace his father with the mattock or at the plow, his lad is taken away by the army, and if he returns healthy, it is to dream of other horizons: the delivery bag of the rural mailman, the policeman's or country guard's uniforms, the railway employee's cap.

The iniquitous General Government of Europe weighs on all rural cottages with its permanent conscription and a permanent tax.

But, failing to connect the effects to the real causes, it is on their own inhabitants that the village or suburbs politicians direct their attacks.

And bottom line, only those local politicians make the

effort to speak to the paysans. He listened in 1793, and he will listen even better, when the wheat and the cattle of *America and Australia* will make him leave his fields fallow.

In the village there is no gymnasium, no theater, no public games, where the other classes of society would come to mingle with the countryman, comfort him and encourage him in his isolation from all social life.

But there is the cabaret, owned by the local politician, amorphous tavern, where the hatred of rival parties infuses the spirit of civil war with ballots, while awaiting the war of the rifles.

For a while, the peasant can still be encouraged to nominate a representative rather than another, as long as he believes that this one will be serving his interest, can help him prevent war, reduce taxes, build more roads, improve the local life of the Commune or Canton

The day the rural laborer forsakes this illusion will bring a terrible awakening, and he will take a revenge much more severe than would city workers, who are more restrained and more civil than commonly perceived.

What other benefits does the peasant owe to the city?

The disgrace of his daughter, if she is beautiful, the short visit of hawkers and of shapeless acrobats howling in the fairs, deafening the air with some barbarous music, and that's all.

It is very little, and it is not enough:
this carelessness denotes a civilization without faith and law worthy of the name, a governmental policy without any kind of social authority, without science, without art, without intelligence and without heart.

THE ALDEA ORGANIZED BY RAM 8,600 YEARS AGO

That said, let's go back to the Cycle of Ram, 8,600 years back, and observe how this pure theocratic genius had organized the Aldea, both legally and economically.

Through its Taleari and its special counsel, the Aldea adjudicated the first instance trials, organized its own local police and its own roads, arrested the perpetrators, built and armed forts to secure its main strategic position, exercised its men at the gymnasium, practiced the art of defense, insured protection of inhabitants against all arbitrariness of the Central Power, controlled and guided foreign travelers.

Due to the nature of his functions, the Taleari could let himself become arbitrary, or be bought by the central Power, therefore he was chosen from among the poorest, and deprived of remuneration by the Kaaldry at the slightest infringement on the freedoms of the Aldea.

Let's move on to economic power.

By the Scharaff and his assistants, the Aldea freely taxed itself for its own expenses, independently administered its own affairs, levied the state tax in proportion to the goods and properties of each inhabitant, and determined the tax quota in plenary assembly of the three councils, or Kaaldry.

The Aldea was jointly responsible for the State tax; in return priestly engineers carried out the great provincial works, whose ruins are still admired by modern travelers: canal and lake water management for agriculture, paddy fields, and transportation, great paved roads up to the highest mountains, shelters against big wild animals, stock of plant seeds and consecrated stallions, technical guidance of agricultural work, etc...

Thus, the Aldea was a small free society, complete in itself, a true Trinitarian Synarchy, appointing its own magistrates, having its own local jurisdiction, its autonomous economy, paying for itself its social offices: Pundit, Rapsoada, medical Doctor, Musicians and Devadassys, as well as Thasildar, Raiassom, Taleari, and Scharaff.

Religion had no political power, as it embodied the Educational Authority. It resided in the communal hearth only to elevate intellectual and moral life: Science, technical Art, legislation combining into Religious Unity a set of Healthy Laws, applied by the Public Wisdom itself.

Nobody in particular governed the Aldea; all consented to the reign of the best possible social principles, that is, to an organic government, impersonal, ruled by pure intelligence.

Such is the ancient rural commune of the Aryas, from Tibet to Hindustan and Ceylon, from Iran to Egypt.

The genius of Ram instituted it by *amalgamating the traditions of his Race with that of all the Races and successive Civilizations* of the ancient Austral Continent and the Gians or Jainas of Bharat-Versh.

With regard to the social organization of Iran, we have detailed how Ram hierarchically linked the circumscriptions of the Kingdoms encompassed in his theocratic empire.

I wished to begin this analysis by the Commune, the first organic molecule of the Social Corps; it is on this constitution of the regional freedoms that the universal Synarchy will be able to be established; because if one wants the organization of a general, impersonal, intellectual government to occur in the totality of the human race, it must be in direct correspondence with similarly regulated local customs.

In order to focus on his social work, Ram gave up his crown as judicial Emperor of all the Kings of Justice, crowned the first Kousha of India whom he consecrated by giving him the banner of Aries.

Ram therefore took the oriflamme and the name of Lamb, morphed into "Lam", and assumed only his role as universal Supreme Pontiff. The territory he chose for residence was situated between Balk and Bamyan.

He declared his territory neutral, consecrated it and put it under the protection of the Divinity, in the custody of his Judicial Emperor of all his Kings of Justice and all the local Assemblies.

SOCIAL ORDER OF RAMA – DIVINE ORDER OF LAMA

This neutral country received the name of *Para-Desa,* meaning *Divine Land,* and that is where we got the notion of Paradise, and not from Gan-be-Heden, which means, as I said previously, the organization of the whole Temporal Order, not only on the Earth, but in all the Heavens.

It was then that in all his kingdoms and all his colonies Ram-Lam similarly organized the independence of his Pontiffs, in equally consecrated territories.

In addition to the name of his theocratic emblem, he also assumed the name of *Pa-ʐi-Pa*, or *Pa-Pa*, Father of the fathers; the other pontiffs bearing the name of *Pa*, and the entire Pontifical Order was named Pa-han-sha, Pansha, Pan, etc.

The most famous shrines of this ancient lamaic cult were, in India, those of Lanka, Ayodhya, Guyah, Methra, Devarkash; in Iran, those of Vahr, Balk, Bamyan; in Thibet, those of Mount Boutala and Lassa; in Tatarah, those of Astrakhan, Gangawaz, Baharein; in Kaldea, those of Ninweh, Han, Iloun; in Syria and Arabia, those of Askala, Balbeck, Mambyce, Salem, Rama, Mekka, Sanah; in Egypt, those of Thebes, Memphis, Ham-Môn; in Ethiopia, those of Rapta and Meroë; in Thrace, those of Hœmus, Balkan and Caucayon or Gog-hayoun; in Greece, those of Parnassus and Delphi; in Etruria, that of Bolsene; in Osk-tan, former Occitania, that of Nîmes; among the Iberians of Spain, brothers of the Hebrews and Iberians of the Caucasus, those of Huesca and Gades; among the Go-laks, or Gauls, those of Bibracte, Perigueux, Chartres, etc., etc. To avoid overloading this book, I must limit the list of my quotes.

Let us now go into some details of the ancient lamaic Cult. Its forms and rites are still found today in Tibet.

SIMILARITIES BETWEEN WEST AND EASTERN RITUALS

It is pleasing to me to take this opportunity to do justice to the perfect loyalty with which Father Hue, of the Society of Jesus, has dared to say in his traveler's books the pure and simple truth.

This conscientious abbot was not afraid to indicate the close *similarity of the Buddhist rites and those of the Catholic and Greek churches*. The episcopal staff, the miter, the dalmatic, the round hat the Lamas wear on a journey, the ceremony of the mass, the double chorus, the psalmody, the exercises, the censer with its five chains, the manner of blessing the right hand raised on the heads of the faithful, the rosary, discipline and retreats, the worship of the saints, fasting, litanies, tonsure, relics, the confessional: *those are the points of resemblance* that have struck the mind of the eminent and excellent Abbot.

Nonetheless, the book recounting his travels to Tibet had the honors of the Index, and the poor man was rewarded for his efforts and his great worth by being struck off, at Rome, from the list of missionaries. The present book will absolutely prove that *Catholicism and Christianity* as a whole, has a lot to gain and nothing to lose by recognizing that *their source lies within the esoteric legacy bequeathed by the Abramids, Moses and Jesus Christ*, thus reacquiring a *profound link* with all the ancient religions of Egypt and Asia and rekindling their ancient former Social Order.

Later I shall provide analogies between our cults and the ancient religion of the Lamb, to which not only the reformers of India, but those of Kaldea, in the person of Orthodox Abramids, those of Egypt who, like *Moses*, were priests of Osiris, O-sir-is, the intellectual Lord, the Synthesis, the Law of Ram. We will finally see *Jesus* renew to the benefit of Humankind as a whole the moral and social exoteric values; these were part of the ancient initiations to the original *Religion of the Lamb* and the original *Arbitral Synarchy of Aries.*

MORPHOLOGY OF ANCIENT SYNARCHY

From one end of the Earth to the other where the Lamb's Cult and the Empire of Aries reigned, this Synarchy was established in the following manner.

The Sacerdotal Body, *guardian of the Esoteric Synthesis of Science*, was the *Teaching Body par excellence*, the totality of the Teachings, and constituted the first High *Council of God.*

The Corps of Lay Initiates with universal control over all secondary institutions formed a second High Council, or the *Council of the Gods*, arbitral judges of the *Supreme Court of Appeal.* Finally, the third Power encompassed the *Public Mores* themselves and the hierarchy of all the delegations of fathers and mothers.

The Sovereigns, Viceroys, Kings or Emperors, were part

of the Second High Council, and as such, they represented the *Arbitral Justice,* hierarchically constituted so as to adjudicate cases not only of individuals, but of kingdoms themselves.

The last representative of this ancient Arbitral Order of Aries and Lamb, representing this ancient *sacerdotal Sovereignty of Justice,* will be *Melchizedek,* residing in *Salem.*

ABRAHAM, MOSES, JESUS, PERPETUATE RAM'S MISSION

This is why the *Orthodox Order of the Abramids* or neo-ramids of Kaldea will bow to this kingship, after fleeing the arbitrary Empire, the universal power of iniquity that *Moses* will stigmatize under the hieroglyphic name of *Nimrod,* the tiger's way, *the path of the Beast.*

Wherever the Lamaic cult reigned, one finds the same mores and behaviors, even the details of the rites.

The altar of the Ancestor at home, the slaughter of cattle according to certain hygienic practices, regulated by worship in the tribe, and lastly Communion under the "species of wine and bread", reserved for priests and initiates: such are the distinctive features that we will find in all the divisions of the ancient Aries empire.

Even after the schism of the year 3200 BC, we will still see in historical Greece proper (Acheans), the Holy Mysteries of Delphi and Eleusis open and close as in India by the words: *Kansha, Aum, Pansha,* that the Brahmans pronounce today *Kanska Om Pakscha,* and that the Greek hierophants altered into: *Kanx-Om-Panx.*

It was the *Domine Salvum* of the Aries Empire, or his *Ite Missa est.* We will see Moses again communing with His master Jethro, like Abraham at Salem with his Master (Melchizedek), "under the species" reserved for the priest and the Initiate.

I cannot reiterate enough here that the brotherhood of the Initiates belonging to the old Order of Things persisted from one end of the Earth to the other until Jesus Christ, in spite of the schism and the ensuing general decadence that caused the ancient Order of Aries and Lamb in Kaldea to give in to the previous order of the Taurus, former Power which allowed the proliferation of arbitrary dominions.

It is this second Council of the ancient Aries Synarchy which, in Asia as yet, preserves the ancient esoteric Science, venerable remains which are revealed or rather hinted at, in the letter which I have published in Chapter IV.

In the Gospels and in the book of Apocalypse, the spirit of the ancient Initiations surges at every moment under the literal meaning, and the tradition of the Lamb and Aries is just as evident there as in Moses' book itself.

I shall give more details in the next chapter; but, before closing this one, I wish to pay a religious homage to the founder of the Ram Cycle of which we have just seen the emergence 8,600 years ago; also, Israel and Christendom, thanks to the Abramids, to Moses and Jesus, are waiting and preparing its *universal reconstitution and transfiguration.*

Such was the primordial Synarchy, the trinitarian impersonal General Government in its youthful vigor, which the heavenly Genie Protector of the Kelts incarnated in a providential man, actualized it all over Asia, all over Africa, and a large part of Europe.

It was through this wise and savant organism that the peoples of the Universal Theocracy of the Lamb, the Universal Empire of the Aries, experienced for 3,500 years the *actualization of Divine Unity,* the peace of the Social God living through all the members of Humanity's Spiritual body here below.

No doubt all men and women were not perfect; but the institutions were as perfect as possible, and that's the important thing. These institutions were as perfect as possible for they corresponded to the threefold nature of Humankind, whether individual, collective, or universal.

This triple nature is *intellectual, moral, physical;* and this triple life has for its necessary organs 3 Bodies, namely Religious Synthesis of the Teachings (1), Justice (2), Economy (3). The *Hominal Kingdom* with all its subdivisions, whose flesh and bones are only the visible submultiples, is an immense Spirit, living in an invisible Body, male and female, and the institutions of our Societies are its organic shades.

The eternal glory of Ram will be to have known in his true essence this *Hominal Kingdom*, this *Adam-Eve*, to have recognized its main organs, its cosmic laws, and to have conformed to them his hierarchical institutions.

I do not want to be clearer here than necessary; but I ask the reader to keep in mind that *Moses*, priest of Osiris, that is to say of the Intellectual Law of the Lamb and Aries, will be compelled, after the schisms, to form a *special new people*, an *Israel* or *Royal University of God*, in order to avoid the sinking of the ancient institutions, the vanishing of the Science of the Physiology of the Universe, or Cosmogony, and consequently the decline of the Science sustaining the Social State.

The form of *government which Moses will give*, in the wilderness, to his people, and which that people will safeguard for more than 400 years, will be *the Triune Arbitral Synarchy, with its three Councils.*

And finally, in his mysterious prayer, *Jesus* summoning the entire universe to obey *the Law of the Kingdom of God*, will clearly reveal his purpose, that is the restoration of Universal Synarchy. For, as St. Matthew tells us, Ch. IV, verse 23: *"Jesus went all over Galilee, teaching in the synagogues, preaching the Gospel of the Kingdom."*

This evocation of the Gospel of the Kingdom is to be duly noted, and we shall recount later in this book how *Abraham* and all his order of orthodox Initiates will bow before the King of Salem and receive from him the Communion of Bread and Wine, because that King was one of the last representatives of that Reign and Kingdom. *Ram, the divine founder of the Empire of Aries*, of the Theocracy of the Lamb, of the Trinitarian Synarchy, reached, according to Tradition, the extreme limits of age.

Before passing away, Ram saw the Synthesis of his vision

almost completely actualized; and in the sanctuaries of the *Para-desa* he regulated the succession to the tiara by means of secret contest.

Every Initiate being followed, even at a distance, throughout his whole life, fulfilled, without suspecting it, the conditions of this contest. Moreover, Lam announced that *he would return*, when needed, to *undergo reincarnation* here below, and to take the tiara again if necessary. This Tradition still exists today among the Lamas; but it is fitting for me to respect their Mysteries, by deferentially revering and glorifying the holy memory of the Genius who became the *first Lama*.

We will read this name on the lips of Jesus expiring:

Lama Lama

Lama Lama Sabakhtani.
The common translation is:
"Why Why have you abandoned me?"
If Jesus had wanted to say *"abandoned me"* he would
have pronounced *"Azavtani"*.

But Jesus said *"Sabakhtany"*, which means:
You gave me the mission to *awaken (Sabakh=the dawn)*
in me and around me the twin crown of the Lamb
(*Lama Lama*),
the dawn of a new era
of social evolution for humankind,
which minimizes violence
and maximizes the spirit of pacific leadership.

Note by Simha Seraya

CHAPTER VII
RAM'S CYCLE (Continued)

RAM'S CYCLE BEGAN 8,750 YEARS BEFORE 2018 AD

There are three ways to set the date of the Cycle of Ram: the *chronology of the Brahmans*, the *chronology of the historian Arrian,* and finally a *document inscribed by Ram himself* on the vault of Heavens.

Deçaratha, the Rawhan dethroned by Ram was the fifty-fifth solar monarch since Ikshaukou, son of the seventh Manu, son of Vaivasouata, who was saved from the last flood.

Now, the *Brahmans count 12,000 years* for each Manu or inter-diluvian Organic Law; and they date the reign of Deçaratha at 2,100 years after the last cataclysm.

These calculations give a little more than 8,600 years before the present year 1884 AD. According to the *data of the Greeks,* Tyrians, and Egyptian sanctuaries, Arrian says that from Ram to Sandrocottus 6,400 year elapsed. But Alexander defeated Sandrocottus 326 years before our era, which gave the foundation of the Cycle of Ram, Dionysus, Osiris, 8,600 and a few years (before Saint-Yves' time). Pliny agrees with Arrian.

Finally, *Ram* having himself written one of his *books in hermetic language, in primeval hieroglyphs, in the Starry Sphere* he structured for humankind, he deliberately indicated the date *astronomically*, by designing the *Zodiacal Aries forward, face back, fleeing the West.*

At that time, the Keltic year was lunar, and although Ram knew of the solar year, and while confining the total knowledge of the World's System to the domain of esoteric teaching, he let his people use the lunar year to which they were accustomed. That lunar year began at the *Modra-Necht*, at that M*other-Night* of the Winter Solstice, where the festival of *New Salvation, New Health, New-Heyl,* our *Noel-*(Christmas), was celebrated around the Dolmens and Gromlechs.

That night, the starting point of the zodiacal Order of Aries, today corresponds to Sagittarius.

This gap of nearly 4 signs gives us more than 8,600 years at present (1884 AD). This quadruple chronological concordance of the Brahmans, Arrian, Pliny and Ram himself, *dates exactly the opening of the Cycle of Lamb and Aries.*

Now it is interesting to observe that the *festivals of Hammon and Osiris were celebrated at Noel,* like that of Bacchus, Devanahousha, Gian-Shyd, etc

As for the place where our Ancestor, the *Ancient of Days of the Aryas,* wrote his heavenly book, it is certainly the Divine Land, the Paradesa, where he resided as Sovereign Pontiff.

Indeed, the circle traced towards the South Pole by the constellations of the Ship, (Argo Navis) the Whale (Cetus), the Altar (Ara) and the Centaur (Centaurus), as well as the emptiness left below in the most ancient Spheres, precisely draws the horizon of the thirty-seventh degree of latitude, that is to say the region between Balk and Bamiyan, where this heavenly and most mysterious book was written.The date of the opening of the Ram Cycle is therefore unambiguously fixed.

The *unicity of the institutions of this Cycle from one end of the World to the other* is also unmistakable, and the diversity of names only confirms in different languages the religious Unity, the Synthesis of this former Social State.

It is this Principled General Government which is evoked by Moses, when he reports about certain Patriarchs, as collective and not individual symbols, and it is the total duration of this Arbitral Empire which he characterizes under the name of Kush.

FOUNDING PRINCIPLES OF ARBITRAL GOVERNANCE

Here, I ask the reader to re-read carefully in the *Sovereigns' Mission* the chapter on the definitions of different forms of government.

But as that book might not be available, I will recall, by summarizing them, the passages relating to the Theocracy.

"The principle of pure Theocracy is the Unity of Science and Life".

The goal it proposes is the universal Culture of consciences and intelligences, their union and their social peace.

The means by which this Principle tends towards its end is the tolerance of all Cults and the emphasis on their common Principle.

The necessary condition for implementing these means is the voluntary free assent of the legislators and the peoples, all recognizing the practical efficacy of Science combined with the Virtue of Universal Religion.

The guarantee of success of this form of government resides in the *incessant actualization of Divine Perfection* through the continual development of human perfectibility: Education, Instruction, Initiation, Selection of the best.

Before the schism of Irshu, Asia, Africa, Europe, were governed by a Theocracy; all the later religions of Egypt, Assyria, Syria, Persia, Greece, Etruria, Gaul, Spain, Great Britain, were but fragments and dissolution of the original Theocratic Synarchy.

This Theocracy is clearly indicated in the sacred annals of Hindus, Persians, Chinese, Egyptians, Hebrews, Phoenicians, Greeks, Etruscans, Druids and Keltic Bards, and even in the songs of ancient Scandinavia and Iceland. This Theocracy was founded by the Keltic leader, *Ram*, celebrated by the *Ramayana* of Valmiki and the Dionysiacs of Nonnus.

Many ancient temples preserved the Tradition of this first Unity, of which we find everywhere positive traces, as reported by Philostratus and Apollonius of Thyane - the latter contemporary of Jesus Christ - as they conversed with all the priests of all cults while traveling and visiting the World's religious centers, from Gaul to the depths of India and Ethiopia.

That same *Apollonius*, last *voluntary Initiator of the Rulers*, endeavored to reorient and guide all the Roman emperors who, during his long career, succeeded one another to the General Government of the World.

As reported by his biographers he accomplished this mission risking his freedom and life, as similarly have the Council of the Gods, the Council of Lay Initiates, in Israel and in Judea.

PRINCIPLES OF TRUE THEOCRACY

Even more brilliantly *Jesus Christ* himself has performed this same duty vis-à-vis the governing institutions of his people.

Daniel had done the same in Babylon; and the more we dive into the past, the more we find out that the control of public Power when effectuated by Initiates has been frequent and effective.

That type of control is impossible outside of a Theocracy, in a particular nation as well as in mutual or intergovernmental relations between nations.

Where rules a form of purely political government, be it an oligarchic power or the power of one, where Anarchy reigns, whether represented by an assembly or crowned in the person of a sovereign, then no social perfectibility is possible; and it can only result in the overthrow of one form of political government by another, nothing that matters can change in the structural fabric of Society.

It is quite different when Trinitarian Synarchy reigns, and arbitrariness is as intolerable in the internal government of a people as it is in the General Government of groups of peoples thus organized by the unified Theocracy.

Since more than a century we have misused the names given to realities, *taking the effects for causes*, calling Religions what are only Cults debilitated by Politics; unfortunately, the *promotion of unscientific ignorance*, fruit of this debilitation, *is obscuring the ancient primeval Ultra-Spiritual Science foundation of True initial Religion.*

The rational, superficial criticism perpetually rehashes the same *half-truths, soon becoming patent errors, then eventually are imposed as dogmas.*

I have already done justice to the most important of these errors, in the first chapters of this book.

I have shown that, far from being the fruit of ignorance, *true Religion* has been the very *Synthesis of the antique Sciences,* and that the twofold aspect of *physical Science and spiritual Truth can and may be united,* synthesized and known only through True Religion.

In *Mission of the Sovereigns,* in *Mission of the Workers,* I have aptly proved that not only among the people, but mostly in regard with the mutual relations of governments, the social disorder of Europe cannot be resolved by pure Politics, either monarchical or republican, since this disorder is the fruit of that twin political form, and of it alone.

By contrast, I have proved that this armed and revolutionary anarchy of the current form of sovereign Powers is a perpetual dereliction of the Religion of Christ, and that, in truth, this latter religion unequivocally implies the necessity of a Trinitarian social government, of an impersonal triple Arbitration.

Nearly three thousand volumes of these works have been spread in the public for two years. They correspond so much to the secret assent of intelligences and consciences, that no serious refutation has been made of them, and that in certain countries where arbitrariness reigns, the press has been forbidden to discuss the subject of these questions, ideas, and even booksellers are forbidden to sell these books.

But in personal letters, in messages sometimes sent from far away, in private conversations, the adhesion of the most eminent minds has come to light.

From the top to the bottom of the ladder of social responsibility, I have received valuable testimonials, of which I am deeply moved and grateful, and to which I try to respond as best I can with this book.

Later, we shall see how, the High Council of God and the High Council of the Gods, fruits of the Synarchy instituted by *Moses* in ancient Israel, was firmly admonishing the Political Power, as soon as the latter, coming out of its boundaries, was attacking the Authority in order to escape all Principle and all control, and replace Theocratic Arbitrage by its kingly arbitrariness.

PEACE AND GENERAL HAPPINESS FOR 3,500 YEARS

All this intellectual and moral knowledge, in matters of general and particular governance, originated from the pure Genie who opened and organized the social state of the Cycle which we have been studying, and of which our present Social forms are mere fragments.

We shall see later that this dismemberment of the ancient Osiris, the ancient intellectual government of Aries and the Lamb, was the works of Politics.

For the moment, we have to consider how, thanks to Ram, the Theocracy gave to the whole World the public peace, the general happiness, the prosperity, *the Reign of God finally on Earth as in Heaven*, during more than 3,500 years.

TRINITARIAN SOCIAL ORDER

Ram decreed the three Councils representing *Science, Justice* and the *Social Economy* of his Empire to be absolutely free, independent of all political Power.

The *Economic Council* was composed of the Assembly of Elders, fathers and mothers, with all their hierarchical delegations, from the rural districts to the central districts.

We saw how wisely this Social Order was organized, with its arbitral tribunals and its executive adjudications.

The second Council or Council of the Gods formed a real Court of Appeal. The lay Initiates belonged by right to this second social order, which controlled all the delegated public authorities. The sovereigns themselves belonged to this Council, to this Arbitral Court, and they held from it their Powers as Kings of Justice.

After his consecration by the Sacerdotal ministry, the Sovereign thus authorized by a higher power than his own was officially and publicly treated by the Initiates with the respect due to his impersonal function and not to his person alone.

However, the Initiates remained his peers, and could always make him appear at the bar of their closed door tribunals, whenever he was derelict in the application of the laws of the Order, whenever he inclined towards personal Power, whenever, as King of Justice, he was tipping his scale toward arbitrary decisions.

The *third High Council, the Council of God* was formed, not only of the official priesthood, of which all ranks were obtained by exam, other members were chosen among those of the Initiates who had attained the highest level in the double and quadruple *Knowledge of the visible and invisible realms.*

Later, in Judea (4th cent. BC) at a time as recent as Esdras', we still may observe in the Talmudic book "Gemara" that the most important secrets of the Mysteries were not available to all priests and could be revealed only to the wisest and most educated.

Moreover, in the *Mishna Hagiga,* Part II, it is said that even the table of contents of the Merkaba can be communicated only to the most advanced Sages.

I could show that these esoteric rules of accession to the higher degrees of Science have been preserved almost intact, where Ram established them.

The same rules exist indeed in books of Buddhism and reading the *table of contents listing some of the Sciences and applied Arts,* would by itself seem to Westerners a fabulous dream like the Thousand and One Nights.

SUPERFICIAL WORSHIP VS ENLIGHTENED WORSHIP

Among the Europeans who think they are religious because they worship on Sundays, three-quarters perceive Divinity, not in the form of a quadruple hierarchy of Truths and subsequent Sciences, but as God the Father, in the form of an old man with a white beard, God the Son in the guise of a handsome Rabbi, the Holy Spirit under the plumage of a dove. Few are the brave faithful who venture beyond this anthropomorphism and zoomorphism.

Accustomed, as regards religious matters, to utter names whose meaning and value is *not scientifically analyzed* and ascertained for them, they would not believe it possible that *the Soul,* for example, is *experimentally demonstrable,* and that through

Wisdom, Science and applied Art, the Puissance of the Soul can master the Space of our Solar Whirlwind, and manifest the full intensity of its spiritual vigor across all planetary circles of our solar system.

Conversely among Brahmans and Buddhists, the *esoteric* Science of which I just spoke was not and is not limited to that knowledge. And similar centers of *Initiation*, representing higher or lower degrees of ancient science, still exist in other communities of the East. So, the educated Oriental understands and feels Life differently than the European.

His thought, his soul, his very sensations, live in what is for him the *"main (spiritual) side of Nature"* whence he has exiled himself; and the reverse side of this place, which we name "the real", has only a very relative value to the eyes of the spiritual scientist of the East.

All the current resources where the fragments of the ancient Synthesis are kept, come from the Cycle of Ram. This esotericism and the subsequent Initiations are but the broken extension of the ancient High Council of the Gods and the ancient High Council of God.

Politics, Powers becoming personal, conquests, arbitrariness, may have depressed in the East the ancient Social Corps organized by Ram; but the original spirit still resides there.

The Brotherhood of Priests was as autonomous as the organization of the initial Commune.

It formed a special jurisdiction, and its temporal power, administration and property, was its own entirely.

We find the same organization in Egypt and in all the colonies of the Kousha. Before the schisms, the class of warriors had no prerogative as such.

The military officers received their teachings from the temples, and enjoyed the rights conferred by the Initiation. As such, they formed a court of first instance in military matters; but the Court of Appeal was the Council of the Gods, and the Supreme Court of Appeal, the Council of God. The officers of the army were chosen among the gymnasts of the communes, and every year, around certain temples, the army met for the great maneuvers, coinciding with the public games of certain Astronomical Festivals.

RAM'S LEGACY ENDURES AFTER THE SCHISM OF IRSHU

We shall see in Egypt this organization persist, in the service, not of the spirit of conquest, but of the General Government of the World.

In the Spirit of the Ram Cycle, the army was only a national police force, intended to bring to Order any royalty or international viceroyalty that was trying to escape the religious laws of the Universal Empire and to replace by arbitrariness the General Arbitration and its three Councils.

All the wars of India, from the Schism of Irshu to the constitution of the personal Government and the arbitrary Empire of Nimrod, had this corrective character. And when India was conquered by this power of iniquity, when Ninus and Semiramis crushed the metropolis, when the new, arbitrary empire also assassinated the former Iranian Arbitral government, when it sacked the Para-desa, and went so far as to assassinate the Sovereign Pontiff in order to silence the Ancient Authority, then we shall see Orthodox Egypt raise the sword, and, faithful to the ancient Order, remind the Assyrian Schism, the arbitrary Empire, the crowned Anarchy, their duty to respect the ancient Constitution.

No trace of communism to be seen in the scholarly organization of Ram, except among certain religious orders, prototypes of ours.

In all other social classes, the sacred books show family and property safeguarded by institutions one finds everywhere, in Egypt, Persia, Kaldea, Japan, China, Touran, Syria, Judea, Etruria, in the laws of Solon as in those of the Twelve table.

Celibacy was struck by a sort of civil death.

As to death, Ram marked his legislation with a character, where the inviolability of human life is found at every step. As far as in Greece, the crime involving the death penalty could by law be converted into exile at the request of the convicted person. From those out-law exiles originated the caste of *pariahs*, with all its subdivisions, thousands of years later.

The same spirit will inspire all the reformers who, like Sakya-Mouni (famous Buddha), will attempt to bring back the institutions of Ram to their original scope.

Even today, the Buddhists, when they can, pull back the condemned from the hands of the executioner.

The priests, in their Brotherhoods, did not immolate victims; and the bloody animal Sacrifices were performed by the butcher of the tribes, guided by the principles of anatomy and hygiene, and the animal of the holocaust was selected as a living symbol dedicated to the corresponding cosmic Divinity.

The Highest priesthood offered the Divinity only symbolic victims, cakes bearing the *imprint of Aries* or Lamb.

The holy sacrifice of the Mass was called *Avahna-Pudja* or *Feast of the Real Presence*, and was composed as follows:

Hassanah, whence *Hosannah, Invocation*;

Souagatta, *Elevation*;

Arkia, *Consecration*;

Madou-Parka, *Communion* in the golden chalice;

Atchamavia, *Washing hands* in the silver ewer;

Doupa, *Fragrant incense* on the altar and the tabernacle;

Niveddia, *Communion of the faithful*;

Asservadam, *Blessing* of the faithful and sprinkling with lustral water.

These rites were almost the same throughout Ram's Theocratic Empire. The peoples most attached to the ancient symbols of the Black Race, Ethiopia and Egypt for example, kept the round form of the Host with the image of the Sun, stamping it with the image of the Aries or the Lamb.

These are the same rites observed by the priestess of Eleusis, the priests of Delphi, those of Etruria; rites which Ammonius Sacchas will transmit to the Christian priests.

The priests, later in time, have borne various names; but they long kept that of *Druid*, softened in *Dwidja*: Manu, Book.

IV, sloca 2 and following. The *knowledge required of the simplest Dwidja* was vast: Tarca-Sastram, Bouta, Mimousa, Dotkioa-Sastram, Veiddia, Dharma, respectively *Logic, Psychology, Ontology, Astronomy and Cosmogony, Medicine, Jurisprudence.*

Apart from this sacerdotal knowledge, or *Vedas*, came the 18 books of history, those of the encyclopedia of the other Sciences, a total number of 64.

Thus, were formed the *Puranas* and the *Kalais*, or rather *Kaal-Ais, Convergence of all Intellectuality.*

The books which are known to Europeans represent only the median or allegorical meaning transmitted by the schools of the Bards.

At the present time, all *esoteric* books are *carefully protected* from the profanation of our missionaries and scholars.

However, even with what Europeans possess, when paying attention to proper *names, hierograms, mentrams*, one can penetrate to a certain extent the scientific meaning, provided one knows by what *ideographic rules* these names have been composed.

Let's keep in mind the *Sanskrit song* so popular in India, about the importance of the mentrams.

Studying texts produced during a period of 8,500 years, we shall find this scientific Truth well safeguarded, where the secret meaning is carefully distinguished from the apparent literal sense.

And even when politics and local ambitions have separated themselves from the Theocratic University, from the intellectual and social Universality, Ram's legacy to all humankind, the divided members of the old Council of the Gods who will testify publicly by teaching certain branches of Science will be very careful, including Plato, Aristotle and Hippocrates, to *distinguish what can be said in public and what should be taught only in secret.*

NECESSARY SECRECY OF FUNDAMENTAL KNOWLEDGE

Revelation was therefore not an empty word, since total Science was the very Religion of the temples, since the

Knowledge of Life at all its degrees was accessible by Initiation, since the Tradition was *transmitted for more than 80,000 years continuously from deluge to deluge, from a metropolitan temple to another metropolitan temple.*

I have said over and over why the *Sciences of the Intelligible Order* are taught only under the seal of secrecy.

I would add here that, even in the Physical Order, some sciences that have reached a certain high level will have to be the object of the same secretive security measures on the part of the Europeans, in the presence of public and private dangers that the possession of this knowledge will surely bring, if it can be acquired by men without wisdom, without virtue, driven by passions and ambitions of all sorts, political and others.

A fortiori, the *Ontological, Cosmogonic and Theogonic Sciences* should have been and still should be revealed only to souls and intelligences absolutely inaccessible to evil in all its individual and social forms.

That is why we will notice complete compliance to this Law of Mysteries, not only by theocrats like Moses and Jesus, but even by the founders of Orders or Public Schools, such as Thales, Pythagoras, Plato, Aristotle, Hippocrates, Theophrastus, Archimedes, Euclid, Apollonius of Perge, Hipparchus, Ptolemy, Apollonius of Thyane.

All preserving the *esoteric doctrine* for themselves, never entrusting it to vulgar writing.

This is why one must not lightly judge neither the Sciences of the Antiquity, nor the ancient Religions which were the Social applied Art, deriving from these Sciences.

It is a vain enterprise to judge them, either from symbols of which we seldom have the key, or from what the vulgar said, thought or wrote about them.

Now, this prudence must not stop there, and it must be redoubled when one studies what the Heads of Schools themselves have confided to phonetic writing.

For their books only came to us through copyists, on whom the College of the Gods had their eye, and through translators, either ignorant or sworn in such a way as to deliver only the *exoteric strata* of these writings.

All these Heads of Public Schools, whether Lay or Sacerdotal Orders, even during the period of decadence which produced Judea, Greece, and Rome, -the religious and academic past of present day Europe- all these Masters still belonged either to the Lesser Initiation or the Great Initiation Centers of Asia and Africa; and, as Aeschylus says, they had the 'Seal of the Taurus" on the tongue.

The same fact is observable in the records of Herodotus, the so-called father of history, when he evokes certain names reminiscent of the ancient order of things, the ancient intellectual and social Synarchy, that the new governments wanted at all costs to forget, because they had all become, since Ninus Nimrod, personal, arbitrary, anarchical.

For want of knowing the Constitution of the Universal Empire of Ram and its subsequent branches, it is impossible to grasp the true Spirit, safeguarded everywhere by the remains of the ancient University and its first two High Councils.

So, there is no foolishness that has not been freely attributed to antiquity by European criticism, from the decadence of the Roman Empire to our time.

What happens as to Moses' legacy?

Some affirm that he had received his books directly from Jehovah himself; and they show you the Targums (Translations), the Version of the Septuagint, that of St. Jerome, and finally *the Bibles translated from these former translations.*

Others, in the camp of the naturalistic critics, namely the "Ionian" exegetes, have it easy to mock these Dorian and Science traditions deformed by the translators.

That wild group of naturalist critics -like in a "medieval black Sabbath"- fall on these venerable texts, peels their alleged gross errors, abuse the Revelation, and puncture, without knowing it, the right eye of the *Great Face*, the Partzufim of the Kabbalists, or rather they puncture their own eye, that is to say they mutilate all the side of the Human Mind that corresponds to the *Science of the Intelligible Order.*

What happens as to *Jesus' legacy?*

Some say that Jesus was the son of God in the anthropo-morphic and modern sense of the word.

That debased religious claim makes the Gospels fair game to the muddy naturalist exegetes, who delight themselves by easily exposing the similarities of the New Testament with the more ancient sacred books of many other peoples.

But all of them, under the mere letter of the second as well as the first Testament, choke the ancient Spirit of Ram's Cycle and all its subsequent intellectual and social fruits, which remain inaccessible to them.

KEYS FOR EFFICIENT READING OF THE SCRIPTURES

Volumes pile up on volumes, and during this time, political evil and social disorganization go unhindered, while the original marching order and the scientific-religious formula of the Good is not given an opportunity to triumph over the anarchy of the teachings and political powers.

To "flay" Matthew, to "depilate" Luke, to "shred" Paul, to "dissect" John, to proclaim that Jesus was a gentle innocuous dreamer are easy things to do.

Yet *Christendom* exists, *eppur si muove, and yet it moves*, and it has *all Israel* behind it, *Moses* in front.

Now, these great spiritual bodies called *Social States*, are not self-created, nor are they existing without the assistance of a *Creative Power*, nor without an *animating Spirit*, nor without an *organic Soul* individualizing their Life.

And I challenge three of those exegetes to come together and originate a Social State that lasts eight days.

This profane and barbarous way of judging the Spirit contained in the Testaments of Moses and Jesus only at the exoteric level, without complementing it with knowledge related to the Creation or the Organicity of Societies, is applied to all contemporary study of ancient Judaism or anything anterior to it, by even ignorant scholars..

We will not find the keys to the truth by examining the texts of Virgil, Homer, Hesiod, the remains of Greek literature, the rituals of Orpheus, the emerald table, the bardic works of the Avesta, the Y-Kings, the Vedas, Puranas, stelae, papyri, hieroglyphic, cuneiform or other inscriptions; nor will we be any more successful by collecting their dust, by separating their phonetic meaning, by analyzing these graphic forms, than the anatomist who dissects a corpse to become a physiologist, or a barbarian vivisector who tortures unfortunate animals to study biology.

And as one finds nothing, or at best only shreds of ideas whose thoughts and mental categories escape our understanding, one lends liberally to Antiquity an ignorance against which successfully protest the Sages of Asia who have preserved its Science.

Simple common sense should clearly demonstrate to all sound intelligent minds that if, in barely one hundred years, we have been able to come out of barbarism and catch a glimpse of a considerable sum of the truths of the physical and natural order, all the more so *the 74,000 years of human cycles that preceded Ram*, must have bequeathed him at least a good amount of scientific certainties of all kinds.

For, Ram, this great man, no more than any other on Earth or in Heaven, created nothing; *he transformed, by reviving it, the quadruple hierarchy of Knowledge* which I have spoken of, and he applied its Principles to the construction of a Social State as perfect as possible.

The *similarity of the doctrines* and institutions of the different religious founders of human societies *does not prove that they have plagiarized each other*, no more than the construction of a bridge by an engineer shows that he wanted to steal Euclid's ideas.

EVIDENCE OF ANCIENT WORLDWIDE CIVILIZATIONS

Thus, the exegete and the archaeologist do nothing but confirm Moses' data, when they show the correlation which exists between their exoterism and that of the Egyptians, the Kaldeans, the Persians, the Hindus and the Chinese. No doubt, Judeo-Christianity came from somewhere and for a definite purpose; but it is precisely for this reason that it conceals a truth deeper and more real in scope than is supposed.

Yes, their exoteric Revelation is a Revelation, and hides another more positive one, for in the sanctuaries of the Ram Cycle, all esoteric Teaching was called Revelation.

But in such an Order of knowledge and consecutive social evidences, *the rational study is simultaneous with the exercise of all the psychurgical, intellectual, spiritual powers* of humankind.

Thus, surpassing the static study to enter the realm *of actional thinking*, reinserting organic memories into the Ocean of the Peoples' Life, it is truly an act of creation, it amounts to *bestowing the force of Life* to what was no more and that is still to be. This *actional thinking* allows for organical *cooperation with the Intelligent Puissances of the Cosmos*, in order to alleviate the burdens of the whole of Humankind which keep it captive in front of the closed gates of the Kingdom which is its rightful inheritance.

The first line of Homer's Iliad is borrowed from Orpheus' Demetreide; its fundamental data, entirely psychurgical and cosmic in nature, is extracted from the Eons' War found in the priestly library of Tyr.

The Odyssey is the story of Hanuman, Ram's lieutenant, dressed in Greek clothing. This does not prevent Homer's work from being marked with the stamp of genius, that is a life-giving power of which is capable only *an individual united directly with a Celestial Puissance.*

And as for the modern sophists who, finding such great men a challenge to their own mediocrity, have denied their existence, and attributed their works to a group of anonymous individuals, they can be refuted by virtue of the absurd, by assembling them together, handing them a pen, asking them to compose a sonnet bearing the mark of genius.

What I say here about Homer can apply even more to Jesus Christ and Moses.

TIMELESS KNOWLEWDGE VIA SCIENTIFIC WORSHIP

So much the better, if in the astronomical symbolism of the festivals, in the rites of the Worship where I was born, I find the ceremonies, the sacraments, a hint of the Mysteries of Delphi and Eleusis, of Bolsena and Thebes, of Kaldea and Paradesa!

For, provided that at the pulpit the contemporary feeble theologian does not betray the sacerdotal Spirit of Jesus, provided that over the organ and choir presides a religious artist, a Sebastian Bach, a chapel master who does not impose on me the annoying music of an opera maker, I will cherish all the more the ritual of my church if it allows me to communicate in a more universally aesthetic manner with the Souls of all those who worshiped in all forms and all kinds of ancient temples.

So much the better, if I find in the Talmud, in the Prasada, in the Bagaveda or elsewhere, the parables that the Evangelists put on the divine lips of Christ!

Esoteric Tradition teaches me what this precious similarity means; and I become an observant with greater piety; and in the founder of my Religion, I revere and worship the real presence of the cosmic Holy Spirit and the manifestation of his breath throughout all the earlier Humanity.

So much the better, even from the exoteric point of view, for then Christendom, the masterwork of this Christ, leans on a base all the more extensive in the past and in the future.

The same thing with regard to Moses, his written work and his social work. The same thing, with regard to the Order of the Abramids or neo-Ramids, expatriates from the arbitrary empire of Babylon. Yes, the founders of these three social movements had in their mind and heart the intellectual light of Ram's Cycle, the resolve to will its resurrection!

That is why it is *so important this Cycle is revived in the memory of Westerners*, as it lives in the memory of all Asians who secretly keep its light on. There are no two ways of constituting a cyclical self-renovating General Government.

Nearly 5,000 years since the schism of Irshu, followed by the crime characterized under the name of Nimrod, whenever a man of instinctive genius lends to social administrative mechanics the temporary force of his vital energy, fragmented governments are constantly attempting to impose Universal Empire by means of pure Politics; none has been able to succeed, and none will succeed, because cunning and pure force will never reach the Universality, without being chastised for their folly.

To achieve such a cyclical goal, one must be totally inspired with an invincible love for the True, the Good, the Just; and only a man of religious genius could thus build a Universal Empire, and endow it with great Life force, by *uniting himself with all the intellectual and moral Life* which Humanity can receive.

Such was *Ram,* immense prototype of all the religious and social reformers whose influence, 3,500 years after him, arose everywhere from the bosom of the Council of the Gods to repair every kind of disasters unleashed in the World by Arbitrary Politics.

PURE POLITICS UNLEASHED

After the intense display of iniquity of which Assyria was the theater, kings and viceroys everywhere shook the power of the first two High Councils, enslaved the third,(communal and familial), transformed the priesthood into a political instrument, *forced Science to silence,* tied the hands of Religion, overturned the Kousha, persecuted the regional pontiffs and even the Lamas of Paradesa, thus making arbitrariness prevail by refusing all form of arbitration.

Then, peoples, crushed with exactions, clashed in wars, reduced to military slavery, experienced the Hell of political and personal governments, and gradually forgot that Heaven had reigned over the Earth.

They remembered the reign of Heaven only in the temples, and they exchanged these divine memories and divine hopes only under the seal of oaths; and from the height of 3,500 years of happiness, the triumphant Beast rushed them back to our days in 5,000 years of oppression, in this General Government, now occupied by the armed Anarchy, where Peoples, Races, Social States, Religions, Sovereignty, are still stupidly enchained today.

Plagues were unleashed by the rupture from the old Universal Alliance, by this criminal madness of the kingly Powers detached from independent Authority of the ancient Trinitarian Synarchy.

LOCAL REMEDIES TO MANY EMERGENT TYRANNIES

Locally, seeking remedy, the debris of the second High Council will rise in India with *Christna*, in Persia with the first *Zoroaster*, in China with *Fo-Hi*, in Egypt and on all the littoral of the Mediterranean with the *reinstatement of the Law of the Mysteries*.

Everywhere the marching order of the Initiates will be to hunt for the local symptoms of the universal disease of the ancient social body, until, in the course of time, the ancient health can be restored with the hierarchy of organic functions.

The apparent diversity of the cults, great vector of social culture, will emerge from the diversity of milieus, from the more or less profound alteration the armed anarchy of viceroys and kings will have forced on the official priesthood, also on the remaining ancient public Powers, and on the intellectual and social mores of colonies and kingdoms.

That is why the works of Christna, Zoroaster, Fo-Hi, then later the *Neo-Ramids* or *Abramids, Moses, Sakya-Mouni* (known as Buddha) and finally *Jesus*, will differ as to the forms, though identical in substance in their Principles and in their scientific and social goals.

One would find inept the physicians who would treat in the same manner diseases varying with the physiological characteristics of individuals and with the hygienic conditions of environments or climates. Their different therapeutics in no way prove that medical science itself is not one in its Principles and in its Ends, which are Life and Health.

But before discussing the history of these partial renovations, before showing their concordance, their common tendency towards a universal renovation by the restoration of the harmonic Law of Societies, let's not leave the study of the

Ram Cycle without deeply impressing the reader's mind with its reality and import.

The incomparable grandeur, the general health of this regime of the Lamb and Aries is inherent to *the intellectual character of its Constitution.*

That Constitution could only be Trinitarian, because the individual or collective human is marked by this irrefutable sign of a *triple Life.*

Genuine Authority never emanates from Force and, as I said in the *Mission of the Sovereigns*, it is necessary to look for its first symbols in the family home, in the mother and in the grandparents, ultimately in the dead ancestors.

This real Authority has the character of being without executive consequences, for the father of each family is the one who holds the baton of command, possesses the Power to operate *under the control of Higher Authority.*

That *Authority made solely of Intellectual and Moral force*, of Wisdom and Love, instructs, educates and vivifies; it judges only to perfect, it chastises only to heal, never condemns.

In the Social State, so is the true Authority, the only one before which, from the sovereign to the last of the artisans, all can and must, from one end of the Earth to the other, bend, flex the knee, then rise, instructed, educated, enlivened, ready now to obey, by accomplishing their duty, and thus living happily, each according to their rank.

Now, the totality of the Teaching Bodies alone bears this divine character of the Authority, for *integral Science extends from the center of the Earth to the summit of the Heavens, from Physical Nature to Intellective Nature which is the Confidant of the Spirit of God and the Mother of Human Intelligence.*

This is how Ram understood the Authority, and there is no other way to understand it without departing from Integral Science and Life itself.

That is also how, after Ram, all the members of the ancient Council of the Gods understood the essence of Authority when endeavoring to achieve social therapy anywhere.

As to Power, its genuine true character is to be absolutely submissive and obedient to Authority; without such obedience it loses any intellectual or moral authorization vis-à-vis the public Mores; without submission to organic Authority it also loses its legitimacy in regard with the part of the intellectual or moral Forces of the Universe which are represented and present in the Organic Life of Societies.

All sovereign powers, which separate themselves from these biological organic and intellectual conditions, enter into a deep state of malady and make that disease prevail throughout the Social Body.

Whether represented by a republican oligarchy or by the head of a monarch, it no longer offers the slightest intellectual or moral character, and it is called Anarchy, without a crown in the Republic, crowned in the Monarchy.

HOW RULERS ARE CHOSEN UNDER RAM'S LAW

Here is how Ram understood the sovereign power: from the last of the viceroys, from all the national kings to the emperor, he had organized the hierarchy of these Powers, as an ascending series of judicial constituencies and arbitrations, either national or supra-national.

But kings and emperors of justice bearing this character cannot be improvised; they are selected. Though they may not select themselves by themselves, let alone by trickery and violence, carried up by military conspiracies, coalitions of interest or coups d'état.

It is not in such darkness that true sovereigns can be born; it is in *the full light of Intelligence, Conscience, and public Morals* that they can be born of Life and serve the organic Life of Societies.

That is why Ram wanted the three assembled Councils to appoint these Royal and Imperial Powers, under the guidance of Authority, and that the individuals who represented them should be impersonal agents of those Powers, *the arbitral enforcers of a code of national and international Justice*, which they could not attack at their whim with impunity.

But the only way to prevent this form of attack on the Authority is not the one promoted by revolutionaries, political iconoclasts, social destroyers, because it needs creating, not destroying.

There is only one way to create such kings and emperors: to instruct them, to educate them, to vivify them, to circumscribe their impersonal function in its proper place in a social organism so true, so fair, so healthy, that public Mores connive with the social organism in order for the people to preserve their liberty, that is, their organical accord.

This is why the king, *before being crowned*, had to go through all the *examinations* of the High Council of the Gods and the High Council of God.

Only then, *being a king within his inner self*, could he be king outside; only then, having acquired *Wisdom and Science, which was called the Royal Art*, and which gave the title of King and even of God, he could, after having sworn allegiance to the first two High Councils, that of the Teaching and that of Justice, receiving on its head the entrusting representative crown, one kneel on the ground, under the raised hands of a Pontiff, in front of the three assembled Councils.

Moreover, public mores themselves cannot subsist without organization either, and that organization finds its laws and Principles in Life and Science, like everything in the Universe.

That is why Ram focused so deeply his attention on the Municipal Assembly, the first molecule of the entire social Economy. That is why he vested as much intellectual genius, science and art, organizing it as to constitute the whole ensemble, the whole *Spiritual Body of his Empire*.

We have seen in Iran and India how he made the family the condition of the electorate, the suffrage, which cannot have any other base.

With such a point of departure, with the woman next to the man at their proper place, the elected representatives of the municipality had necessarily to meet the required conditions as to their moral life, and thus attach to their economic status the guarantees which one would seek in vain elsewhere.

From this origin, the whole series of successive delegations, having for electors those first elected representatives, constituted a pure and lively wellspring, drawing from all the special branches of the economic life -vice-kingdoms, kingdoms and Empire- its highest representatives to form the great assemblies of the Third Council.

It should be noted that a great deal of attention had been paid to the county district.

The Third Council of Communes in turn received from the High Council of the Gods its Code of Arbitral Justice, from the High Council of God the Principles and Canons of all Sciences and all the applied Arts of economic activity.

Thus, thanks to these three social Powers, the civil and administrative organism, like the circulation of the blood and the nervous system, had its double movement, its systole and its diastole.

Centralization and decentralization were *geometrically parallel,* born from each other, and lent each other mutual aid.

As to forms, it should be noted that Ram's genius had determined and applied them according to their nature.

He had given the republican form to the municipality and the county, the royal monarchical form to the impersonal centralization of the powers of Justice, the imperial monarchical form to the General Government of the Kousha, the theocratic form to the supreme control of the whole, control supported directly on the public Mores below, on the religious Synthesis of the Truths above.

Conversely, the caste system, as it was subsequently established, the predominance of the personal monarchical power, and the consequent demeaning of the official priesthood, were the result of the series of public crimes committed by the rising of purely political governments.

SOCIAL ORGANISM BASED ON UNIVERSE'S HIERARCHY

Classes exist and will exist forever, they will eternally constitute 3 different categories, whether or not these classes are socially and formally constituted:

1-*Instinctive* individuals, with weak intelligence and *underdeveloped moral faculties,*

2- Individuals of *passions,* nevertheless able to *understand* the external *causes* of things,

3-*Intellectual* men and women reaching to the very *Principles* of these same things.

And these 3 ontological kinds of humans will always tend to apply their vital energy to 3 distinct orders of facts in the hierarchy of trades, technical arts, and sciences.

In a formless Social State like ours, these 3 ontological categories are everywhere mixed, their destinies and attributions confused, creating evil or discomfort for each and every one.

But their isothermal lines, so to speak, exist nonetheless, hence the proverb: *Those who resemble, assemble.*

Now, the *Triune Synarchy* has precisely for purpose to institute the 3 Assemblies corresponding to these 3 degrees of similarities.

But it is obvious that an individual of the first ontological category can as well be born at the bottom of the social ladder as above, especially in our confused Societies, without organic forms, without physiological harmony, where the *reentry of the souls by the gate of the Generations is not more religiously nor scientifically enlightened than their return to the Cosmic Order, invisible, through the gate of the tomb.*

Ram has never instituted imperviously separated castes for the attainment of individual values, wherever they came from.

Anyone could be part of the Economic Council, provided he was carried there by the esteem of the circles in which he lived.

Anyone could be part of the High Council of the Gods, provided he had gone through the series of examinations that led to it.

Anyone at last could be part of the High Council of God, provided that belonging to the previous one, he wanted to pass into the official priesthood or the learned bodies of the temples.

The inheritance of the monarchical functions in the Order of Aries and Lamb, was extremely problematic: Egypt until Menes had no king and was governed by a Council of the Gods with a president functioning as Grand Judge. Above that Power was the Council of God, and below it the Council of Elders.

Moses, who, like the Abramids, aimed at the resurrection of this Order of things, did not institute kings, and allowed the three Councils alone to reign. Moreover, when he reports on the Order of the Abramids and its 300 Initiates bowing before Melchizedek, the last representative of the ancient Tradition in Salem, he presents him to us as being without ancestors.

He would certainly not have done so, if this priestly royalty of Justice had been hereditary, and the crown not offered on personal merit.

As for the official priesthood, it was only a part of the Council of God and not the most important one. The Savant priests had precedence over that sacramental administration.

Moreover, the Council of the Gods, that is to say, College of lay initiates, was there to counterbalance possible ritual monotony, and to fight with the *forces of Life* the special maladies developed by every constituted body, the official priesthood among others.

SOCIAL ORGANIZATION OF ANCIENT CHINA

Apart from India, Persia, Tibet, the kingdoms of Siam, Kambodia, and Japan, the Celestial Empire of China is an irrefutable proof of this ancient organization.

Founded, as we shall see, or rather reformed nearly 4,000 years after Ram, and following the great Hindu schism, it bears the undeniable mark of the ancient Order of Things which *Fo-Hi* was contemplating, as did the first *Zoroaster*, like the *priests of Osiris,* like the *Abramids,* like *Cadmus,* like *Moses,* like *Orpheus,* like *Sakya-Mouni,* like *Jesus.*

I will later be more detailed about the Chinese Social State. For the moment, I only want to note the *organic similarities with the Empire of Aries.*

The Chinese Commune bears the certain mark of Ram, in its organization based on the Cult of the Ancestor in the home, in its spirit of justice and arbitral associations, in the constitution of its powers and its local liberties.

Fo-Hi, a member of the Second Council of the Hindu Empire, part of the military officers' school attached to the temples, traveled from India to China, with a hundred families of the same rank, to reform the Celestial Empire.

Hence, we find the imprint of the College of the Gods represented in the *College of Literates*, that is to say, in Chinese, the Savants.

Indeed, it is to this Assembly that, in principle, belongs the Authority. In this College, all the degrees giving right to control or exercise *all public functions are still obtained by exam and merit.*

Appointments according to abilities, advancement by merit, *chu hien jin neng, "Employ the able and promote the worthy"* is Fo-Hi's old maxim as reported by the ancient Sages; and in 2200 BC, Emperor Shun is still presiding over the examinations of his officials every three years, and lowering or elevating their rank according to their merit.

The social constitution of China is above all Intellectual, and one feels there everywhere the care with which the founder endeavored to neutralize the inefficient interference of Politics, that is to say of Power without Authority, passions without legitimate authorization of intelligence, without purpose specified in and for public order.

The *Esoteric Principles, extremely scientific,* contained in the *Y-Kings*, may not have been understood for 3,000 years, though they have been no less efficient in the fundamental institutions they have shaped.

The character of these institutions is, above all, Intellectual, Moral and Social. Their main purpose has been and still is to cultivate and exert public intelligence, to solemnly observe the various degrees of progress, and to officially reward their efforts, opening for them the entrance to all the hierarchy of functions up to the dignity of viceroy or prime minister.

In the village schools, among the sayings that are repeated

or dictated to the children, is this significant saying: *Tsiang siang pun wu chung, the general and the prime minister are not born such.*

Thus, the general allocation of offices has been, from the very beginning, taken away from the political Power proper, to be at the sole mercy of the Authority, that is, the Teaching Bodies. The General Assembly of the Literates (Savants) still retains to this day the four divisions of the ancient Mysteries, although the esotericism of the ancient sacred books is hardly heard more in China than in Europe, and that since a long time.

To the four hierarchies of the sciences, lost almost in their entirety, correspond the four degrees of Siutzai, Chu-jin, Tseuchi, and finally Kouatzekian.

70 MEMBERS FORM A HARMONIOUS ASSEMBLY

Even today, another similarity to be noted is that the Supreme Council of the University consists of 70 members.

We will find this number (70) applied similarly in the Order of the Abramids, symbolized by the name of Jacob-Israel,

That is the Supreme College of Lay Initiates whose Jethro advised Moses to create; same number (70) later found in the College of the 70 translators who gave their name to the Exoteric Version of the Septuagint, and finally the 70 envoys of Jesus. (See St. Luke, x, v. 1, and St. Matthew.)

The very name "College of the Gods" is found even in the examination sheets of the candidates, where we see questions like the following: *"The public use of firearms recommences under the Chaw dynasty (eleven hundred years BC); in what book do we find, then, the word expressing the idea of a cannon?"*

"What is the difference between the two classes of death machines to which this word is applied?"

"Is the defense of K'aifungfu the first feat of arms where we find this memory reported?"

"Koublai Khan had cannons of a new kind, where did he get them from?"

"The Sungs had many varieties of small caliber cannons: what was their advantage?"

"The Mings under the reign of Yungloh invaded Cochinchina; they

employed there a kind of cannon, called the "arms of the Gods": can you give the reason of their origin? "

If we recall what I said in the chapter dealing with Science in Antiquity, we find in the foregoing a new confirmation; but here I want to point out only one main fact, that which is relative to the *similarity* of the *Body of the Literates* with the ancient *Council of the Gods*: the weapons of the Gods.

That Body of Savants, veritable assemblage of selected individuals representing all the founding values of the hierarchical Empire was not, in the past no more than today, in the hands of the Emperor; for according to the ancient Social Constitution, the public offices must be allocated only by exam, and the Emperor himself is but the representative of that Constitution, its head, its ritual leader, without legal power to oppose that Authority.

Indeed, from the earliest antiquity, the more we move up the course of the centuries, the more we see that Body of Savants stand against any emperor attempting to become arbitrary, with the same courage, with the same selfless sacrifice demonstrated by all the Councils of the Gods in the Ancient World, up to the more recent Council of Israel, the larger part of it having been murdered, the remaining fragments from which the Order of the Prophets rose again.

A thousand years before our era, the Authority of which I speak was still in full force in the accomplishment of its duties vis-à-vis the Imperial Power represented by the House of Chow.

In the thirteenth book of the "Chowles", we still find the same intellectual mastery and its rules recounted in every detail.

The Kouazeken Supreme Council was admonishing the Emperor about the rituals, what is good and what is right.

The Emperor was to attend the teaching of the Presidents of the Council, attend his lessons in moral aesthetics.

The vice-presidents had to fulfill their duty of Intellectual assessors, by reproving the person of the Emperor about the public faults he could commit or had committed, and by reminding the discipline of the sovereign Authority, Wisdom and

Science, to *the sons of the State*, the members of the imperial family.

Fo-Hi, a member of the Council of the Gods, fleeing from India disrupted by the schism of Irshu, evidently manifested the spirit of his Order, by confining the rituals of the Priesthood to the *esoteric Science*, and thus not establishing an official priesthood separate from the rest of the Assembly of the Teaching Corps.

It is in this respect that initiated to what remained of the ancient esotericism, the Emperor practiced in his palace and in certain public ceremonies a Ritual, a form of lay Sovereign Pontificate, whose Art had obviously its source in the ancient priestly Science.

Inside the southern gates of the capital, surrounded by a sacred woodland so thick the silence of its shadow stops the distant noises of the active world, stands the *Temple of Heaven*.

It is a simple tower whose resplendent azure symbolizes the *color of the Ethereal Space*.

No image there, and few men know the rites that are accomplished here; but opposite is a marble altar for a certain annual sacrifice, where the fire plays its role, while the master of the Empire, prostrate, barefoot, worships *the Spirit of the Universe*.

Only the tablet on which is inscribed the name of Shangte, the Supreme Regulator, represents the Divinity.

This analogy with the ancient king of Salem (Melkitzedek) did not fail to strike the attention of many attentive travelers.

As for the Third Council, it is found in China everywhere: hence the indestructibility of the Chinese Commune, the biological organization of the Family founded on the Ancestor's Cult; hence also the absolute freedom of association which supports the economic strength of this empire, debris of the Ram Cycle, which, despite its colossal past, is even more vigorous than Christendom and all the rest of the World.

Thus, compared with the anarchic constitution of Christendom, China's synarchical organization offers this singular character of perfectly matching its intellectual state. Such is not the case for Europe which has renovated its intellectual state through more advanced physical and natural sciences, (Renaissance) without the social synarchical organization to match it.

This can only be explained by the fact that the learned system of the essential institutions of China *originates from an ancient epoch*, when the social organism itself was in perfect *correspondence with Integral Science.*

China today (1884 AD) is an *Arbitral Empire nested in a lay Theocracy.* The communal bases which are republican in nature, the royal provinces, the imperial center on which a tiara is laid by the Teaching Authority, all this triune social organism is the weakened *reproduction of a prototype*: *The Empire of Aries, the Theocracy of the Lamb.*

The excellence of the Principles which presided over the social institutions of the Empire could not fail to be noticed by impartial observers.

AN AMERICAN TRAVELS TO CHINA IN 19ᵀᴴ CENTURY

The most educated American travelers turning their attention towards this ancient replication of a primordial model, more ancient and more learned than theirs, are detecting the flaw of their own constitution, its lack of social viability, due to its mode of Universal Suffrage opening doors to chance politicians.

After insisting that public education and popular education are absolutely free in China, Mr. Martin, from the United States, president of Tungwen Middle School in Beijing, adds the following:

"Such is the system of intellectual competition in China.

More consistent than any other with the spirit of our freedom-based government of the United States, it could bring there even better fruits than in the Celestial Empire.

In British India this system has excellent results.

In England, diplomatic and consular services have finally been put on this footing; and an effort in this direction must be made, if we want our American influence abroad to be correlated to our greatness and our prosperity within.

When will our government understand that a good consul is worth more than a warship?

To have good agents, they should be recruited from special institution where they receive a special instruction."

Further on, the same author adds that this Chinese system, which could be defined *all by exam*, is applied according to such a grandiose scale of proportions that no nation on Earth can compete on this point with the Celestial Empire.

"Lord Mahon, in his *History of England,* speaking of the patronage accorded to the learned world during the period preceding Walpole, observes that the Sovereign might not have been an Augustus, the minister was always a Maecenas. Newton became director of the mint; Locke was master of petitions; Steele was guardian of the seals; Stepney, Prior, and Gray received important and lucrative embassies; Addison was Secretary of State; Tickell, Secretary of State in Ireland; Congreve, Rowe, Hughes, Ambrose Philips received rich sinecures."

And this historian goes on to show how the decrease of these liberalities brought about a comparable decrease of the popular favor under the following reigns.

This method, Martin adds judiciously, is not that of the Celestial Empire.

"Less arbitrary than Western monarchs, the Emperor has not the freedom to reward a scholar or a savant with an official office; and his prime minister cannot either. Neither can the popular favor elevate anyone to public office."

The only Institution that has this Power is, once again, the *Authority,* that is to say, as I have repeated many times, *Science itself* and the Teaching bodies *empowered by exam.*

That is why in *Mission of the Workers*, after proving that there was no other imperative mandate than the professional value of the agent, I demonstrated that there is no other national representation capable of ending our anarchies and our divisions, fruit of our incapacities, than the institution of 3

Chambers of elected specialists corresponding to this triple social life, eternal through all the Societies: 1-Instruction and Education (public, civil, religious, military), 2-Justice, 3-Economy.

Mr. Martin having observed the system *all by exam*, insists on the profound error of the Westerners when they claim that its value has been overrated, and that it must be held responsible for the defects in mental culture of the Chinese people.

"It is precisely the opposite that is true, and it is to other causes that these defects must be attributed.

For more than 2,000 years, the renovation of this system has been both a stimulant and a preserving agent, to which are owed, not only the merits of the national education, as it is, but the existence even of the Nation.

The political fruits have not been less beneficent than those of the social order; and this renovation has done even more good from this point of view, than the Corps of Literates could have expected.

By giving back to the people its ancient freedoms, it has strengthened the State. By opening all public offices to national energies and ambitions, it has shown that it is the best way to ensure general tranquility. This system is the safety valve of the social order, and without it the ambitions and the individual wills, instead of being distributed in the hierarchy of the capacities and the specialties, would break out in conflicts of classes, parties, chance politicians; and by all the cracks of anarchy, the bloody revolutions would have been perpetually made."

Now, if the reinstatement of the ancient synarchical institutions since Confucius can even today strongly strike the minds of attentive observers, all the more all the writings of Sou-Wang, *the king without scepter*, are here to affirm the incomparable grandeur and the excellence of the Principles and the model, which he had studied in the Y- Kings of Fo-Hi.

And Fo-Hi himself, a sort of genius protestant, only endeavored to laicize, by simplifying it, *the primordial prototype* that the schism of India had altered, the Synarchy of the Lamb and Aries, which the sudden emergence of Politics had weakened.

ONLY ONE AUTHORITY PROVIDES UNIVERSAL PEACE

For, Ram's work, scholarly and complex, did not only aim at the organization of an isolated empire and singular people, but to a whole *series of sovereignties and nationalities* that had to be *united by common Principles.*

Acting in China alone Fo-Hi was able to laicize the sacred Science, the Teaching and Worship itself; but it would have been quite different if he had been dealing with the General Government of the World.

If such had been the case, he should have maintained the upper level of the structure, the priestly body and the Sovereign Pontiff at the head of the Council of God.

This is what *Moses* understood perfectly, when he yielded to the High Priest *Jethro,* himself *yielding to the Lamas of the Paradesa.*

There is *only one Puissance in the World* which has sufficient eminence to bend under its hand the menagerie, the beastly circus of royal or popular sovereignties in their international relations. There is *only one Power in the World* which has the right to demand universal Peace, Moral and intergovernmental Justice, from those who, at the head of the nations, regulate not only their internal organization, but above all their international relationships.

There is *only one Force in the World* which has the right to remove from its throne, to shake in the Heavens and to crush on the Earth any sovereign, king or emperor, who allows himself to perpetrate vis-à-vis of a neighboring king or nation, the crimes -theft and murder- he punishes in his subjects.

This Puissance is *Providence, Intelligence of the Universe,* reflected by the religious intelligence of the priestly man, ideally able and empowered for chastising, not only in the visible Realm, but especially in *the Invisible Realm,* every ruling anarchist, every felon, whose responsibility grows with his Power.

That Puissance, supra-sovereign and supremely pontifical, Ram had felt to be so indispensable, that, abdicating as Emperor of the World, position which had served as a stepping stool, he ascended to the supreme Altar, and leaned on the Universal Consciousness of all peoples, bore the tiara to watch over public Peace, and to insure that it would be watched over after him.

For 3,500 years indeed, Emperor, kings, viceroys, remained in their role of rulers of Justice; the triune savant Arbitrage instituted by Ram was built in such a way that it contained and limited all arbitrariness from above, while the sovereignties themselves contained and limited all arbitrariness from below.

But that would have been impossible without the three social Powers, foundation of the arbitral Synarchy, equally impossible without the Council of God, guardian of Public Law, itself solemnly placed under the protection of the living Constitution of the Universe, like all Sciences and all applied Arts.

This would have been impossible without the Council of the Gods, whose Fo-Hi's empire will only be a mere reflection.

Finally, it would have been impossible without the Third Council representing the religious acquiescence of the Social Economy to its own Principles of life.

$$\infty$$

CHAPTER VIII
SCHISM OF IRSHU

THE BEGINNING AND EXPANSION OF CIVIL UNREST

A little before the Kali-Youg, say the sacred books of the Brahmans, nearly *3,500 years after Ram's pontificate*, a little more than *3,200 years before Christ*, the universal Empire of Aries received, at its very center, its first *germ of disease and dissolution.*

The function of the Kousha of India had become hereditary, and the imperial family was in dissension, due to two brothers, whose exoteric legend can be read in the Puranas, and mainly in the Scanda-Pourana and Brahmanda.

The Emperor Ougra had just died, and his eldest son, Tarak'hya, had succeeded him. The younger son, *Irshu, Regent of the Provinces*, was extremely ambitious, and not being able to reach the sovereign Power by legal and legitimate means, he provoked a schism, in order to grasp the scepter by means of a revolution.

After having filled his general staff with ambitious and dissatisfied members of the upper classes, he aroused the disaffection and revolt of the lower classes of cities and rural areas.

Tarak'hya, at the head of all the regular organization of the Empire, had to repress and expel from the land this *revolutionary movement* which will in History be known under various names, according to nations.

In India, it will be called the *Yonijas civil war.*

On all the coasts of the Gulf of Oman, the Persian Gulf, and the Arabian Gulf, it will be known as *the movement of the Phoenicians, Eritreans, and the Reds*, because of the purple flag on which was stamped the poppy-red Dove, the imperial rebels had adopted as emblem on their banners.

In *Egypt, later*, the invasion of the *Hiksos, or Irshuists*, will give to this country the arbitrary Pharaohs, the schismatic despots, known under the name of Kings Pastors.

In Assyria, in Syria, these Yonijas of India will found all the

Ionian naturalist temples, and will everywhere provoke revolts with pseudo-republican tendencies, until they seize the military Power, to constitute the Caesarism, spurned by Moses under the name of *Nimrod, the way of the tiger,* the Cycle of arbitrariness, Might dominating Right.

In Syria, as everywhere, they will crush the ancient Synarchy and its Trinitarian powers, to infinitely multiply personal, monarchical or oligarchic powers.

And their history will be perpetuated in the memory of humankind under different names: *Idumeans, Pallantis, Philistines,* etc., etc.

To the ancient rights of the people of the Theocracy of the Lamb, to the antique hierarchy of Kings of Justice within the Empire of Aries, they will oppose a new law, marked by the character of *Public Anarchy.*

This Law was known as the law of Taurus; and indeed, the Caesar of Babylon will conquer the Turan and the Turanians already dissociated from their ancient Covenant with the Aries Arbitral Empire, and from all its judicial organisms.

This arbitrary Caesarism will go further still, and when allied with the Kelts of Northern and Eastern Europe who had remained faithful to the old bloody Law of the Zodiacal Taurus, it will wage war even in the Southern European colonies of the Empire of Aries, which still had for "heart and brain" the temples of the Theocracy of the Lamb.

Such is the universal revolution by which, until today, was broken the ancient hierarchy of sacerdotal and legal Powers, which *for so many centuries had provided the world with the greatest amount possible of international peace, local freedoms and general happiness.*

ROOTS AND CAUSES OF THE DIVISIVE CRISES

Before starting from the social sciences viewpoint the analysis of the consequences of Irshu's schism, I must acquaint the reader with their causes, not only as reported to us in the ancient exoteric books of Asia, but as they are known to the religious Savants of today's Asia, who, I am sure, will not disown me.

But here I ask the reader to remember that at the time of History when these undeniable facts are taking place, the ancient World, the ancient Cycle founded by Ram, *had reached a degree of extraordinary scientific culture.*

That is why we are going to see the dissident Irshu, before resorting to weapons, affirm his opposition on the level of pure Intelligence and in the realm of the most transcendent Principles.

Like all schismatics, all sectarians and revolutionaries of the World, with very few exceptions, Irshu was an ambitious man, powerless when it came to reconstruct and to replace that what he endeavored to destroy. Like Luther, but on a much larger scale, he was only a firebrand more or less aware of the immense fire his spark ignited. The intellectual cause that made this schism possible, goes back earlier than Irshu, and we must stop awhile and examine the facts.

The *quadruple hierarchy of Sciences* bequeathed by the temples of the Red Race to the Priesthood of the Black Race, and by the latter to the Theocracy of Ram, made mathematically and geometrically all the Sciences and applied Arts *converge towards the Divine Unity, Iod, Wodh or Boudh (Hebrew/Arabic Wahed).*

The method of that Science, which I shall designate under the names of *Qualitative Arithmetic* and *Qualitative Morphology* is the only one, in fact, which allows the human intelligence to ascend, step by step, every level of the Truth, with exactitude, and not in the mere imaginative mirage of the exoteric fantasies of Theology or Metaphysics.

Now, if that method of *Qualitative Science* was accessible only in the temples, the experimental Art which resulted from it, and which is itself mathematical and geometrical, was put in the hands of everyone.

I will neither name this Art here, nor raise the veils covering it more than it is appropriate, and I will resume the history of the causes of the Schism of Irshu,

The Divine Unity represented by the name of *Wodh* was considered ineffable in its Essence, except by savants initiated in the Synthesis of Sciences.

DIVINE DYAD MASCULINE-FEMININE

The first manifestation of that Divine Unity, the only one that was organically accessible to the human Soul and Spirit, was envisioned as an eternally and *indissolubly united Androgynous Dyad.* This Dyad, this Union manifesting the inaccessible Unity, was called in the sanctuaries I-ÊVÊ, Iswara-Pracriti, Osiris-Isis, etc., etc.

It is this Dyad that Moses will later draw from the sanctuaries of Egypt and Ethiopia, and that the Hebrew high priest, once a year, in the presence of the priests only, pronounced in the antique way, in three sounds:

IOD-ÉVAUÊ;

IODÊVÊ;

IEVE.

Such is evoked the God of Creation, Father and Mother, whose four letters I E V E corresponded, as I said, to the four hierarchies of sciences; whose first letter (Iod) expresses the *Universal Masculine Principle* or the Spirit of the Universe; and whose three other letters(E V E) express the *Universal Feminine Principle* or the Soul of the Universe, the Life.

The whole suite of numerical or mathematical symbols, after the Monad and the Dyad, formed the indisputable chain of *qualitative arithmology,* having its *qualitative equivalents* in the world of *hyperphysical forms* and, consequently, in what we improperly call Geometry, whose real name is *Morphology.*

I cannot go into the details of these *lost Sciences* here; but they were by no means despicable, even and especially for the most ambitious Savant Scientists, seekers of Truth

For us Judeo-Christians, this *qualitative aspect of the mathematical and geometrical sciences* is indisputable, since, to their application to sacred architecture and to all the symbolism of worship, we also owe it certain theological terms, which, without those same sciences have no positive foundations or viable explanation.

Indeed, we are still making use of words such as *Unity* of God, *Dualism, Trinity* or Trinitarianism, etc., which express something other than the quantities relating to these numerical symbols.

That being said, I will particularly insist on the fact that the *Divinity considered as Creator of the Universe* was in no way envisaged under the aspect of a Dualism, that is to say the confrontation of two opposing Principles, as will soon in time be asserted by the first Zoroaster.

I reiterate, Iswara-Pracriti, Osiris-Isis, I-EVE, were regarded as an insecable Dyad, as the *indissoluble Organical Union* to which the Universe owes its existence.

In fact, all the Sciences made it possible to observe the two *concordant*, though *inversely proportional*, aspects of Truth, the one *intelligible and descending*, whence the purely scientific idea of the Fall, the other *sensible and ascending*; so Perfectibility is increasing in proportion of the descending in us of the Intelligible Perfection.

In the Indian Empire, in its kingdoms and colonies, the somewhat educated socialites had no more doubt on these Principles religiously and scientifically demonstrated, than the members of the High Council of the Gods and the High Council of God itself.

All men and all women also could reach the state of this certainty, which founded, in the Mysteries, the great and holy authorization of the Marriage, the interior illumination of the Life from below, with its door of light open to the Life above: Cult of Ancestors and Generation, Veneration and Love.

All knew that, from the Universe and the great Cosmogonic Beings to the lowest of the humblest animals and plants on this Earth, *all existence results from a double genesic and generative movement, intelligible and sensorial, spiritual and hyperphysical.* So far, no cause of schism.

THE DISSIDENT PROCLAMATION OF IRSHU

But Irshu, not having reached the higher degrees of Initiation, wanted, without science and without a guide, to go beyond these data.

The Eternal Masculine and Eternal Feminine are Unity, Universality; they are expression of Creative Union, Spirit and Soul, Essence and Form, Unlimited Time and Unlimited Space; in spite of this fundamental truth, the schismatic Irshu, asked, outside the temples, the following questions:

"To whom belongs Excellence, Primacy in the Generation of the Universe and in all life and in all things hyperphysical or physical?

Is it to the male God or to the feminine Nature, to Iswara or Pracriti, to Osiris or to Isis, to IOD or to EVAUE?

By falling on our knees before the greatest God that is accessible to us, by evoking the fire of Heaven on the altar, must we first say our Father or our Mother? The Holy Name, how to sanctify it in Science and in Life, in all their visible and invisible degrees?

The concordance, the union, the inseparable harmony of the two Organical Principles, do not imply either that the One cannot be superior to the Other, that the One has not been and is not more accessible and more directly beneficent than the Other for existing beings, including Humans."

"Furthermore, added the sectarian, *why would Man have preeminence over Woman, not in the exoteric law, but in the esoteric law; not in civil and political life, but in religious and social life, at the altar of the hearth, at that of the temples, at the supreme altar of the Sovereign Pontificate? Is Woman less than Man worthy to love, to understand, to adore, to celebrate Unity, the Union of the Universal Spirit and Soul, of the Bridegroom and the Bride?"*

"Since when, continued Irshu in his orations and in his writings, *has the Divinity revealed, by any sign whatsoever, that the lips of women were unworthy of the liturgy, their hands unworthy of touching the chalice and tabernacle, their knees unworthy to climb the holy steps, their hearts, their souls, their spirits unworthy of the Pontificate, their heads unworthy of the miter and the tiara?*

No priest, no founder of worship, has ever dared overtly formulate such an exclusion, and the question has always been suspended, retracted thus benefiting the man only: why?

Is not the Heavenly Nature, our Mother, indissolubly united to God, isn't she, up to the Infinite and to the Absolute, indivisibly associated with its living thoughts, which are the spiritual sparks Spirits of all solar Systems?

Celestial Nature, our Mother, testifies to the contrary, by making these thoughts manifest, and by lending them the force of Life and their cosmogonic existence.

Why, then, would the Masculine and the Feminine not be equal in religious law, and would they not also render the same sacramental homage to what authorizes them from the Heavens?"

Thus spoke and wrote Irshu; and the troubled conservatives responded as follows to this ambitious revolutionary.

DIALOG BETWEEN INITIATE SAVANT AND DISSIDENT

Savant: - If the Woman rises to Public Priesthood, will she go up to the altar of the temple at the same time as the Man, or will she offer her sacrifice to a different altar?

Why raise such questions outside the Council of the Gods and the Council of God?

The dissident rejoined: - *In Europe there were always Druidesses, and in India, before Ram, the Feminine Lunar Dynasty has existed jointly with the Masculine Solar Dynasty, as far as the time of Daçaratha.*

Savant: -The problem had once been not only posited, but resolved in favor of equality, in Europe through Intuition, in Asia through pure Intelligence and Science. I could give mathematical proofs of the astonishing science in which the resurgence of this problem occurred again; but I do not permit myself to do anything other than to open just enough the veil of esoteric Tradition, not more than is necessary to illuminate the exoteric external facts.

Author St Yves: As these interrogations took place within full public opinion, within intellectual and moral circles absolutely sincere in their information and in their convictions, as the Scientific Religion of that time supported universal tolerance and righteousness, the solution would have been found by Science and Religion itself, if Irshu's interest had not been to precipitate everything.

Was he sincere, but blind, or did he play a game of power?

Anyway, with a passion all the more dangerous that it was seductive, *he suddenly took side for the superiority of EVE*, Pracriti, Isis, the Eternal Feminine over the Eternal Masculine, Nature over God, Soul over the Spirit.

He systematically did in the realm of Sciences, - rather in the high Technical Art, which was then in the hands of all – what our modern experimentalists are doing since Francis Bacon in the West, namely positioning applied natural and physical Sciences besides, outside and in opposition to theology and the dogmas of the priests.

Without denying the *Spiritual Realm*, which was then scientifically demonstrated, let alone the *Soul of the World* whose proofs of existence were everywhere, Irshu claimed as more directly beneficial to all living beings the *Realm of Forms*, the *Universal Feminine*, from which come immediately all the manifestations whatever they are.

NATURE FIRST EQUALS WOMAN FIRST

"It is the Mother, above all, that must be invoked, Irshu declared in the assemblies.

It is Nature that gives to all beings and things, a space, a proper formative medium, a substance and a sustenance, the Soul, the Body, the real individualized Life, the Law of all Life and all things.

Without Her, what would be the Universe and all the infinite worlds and all the billions of beings who participate in its Life, from the subterranean Daimon to the Gods of the higher Heaven?

What would they be? An occult thought, a proto seed enclosed in pure Spirit, a possibility in Iswara, but by no means an act realized by Pracriti.

All, then, would be Nothing; and the Universe would not be existing, no prayer of existing being would seek the One, who would never be a Father, being not a Spouse.

It is therefore to the Mother that we owe prayer first of all, since it is

through Her that the entire Universe owes the power to exist, live, feel,
and assent.

Did not Ram say in old times: "The field is worth more than the seed,
the maiden than the young man, the wife than the husband, the mother
than ten thousand fathers?" He said true; but now we must draw the right
consequences."

BALANCE BETWEEN MALE AND FEMALE PRINCIPLES

The first two High Councils cited Irshu in their court; and
the Pontiff answered him as follows:

"Whatever the feeling that inspires your speech, the substance of your words is not invalidated, neither by the Science
of the Principles, nor that of the Origins, neither by the intelligible descending method nor by the ascending sensorial
method.

Yes, the Universe is the living Son of the Union by which
is created the unfathomable Unity.

Yes, on all Its suns burning with a fire and a light which are
not only physical, but hyperphysical, the Universe is forever
celebrating the eternal Union of the Two who are One.

But from a sound premise and true Principles, a mind mis-
guided by a passionate soul can draw false conclusions.

And passion obscures your thought, when you want the
prayer to rise first to the Mother, to the universal Soul, to Life,
since the Creative Power of the Universe is Father and Mother
as one.

Why are you dividing the indivisible, the Indissoluble Union of the universal Spirit and Soul, of God and Nature?

Why do you want us to pray to One before the Other,
when their mutual Wisdom and Love make One and the Other
united in the same Spirit of Life and Truth?

You need to come here again and for a long time, learn and
meditate among us.

You need a few years of training in the Sciences and in the
psychurgical Arts, thanks to which, from the depths of our sacred crypts, eyes open and in full possession of yourself, your
soul freed from the bonds of the body, can go back in this

universal Soul, and, making use of all its inner senses, seeing, hearing, and feeling the lessons of the Higher Gods, the direct teachings of the glorified Spirits.

For it is only at the cost of this immense effort that one can organically reach the Unity of Life and Knowledge.

For if one does not pass thus, from this existence, through the gate of Death, to be reborn in the Universal Cosmic Life, how can one speak with experience and accuracy on the topics you raise so recklessly!

Before judging you, we would like to heal you; as you need it surely; and we can heal you, if you will it determinedly.

The Soul, in order to reflect the Heavenly Life and the Divine Truth, must be calm in its triple sphere, in its intellectual heights, in its emotional milieu, in its instinctive depths.

Otherwise, fear to carry outside the tempest which agitates you inside, and to change in civil discord the Peace of this Empire, head of the Social God, realized by Ram on this Earth as in Heaven.'

MOTHER IS SUPREME. EMOTIONS AND FEELINGS REIGN

"Yes, war is in me, replied Irshu*; but what can I do?"*

"If I feel to be the son of the Woman, before I feel to be the son of Man, if my heart beats for our Mother Visible in Heaven and on Earth, before it beats for our Invisible Father, what can you do?

I cannot change my will, and you may not do so, not without my own assent: what can be done? It is to the first endowment we owe our first love.

This gift is not a Principle, but an Origin; it's Birth, Life.

It comes to the Child by the Woman, to the whole Universe by this Woman of Women, Nature.

You will argue Woman and Nature give birth in pain, the Mother of the child for terrestrial duration, the Mother Nature for boundless Time.

Of that I know; but this pain is a reason to cherish them a thousand times more, and to wish their glorification and my adoration to be a thousand times more intense.

It is not my intent to disrespect you; but why is it you wish to avoid before the public the debate which has arisen for so long within intelligences and souls, temples and homes?

You hope to procrastinate unceasingly, always relying on what was and what is, for want, perhaps, of being certain of what should be, and for want of ways to reconcile with what should happen.

But what your Science can not or will not solve, my Love knows enough to will it and do it.

I want Women as well as Men to have their own Priesthood, miter, tiara. I want Nature, Soul of the Universe, the Life, to have its separate altars served by a female Priesthood.

Am I ungodly, say it; am I unfair, dare to express it publicly!

I will call on everyone, and those who love me will follow me."

SEPARATION MALE-FEMALE: TRAGIC CONSEQUENCES

"Ah! responded the Pontiffs, if Love alone directs them, woe to the peoples; for Hatred will without recourse surge among them.

Love is the Cosmic Fire itself, whose Wisdom is the Light; and you want to remove this Light from the Government of Souls.

Universal Truth and Life dwell in our temples; Integral Science has, like this Truth and this Life, four hierarchies; the ineffable four-letter name; and, of these four, you want to delete the First, which you do not know.

Listen, and if you can be returned to the Light, meditate, after listening.

It is to avoid a thousand public and private evils that we are delaying what you want to precipitate.

Wisdom is slow moving; it manifests itself in new rites only if mores absolutely demand it. Precipitance is a mark of madness, and neither Love nor passion will ward off its dangers.

These dangers are immense, and waiting is a lesser evil than running toward them.

Should we enlighten you again? So be it."

REIGN OF MATERIALISM AND SOCIAL ANARCHY

"From the day when you will have divided the indivisible, dissolved the indissoluble, not in itself, for you cannot do it; but in the minds of the ignorant, from the day when, thanks to you, Nature's altars becoming separated, standing in opposition to the altars of God, when a college of priestesses, will stand in opposition to the colleges of priests, then the Social Order will crumble on the foundations of its arbitral hierarchies, established since 3,500 years.

In Science as in Life, the terrestrial social God, the ancient Unitary Synthesis, will be dismembered, and a dreadful disorder will inevitably follow. Deeply unequal in intelligence and will, most men and women will misunderstand the truths they cannot attain, truths which you will have brought down at the level of public opinions and passions.

They will perceive as true only the superficial aspects which sensations or emotions will be presenting to their reason; and they will become the plaything of superficialities, and then they will distance from us, who alone could correct their lack of knowledge, by a gradual advancement through teachings and revelations.

Below the category of rational men and women, a greater number will inevitably confound celestial Nature with terrestrial Nature; they will confound effect with cause and will find themselves lost in an unreal and bottomless materialism.

The arbitrary willfulness, in the rational group, constantly shall rive itself against itself.

In the emotional group, the primitive and savage instinct of the earthly man will resurge full-fledged.

Some will lead others to ruination, beginning with the onslaught on the social and intellectual Order which solely keeps them at peace; and on the debris of the Social Intellectual Order, they will devour themselves in a competition for an impotent Power, lacking the Authority to enlighten it.

Beware, son of the Woman!

You know from your own family how difficult peace is to maintain, when jealousy and ambition are unleashed.

That is what would happen, not only on Earth, but also in Heaven, the Ideals on which the Souls are here modelling their own self-image, if in these Souls the living idea of Nature was separated from God's Ideals.

Only a small number of men and women can ascend to the first letter of the sacred Name (Iod), to the fourth hierarchy of Life and Science, and this, by the strength of their meditation, by the power of direct observation and experience, and only when and if the intelligent Powers of Heaven desire it to be so, only *when Divinity transfers its Spirit of Wisdom into their intelligence* and *acquired knowledge.* Know what full Science, mirror of all Life, image of all Truth conveys: *Synthesis, Union, Unity.*"

LOSS OF COSMIC CONSCIOUSNESS

"And, if all of this is manifesting in the Realm of Intelligence, wholly informed by Science and Life in the Supreme Marriage of the Heavenly Husband and Bride, it is because it is eternally inherent in the Divine Wisdom and Divine Love, without which, as you said it yourself, Totality would be Nothing.

The *ascending Order* of existing individuals and physical facts is accessible to the senses; and few yet understand this order, which constitutes from below the first hierarchy of Sciences.

All people, through their adoration of Pracriti separated from Iswara, will at most, see only this physical, terrestrial Order. Yet it is only the first ladder's step of total Nature, whose apex reaches the top of Heavens. Such is the true height of the Divine Mother, whose heels will be the only part they see.

The *descending Order* of the Father, the pure Spirit through the cosmogonic reigns, from the cyclic Spirits of all flesh to the physical individuals, is pure Intelligence.

Not one in ten thousand men and women can approach the hierarchy of sciences that corresponds to this masculine Order, nor understand it without symbols, product of a precise Art allowed by this transcendent Science.

Your form of worship will obfuscate this entire Order of beings and things.

Subsequently, no universal Truth will be shining in the realm of pure Intelligence, no Principle will enlighten Science, and no truly scientific causation illume Reason.

For you, Irshu, know as well as we do, that reason can

derive logical consequences from a true or false premise, but that Reason can never find, in and by itself, a Universal Cause or Principle, if Intelligence does not provide them.

Now, how will it provide them, if, at the summit of the Worship and the University that you want to create, you put Love before Wisdom, the Soul before the Spirit, the Bride before the Husband, the heavenly Nature before the God of Heaven.

All non-phenomenal science being extinguished, all initiation of Intelligence to the cosmic Principles being closed, every thought of Universality becoming particularized, no intelligible hierarchy, no intelligent government of Societies will soon be possible.

All elevation will be reduced to common mediocrity, all non-personal delegated ministry will shrink into mere selfish individual power and result into governmental materialism.

In the Sovereign Pontiff, we will no longer be able to see the Sovereign Pontificate, in the Priest the Priesthood, in the Emperor the Arbiter of Kings, in the King the umpire of the Viceroys, in the Viceroy the umpire of the Economic Council of Elders, and in the Council of the Gods we will no longer see the Mastery of Initiation, in the Council of God the Authority of all Teachings at once, and in the rich man one will no longer see the Public Wealth.

Now, all these things, Pontificate, Priesthood, Royalty, Teaching, Justice, Wealth, are only Intelligible Forms, invisible, impersonal organs of this Spiritual and Living Body of the Societies you are going to annihilate.

In the man in his function of Pontificate, Priesthood, Empire, Kingship, Mastership, Wealth, the naturalists will see only a flesh and bone costumed individual, the symbols attached to his dress having lost their Intelligible Virtues.

One will cease to see the heavenly adumbration of the impersonal functions of the Family Order, at home, in the Ancestor, in the Grandparents, in the Father, in the Mother, in the first-born Brother.

A father will be merely a man, like all other men; a mother, a woman, like all other women; and the child, shaking off all real duty dictated by Wisdom, will claim all the fictitious rights of his folly. The Souls of the Ancestors will cease to shine in the minds of their descendants and become obliterated in their weakened intelligences.

The past no longer containing the present, everything will fall to the future, become a pure nothingness which human beings will manifest in their self-image; and this future will become the unknown and the unforeseen.

For, instead of determining events, instead of scientifically directing the course of social and individual things, we will be more and more its toy, thanks to ignorance, thanks to the break-up of the Unity of Knowledge and Life."

LIFELESS COSMOGONY

"In broken science, the Universe will die, or rather the human Spirit will cease to know the Universe in its triple Life, to feel its Soul, to live in Harmony with its Vital Spirit.

The inanimate skeleton of Cosmogony will scarcely survive in Cosmography, purely rational, mechanical, mortal conception of celestial phenomena.

The ephemeral mind will doubt that the Universe is a Living and Intelligent Being, the Being of beings.

The Earth will appear to him as a machine inexplicably engendering Life for Death, as a raw material from which atoms come and go solely in the grip of brutal Forces.

The biology of this Globe will no longer be understood as originated from the Universe; it will no longer proceed divinely from top to bottom, nor from the Principles, but materially from the bottom up.

So that all the notions illuminated by a fantastic, infernal light, will spring, not from the celestial peaks of the Intelligence, but from the demonic abyss of the Instincts.

The immediate Father of human Life will be the monkey of the forests; the Father of all life here below will be the vibrating infusoria; the Mother will be the marine glue, the earthly mud.

And the chain of beings rising up to Man will keep him captive in animality, on the other side of his soul, alienated from his own mind, a prisoner of Matter; Man having become an incomprehensible sketch even to his own eyes, being placed at the edges of two worlds, and when one of them will no longer exist, Man will be a half-thinking monster excited only by visible things, idiotic being as he becomes disconnected from them; commonly deemed to be perfectible, while nevertheless incapable to love and to understand Perfection.

And if we wanted here to show the consequences that your madness will cause in the invisible Order, perhaps would you experience genuine remorse.

Man and Woman create their beyond-the-grave Heaven, starting in this life on Earth, and in accordance with the creative energy of their life on Earth.

At present, the Astral realm of the Souls, reflection of this Earth, is a Divine Society, happy, harmonious, united as the earthly Social State that Ram founded, and which we preserve.

But as soon as the hierarchy of arbitral Powers, along with the present kingdom of Trinitarian Constitution, will break into pieces under the blows of Anarchy, then the earthly powers, in conflict with each other, will oppose their collective Spirits, and the Dominions will devour each other in the Heavens' realms allocated to the humans of this Globe, as well as they do fight on this very terrestrial Planet.

So you will bring Hell in the Invisible Order as you will in the visible Order of this Human Cycle, by giving way to the individual passions over the Intelligences who had consciously and knowingly rallied into the universal Order.

But let's leave this vast subject and limit ourselves to Earth alone. Each form of Intellectual teaching brings about its own form of Society. According to the kind of ideas sown, one will harvest social order or social disorder.

Men and Women emulating your conducts will necessarily be of the third ontological lower caste. The circle of their life will be limited to the speculation of phenomena and material interests.

Analysts in essence, they will be incapable of any Religion, or, in other words, incapable of any intellectual or social Synthesis.

Anarchists for lack of Synthesis, they will however want to dominate what they cannot govern.

Also, crushing the head and heart of the ancient Social God, will they establish their bloody arbitrariness on the ruins of our Arbitration, their governmental Anarchy, their Personal Powers, on the debris of our three Powers and our Social Synarchy.

Ah! Irshu! Irshu! If you had like us the direct vision of the Spirit, you would cry over yourself and over the Race of men and women that your thought will procreate.

You would see those humans fall from the Reign of Providence into the tyranny of Fate, into the disunion of the ruling wills, into rivalry and mutual devouring, and at the same time become, from one end of the World to the other, executioners and victims.

They will no longer understand Liberty in the organic and healthy sense of our Principles, where the good of everyone emanates from the good of all and from the Sovereign Good.

Their freedom will consist in bringing down Social Heaven on their own heads, while running at random under the rain of the calamities they invoked.

Why a Sovereign Pontiff above us? will say the Pontiffs.

Why an Emperor above us? will say the Kings.

Why a King above us? your people will say.

Why a Truth Above Me? will say the ignorant or half-learned. Why a judge above me? will say the criminal.

And the Social State, dissociated, will oppose to each other its bloodied members, mutually inflamed by your mad fever, in wars and in endless revolutions.

In this universal disease, everyone will seek his good in the common evil, the Pontiffs at the expense of the Supreme Pontiff, the priests at the expense of the High Priests, the Emperor at the expense of the three Synarchic Powers, the Kings at the expense of the Emperor, the lowliest of the ambitious at the expense of Kings, the children at the expense of the parents, each against all, all against each.

And one day the people having fallen back into all the divisiveness of social death, groaning in the night of ignorance, under the sword of governmental iniquities, under the chains of military slavery, under the crushing of all their ruins, will not attach any scientific value, organic intelligence, living significance to these words: Religion, Justice, Economy.

They will curse any Authority mistaken with Power, they will even erase the memory of the past Wisdom, of the ancient Covenant, the former universal Peace, and cursing each other from creed to creed, curse their governments and their own life now worse than death, as if already residing in Hell presided over by Evil and governed by Night.

We could strike you down right now, but we are Authority and not crude Power; and, if we have the duty to enlighten your thought, we have no right to prejudge your actions by threatening your freedom or your life.

We invite you to join the Universal Order of Aries, the Universal Peace of the Lamb.

You are free to stay there, or to surge out sword in hand, with the intent to murder the *Social God*.

As for us, we will not forestall the time of a religious innovation, which mores do not require; *but when the time has come, we will know what must be done, with Wisdom, with Science, and Art.*"

ABOUT RELIGIOUS EQUALITY OF THE SEXES

In the previous dialog I wished to give ways to the direct strong expression of the Naturalistic viewpoint of Irshu when confronting the Trinitarian and Synthetic Unitarianism of Ram's Priesthood. These *same questions return cyclically, at their time, within all societies*, from the infancy of the human Races to their maturity age, from their old age and to their renascence; and no social Synthesis, no positive Religion can avoid them.

Intact for almost 3,600 years, the Social State of Ram was essentially vulnerable only on this one point: the *religious equality of the Sexes* up to the tiara inclusively.

Now, as it was impossible to prove that the Living Universe was or was not the product of the living Union of a twofold Puissance, One mindal, the Other insightful, there was no reason why the two Sexes should not be equal even to the summit of the Social State itself, unless there was scientific proof that, in the generation of human beings, as in that of the Living Universe, the Masculine had a greater physical, moral, and intellectual share than the Feminine.

RESURGENCE OF AN ANCIENT PREDICAMENT

While responding to the dissident Regent Irshu, Truth was spoken by the Pontiffs, when they said that the divine Androgyne, of which the heavenly Adam-Eve is the image, is indivisible and indissoluble; but, in the end, it was vindicating the self-interested demands of Irshu the Imperial Prince of India.

Above the Dyad, the Brahmans and Lamas could have appealed to the unfathomable *Wodh*. But that *First Principle*, even more inaccessible to the masses, cannot give rise to any exoteric worship; and, considering that inaccessibility in itself, it would definitely lead to governmental and individual atheism. In order for the conscience of the Unity of God to protect human societies from falling into governmental and individual atheism, they must be sufficiently scientifically enlightened not to stray away from the Synthesis of Sciences based on this Principle; or, alternatively, societies must be maintained in a form of partially veiled ignorance, sufficient to prevent the thorough scientific examination of the Synthesis leading to this Unity, except within savant sanctuaries.

The *balance between these two extremes is almost impossible to achieve*. That is why, instead of emphasizing that inaccessible Unity, *Moses* himself will posit at the summit of his Cosmogony the ancient Organical and Creative Union, IEVE (I+EVE).

As for Irshu, he was not *sectarian* just for having proclaimed the absolute equality of the two Masculine and Feminine Principles in Heaven as on Earth, but *for having separated them*, in spite of the fact they are Indivisibly and Indissolubly United, and moreover for having proclaimed the supremacy of the One over the Other.

At the time I am writing these lines, exoteric Judeo-Christianism, as presented by Talmudists and Theologians, is suffering the same assaults from naturalists, oblivious followers of Irshu and of the Yonijas of India. But the Judeo-Christian Exoteric Synthesis is not strong enough to defend itself without resorting to its *esotericism*, direct *extension of Ram's Scientific Religion*.

REVIVAL OF THE ESOTERICISM OF JESUS AND MOSES

In the first chapters of the present book, I tackled these difficulties head on, and proved that one could easily take away all modern science, all contemporary naturalistic Ionism, and invigorate them by empowerment with Heavenly Dorian Principles, which have been transmitted to us by the Abramides' and Moses' Tradition.

Beyond this path, let it be known to the theologians that, for lack of understanding the *esotericism of Jesus and Moses*, they have no sustainable social science or test-proof cosmogonic science.

Let them know, once and for all, that their information and their religious teachings are purely elementary, and because of that, they are at the mercy of the domination of lay secondary and higher education.

Now these two higher degrees, which take precedence over the third, belong to the secular world and to it alone for the moment. By giving the same elementary education to its priests and to the whole social hierarchy down to the little children, *Christianism thus necessarily is diluting, inevitably lowering all Christendom to a childish expectation* of longing and vague love, which can have no other practical result than pursuit of unspecified progress, recurrent revolt without a definite goal, against which, nevertheless, the clergy are protesting with all their might.

CRUCIAL RECONNECTION WITH THE TRANCENDENTAL

The organic challenge of societies always arises in the realm of pure Intelligence, before eventuating in the realm of facts. That is why, although I write my books only from the point of view of the social sciences, I am driven to ask assistance from the purely Intellectual Sciences, which alone can enlighten them; ancient Religions-Syntheses bear witness to those Intellectual Sciences.

Now, as in these culminating elevated regions, from which the genesis of the Societies originates, Truth is One, as Science itself; those who have charge and responsibility of Judeo-Christianism and Judeo-Christianity, will have to reach that Science by following the way I showed them, because it is *the way of the Abramids, of Moses, of Jesus.*

And then, the arbitral resumption of Universal Education in all its degrees becoming accessible again, Authority and social efficiency will be given back at the same time.

In *Mission of the Sovereigns* and in *Mission of the Workers*, I have made a great effort to endow the Judeo-Christians with an organic method, as regards the past History and the present organicity of their Social State.

In the present book, I am striving even more, elevating both the Lay Savants and the Theologists themselves high in the reality of *Integral Science and Religion*, which are, in their Essence, only *One and the same thing*, and, also, allowing readers to breath in deeply this religious and scientific Spirit which has defined the Life of the Universal Theocracy and the Universal Empire of the Lamb and Aries.

We will witness that the consequences of the schism of Irshu have been to open the door of the future to personal governments, while shaking the institutions which bound them to mutual Peace, and which constrained them to respect the public freedoms, guaranteed by the three Social Powers.

The analogy with Christendom will be obvious to all; and all will remember, by reading what follows, the words of

Montesquieu: *"Europe will perish by men of war"*; for so perished Asia. Now Anarchy resides in the General Government of Europe only because it already resides in the Judeo-Christian Intellect.

Let it cease in the latter, and the lion's den of personal governments, armed against each other, will soon be pacified by the Authority separated from Power.

But for Anarchy to cease in the Judeo-Christian intellect, the religious and civil faculties of public education must be reconciled; and only Truth can bind them to Peace; and *Truth is called* in the Spirit of Man the *Integral Science.*

If this reconciliation does not take place, one must expect to see the physical and natural sciences lead to a religious conclusion *sui generis* as I showed in the first chapter of this book.

It is to be expected that a new Irshu will, sooner or later, raise in Europe the sectarian banner that has bloodied the World since the year 3200 BC, and resulted in deplorable governmental and political consequences, both in the General Government of Societies and in their internal organization.

IONIAN REBELLION VS DORIAN ORTHODOXY

For the Regent (Irshu), after having constituted the particular synthesis of sciences and technical arts specific to Ionism in all its forms, gave the signal of the armed revolt.

After a bloody civil war, Irshu was driven out of the Indian Empire by Tarak'hya.

Irshu had repudiated the white color of the ancient Dwidjas, Brahmans, Lamas, and all the Priesthood of the Lamb, replaced by the red color which will evolve into the purple of the Caesars of Babylon and Rome.

On its banners, as we have said, the Red Dove replaced the Lamb and the Aries, the Crescent of the Moon replacing the Sun, the Yonah Dove replacing the Omphalos, the Violet of Juno and the Rose of Venus replaced the Lotus and Lily of Brahma, Osiris, and Jupiter.

Driven from the frontiers of the Metropolitan Empire, he enlarged his armies with a huge contingent, supplied by Rural

Communes. Hence his name which, in Sanskrit as in Egyptian, signifies the *Regent of the Pastors.*

I am completing here what I have said about the various names given to these sectarians, according to different countries.

The plastic Faculty of Nature, called in Sanskrit *Yoni,* in Ethiopian, in sacred Egyptian *Yonah,* and consequently the schismatics were named, according to the local dialect: *Yonijas, Yawanas, Ionioï, Ionians.*

As people of the red flag and red color, they were called the Reds, Pinkshas, of the Keltic word Pink, which still means" Ponceau", and origin of the word *Phoenician.* The name *Idumean* means the same thing.

As for the most part they belonged to rural Communes, they were named, with contempt: provincials, peasants, pastours, pastors, Palli, from the word Palla, shepherd.

They adopted this insult as a title of glory. In Kaldean, in Arabic, in Egyptian, that name became Balli, and later turned into meaning governor, sovereign, lord.

In Europe, the same glorified insult has survived in the names of Pallas, Palaces, Bailli, Palladium, Palatine, etc.

In Asia Minor, this sobriquet was carried by the Phili, the friends, the lovers of the Feminine Principle, the Pallantis, the Philishtani, the divine shepherds.

The Red Dove found on Coat of Arms and in ritual symbols gave the name of its color to the Phoenix, emblem of the Universal Soul and Life, burning with love and reborn from its ashes, sacred emblem of Io, Ionah, Aphrodite, Astarte, Venus, *Milyddah,* exactly replicated in *Milady,* the Lady par excellence, the great Goddess.

Repulsed by the Kousha, condemned by the great Lama of the Paradesa, Irshu and his Rurals had, beyond the borders of the Indian Empire, dazzling successes on all the coasts of the Gulf of Oman and the Persian Gulf, in all Arabia, from the mouths of the Euphrates to Syria, on all the coasts of the Red Sea, to which they gave their name.

Breaking the ancient alliance of Touran with the Empire of

Aries, the schismatics allied themselves with the Turanians, calling them for help, and these came indeed surging from the North, attacking Iran, Armenia, Paksha, Syria and Kaldea, thus supporting the military effort of the great revolt in the South.

SCHISMATIC IONIANS PROMOTE GENDER INVERSIONS

It is not unimportant to note that the *feminist and naturalist schism* has left its undeniable imprint even in the languages of the peoples who have espoused it.

Thus, the ancient Touranian Scythians, brothers of the Tatars, who will constitute, many centuries later, the *German* invasion, still *bear in their language the seal of the schism.*

Indeed, in German, the Sun has become of the feminine gender, the Moon of the masculine gender, expressing the strong Love for the feminine.

This *reversal of attributes and sexualities* was particularly characteristic of the Turanians, Tatars, and Mongols, or at least of those who emigrated to China.

This reversal is most striking in the Y-King symbols of Fo-Hi, on which topic I shall comment later.

Other divisions of the Scythian Turanians which will constitute the origin of the *Saxons, will suppress* in the Keltic-Scandinavian languages of England *the symbolic sexuality of the genera,* and not only *Life will thus be degraded in the Language,* but among the Angles themselves the grammatical future tense proper will disappear, as well as the distinction between the various tenses of the past.

But this is only one of the subsequent disruptions, one of the signs of the *turmoil of ideas and facts* caused by the schism of Irshu among the Turanians.

Conversely, among the Yonijas or Phoenicians proper, the naturalistic synthesis of ideas, remained rather clear in its symbolism and its manifestations.

It engendered everywhere a *kind of double language*, parallel to that of the Orthodoxes.

In India as in Greece, Ionism positioned itself in all things beside Dorism; but in the language, its primordial character consisted first and foremost in giving precedence to phonetics over ideographism, to analytic forms over synthetic symbols.

For several centuries, all the temples of the Theocracy of the Lamb, all the kings of Justice of the imperial order of Aries, fought against the growing fortune of this federation, whose Cult was everywhere enthralling the souls more passionate than wise, artists, young men, women, and even scholars more enamored of the sensorial Order than of the intelligible Order.

TRAJECTORY OF THE IONIAN CONQUESTS

The people, always more or less at the mercy of novators, were easily seduced everywhere by the suggestions of the anarchists promising them wonders.

On land and sea, there were gigantic and constantly renewed combats, striking three Continents at once, with cries and songs a thousand times retold by the bards of every country.

The old military ferocity of the Kelts of Europe, the old jealousy of the Druids and Druidesses of the Order of the Taurus towards the Empire of Aries and the Theocracy of the Lamb, did not fail to take advantage of the falling-out within the ancient Alliance, the ancient Peace.

A formidable thrust took place from the Atlantic to the Kourou (modern Ukraine).

The military leaders of the Varaha rushed towards the colonies of the Empire of Aries, from the Eastern Danube to the Caucasus.

They attached themselves and their troops to the Yonijas masters of Assyria and Syria, thus further strengthening the formidable support to the schism provided earlier by the Turanians of Asia.

Meanwhile, another surge of ferocious energies was still taking place from the North to the South of Europe on all the Southern Colonies: Portugal, Spain, the south of present-day France, Italy, and Greece.

From the harsh embrace of an ever-renewing war, from the streams of blood gushing out of the wounds of the old

Covenant, emerged, however, in the East, songs, harmonies, new architectural creations, an artistic movement, a half intellectuality passionate, lively, feminine.

Established in India in the general staff of Irshu, this School marked all its creation with this Ionic stamp, which the moderns today recognize only on architectural monuments.

Answering the appeal of the Sovereign Pontiff of the Paradesa, all the regional Pontiffs of the world stimulated the Kings of Justice to resistance, encouraged the ancient wisdom to master this torrent of fire, this deluge of love maddening all intelligences and unleashing all instincts.

The League of the Orthodoxes is, everywhere, asserting itself in the names of the symbolic color that distinguishes it and in a thousand other emblems.

Argians and Hellenes in Greece, Albans in Italy, Whites fight against the Reds, the white standard of Aries opposed to the red Dove on purple background.

And yet, even among the schismatic Kelts, the color *white* will remain symbolic of the ancient Sacerdotal Wisdom: *weis*= white, *weise* = wise, *wissen*= to know, *white*=white, *wit*= wit, *wise*= sage, *Wisdom*= Wisdom.

This struggle of the two dissociated Principles still shows its adverse colors until the Christian era which interrupted it.

Caesar and Pompey are the representatives of the last antagonism of the temples; the first is Ionian, the second Dorian, the first has the color red, the second the color white.

The family of Caesar, belonging to the Yonijas of Troy, claimed to be descendant of Venus, and Troy itself bore the golden sow on a purple background, this hieroglyphic animal being dedicated, because of its fertility, to the Plastic Faculty of the feminine Nature

We shall demonstrate later that Rome was founded by schismatics rallied to the arbitrary Order of Nimrod.

All its wars were basically the continuation of those of Assyrian Caesarism.

When Caesar committed the crime for which he perished,

when he placed the pontifical tiara of the Etruscan priesthood on his head, he united the two colors, red and white, which the roman catholic Popes still wear today.

As for Caesarism itself, its conception of personal government of the societies, the predominance of arbitrary power over the ancient arbitral constitution, guardian of the ancient civil liberties, it is still the legacy of the schism of Irshu, which governs present Europe, unaware of this fact.

This is the complete trajectory of the Yonijas movement and its consequences in History.

We will continue this study in the next chapter, descending more slowly the course of time and historical events.

We will then stop the reader's attention on all the efforts that will be made by the High Council of the Gods to repair locally, in each country, the frightful disorders introduced by emotional Anarchy, also called Politics, through the overthrow of the ancient Institutions, which, socially and intellectually, linked the peoples together.

∞

CHAPTER IX
THE SHISM OF IRSHU continued
CHRISTNA. FO-HI. MYSTERIES OF ISIS.
ZOROASTER.

GENERAL SOCIAL DECAY BEFORE THE SCHISM

Societies and individuals alike, are born and grow, decline and die, to be reborn and to live again.

They are subject to the law of existing beings, submitted to Duration and Extent.

When Irshu appeared on the stage of the World, the countries his schism was to conquer were more or less aggressed by the causes of death which attack all Life, even the best organized.

Controversies agitated the Empire of Aries, from its center to the furthest of its Colonies. If those debates had not happened outside of the two High Councils, they would soon have been terminated by Science itself.

But from the level of scholars, thinkers, bards, those debates fell into the public chatter of half-savants, half-philosophers, half-literates, in a word, amidst the unavoidable hornets of the hive of intellectual labor. Like all Theocratic Societies, India has kept all its memories intact.

It is impossible not to recognize in the most remarkable philosophical treatises of India, in the Darsanani, the results of the agitation of secular thought outside the temples, that is to say, outside the ancient universities.

The Vedanta of Vyasa, the Mimansa of Djaimini, the Veiseshika of Kanada, the Nyaya of Gautama, the Yoya of Pantadgali, the Sankhya of Kapila, still accurately reflect the debates of that epoch and the phases by which exoteric intellectuality, though diluted, has since passed into Greece, Rome, Alexandria, Byzantium, into scholasticism, into the philosophical literature of Christianity, from Scott to Buchner and Moleschots.

Among these schools and systems, which eclipse singularly those of Europe, the *Sânkya* is certainly the *oldest manifestation of Naturalism and Ionism* opposed to Dorism.

The whole hierarchy of Divine Sciences proper, is suppressed in the Sankya, with a clear affectation of not borrowing anything neither from Tradition nor the sacred books on this radically banished subject. Same observation for the schools of Yoga, Nyaya, Veiseshika.

What remains is the Soul of the World, Life, the triple Nature, E V E finally presiding entirely and solely on its three hierarchies of Sciences, physical, human, universal, in the visible Order and in the Invisible Order.

Mimânsâ and Védânta will come only later to fill in the Public Spirit the abyss that Ionism will have put between the Universal Spirit and the Soul, between Iswara and Pracriti, between Iod and Ê-Vau-Ê, between the first hierarchy of ancient Divine Science and the other naturalistic three.

It was this philosophical "chaff" (EVE's superiority), separated by the Ionism from the scientific "wheat "of Dorism, that Irshu ignited to start civil and political passions.

Same symptoms at that time in Iran.

In the Varkhanat, say the sacred writings of the Persians, almost all the great cities were also agitated by the buzz of the philosophers and the corruption of idle people, before being shaken by the schism itself.

The city of Merw distinguished itself by its passionate controversies, Niça by its rationalism, Seystan by its spirit of anarchy, Herat by its contrasting luxury and misery.

And when the schism came, Ourva was filled with scandals, Hyrcania filled with unbridled debauches.

ORIGINAL HEBREWS RESISTING ALL REFORMS

The *Hebyreh*, says Kush-Nameh, remained faithful; it was *the land of Pure Law.* This land of the early Hebrews will itself be shaken later by the revolution.

Its main families, such as those of the Iehoudim of India, the orthodox Bodhones of Arabia and Kaldea, will be driven out by civil wars, will roll with the waves of Yonijas from one country to another, keeping faithfully their old memories, which became more and more blurred as they moved away from academic centers. But, irresistibly tenacious in their stubbornness, refusing any new doctrine, they will thus make themselves odious to all, to the followers of Irshu and to the faithful of the religious reformers of India and Iran, Christna, Zoroaster.

When the worm is placed in the tree, it swarms there, and its work is unstoppable. Thus, in the Empire of Ram, following the anarchy of ideas and even before Irshu appeared, the factual social decline had already manifested itself.

From Assyria, says Myrkhonde, in the Rouzet-Essefa, *the faithful of ARam* came to reestablish the order altered by the corruption of the high class and the debasement of the princes.

TURMOIL IN ORTHODOX EGYPT CIRCA 3500 BC

In Egypt, more than 200 years before Irshu, extreme prosperity had already produced decadence.

After the great peace of the fifth dynasty and its nine Memphite kings, internal dissensions had broken out.

In addition, the international law enforcement had to go to war to bind viceroys and turbulent kings to the Universal Peace of the Empire of Aries.

The first two High Councils made the greatest efforts to maintain or re-establish the social concord, within Egypt among the *erpads* members of the Third Council and their tribes of different races, outside Egypt, among the peoples and vice-kings of the North and the South.

The Black Race had never forgotten its ancient supremacy; it was, like the Red Race and like the Yellow, attentive to the slightest signs of weakness among the Kelts of Aries.

Besides, it had in the Bodhonian Kelts of Arabia of the African Coasts, in the Oases and Mediterranean Colonies, friends always ready to give it a hand against any governor, against any viceroy, against any king inclined to transform his arbitral and synarchic power into arbitrary and personal power.

For their part, the Turanians of Asia were no easier to be kept loyal to the ancient Alliance, no more than the European Kelts of Thor, due to their fierce jealousy against the Empire of Ram; neither was it easy to limit them in their enterprises against Ram's European colonies.

Due to all its difficulties, the sixth Egyptian dynasty had begun with a civil war several centuries before Irshu.

In the South, the Black viceroys and Bodhones had pushed to the throne Ati at Elephantine, while in the North, the first Council would in Memphis crown Teta, a sovereign conform to the Indo-Keltic Tradition of Menes. Ati had been killed by a military revolt, and Papi 1ʳˢᵗ had succeeded Teta.

As the names were given to the sovereigns after their initiation, that of Papi 1ʳˢᵗ indicates the resumption of the Dorian priestly tradition of the Paradesa and Pa-zi-pa, as we shall see.

It was then, in fact, that the chief of the Council of God, Ouna, aulic auditor, took the reins as grand chancellor of the Pharaoh, and reorganized the Synarchy, the interior services, the assemblies of the Third Council, with all the economic prerogatives of the latter, local administration, regional police, cantonal army, collection of taxes.

The Egyptian Pontiff, Overseer or Episcope of the Prophets, thwarted the politics of the Black princes, the bodhones haks, and once again reestablished peace within the turbulent Khenterah (Ethiopia) and its four Nomes.

In the North, the Grand Chancellor defeated the league of Syrians and Bodhones of Arabia, Aramous and Herouschas, who had invaded the mines of Sinai.

In Egypt, as in all of Ram's Empire, the army was at the service of the Law of Ram and the Peace of the Lamb.

It consisted of three distinct elements: 1-the general staff of the temples, the whole initiated Corps of special armament, attached to the sanctuaries; 2-regular officers, maintained by the Communes, under the orders of the Third Council; 3-the mass drafting and mercenaries completed, in time of war, the framework of the regular army.

Thus supported by Ouna, Papi, a giant nine feet tall, reigned nearly a century, and reached the age of 120 years. The leader of the college of God still exceeded him in longevity. He put on the throne Mérenra, son of Queen Raoumeri Ankhnas.

He was thus able to consolidate his restorative oeuvre, before going to rest at Abydos, and to make, in the Amenti, the great cosmic journey of souls.

The life of this Overseer of the great Pyramid Prophets is summed up in fifty lines on his tombstone.

When Irshu brandished his incendiary torch in India, Egypt was in trouble again. From the time of Queen Nitaqrit, who died in 3500 BC, kings do incline toward arbitrariness; but as soon as they are sitting on the throne, they are broken and sent away by the first two High Councils with the approval of the third Council.

In 70 years, says Manetho, during the seventh dynasty, 70 kings come and go.

In 146 years, the eighth dynasty counts 27 kings: Nowerka, Nowerous, Ad, each reign only a few years.

The third Council of the kingdom is agitated by the opposition of the chiefs of the different races, Keltic Tamahous, Reds Rotennous, Blacks Nahassous, Keltic-Indians Manous.

Thirty leagues south of Memphis, a military group of tribes belonging to the Kelts of the India's General Staff, were sent everywhere, under the name of Harakala, to preside over the great public works of the Aries Empire, created a new city, and founded the ninth and tenth dynasties.

Standing on an island of the sacred river, this city built by the Harakala military engineers, which the Greeks will name Heracleous, was resisting the Egyptian anarchy, and was attempting to reestablish the Synarchy of Aries, when the schism of Irshu and the civil war of India broke out.

MAYHEM IN KALDEA CIRCA 3200 BC

In the ancient Kaldea, the mixture of races had been maintained at peace, as everywhere, only thanks to the free institutions of the original Arbitral Synarchy of Ram.

It is that Law of Aries, that social organization, which we find again, later, deified on the banks of the Tigris and the Euphrates, under the name of *Na-Ram-Sin*.

At that time, the king of the four regions of the Tigris and Euphrates, the representative of the Kousha reigned at Ilou, the City of God, which will later become Babylon.

The populations, as says Berose, had been from the beginning composed of widely diverse races. The Communes, governed by the Third Council, were shared between the Turanians, ancient allies of Ram, and the Aryas or people of Aries, also called koushistes or imperial. The former referred to themselves as forest mountaineers, or *Akkads*, the latter as agricultural communities or *Soumirs*.

The second High Council, headed by its King of Justice, was composed of these diverse elements, into which the ancient Bodhonian Kelts still participated.

The first High Council or Council of God, especially the erudite priesthood, belonged to the pure Kelts, as shown by its name Kaldeans.

The intellectual agitation that brewed in other countries was happening in the Four Regions as everywhere, and the impersonal delegated ruler who reigned under the name of Na-Ram-Sin had all the more to do to prevent these ferments of discord from degenerating into political anarchy, that the races were different, and each had preserved, even in their language and in their ideas, even in their rituals and in the lower priesthood of the tribes, their physiognomies and their own liberties.

When the exoteric philosophers had agitated India, by *opposing Naturalism to Deism* properly so called, the cities of the Tigris and Euphrates took sides for or against.

It was then that, in order to yield to the novators, and to reconcile it with the old Order of Things, the leaders of the first two High Councils emphasized the double sexuality of the cosmogonic Principles, under the invocation of which each of the cities was placed.

In Erech, in Nipour, in Eridou, in Ur, in Larsa, in Sippara, in Ilou, in Borsippa, in Cutha, in Han, the feminine faculties Ana, Davkina, Anounit, Zarpanit, Laz, were adjoined to the male cosmogonic Princes, Anou, Nouah, Sin, Samas, Marduk, Nebo, Nergal, etc., etc.

As the agitation continued, the Kousha of India put the Powers of King of Justice as much as possible in the hands of the pure Kelts: hence the *Ur dynasty*.

Finally, when the civil war broke out in the Metropolitan Empire, when Irshu was rejected by Tarak'hya from the frontiers of the Indus, Irshu's policy spread everywhere the seeds of discord, between the conflicting doctrines and ambitions of the rival races.

MOSES DEFINES ESOTERICALLY THE SCHISM

Without reiterating all that I said in the preceding chapter, as to the course and political fortunes of the naturalistic schism, I will let *Moses speak* concerning the new Form of imperial government which Irshu introduced into inter-relational life of the peoples, by overthrowing, wherever his power was exercised, the free and savant Synarchy of the Lamb and Aries.

Here, in part, is the hermetic meaning of the verses, in which the future legislator of the Hebrews will characterize this emergence of Caesarism in the World: Genesis Bereschit, Ch. X, v. 8, 9.

We Koush ialad œth Nimerod houâ hehel li-heyôth ghibor ba-Aretz.

Houâ-hayah ghibor tzaïr li-phenei IÉVÊ: Hal-khen iêamar khe Nimerod ghibor tzaïr li-phenei IÉVE

"Koush degenerated into Nimerod, who tried by violence to be North Pole, domineering on Earth".

"In him the North Pole Domination was contrary to the image of IEVE. Hence this comparison: as Nimerod, the Dominating Pole, was Adversary to the Face of IEVE."

Above is, word for word, the ideographic sense of the exoteric text of Moses. This is how he characterizes the kind of General Government which replaced the Theocratic Synarchy of the Lamb, the Arbitral Empire of Aries. Here is the translation of this ideographic sense into an analytic language:

"The arbitral empire was replaced by the arbitrary empire, whose characteristic name is the tiger's way, Nimerod, the Caesarism.

"This type of government wanted to dominate by military violence the terrestrial social state, like the North Pole dominates the planet.

"In this type, the Government Pole, the Anarchical or Personal Power defied the Reign of God, the Social Order which is the reflected Face of IEVE within Humanity."

Hence the axiom of the Orthodoxes:

"Nimerod, the Arbitrary Government, the Personal Power and all that pertains to it, is the Opposite, the Antipode of the Reign of God, the Opponent preventing the physiognomy of IEVE from reflecting itself in the Social State."

The three main hierograms of these two verses are Kush, Nimerod, Ghibor.

Moses, priest of Osiris, the Orthodox who will constitute the Hebrew people and give it the mission to carry through the centuries the cosmogonic Science of the temples of the Lamb and the social marching order of the Synarchy of the Aries, with the names Kush and Nimerod will oppose, not two actual persons, but two types of General Government.

One is the Imperial Arbitral type, the Kousha of India, sacred by Ram; the other is the arbitrary Empire of Assyria, such as Ninus will institute it, after Irshu defined it in principle.

The first (Kush) which signifies *Spiritual Principle, igneous, fiery,* of which Aries was the hieroglyph, is the Synarchy empowered by the High Lama who crowns the Emperor of Justice, Supreme protector Magistrate of kings and Rights of the People.

The second (Nimerod), whose emblem is the Taurus, hieroglyph of Water, of *the plastic Principle*, is Anarchy, crowning itself as a Caesar of iniquity, as a despot who follows the path of the tiger, who crushes underfoot and lacerates under his military might the Rights of the People, the regular delegations of this Law, the moral Unity between the rulers and the governed, and the triple organism which guaranteed their triple life in three distinct Social Powers.

The first (Kush), delegate of these three Social Powers,

had above him the social Authority par excellence, the Council of God and the Council of the Gods: therefore, the Emperor was the organic reflection of the face of IÈVE, Creator of the Universe, that is to say, the representative of the General Government of Society by Wisdom and Science.

The second (Nimerod) quashes Authority, crushes under the iniquity of personal Power the Council of God, the Council of the Gods; thus it embodies the Principle of Social Disorganization through arbitrary Politics, that is to say, the exact opposite of the Reign of God in Humanity, and it represents only the General Government of Societies by madness and ignorance.

MISSION OF THE ABRAMIDS OF HEBYREH

This is how the *Abramids, members of the ancient Council of the Gods in Kaldea,* and how *their inheritor Moses,* a member of the Council of God *in Egypt,* will stigmatize the entry on the world stage of a Power without Authority.

This is how they will imprint the Kain's symbol, sign of God's disapproval of Politics, since its beginning in human History. With that same symbol they will stamp the forefront of the crowned Anarchy, the personal Monarchy.

Serious fighters, the Abramids! They know the strength of the Adversary of the Kingdom of God, they also know the weakness of his false right to rule men by force, starting with the Sovereigns themselves, first prisoners of war of such a system.

Therefore, it will not be in the name of Politics that they will seize by the horns the winged Taurus of Assyria.

It will not be by a republican babbling that they will oppose the march of governments on the path of the tiger.

Every tribune leads to Caesar, every political form leads to another.

Poor anarchists of all times, who believe they are fighting against Caesarism, by opposing it the rhetorics of the forum!

Poor sheep bleating under the steel claw of the Government Beast!

The members of the first two High Councils were never

mistaken on these questions, nor on the impossibility of solving them by Politics alone. So, *they always used precision weapons and a weaponized Verb,* with long effective range, to fight the Evil and to resurrect the Good. These weapons are the social Sciences; this verb is the religious autonomy of the universal teaching, recognized or concealed, for the happiness or for the misfortune of the few, starting with the Governments and the Sovereigns.

CHRISTNA ENTERS THE STAGE OF HISTORY IN INDIA

Seventeen and a half centuries before Moses, that is 5,034 years ago (before 1884 AD) a *member of the Council of the Gods, Christna,* had already manifested itself in India.

As always, the Kousha had taken advantage of the civil war of ideas and facts, to install an arbitrary power in lieu of the Arbitral Imperium.

Seeing politics bloodying his country, witnessing the clashing of the Suras with the Asuras, the Pandus with the Kourus, the Yonijas with the Lingayas, seeing that, because of this tumult, the Emperor betraying his oaths vis-à-vis the two High Councils, confiscating the liberties of the third Council, assembly of the people, and thus authorizing, unknowingly, all the kings, viceroys, and governors of Provinces, to make themselves independent of him and to throw themselves into the feudal revolution, *Christna* took to task to *face the intellectual cause* of this social evil. Although born among the schismatics, within a royal family who had sided with the dissident Yonijas, *Christna* chose to side with the Orthodoxes.

His Initiation made him a member of the Council of the Gods, and he went out to present his knowledge, creed and wisdom to the people of the outside world, out of the temples.

His testimony can be summed up in the magnificent Trinitarian Synthesis which has preserved up to our days, in spite of all the foreign dominations, the intellect, the soul, the organism, the faith, the law, the mores which constitute the Hindu Society to this day.

How much strangely mistaken are those who attribute to

religion the decadence of the Societies, for the cause of this decadence, as we shall prove superabundantly, is found solely in Politics.

It's been 5,030 years (based on 1880 AD) since the head and heart of the Hindu Society were preserved from Politics by this member of the Council of the Gods, *Christna*, despite all the conquerors: Assyrian, Egyptian, Macedonian, Turanian, Mongolian, Muslim and English.

The same fact is true about *Fo-Hi's China* for 4,850 years (since 1880 AD)

But observe, on the contrary, in History, within this great laboratory of the social experiments of the human regnum, the weak viability of the societies, since the moment Politics alone has governed them, and make comparison.

Kaldea or rather Assyria since Ninus, Iran since the same epoch, Egypt since the invasion of the Hyksos, Asia Minor since the Phoenician republics, Greece since the predominance of the Third Council in the Assemblies, Italy since the foundation of Rome by anarchist members of the Third Council to the exclusion of the two others: all these experiences, all these facts will be many lessons to pick from.

And as for the whole of Christendom, suppose, which is not impossible, that China is determined to follow its example, to establish permanent taxes, to issue government loans and thus to maintain a tenth of its population under arms, that is, 45 million men.

Continue the supposition and let this army of 45 million men come to submerge Europe, from the Caucasus to the Atlantic. What will remain, at the end of half a century, of the thought, the soul, the body, the faith, the law, the mores of Christendom?

Absolutely and radically nothing; for the physiological force of the social organism and the institutions of China will have engulfed everything in a superior synthetic spirit, our science and our industry, like all our other disassociated social groups. That said, let's go back to *Christna*.

Like all reformers out of the Council of the Gods, he

worked with the exoteric Society as and where it was.

The fields are seeded according to their current state of receptivity for a particular crop.

Hence, the difference of the Rituals, according to the different countries that social Anarchy had transformed in various ways.

After having consecrated *the double sexuality of the cosmogonic Principles, Christna* revived the knowledge that in all things the *Organic Union* of these two Principles manifests their ineffable Unity through a third term: The Triad or Trimourti.

I will not repeat the intellectual teaching that I put in the mouth of the Brahmans responding to Irshu.

CORRECTIVE TEACHINGS OF CHRISTNA

Thus taught *Christna*, while endeavoring to cure the dualistic schism through the Principle of Trinity:

After reformulating the moral education of the people, spreading and commenting everywhere on the Divine Verb of Ram, he reinforced his allegoric teachings by the miracles of the Therapeutic of the temples, developed to infinity in a marvelous language, the Principle of the Triad, of Harmonic Unity, Principle just as true, in its place, as the Dyad, as the Monad, as all the Qualitative Science of Numbers; Christna thus sealed an alliance with the members of the High Council of God for the purpose of reforming the outward symbolism of the Worship.

He resuscitated the Lunar University and Dynasty, thus giving a measure of victory to the Yonijas. He even accepted the substitution of the zodiacal hieroglyph of Taurus or Cow with which Irshu's followers had iconized the new Law.

He appeased the fanaticism of the Turanians of Asia and the European Druids of Thor.

In addition to the Code of Manu, - which Politics will nevertheless alter in regard with the Castes- he kept inside, by protecting in the temples the complete Aries Social Tradition, all the *scientific esotericism of the Lamb*, and conversely he brought outside in the public, as a symbol of his new Covenant with

Ram, the Sun on a background of Azure, the Mediator Star that hosts the glorified Souls, the source of Light, of the Life and Peace of our Heaven.

He moved out of sight as much as possible the separated emblems of Ionism and Dorism, and accepted them only together side by side, a decision which gave rise in the realm of symbolism to new Orders or new Styles, which the moderns distinguish only through the architecture.

He adopted mainly as the reflective correspondence of the man from below with the Man of Heaven, the Omphalos or Umbilicus, because of the particular role of the solar plexus in the psychological sciences and in the psychurgical applied arts, and because of the similitude of the role of the solar plexus with that of the direct Light of the World Soul, a Light invisible to the physical eyes.

His Trinity representing this universal Soul, symbolizing the three hierarchies of Sciences of the Holy Name of EVE, was *Brahma, Vishnu, Shiva, Intellect, Verb, Instinct*, to which he added the Shaçti, the triple feminine faculty, the triple conceptive Power, *Sarasvati, Laksmi, Bhavahni, Intelligence, Intuition, Sensation.*

Of these three Persons, he indicated to the adoration of the faithful the Median, *the Mediator: Vishnu and Lasksmi.*

Having thus reestablished harmonic Unity through Trinity in the public worship, purified reason and morality in all elementary education, *Christna*, at the same time vitalized the state of ancient Liberty, the three Social Powers, the former Arbitration who had attached to Ram, up to his European colonies, the religious nickname of *Liber,* the *Liberator, Lyæu*s, the *one who unknots.*

But the Kousha, who had become all the more arbitrary as this triple arbitration had been more ignored, due to the civil war, felt that through the discourse of *Christna*, Science, Justice, Social Economy, in brief the three Councils, would bring him back to his duty, and incite him to restore the control of the pontifical Authority over his imperial Power. This is why the Kousha never stopped pursuing *and persecuting Christna.*

THE ASSASSINATION OF CHRISTNA

One day, this divine man *Christna* had walked away from his disciples to meditate and to pray. He had left them behind, along with his favorite pupil Ardjuna, and the holy women Nichdali and Sarasvati.

Angada, an emissary of the tyrant Kousha, followed him at the head of a gang of archers, had him tied to the branches of a tree and pierced with arrows.

Nevertheless, this holy life bore its divine fruits in the Cult and Society, not only of the Hindus, but of all the peoples of the world.

In India, his sublime morality brought the Souls back to social Peace through Goodness and through Virtue, extended to the point of absolute renunciation.

Here are some weak echoes of his luminous teachings aimed at the poor people, before whom he, *like Jesus*, testified:

The tree assaulted with a black swirl of pebbles
Takes revenge, responding with a gentle rain,
Beautiful flowers, pure perfumes, excellent fruits;
The shell of the seas, when the diver kills it,
Answers by laying pearls in his hand;
The rock the miner's pick strikes and breaks
Enriches him with rubies and adorns him with sapphires;
The ore melting in the fire's cup,
Cry, and drops of gold remain when it is no more.
Man lonely, oh Lord! but, oh sweet Wisdom,
Whoever loves you may feel hated:
In vain hatred attacks and tears his life;
Even in the torture, he never ceases to love;
He blesses the bloody arm torturing him,
And dies of love, like the Sandal tree
Which, while falling, perfumes the iron of the ax.

Such was, in India, the pure manifestation which issued from the Council of the Gods, to remedy public evils, to purify common morals and reason.

As the reformer was born in the sect of the Yonijas,

whence his name *Go-Palla, itinerant Pastor*, he was associated by the Hindu apotheosis with the sign of the Bouvier, Cow herd.

His name became *Christna* the *Sacred, Iezeus the Savior*: see the Bagava Vedam and the Bagava Ghita in the Pouranas. We will see his doctrine of the Solar Verb travel like a beneficent trail of ritual light and social warmth towards all the ancient temples of the Lamb shaken by schism.

In Persia, this doctrine will be carried by the *first Zoroaster*, in China by *Fo-hi*, though modified by the special genius of these two men and by the condition of the milieu they will have to reorganize. In Egypt, the same doctrine will inspire the worship of *Horus*, in Greece that of *Phanes* and *Apollo*.

The Greek temples will also give the apotheosis to Christna in the Bootes constellation (the Herdsman), and often merged him with Ram himself when renovating the Mysteries of Bacchus and Iao.

Finally, the *Arabs (Sufi Initiates)* revere him today in their cosmogonic esotericism, under the name of *Muphrid-al-Rami*, the *hierophant or commentator of Ram*.

FO-HI ENTERS THE STAGE OF HISTORY

In 2950 BC (4,970 years ago), another member of the Council of the Gods, *Fo-Hi*, one of the chiefs of the Hindu general staff, went to reform the Society of Tien-Hia on the banks of the river to which he gave the name of its symbolic color, Hoang-Ho, Yellow River. The name of *Fo-Hi is of Keltic origin*; it means *Living Father*.

Inspired by Christna's trinitarism, he condensed his own intellectual and social Synthesis into five hieroglyphic books, a sort of memorandum of initiations. These books were the Y-King, Chu-King, Chi-King, Li-King, Yo-King.

All consisted mainly of mathematical or morphological series of Principles represented by hierograms.

The Y-King was related to *Cosmogony*, Chu-King to *Androgony* or Science of the Principles of the Social State.

The Chi-King contained three hundred symbolic

theorems summing up all the esotericism of other *intellectual, moral and physical knowledge.*

The Li-King contained the canons of *social aesthetics*, the rules of ceremonies and the hierarchy of duties and human relationships.

The Yo-King expanded on *Science and on the Art of Analogy*, which the ancients called Music, and which the moderns understand only from a purely sensorial point of view.

At the head of the Y-King, *the Unity of the Unfathomable Principle, Tai-Iki, the Universal,* was manifested by the Dyad, Yin and Yang, within the Triad, Pa-An-Kou.

The Triad Pa-An-Kou contained the three Realms corresponding to the three hierarchies of Sciences of the sacred name ÊVÊ.

The first Realm, Tien-hoang, was the Intelligible Universe, the last, Ti-hoang, the Sensorial World, mineral, vegetal, animal; the median realm, the Gin-hoang, the Mediator was the Hominal Realm uniting the other two.

Noteworthy: having to reorganize the Mongols and Turanians, Fo-Hi accepted their *transposition of sexualities*, attributing to Yin passivity and rest, to Yang activity and movement.

This fact is similar to what I have said about the Turanian and Tatar characterization regarding the transposition of the sexes into the genders of the Sun and the Moon, as shown today in the symbolism of the German language.

This is why Sanskrit books characterize China by this very transposition: Tchandra-Douip, the country of the Masculinized Moon, of the Feminine that became Masculine.

It would be too long to explain here the crucial importance of these symbols which, from the top of the four hierarchies of sciences of which I spoke so often, extended their arithmological and morphological progressions, specialized, according to the divine or natural order, male or female, up to the systems of Numbers, Weights and Measures, including the Currency Standard.

The *schism of Irshu* had in this respect, as in all the others, *confounded the ancient ascending and descending methods, broken the concordance of the double aspect of Science, broken the ancient Synthesis, dismembered the ancient Unity,* whose great Pyramid had been the gnomon for all the Empire of Aries.

It is in this sense that Moses says, Genesis, Ch. XI, v. 1: "*(at that time) the Earth had only one Verb, only one Ideography.*"

In Babylon, the famous Tower was nothing more than a failed attempt at a new Synthesis of Sciences, asserting itself on the outside in a new gnomon. They did not want to return to the Law of Aries, and never could the savant Corps bring back to Unity the Law of the Taurus. Hence the so-called division of languages which the exoteric translations attributed to Moses: in *Genesis*, Ch. XI, v. 7.

However, in the *esoteric text of Moses* the Orthodox who will choose the people to become the Hebrews, the topic is not the phonetic languages, nor the verbiage of the talkers of the time, but it was about the sacred *Science and scholarly Ideography*, from *Astronomy* up to *Geodesy*, from the *Cosmogonic System* to the *Metric System* and up to the *Monetary Standard.*

On this point, as on all others, the Universality of Knowledge and of Social Life of the peoples, from one end of the Earth to the other, had received a fatal blow from the schism.

This is why the Hindu Pontiffs always blamed Fo-Hi for having made a concession as serious as the inversion of sex genders, so generalizing the Turanian mistake.

The name of *Tchinas*, which the Brahmans still give to the peoples organized by this reformer, means *schismatics.*

The Chinese themselves call their own country *Tien-Hia, Celestial Society*; but the Emperor's annual sacrifice at Shangte is indeed that of the Zodiacal Taurus, hieroglyph of the Wet Element devouring the fire of the altar.

In the Greek temples, the symbol of the abduction of Europa by the Taurus is referring to the same facts.

I will not go back to what I said about the Celestial Empire. Like a World in a seed, it was contained in principle in the sacred books of Fo-Hi.

THE TEACHINGS OF FO-HI

This is the whole social organism that Fo-Hi determined: the Y-Kings, the Cult of the Ancestors, Authority given to the Teaching Body, all the public offices assigned on the merit, the Council of the Gods under the name of Literate Corps, the Council of Elders with its freedoms and local powers, no Council of God or Official Priesthood separated from the secular world.

This form of organization instituted by Fo-Hi is *insufficient to assume the General Government of the World*, and to sustain a social constitution facilitating the interrelations of Worship to Worship, State to State, Nation to Nation; this secondary intellectuality, this bourgeoisie of the ancient Synarchy, this masterful Prudhommie of the old University of the temples of the Lamb, nevertheless evidenced the strength it had appropriated from the complete edifice of the Aries Empire with the ancient Trinity of its Social Powers.

In the *absence of a Council of God*, the Corps of Literates was without power to appeal to supranational authority against invasions, and within its regions this Corps was unaided to conduct its struggle against arbitrary imperium.

But to the honor of this *Corps of Literates* and to its eternal glory, as well as to that of the ancient Council of the Gods, of which it was a weak substitute, it has remained for 4,000 years, erected as a column of light against all emperors inclining towards their own personal power and attempting to shake down the only true Authority of the Chinese Empire, that of Wisdom and Science guarded by the teaching Corps.

At the head of the Sacred College, it is Tching-Tang who will expel the infamous Kie from the throne; it is Wou-Vang which will raise the conscience and the public liberties and will dethrone the tyrant Tchiu.

PERSECUTION OF THE LITERATES AND INITIATES

But this noble struggle of the Literates will not be without perils, and, on many occasions, they will be decimated and drowned in blood, like the Council of the Gods of all other countries, from the Initiates of India to the Pythagoreans of Great Greece, to the Gnostics of Alexandria, through the College of the Gods of Israel.

In China, the most atrocious persecution was that of which the miserable criminal Tsin-Che-Hoang afflicted the Literates; tearing not only their life, but also their soul, by having the books Chu-King and Chi-King thrown to the flames.

Which of the constituted Corps of present-day Europe could show, in the defense of the Social Authority against Political Power, services comparable to those of the Corps of the Literates of the Celestial Empire, unshakable guardians of the strong intellectual, moral, and civil constitution that Fo-Hi provided from the beginning, and to which constitution all what is needed to resurrect its ancient spirit, would be to incorporate all of our modern sciences?

OSIRIS, ISIS, HORUS

In Egypt, Christna's Trinitarism also had its beneficent influence in setting apart the Trinity Osiris-Isis-Horus.

But the politics of the schismatics, as soon as year 2703 BC., relegated in the deepest core of the temples the ancient Synthesis, the first Hierarchy of Sciences, Osiris, whose name, when pronounced, was making Herodotus tremble.

At that time started the spreading of the exoteric legend of the dismemberment of *O-Sir-Is*, the intellectual Lord Master, the God of the ancient savant and universal Alliance.

Holding in her arms her son, solar haloed Horus, the crescent adorned Goddess, Is-Is, double Intellectuality, hyperphysical Nature, was herself and all her sciences and all her arts, covered with the veil of a double Initiation: Lesser Mysteries, Greater Mysteries.

From this period dates the moral test and the oath applied to all levels of Teaching and Knowledge, starting at the level of secondary studies. From this period, in Egypt as in Assyria, dates the replacement of the hieroglyph of Aries by that of

Taurus; nevertheless, the Orthodox Pontiffs kept the head of Aries carved on their crosses.

Tradition says that the equinox of spring occurred on the first degrees of Taurus, when the Mysteries of Isis where instituted.

However, the festival of Osiris remained fixed at Noel time, that is to say at the time when Ram's Aries, 4,100 years earlier, coincided with the beginning of the astronomical year. The date of the opening of the Mysteries of Isis matches the first astronomical records of the Chinese Literate Corps. Those records indicate indeed the Polar Star, *Yeu-Chu*, the Pivot of the Right, in the Constellation of the Dragon, Alpha.

It is nearly 4,600 years since these events occurred.

THE CONQUEST OF EGYPT BY THE HIKSOS

The cult of the Ancestors recorded in the very ancient Book of the Dead, the withdrawal of the Council of God with its ideographic libraries in the depths of the esoteric Science, the withdrawal of the Council of the Gods in the secret of the Mysteries of Isis, saved Egypt's intellectual and social existence, that is, the soul of its national life, until an orthodox king, instructed in the temples, was able to drive out the *Hiksos*. In vain, the flood of the *Ionian* invasion had rolled its waves on this country.

The invader did not dominate Egypt; the invader was dominated by the power of the institutions, of which the first two High Councils, though bending their heads, remained the invisible Spirit and Soul.

EGYPT CONQUERS ITS CONQUERORS

In vain did the Hiksos pastoral kings strive with all their strength for pure Caesarism; they always had to reckon with the opinion which constantly disdained them, watching their illusory power pass, and admitting no other authority than Religion.

Religion, the Teaching of Wisdom and Sciences of the Visible World and the Invisible World, remained elusive under its veils, while cultivating in the people the sacred fire of its hopes by the pomp of ceremonies and the rich symbolism of public festivals.

Thus, thanks to its two High Councils, Egypt saved its civilization and conquered its rude conquerors.

These conquerors, in order to assume their Power with a minimum of Authority, had to ask for it in the teachings of the sanctuaries; and from then on, they were in turn civilized, submitted themselves to the Ethics and Intellectual leaderships, and exercised only a diluted Caesarism.

Finally, despite 470 years of apparent domination, they were driven out by Amos, so much had the National Soul of Egypt been preserved within the Temples.

ZOROASTER ENTERS THE HISTORIC STAGE OF PERSIA

Another member of the Council of the Gods also went out of the Universities of India to reform the Varkhanat.

His Initiate name, *Zaratoushtra*, had formerly been applied to a whole part of the esoteric Dorian teaching; the name Zaratoushtra meaning *Solar Revelation*.

Historians Hermippus and Eudoxus thus designate as Zaratoushtra the Priestly School of *Ram*, himself being called, as we have seen, the *Head of the March of the Stars*, that is, *Head of the Cosmological and Astronomical Colleges*.

These two authors mention, in this regard, the date which corresponds to the foundation of the Empire of Aryas, or Aries, the Ram. It is also the period indicated by Plato.

But after Christna, the first renovator who raised this Dorian school in Iran, lived, says Pliny, about 2,450 years before our era.

The name *Persia* did not exist then. A contraction of the name of Paradesa or Parathesa, this name was given to part of the old Varkanat by the Mongolian and Turanian schismatics only as a mark of contempt. That is why Berose, Pythagoras, Suidas, will represent the renovator of the Solar Initiation, which is our current subject, in turn as *Mede, Persian and Persomede*. But these names do not correspond to the time when this great man unfolded his social reform.

It was at Balk that the action of *Zoroaster* the *reorganizer* took place, in the midst of the University Center, in the middle of the *rivalry between the Deistic and Naturalistic schools*, respectively *Dorian and Ionian*.

In the Esoteric Synthesis which motivated his social reform, and of which *Zend-Avesta* contains only the symbolic abstract, often altered, *Zoroaster did the opposite of Fo-Hi*.

He exaggerated the radicalism of his opposition to the schism.

In India, Christna, far from denying the Sexual Dyarchy in the Organic Creation of the Universe, had scientifically solved it by the Trinity.

Yonijas and Lingajas, the two parties which agitated the Empire of Kousha, were sufficiently enlightened, sufficiently merged as races by the ancient institutions, and *their motives were above all intellectual*. They could therefore reach the Truth, provided a man of religious genius showed it to them.

That's what Christna did.

In China, dealing with a majority of Turanian and Mongolian peoples who had reversed the order of ideas attached to sexual symbols, Fo-Hi had conceded this error, endeavoring to bring them back to the Trinitarianism of Christna.

In Persia, Zoroaster, a man of Aries, an Aryan and Dorian Initiate, was face to face with a turbulent thrust of Turanians.

The Turanians stirred troubles in the temples, the universities, the public discussions.

But far from being motivated only by pure intelligence and concern for the truth, *they were full of passions and political appetites*.

The Aryas, the ancient European Kelts, had everywhere prevailed in the Empire and in the Temples, outside the Turan proper. Thus, the schism of Irshu was for a long time a good opportunity that the people of the Taurus had seized in order to supplant the peoples of Aries.

Naturalism in the temples, republicanism in order to

dissociate the Aryas, then military Caesarism for their own profit: this was the game of the Turanians to infiltrate the magnificent kingdoms and the beautiful colonies of the ancient Synarchy of the Lamb.

This is why Zoroaster had to worry less about absolute Truth than about relative order.

This is why he turned his race back to an exaggerated Dorism, more certainly inspired by the necessities of national defense than by Science itself.

THE TEACHINGS OF ZOROASTER

Like Christna and Fo-Hi, he put the Divine Unity out of debate, placing it within the deepest mystery of esoterism, under the name of *Wôdh*.

His intellectual war against the Turanians was especially evident in the Dyad, which had been the primary cause of the division of the minds, and which remained the transcendent pretext for the anarchic and caesarian politics of the invaders.

Therefore, suppressing female sexuality in the Dyad, Zoroaster presented it, not as the Organic Union, but *as two absolutely antagonist Principles*, one good, the other bad, the one Iranian so to speak, the other Turanian. These two Principles, *Ormuzd* and *Ariman*, in *esoteric* initiation were mediated by a third force, *Mithras*, representing the *Mediating Trinity* and the *Solar Mediation*.

But, influenced by the political requirements of the environment he was in the process of reforming, Zoroaster, presented the Dyad *exoterically* as a dual reality, and thus he made the crucial mistake which the first two High Councils of India reproved.

The mistake was to transfer the *notion of Evil* out of its proper domain, that of free will of Man, his faculty to draw inspiration from below in the realm of physical Instinct, instead of drawing inspiration from above in the realm of Intelligence.

The ancient original Dorian Science envisioned the Fall as a descending cosmogonic progression from the absolute Being to the Not Being, from the pure Spirit to the Divisible Substance.

In that scientific notion of the Fall, there was not the slightest idea of Evil; on the contrary, it was designating the idea of *Universal Good descending to propagate Life to Infinity, from the Highest Realm to the lowest*. This downward progression was exactly mirrored in the Ionian science describing the ascending series of existences, from the infusoria to the individual human.

The Ionian science was revealing that, the Human being, reaching the apex of visible beings, can ascend further up to the summit of Heaven, thanks to the faculty, given to him by *Science and Conscience combined*,

1-to develop his body of astral light while living here below, thus avoiding the second death,

2-to preserve his individuality

3-to return to the intelligible sources of Being.

Once his intellectual synthesis made, founded on these irreconcilable Dyadic sectarian bases, Zoroaster radicalized its consequences to the extreme. He raised his adherents against the Turanians, and an armed revolt followed his predications abroad. "*Strike furiously the arrogant Turanian who afflicts and torments the righteous! He does evil: break him; he rises by violence; smash him.*"

Such are the passions of race which are revealed in the *Zend-Avesta*, 50th ha, 45th ha.

The result of the war was the absolute separation of Iran, formerly an integral part of the Varkhanat confederation.

In spite of the well-deserved blame which the Brahmans addressed to Zoroaster from the viewpoint of Intelligence, his Dorism, although outrageous, produced great benefits for the General Good of Humanity.

As his country was on the path to India, or Assyria and Kanaan, thus reacting against the Turanian thrust, he secured the existence of the ancient civilization, and sheltered it as long as its preservation was necessary.

Thanks to Zoroaster, the predominance of pure Politics

in the partial government of his country and in the General Government of the World was counterbalanced by the ancient Synarchy. Indeed, he revived the Intellectual and Moral Authority of the first two High Councils under the names of Maha-Wodh, Mahabad, *Great Wisdom*.

Until the conquest of Iran by Ninus, the royal Power remained subject to that twin High Council Authority, and the peoples were benefiting from public liberties sanctioned by the Council of Elders, and in agreement with the other two Councils.

Surely, those benefits would have been impossible everywhere without the presence of the Highest two Councils of the ancient Synarchy, without Christna in India, without Fo-Hi in China, without the Priesthood and the Mysteries of Isis in Egypt, and without Zoroaster in Persia.

So we shall see Despotism always trying to annihilate, not only these two High Councils always opposing arbitrariness, but also all the fruits of Science, all the remnants of Divine Authority, as it is only on those destructed bodies that Iniquity can reign by means of pure Politics.

Let's observe everywhere the advance of purely political governments, from their start to the time they annihilate the ancient Synarchy.

PROTO ASSYRIANS ENTER THE STAGE OF HISTORY

What is *Ninus* doing in Iran? He decimates the first two High Councils, he annihilates the government of the Mahabad, he destroys all the sacred books, depositories of cosmogonic and social science.

What is Nabon-Assar doing in Babylon? He is aiming at erasing all the previous chronicles, scratching the inscriptions, breaking all the brass tablets, melting all the stelae, burning all libraries. In the mind of this brute, it is essential that all "future Times" be known only as the fruits of his ill will.

What is the stupid Tsin-Che-Hoang doing in China? He forbade, under penalty of death, to be left intact any book, any pillar, any engraved stone; then he exterminated the savant Literates.

What is the Council of plebeian anarchists, which founded the Republic, doing in Rome? They make cunningly disappear the books of Numa, compendium of the Etruscan Sciences and memory of the ancient Synarchic Authority of the first two High Councils.

What are the Caesars of Rome doing? Exactly the same as their Kaldean prototypes. Roman law is fraught with persecutions against the ancient Science, against the ancient applied Arts. From Caesar to Diocletian, Roman politics burned the libraries kept by the first two Councils.

It is Caesar who burns the Ptolemaic library, it is Diocletian who burns that of the Serapeum of Memphis, and who also pursues the same line of conduct vis-à-vis the Persian books. It is Theodosius finally who, after Constantine, hides himself behind the new Christian faith in order to annihilate all the temples, guardians of the ancient Science and ancient Social Tradition.

Now, once one holds *this secret thread of History*, it is no longer permissible to misunderstand the fact that Religion was everywhere the safeguard of Science, of good social organization and of public liberties.

On the contrary, Politics was, from its origin, the anti-social claim of Anarchy with all its consequences: governmental Ignorance, Iniquity in social relations, Fatality substituted for the ancient Freedom.

After having shown in this chapter the efforts made by the ancient Synarchy to fight local government anarchy, we shall expose in the following chapter, how the brutal Assyrian Caesarism responded to the resistance organized by the Synarchy.

The remedy will surge again from the first two High Councils, which had been crushed by governmental arbitrariness in Kaldea. We will spend a moment to observe *the voluntary exile of a group of Orthodox neo-Ramids* known under the ideographic name of *Abram*. (Ab-Ram).

CHAPTER X
ASSYRIAN CAESARISM - ORTHODOX ABRAMIDS OR NEO-RAMIDS

POLITICAL TYRANNY OF NINUS

In 2200 BC, a radical *emperor*, *Ninus*, entered the world stage.

He was inaugurating in the World this sort of Anarchy from above, this arbitrary Power, this General Government by the Force of arms, which *Moses* stigmatizes under the hierogram of *Nimerod (the way of the tiger)*, and which, until today, still governs our Societies.

Ninus, in Kaldaic language *Nin-Iah, offspring of the Absolute Being*, embodied his arrogance in the name he gave to himself.

As a prototype of political Absolutism, he offered himself to the peoples as being directly endowed with a divine right to submit them by force to his will, without submitting himself to any Higher Authority other than his own Power.

Higher Authority, indeed, does not reside in an illusory cloud, nor in a physical sky, or anything alien to Mankind. Authority resides in each human Soul and Mind, present wherever Science and Wisdom inhabit them. Authority is always to be found in the midst of the integral Assembly of all forms of Teaching, Religious, Civil and Military.

So, as *Moses* says, there is no more odious blasphemy than the one perpetrated by the crowned anarchist, who camouflages his governmental iniquity with the hypocrisy of a Divine Right.

At that time the genuine divine right resided in the first two High Councils of Kaldea, in those of India and moreover it was represented by the Sovereign Pontiff presiding over the Savant Colleges in the mountains of the Himalayas.

But the first action of the Despot Ninus was to trample on the two High Councils so as to get rid of the Authority which, by God's Power, had the Right to control his arbitrariness.

From then on, Ninus was able to enslave the Third Council

with impunity and therefore to stifle public liberties and squeeze to the extreme the social Economy, so levying a permanent Tax, caesarian condition to maintain a permanent Army. Moreover, according to the eternal tactics of despots, he also snatched from the first two High Councils their right to designate the laureates of the examinations to public office. And so, Political Power without Authority became the greatest *agent of the moral corruption of peoples, the focus of all abnormal ambitions, of all capitulations of conscience, of all servitudes.*

MILITARY CONQUESTS OF NINUS

Then, freed from all intellectual and moral barriers, Ninus despotically governed his nation, and practiced vis-à-vis other nations and other governments the international and intergovernmental iniquity which, from then on, and because of him, rules, up to our time, the Relationships of Human Societies.

In his own country, to obliterate the memory of the ancient Theocratic Synarchy, he suppressed the name *Kaldea*, and replaced it with *Assour*, meaning *Oneness of the Lord*. Naturally this lord he was designating was no one but himself.

He declared himself "*son of Bâl*", to play his comedy of divine right in front of the naive populations.

But God, I E V E, is a 4-letter word, *Bal*, is a hierogram of 3 letters; and if we (by ignorance) do not add an absolutely scientific sense and draw its geometrical consequences from the Theogony to the Social Science inclusively, we will say like Shakespeare, of these words: only words, words, words!

Now, we have seen what meaning Ram had added to the Sacred Name of Divinity. *Divinity was in the temples the Synthesis of all Sciences:*
1-divine, 2-universal, 3-human and 4-natural.

At the same time, Divinity was the Right and the Law, which the Romans, followers of the Etruscans, will not define in any other way. Moreover, this Wisdom, this Total Science, this Right, this Law, had its representatives in the first two High Councils.

So, let Ninus call himself "son of Bâl", as long as he likes.

The name of Bâl, as he understands it, means only Anarchy and the fancy of Ninus. It is Ninus who attempted a Synthesis of the Law of Taurus, whose unfinished gnomon known as the *Tower of Babel*, signals its destructive impotence.

Believing himself, by the means of his own energy and the strength of his armies, to be called to rebuild Ram's empire, he began his violent career with a military deployment unheard of until then.

Taking advantage of the obstinacy of Arabia's Bodhones against all innovations the schism of Irshu had introduced into India, he contracted an offensive and defensive alliance with their king, whose name, *Ariéus*, symbolized his intransigence against the new Trinitarian law of Christna.

Then Ninus, at the head of his troops, rushed towards Armenia, then governed by Barzanes, King of Justice, subject to the court of the Kousha.

He sacked the cities of this country, striking the peoples with terror; and once victorious over the last resistance, he exacted a treaty from Barzanes, by which this king pledged, like Arieus, to provide him with all his able-bodied men.

It was then that, at the head of larger and larger armies, he rushed towards Media, of which Pharnus was the King of Justice. Victorious, Ninus seized the Queen, her seven children and the King himself, whom he crucified. He established one of his followers as a satrap, and then rushed towards Iran.

After wresting the Dorian key of India from the two High Councils which Zoroaster had reestablished, Ninus erased the sacred name Iran off this unfortunate country and imposed on it the parodic name of *Persia*.

NINUS DESTROYS THE SUPREME PONTIFF'S AUTHORITY

His fury, resentful of all restraint, persisted in destroying the Authority which Zoroaster, 1,000 years earlier, had re-established and superimposed over the royal Power.

This is why Ninus suppressed the *Maha-Wodh*, that is to say the Authority of the two High Councils over the Power of the King of Justice.

Transforming the Teaching Corps, religious and civil, sacramental and legal, into public officials and, consequently, into political instruments, he installed his viceroys under a deceptive name, in order to simulate in front of the ignorant people a faked conformity to the synarchical character of the ancient kings of Justice (Pish-dad). Indeed, his so called *Pishdadians*, bogus Justiciaries, were but his mere Executors.

Those reigned up to the time of Kai-Kosru, whom we know as Cyrus.

Then Ninus pushed through Turan (Caucasus), on the Kourou and the Varaha (Ural and Central Europe plains up to Denmark and on Baltic sea), with his armies swollen with mercenaries, Turanians and European Kelts of Thor.

He thus seized the sanctuaries of the Lamb, throughout all the colonies of Aries, and militarily dominated the nations, from the Caucasus to the Balkans, from the Balkans to the Ligurian Alps and as far as Spain.

It was then that after the collapse of all the tiaras and crowns, after the submission to military servitude of peoples no more shielded by their traditional protective institutions, an immense cry of pain and reprobation went *up to reach the Sovereign Pontiff, then a refugee in the Himalayas.*

This supreme social Authority, although weakened, did not hesitate to urge to duty this most redoubtable anarchist.

A formidable blame echoed from India to Egypt and Etruria, throughout all the sanctuaries of the ancient Empire of Aries. But crime follows closely arbitrariness, and Ninus, far from bending under the supreme Majesty of Social Science and Consciousness, hurriedly returned to Assyria, dragging with him the innumerable armies of his Turanian and European allies, which he was about to hurl on India.

Death stopped him short, seized the soul of this mass murderer, this first political conqueror, this first arbitrary emperor, and carried his soul to the scales of Eternal Justice.

Such was, after Irshu, the most brutal adversary of the Reign of God on Earth, the first energy without Control and

Law that depressed the Spiritual Body of the Social State, defiled the General Government of the Globe, eclipsed the Face, trampled under his feet the Theocratic Representation of IEVE.

QUEEN SEMIRAMIS ENTERS THE STAGE OF HISTORY

His wife followed on his projects, fortunately with a brighter soul. *Semiramis* was born in Bactria. (Afganistan). The exoteric legend says that she was raised by doves, which means she was a Priestess of a Feminine Initiation College. (Ionian).

The headmaster of this college was called *Simma*, and the college was sharing in the Mithraic esotericism, where women had preserved their Ionian Mysteries. It was him who presented Semiramis to Menones, grand chancellor of Ninus.

Menones married Semiramis.

Ctesias and, after him, Diodorus of Sicily, have preserved the memory of the substantial part Semiramis played in the conquest of Bactria.

Ninus' army totaled nearly 2,000,000 infantrymen, more than 200,000 horsemen, more than 10,000 chariots of war. Nevertheless Bactria, defended by the king of Justice Oxyarte, resisted until the moment when Semiramis took the command of the siege troops. It was then that, enthused by her beauty, courage, genius, as well as the extent of her knowledge, Ninus wished to marry her, and offered divorce to Menones, giving him his daughter, Sosane, as a wife.

Subsequently Menonès hanged himself, and Semiramis became Empress of Assyria.

Before letting Ninus pass away and remit his accounts to the Social God of Heaven and Earth, I wish to say a few words on his tomb. This Caesar was certainly a great man; but that does not suffice to insure happiness to humankind, nor to govern with Wisdom and Science, for the simple reason that pure Politics, monarchical or republican, are radically powerless.

Instead of being the head of an arbitrary empire, suppose Ninus was the head of an arbitral empire, as Supreme Magistrate of Laws of Justice, as the first president of the Court of

Appeal of International Law, his great qualities would have displayed all their luster, and his great faults, even his crimes, would not have occurred.

Having above him to reckon with a true Authority, itself supported by the universal morality of the governed, Ninus would have been a powerfully benevolent genius, for he would have employed his greatness, not at the service of his will, but he would have applied Wisdom and Science to the General Government of the world and his own nation.

That is why I repeat here what I said so often in the *Mission of the Sovereigns:* In organic topics of this magnitude, to attack the person of the sovereigns is to lack Science as well as Wisdom. One must do like the Abramids did, like Moses, like the two High Councils of all the Ancient World: rebuild the hierarchy of functions, wrest the Authority from the compromising Power, and place it back on top of that power.

Ninus, before his campaign in Iran, had wanted to rebuild a metropolitan capital city founded on a Synthesis based on the Law of Taurus. (Ashour)

NINUS BUILT A NEW CAPITAL CITY

That is why, choosing the ancient Nineveh, he had invited there Savants of all nations, not for the purpose of circumscribing his Power, but only to exalt his greatness and to conform to his designs.

The Synthesis failed, as I said, because he did not wish to revive the ancient Principles symbolically inscribed within the geometry and proportions of the Great Pyramid.

Nevertheless, from a material viewpoint, the Caesarean City was conceived and erected with colossal dimensions.

Enclosed in a quadrilateral oblong, it was 55 miles in perimeter, 17 miles long and 10 width. The walls were 100 feet high, and three war chariots could pass through the gates. 1,500 crenellated towers 200 feet high, defended these gigantic fortifications, surrounded by floodable ditches.

SEMIRAMIS TAKES OVER THE EMPIRE OF NINUS

As for Semiramis, after the death of Ninus, she certainly governed her empire with a genius that no personal male sovereign has ever surpassed.

Her symbolic name, SEMI-RAM, means *Ram's Intellectual Light, the Smart Dove of Aries.*

She tried, indeed, but only through Politics, to reconcile the antagonistic creeds and to pacify the various sects of her peoples.

As an Ionian, she was the object of the enthusiastic admiration of the partisans of the Feminine Faculty, and indeed she bore as a symbol, on its banners, the famous Dove-Ionah mark of the Feminine Mysteries.

But she changed the banner's background purple color to white, thus providing a form of victory to the ancient Ram's Orthodoxy. She even accepted the Trinitarianism of Christna, with the new symbol known as *Bal-Iswara-Linga.*

The sacred books of India, in fact, say that this return to the Principles was accomplished at that time on the banks of the Kamud-Vati, the Euphrates.

Yet, far from subjecting her power to that of the Emperor of India, the empress of Assyria was projecting to subjugate him militarily.

SEMIRAMIS BUILDS THE COLOSSAL BABYLON

But first of all, she endeavored to found her glory on useful creations; and in order to conciliate the Kaldeans, she resolved to build a city even more colossal than Nineveh, and chose the site of the ancient city that was placed under the invocation of *Ilou,* or *Ilon,* which we shall find again in the name of *Ilion.*

At the head of the Savants who had become public functionaries, she called on the architects, engineers and artists of all the temples. She employed a prodigious number of workers from all countries, millions of men.

Babylon rose based on proportions provided by the

Science of Astronomy, thus revealing the firm intent of making it a metropolitan solar city.

The previous metropolis, (Ninus' Nineveh), was as big as London (in 1883 AD); but it was not a huge dimension for the time. In truth, *in the past, under the Rutas, under the Blacks, under the Aryas, the Earth had seen bigger cities than that.*

Semiramis extended the perimeter of the first enclosure to 365 "stades", that is to say, in ancient morphometry, corresponding to a Cycle, or one symbolic luni-solar Year, of 42 miles perimeter.

The height of this wall was, says Ctesias, of 50 "orgyes" (Bacchic measurement), or 258 feet.

On the summit of the wall, where several horse-drawn chariots could maneuver side by side, stood up defense towers.

Such was the first enclosure Nivit Bel, itself surrounded by Imgoul-Bel, the second quadrilateral enclosure 52 miles long, more than 140 feet high, and 75 feet thick, flanked by towers of 315 feet, pierced by 100 gates.

In the center of the double wall, stood, bridging over the Euphrates river, the imperial city with its gnomonic tower, observatories, temples, colossal palaces, its one-kilometer long bridges and the hubbub of its human crowds.

Four cities like present London would have been comfortably lodged within the perimeter of Imgoul-Bel.

Aristotle will later describe Babylon as an entire country surrounded by walls, rather than a city such as Europeans understand them.

On the imperial palaces, nearly 400 feet high, the towers and walls sparkled in the sun of the Orient with their polychrome bas-reliefs and their bronze statues representing allegorical hunts, heroes and gods.

The entrance to the Empress' palace had three bronze doors, equipped with an internal mechanism which provided long distance early warning, opening on rooms made of the same metal.

Near Babylon she had dug a lake 35 feet deep, paved like a swimming-pool, of red bricks, tarred, its perimeter of 137 miles. She had diverted the river into this manmade lake, to dug in the meantime in the riverbed of the Euphrates a vaulted tunnel 16 feet deep, made of bricks coated with boiling asphalt. This tunnel formed a gallery 15 feet wide and 12 feet high, up the top of the arc of the vault only. In 7 days, the priestly engineers had finished this work, as everything was calculated in advance, according to the capacity of the temporary lake and to the time necessary for the return of the Euphrates to its natural bed.

At the projected time, the river rushed toward the underground gallery which connected the two forts, the two imperial palaces of the east and west.

Two automatic and secret brass doors closed the mouths of this tunnel; they will still exist at the time of the Persian conquest.

There would be much more to say about this city, if I were not limited by the main subject of this book.

I wish I could bring the reader into the life of this colossal metropolis, its palaces, its temples, its laboratories, its observatories. I would like to show how, even *with a broken and hazy Synthesis, ancient Science was still, up to that time, immense in all its aspects.*

I wish I could elaborate on the *esoteric aspects* of this *Science* as evolved into *Alchemy, Psychurgy* and *Theurgy.*

But we must confine our discourse to the main topic of this book, that is to say reveal the structures of the Social Organism disregarded since Personal arbitrary Power had prevailed.

ORIGIN OF THE ABRAMID ORTHODOX MOVEMENT

Babylon is the metropolis where the very subject matter discussed in this book was debated among the orthodox Savants.

Such was the intellectual and political world, from which will depart the *neo-Ramids* Initiates, known by the *symbolic name of Abram, arch-enemies of purely political governments.*

Now, considering good faith readers, for whom the Bible

is something else than a fetish, an idolatric text obscurely translated, I am asking if, presented with that babylonian social
order, Moses would have taken the trouble to tell the story of
an old shepherd fleeing with his wife the city of Ur in Kaldea.

Yes or no, the Babylon of Semiramis, such as Ctesias, Cli-
tarch, Herodotus, Aristotle speak of it, yes or no, does this
metropolis presuppose Corps of Savants, whose engineers at
least equal ours?

So is it permissible for the *Abramid Orthodoxy movement* to
be anything other than the *development of a Scientific and Social doctrine?*

MORE ON SEMIRAMIS AND BABYLON

But let's go back to Semiramis. I will mention only for the
sake of memory the colossal bridges which she had constructed on the river, on pillars spaced every twelve feet; the
cement underwater; the attachment of stones with iron cleats;
the prismatic shape of the piles cutting the waters; the cedar
and cypress floors, thirty feet wide, laid on enormous palm tim-
ber planks; the colossal docks on each side of the Euphrates;
the temple of Jupiter or Belus with his college of astronomers;
the gigantic statue of Semiramis on horseback, threatening
with a javelin a panther, symbol of the Indian Empire; the
statue of Ninus killing with a spear a lion, symbol of Zoroaster's Iran, etc., etc.

A last word about the immense terraces, known as hanging
gardens, and we will have described summarily the metropolitan masterwork of Sémiramis.

But the notion of the arbitral Empire which had preceded
her arbitrary empire, and which remained here and there, like
an ever-present witness and a judge, was haunting this imperial
anarchist.

So, unprovoked, she declared war on Stabrobates, then the
current Kousha.

A war she had been preparing for a long time.

For three years, as the labor force became less necessary in the capital, Semiramis had enlisted in her army all the reserves of her empire. Moreover, she had bound by treaties the whole Confederation of Phoenician Republics to obtain its war navy, and change their merchant ships into military transport, in case of surprise attack by the Persian Gulf peoples.

From Phoenicia, from Syria, from the islands of the Mediterranean, she had brought in maritime engineers to build a fleet for the navigation of rivers, and to strengthen the corps of pontoniers.

In order to counterbalance the tremendous support that the elephants provided to the artillery and transports of the Emperor of India, she had built enormous war machines brought on the back of camels.

At the end of the third year, 3,000,000 foot-soldiers, 500,000 horsemen, 100,000 war chariots and war machines, 100,000 soldiers mounted on camels were mobilized and concentrated in Bactria.

Sabrobates replied by a no less formidable defense organization. His army was even larger, and to defend the Indus he had amassed up to 4,000 bamboo boats.

Then he sent to Semiramis, through his ambassador, a letter from the Sovereign Pontiff, asking the Empress of Assyria to suspend an unjust war, which no provocation had motivated. Ninus' widow responded by launching the boats of war, and the fight began on the Indus.

The dearly disputed victory remained on the side of iniquity, Semiramis' side, which hastened to attribute it, as nowadays, to the God of the armies.

In fact, the Indian emperor had simulated a flight to provoke the crossing of the Indus by Semiramis' army.

An immense bridge was built across the river by the Assyrian engineers, and the whole army crossed over, Semiramis forward.

60,000 men remained on the other bank, to keep the bridgehead from surprise attack.

Sabrobates soon unmasked himself and launched a battle.

After a terrible massacre, the Assyrian army was put to flight, and the Kousha himself tried to capture Semiramis. Her horse saved her, and she joined her troops, who were crashing down, crossing back the Indus Bridge. Then she ordered the bridge destroyed, and it fell under the vanguard troops of Stabrobates.

On the orders of the Sovereign Pontiff, Stabrobates remained on the Hindu side of the river, the crossing of which was considered impure since the time the followers of Irshu had been sent back by the Orthodoxes to live west of the Indus river.

Thus behaved the two types of empires, which Moses will oppose under the names of Kush and Nimerod.

Kush limits itself to the defense of its territory, while Nimerod, essentially conquering, arbitrary and brutal, is however vanquished.

The Kousha granted Semiramis the exchange of prisoners of war, and the Empress of Assyria returned to Bactria, having lost two-thirds of her army, or 2,500,000 men, says Diodorus of Sicily, to which must be added an enormous amount of resources and money.

One must be aware that without the firearms and "lightning weapons" prohibited by the code of the Gentous, to which we alluded when writing in a previous chapter about *Science in Antiquity*, such a loss of life would be absolutely inexplicable and impossible, the loss in our wars currently (1883 AD) not exceeding, on average, seven per cent of the total army. In an *article of the Gentous' code, firearms and lightning weapons were prohibited*, due to the fact they could be killing more than 100 men at a time.

Ancient Science still saved India; and not having been the attacker, it was not deemed responsible for the evils which Semiramis alone had provoked.

SOCIAL AND GEOLOGICAL TURMOILS

Subsequent to the reign of this great feminine figure, the Anarchy was represented by sovereigns without faith or law, such as Aralios, Armatristis and Belochus, who ruled their own subjects and the peoples they conquered with iron fist and bloody politics.

Once again, the Nations prayed to the ghost of the ancient Authority.

However, in order to put an end to this supreme intervention of Science and Consciousness, of Wisdom and Justice, Belochus cowardly murdered the Great Lama, and with his own bloody hands seized the tiara and put it on his head, as Julius Caesar will do nearly 2,000 years later.

Then all the sanctuaries mourned the Social God, in the person of his highest representative, now definitively struck by the personal Power, incarnation and crowning of all the iniquities.

The Pontiffs of Thrace, Etruria, Hesperia, those of Iberia of the Caucasus, those of the ancient Hebyreh, the Tobbas of Arabia, all called upon the Lord, and detached the kings and the viceroys from the imperial jurisdiction of Babel, this "Carnage" Court of Appeal presided over by Assassination and Theft, scepter in hand, tiara on the front.

But, alas! To untie these kings and viceroys from all bonds was to precipitate them into feudalism, into the personal government of men and territories, into military competition, unless they were directly connected with the Kousha, himself deferring to the High Court of Justice and the Supreme Court of God represented by the Great Lama.

The Anaxes of the Thracians, the Larthes of the Etruscans, the Rhèges of the Vasques, did in the former colonies of the Aries what their crowned colleagues were doing in the metropoles. They took advantage of supra-governmental anarchy to impose on their own countries an unchecked power, suppressing, as much as they could, the liberties and the social powers of the three Councils.

The despot of Babylon raised up innumerable armies against them, which, as always, were reinforced by the Turanian mercenaries and the European Kelts of Thor.

That despot forced the Phoenician confederations to provide him with their navy; and for three hundred years the Earth and the Sea drank streams of human blood.

The third of Asia centralized by Assyrian Caesarism, aided by Northern Europe, rushed towards Southern Europe, which had as allies only what remained of the Orthodox temples, in Egypt, Ethiopia, Arabia and the Bodhones of Africa.

This bloody dawn of the presidency of intergovernmental relations by brutal Force, by Physical Fate, manifested with all the plagues at once.

Prohibited weapons were grasped from the temples. The forests of the Caucasus, Balkans, Greece, Italy, and Spain were burned down, and the Hespérians mountains were now called *Pyrenees, burning flesh* (Pyr=fire/nee=human flesh)

The Soul of the Earth was stirred by the fury of the collective Spirits of the Humans and the anarchy propelled by them into its atmosphere. Out of patience and fed up with iniquity, the old *Mother unleashed* in her turn the anarchy of her *worst geological periods.*

The Central Fire shook off the frail skin of the Globe; the Sea rose, and some appalling local deluges went to slap Attica, Asia Minor, and Tatarah. Lakes surged out the Thessalian mountains.

For 7 years the Atmosphere refused to give its rains to arable land. Mount Etna spat in Space its first flames, and the ground rippling like a furious ocean, swallowed mountains, islands, cities and devoured peoples.

Since the year 1930 BC, since the infernal crime of Belochus, the earthly Social State and the Planet itself were like possessed and in the grip of all sorts of convulsions.

In this frightful tragedy famine and plague raised their vengeful heads.

Rivaling fiercely with the Caesars of Babel, the Kelts of Thor, the descendants of the old cannibals of Europe threw themselves savagely on the Phoenician confederations and the debris of the ancient colonies.

When *Providence* presides over the destinies of the peoples, in the institutions which are proper to it, from the highest social summits to the last of the homes, Intelligence, Wisdom, Science, are everywhere present.

But when, in its place, on these ruined institutions, reigns *Fate* attracted by an arbitrary General Government, the bad will tumble down, from the summit to the abyss which, in turn, reverberates towards the social peaks all the destructions they have provoked.

Not only did the kings oppose the new Babylonian empire, and, for lack of superior authority, crushed the peoples; moreover this fatal example influenced the fathers of family, and arbitrariness extended everywhere.

No human collectivity was spared, India and China no more than others.

Here, Sahadeva, captain of bandits, kills the king of Magadha and seizes his crown.

There, another adventurer of the sword, Bogh-Dhant, declares himself sovereign of Sirinagour.

Further on, another troublemaker assassinates a centenarian, the old King of Justice Nanda, and grabs his savant-initiate's crown and his scepter sculpted with the Aries' head.

One could multiply to infinity the characteristic details of this time, but for what purpose?

To get rid of these poorly known times, *due to its ignorance of the Societies that preceded them*, the official teaching of our Universities closed them in a black cabinet and keyed them under the name *Heroic Ages*.

Unsurprisingly the chronology of the Septuagint, of St. Jerome, of Usserius, is in accord with such ignorantism; furthermore, Higher Education and what is commonly called High Studies, render all these capitulations of the intellectual consciousness so obvious, that the pure and simple Truth cannot be avoided any longer.

To qualify these appalling anarchical times with the beautiful name of Heroic Ages is to boldly slander the religious

Universities of Antiquity, who applied the name of Heroes to a whole different class of men than to adventurers and political bandits.

Properly described that Age must be called feudal Revolution of Local Authorities against the Metropolitan Empire of Assyria.

It was at the time of Semiramis that took place, among the Orthodox Kaldean, *the Abramid or neo-Ramid*, the movement which we will now examine.

That movement was consistent with the Universal response of the two High Councils against Pure Politics.

Here we must resort to *Moses' scriptures*.

Chapter XI of his Book of Principles is, properly speaking, the second chapter of a second Book, of a second series consecutive to Cosmogony and deserving the name of Androgony.

This second Decade deals with the *Spiritual Constitution of the Earth*, and, consequently, deals with the occult Principles of the entire Social State.

ABRAM: ARCHETYPE OF A NEW SOCIAL FOUNDATION

Abram is there considered as a *Principle*, as a specific Spirit of Social Organism, of which the man named *Abraham* was only the impersonal representation, comparable to the Hiram of the Knights Templar, comparable to all the symbols summing up the Spirit of the collective Body of an Order, religious, military or other.

This is what the translations of Exoteric Genesis say: Ch. XI, v. 26 to 31.

"Thareh begat Abram, Nachor, Aran.
Aran engendered Lot and died before Thareh, at Ur in Kaldea.
Abram and Nachor took women. That of Abram was called Sarai, that of Nachor Melka, sister of Jescha, these last two daughters of Aran.
Thareh took Abram Lot, Sarai, and brought them out of Ur to go to Khanaan."

If one were to stop the inquiry at that *exoteric sense*, one would rightly ask why Moses, High priest of Osiris, took the trouble to relate the above genealogy.

However, in their *savant ideographism*, those few lines reveal such an *esoteric sense* that it would take a whole book to comment on them. We will not examine here the Geogonic side proper, the teachings of certain Mysteries relating to the constitution of the physical and Hyperphysical Atmosphere of our Globe.

We will therefore stick to Androgony per se, and here again we will remain in the average of the current European understanding; for otherwise we would be intelligible only for a hundred Pundits, Lamas, Tibetan Initiates, Chinese Literates, and Jewish Kabbalists.

First, it should be noted that, faithful to Dorian Mathematics, to the Qualitative Arithmology of temples, Moses never states a Principle, either celestial or terrestrial, without immediately naming its constitutive Trinity or Triad.

He thus presents the Unity or Universality of this Principle in a Quaternary or a Tetrad: *1 + 3*.

Regarding the Organic God, *Iod*: He defines it as *Iod-Ê-Vau-É*.

Regarding the living universe, 1 *Adam-Eve*: He manifests it in three terms, +3 *Kain-Abel-Seth*.

Regarding Life's Principle of our solar system, named Noah: the Triad appears immediately, to constitute with this Unit the usual Quaternary: *1 (Noah) + 3 (Shem-Ham-Japhet)*.

At last, regarding a Social Principle, named *Thareh: Moses* manifests it again in a triune form, *Abram-Nahor-Aran*.

With regard to the main purpose of this book, here is the meaning of the hierograms which constitute the Quaternary of Thareh:

Thareh is a regulating Principle corresponding to Thor and Thorah. It indicates:

1- as historical memory, the zodiacal coat of arms of the ancient European Kelts and Turanians of Asia;

2-as an astronomical reference, it designates the entry of

the Sun at the start of the Spring season in the zodiacal Taurus;

3- regarding the position of the Earth, it is the time when all the Dorian Tradition was overshadowed by this Taurus/Assyrian Sign (Ashour), symbol of the Assyrian schismatic empire.

Indeed, when the Secondary and Higher Studies were reserved to Initiates under the name of Mysteries, the Festival of the Universal Generation, coinciding with the Spring equinox, was occurring as the Sun was entering the first degrees of the zodiacal Taurus.

At that moment, the symbolic seeds, the sacred stallions, living hieroglyphs, came out of the temples, where one preserved with perfect science all the types of the terrestrial Life corresponding to the Cosmic Life. One day, in his prophecies Hermes Trismegistus will say: *"Ignoring our Science and our Wisdom, the future will accuse us to have worshipped plants and animals!"*

Ignorance, indeed, coupled with fanaticism, did not fail to add this insult to so many others.

Then, *emblems symbolizing the position of the Earth and of its Solar System within the Universe*, were exhibited during day and night festivals, which also made current ignorance claim they worshipped the Stars, while in reality it was the Universal Spirit and Soul that was acknowledged there, as well as the living Intelligences, generated by the ineffable Union of Universal Spirit and Soul.

ABRAM'S FAMILY: BIBLICAL EMBLEMS AND SYMBOLS

In truth, the constitutive Triad of Thareh is Abram, Nachor, Aran, signaling the opening of a new Cycle-Era.

1 - *Ab-Ram*, means both *paternity and filiation of Ram*, that is, Renovation of the Aries Social Organization, based on the Scientific Intellectuality of the Lamb.

2 - *Nacho*r, means the Pause of the Movement.

3 - *Aran*, means Occultation of the Generating Fire.

This last hierogram is completed in *Lot*, which expresses the Enclosement of the Mystery, like the "Lut" of the Temple, the Cement of the Sanctuary, the Oath of Initiation.

Thus, the group of Orthodoxes, who had accepted the Law of Taurus in the hope of bringing it back to that of Aries, is expatriating while taking along this scientific and social Synthesis, hierogrammatically hidden in the word "Thareh".

But that Synthesis is fundamentally neo-Ramid, intending at stopping the movement of Anarchy, and at reconstructing the Dorian Initiation, while placing the antagonistic matter of the Sexes well hidden in the depth of esotericism.

The common translations of the first three verses of Ch. XII of *Genesis*, provide a good glimpse of the exoteric meaning:

"Then the Lord said to Abram: Come out of your land, from your Kinship, and from the house of your Father (that is leave the Law and Thareh's regime) *and come to the land on Earth that I will reveal to you. I will bring a great people out of you ... and all the peoples of the Earth will be blessed in you."*

Abram and Nachor take Women, that is to say, in sacred ideography, Souls of Life, Creative Faculties, Genetic Powers, Organic Intelligences.

Abram, renewal of the constitution of Ba-Rama, or Brama, has the same Woman: Sarai, reappearance of Saravasti.

This hierogram means *Sphere-Ray, Sa-Rai.*

This indicates that the Abramid movement, coming from a broken Cycle, tends to its Universal reconstitution in Science and in the Social Order.

Nachor, the pause of the naturalistic movement, has for symbolic Woman *Melka*, Melting of the Earth, *Mel-Ka*, sister of *Yeska, the Life or the Salvation of the whole Earth.*

These etymological definitions, although they do not deliver the scientific vigor of the transcendental sense, will allow us to brush away the details, and *reveal the higher purpose of the Abramids.*

Thus, from the Kaldean Priesthood weakened by the arbitrary government, emerges a synthetic, encyclopedic, initiation movement, that is aiming at saving the entire Earth, merging all its political divisions, and bringing them back to the intellectual and social Unity of the Ancient Synarchy.

LAND OF KANAAN=POWER OF "CONVERTIBILITY".

Finally, as antagonist cults and political governments weaken both the Religious Authority and the Social Order, the neo-Ramid group posits in Principle its Alliance with Life and the Economic classes, meaning in hieroglyphic style, alliance with the *Land of Kanaan.*

It should be noted that this last hierogram *Khana-an* expresses the Androgonic viewpoint of the ancient Emporium, which the English today calls the Stock Exchange, the very principle of Emporocracy.

Conjoined virtues of *Kain* and *Cham*, that hierogram embodies by Kain the grand physical economy of the Universe, in Cham the model of our Solar System and in Khanaan the model of our Globe and our planetary social organism.

At the comparative level, finally, this word Khanaan applies either to the *Convertible forces of the Economy,* or to the individuals who transact with those forces: financiers, industrialists, merchants, artisans.

Thus, in his *Sarai,* in his complete *encyclopedic Sphere,* which Moses, the Prophets, and Jesus Christ will later develop, the Abramid project has calculated in advance, with an extreme precision, by which levers the Orb of human activities could one day be brought back to a common Measure, to a universal Law and Center.

Without revealing more than necessary certain levels of profoundness, I will point out, however, that economic science, barely sketched out today in Europe, was then especially developed.

Thus, the squashing to which the Kaldean Caesarism subjected the Peoples, in this economical plane as well as on all levels, was the object of universal criticism.

Many attempted to escape all the anti-economic conditions created by the vast political and military centralizations perpetually antagonistic one with the other; and en masse, as it happens today towards America and Australia, they fled towards the Confederate countries (Etruria/Anatolia/Armenia), where commerce being the principal concern, *the intellectually minded peoples were free to pursue other goals.*

Consequences of permanent taxes and continual wars, bankruptcy and famine were pervasive in the Kaldean empire, when the Abramid Dorians exited that land pursuant to the defeat of Semiramis by the Kousha of India.

In Egypt, that similar religious order took root among the Dorians of the University of Thebes.

This movement even reached up to a certain extent the Pharaoh who was a member of the College of the Gods, and revealed to him the scope of that scientific and social encyclopedia.

But the Grand Master of the Order in Egypt did not present this Synthesis as his own; he rather presented it as a masterwork, which he would support if necessary.

ABRAM AND SARAI MEET PHARAOH OF EGYPT (1939 BC)

This is how we should read chapter XII of Genesis, from verse 11 to 20.

The translators' exoteric interpretation attributes to Abram a singular character.

Verses 14, 15: *"The Egyptians saw that this woman was very beautiful, and the first men of the land having given Pharaoh notice, and having praised her before him, she was taken away and brought to the king's palace."*

Fortunately, *Sarai* means *Sphere-Ray or Encyclopedia*, and *Abram* means *the Renovation of the Law of Ram-Aries and the Intellectuality of the Lamb.*

The Orthodoxes of Egypt welcomed the reviving project supported by the Abramid Order, but the Pharaoh, warned by the secret police of the Kaldean Empire, soon was made aware that this was an anti-political movement contrary to the Anarchy of his Personal Power. Hence verses 18 and 19 of the same chapter, which must not be taken in their exoteric aspect:

"And Pharaoh sent for Abram, and said unto him: Why have you acted with me in that way? Why didn't you tell me she was your wife?

Why did you say she was your sister, letting me think I could take her for a wife? So here is your wife, I am giving her back to you now. Take her and go away".

It is obvious that, if an *esoteric intelligence* did not exist under these rudimentary translations, those scenes and dialogs would be worthier of a comedy played at the Theater of the Palais-Royal than of a Sacred Book of this magnitude.

Pharaoh knowing that the Reformation movement, which had first seduced him, was specific to the Abramids and not an initiative of the Empress of Assyria, did not want to find himself at war against this formidable opponent for the simple satisfaction of a group of discontent people, which did not matter much to him.

Moreover, even in Egypt, the Pharaoh feared any indiscretion of the Orthodox party, for the invasion of Shalit (leader of the Hiksos) was approaching.

ABRAMIDS MOVE BACK INTO SYRIA-PHOENICIA-KANAAN

This is why he expelled the Abramids' Order, along with the Symbolic Wife (Sarai), meaning *their Intellectual and Social Reformation.* The Order then directed its steps towards the emporocratic confederations of Syria.

Thus, in modern history, we see the free thinkers traveling to the free Hanseatic cities of Flanders or England, in search of a liberty incompatible with the great military states and the personal governments, entangled one with another.

Ancient Syria, which being affiliated almost entirely with the schism of the Yonijas, had not, however, submitted to the Empire of Assyria.

Syria was bound to Assyria by treaties; but, though its vassal, it had kept its independence.

The pattern of emporocratic or trading nations is the same everywhere.

The Emporium was the core of these Societies; while the University, that is to say, the Temple, came only as a second line.

The Third Council, the House of Commons so to speak,

governed under the name of the Senate, with a president, a magistrate, or tyrant, executor of the Law of Thor.

It was the bourgeois democracy of the republics of antiquity as it is nowadays, with a religion purely formalistic on the outside and on the inside reduced to official naturalist teachings. The first two High Councils, Council of the Gods and Council of God, had been abrogated.

Thus the Third Council was at the mercy of the first anarchist demagogue able to grasp a crown.

That part of the world was predestined by its geographical location to be a true country of Kanaan, the land par excellence of trade and economic transactions between the three continents. There, races were mixed as well as languages, although the Phoenician tongue dominated. Prosperity flowed abundantly along with freedom and peace, these benefits growing as one moved away from the large States at war.

Asia Minor was then what it will certainly become in the future: a sort of England and Holland, a Switzerland adorned with a sea and more. In this respect, as in many others, the sphere and the radius of the Abramid Cycle was perfectly oriented, and the exact Kaldean science contours were very perceptible to observers.

In the Aries Empire, Syria, as its name implies, was declared the land of the Lord (Sir-ya), that is to say, neutral and submitted directly to the Kousha and the Lama.

The name of *Judea*, which will later be called *Pilistana* or the land of the *Pallas*, will remind of this ancient theocratic organization.

This name *Judea* is found not only in India, as I said, but in the ancient kingdom of Siam named Judea, which also was directly overseen by the Lama of Paradesa.

THE CITY OF SALEM: CENTER OF UNIVERSAL PEACE

In the midst of the Ionian invasion, coming from India and Touran, only one city had remained as an island with an organization conforming to the ancient Order.

It was the ancient *Salem* whose name means *Universal Peace*.

The organization of the holy city of Salem was such: Temple of the supreme God under the pontificate of an Initiate, who carried, besides the miter, the golden crown of the Royal Arbitrators, the horns of Aries, the symbols of the Lamb, all three Synarchical governing Councils.

Respected by the schismatics, that royal and sacerdotal Synarchy was protecting the freedom of all the temples and all the secondary thrones of Asia Minor. Salem's Synarchy represented the former most ancient Arbitrage, the great scientific and Social God, upholding the Peace of the Teachings and Powers.

There, during worship, the *sacrifices were not bloody*, like those of the Initiates to the great Mysteries. It was instead the *Communion of Bread and Wine*, as practiced in all Orthodox Sanctuaries. The great political storms, which strike and break the great kingdoms, had passed over the towers of this city, leaving intact its original Synarchy.

Like a Switzerland of the East, Asia Minor and Syria were all the more secure because four kingdoms would have contended for them, arms in hand, as soon as one of them would have planted its sword there; and that's what will happen.

However, 1,000 years of anarchic conflict between the great directorates of the ancient Society had not been without consequences, there as everywhere else.

Syria was then undergoing an internal crisis, which Abram and his initiates were watching attentively even more so because they knew the causes of it.

The Assyrians, plotting, casting away their mask of diplomacy, intervened militarily, though often indirectly, in the disputes of the royal cantons of these Phoenician republics.

Twelve years before, a prince of Susiana (in Iran), Kedor Lahomer, a puppet of Assyrian politics, had subjected to his arbitrary Power the senates and their crowned magistrates. That was a disguised violation of the ancient pact which the political regions born of the Ionian schism, comprising the empire of Assyria, the Phoenician republics or federations, had contracted in order to guaranty their mutual independence.

But what are political treaties worth? The history of Europe is here to tell us.

In the presence of this violation of ancient rights which the schismatics themselves had placed under the invocation of their religion, the Melchizedek, the King of Justice of Salem as sole Arbitrator of the ancient Order, kept an attitude of absolute neutrality, waiting for the schismatic kings to resort to his arbitral Authority.

Berah king of Sodom, Birsçah king of Gomor, Scinab king of Admah, Sçenneber king of Tseboiim, and Tsohar king of Belah had already taken arms.

Reinforced by his allies from Schinhar, Ellasar and Galilee, *Kedor-Lahomer* had to confront an almost general revolt. At Hashtheroth-Karnaim, at Hanat Kirjathaim, at Paran, at Mispat, at Hatsatsu-Thamar, he had to crush the armies of this confederacy.

The Rephaim, the Zuzim, the Emim, the Horeans, the Amorites, the men of the plains, and those of the mountains, rose against that Assyrian arbitrariness (led by Kedor-Lahomer).

Finally, in a pitched battle, the five kings of the League of Syrian Independence were defeated in the Siddim Valley by the four kings who were committed to the policy of Babylonian Caesarism.

Meanwhile, Shalit, general-of-the desert, ambitious anarchist, working on his own account, was crushing Egypt and the Theban Orthodoxy, although they had been warned in advance by the Abramids.

At that time the grand master of the Dorian Affiliation was at the head of a college of 318 Initiates: *see Genesis, Ch. XIV, verse 14.*

Taking refuge among his allies Mamre, Escol and Haner, seemingly neutral in these debates, as was the orthodox king of Salem, the Dorian Master suddenly intervened against the Assyrian league.

The Dorian Order, by force of arms, regains the treasury of the Alliance, as well as esoteric books which, under the hieratic name of *Lot*, had been seized by the conquerors.

MELCHISEDEK AND ABRAM

It is at this moment that the *exoteric Bible* shows the Dorian Order openly allied with the vanquished kings; and at that time, in the Bible, appears *the great personage of Melchizedek.*

Jesus and the Christian movement will, 2,200 years later, refer to this luminous Tradition, to this Authority anterior and superior to the Judaism then weakened by its distancing from its core mission and entrapped into the sectarianism and the particularism of a national or political cult.

Follows the biblical text, or rather, the ordinary version of the text, except two salient words of which I will give the esoteric meaning: *"In the royal valley, the King of Justice of Salem brings bread and wine, because he was Pontiff of El-Helion.*

He blessed them and said: Blessed be neo-Ramism by El-Helion, by YHVH, Supreme Male Generator, who regulates and moves (kouneh) the Heavens and the Earth! and blessed be YVHV, Supreme Male Generator, who put the "contraries" in your power."

And the Order of Abramids gave the tithe of the Whole to the king of Justice." Those few words reveal many things. The position of chief of the Dorian Order of Kaldea vis a vis Melchizedek, King of Justice according to ancient Synarchy, is that of an Initiate before an Initiator, a disciple vis a vis a master, a member of the Council of the Gods vis a vis a representative of the Supreme Council of God.

Both are Dorian, and know each other for such; for, from among the sacred names the king invokes the name which signifies Supreme Generative Principle, the Male Spirit, *Hel- Iôn, Principle of Hyperphysical Light.*

The Feminine faculty is *Ionah, organic Soul of the World*, whose physical light is one expression.

Moreover, notice that those two co-present *Lingayas* both

worship by means of non-bloody symbols, *bread and wine reserved for the Highest Initiation and the Highest Priesthood of the Religion of the Lamb* in all the sanctuaries of the ancient Empire of Aries.

But, one must notice, *Abram receives*, and *Melchizedek gives* this Communion, which entails as a ritual and academic consequence, the Highest Initiation, a superior instruction of Abram by the Pontiff-King of Salem, and a testamentary transmission of the ancient scientific and social Synarchy.

Furthermore, this King of Justice has *no ancestors*.

His tiara and crown originate from the ancient Law, through Initiation and Merit, consecrated by the Supreme Pontiff, the great Lama who was then a refugee in the Himalayas.

The principle embodied by Abram goes back, as we have seen, to the College of the Gods, and thus to the Council of God of the Kaldean Priesthood, designated by Moses under the hierogram *Arpha-Chesed*.

Abram pays to Melchizedek, to the King of Justice, the tithe of the whole, the *tithe of the complete Cycle*, because the Pontiff of the City of Peace-Salem was still the representative of the integrality of the most ancient Law.

However, the first two Councils of Kaldea were no longer directly in touch with the Sovereign Pontiff.

Weakened by the bureaucratic government of the Assyrian Empire, they no longer represented the ancient Authority, whose fundamental condition was to curb the Power, and not to be curbed by it.

Belochus was soon to steal the tiara in the blood of a Sovereign Pontiff.

Thus, in order to reconstruct, in the course of time, the ancient Intellectual and Social Universality, to reconstruct the Cycle of the *Lamb and Aries*, the neo-Ramid Order moved to the free countries of the Phoenician Emporocracy, after having its new Synthesis reviewed by the Orthodox of Egypt *who saw that she was very beautiful*; Genesis, Ch. XII, v. 14.

REFOUNDATION OF ANCIENT SYNARCHY

Moreover, the neo-Ramid Order and its 318 initiates, sided with the vanquished of the Syrian confederation against the Assyrian empire, and then stripped their Initiation from the allies of Babylon, initiation which had been distorted by them, and which they used only for political gain.

Finally, holding the treasury of his Order, which had been stolen, the head of this College of Orthodoxy submits himself to the representative of the ancient Authority, and receives the testamentary consecration.

This is the point of connection which *links the neo-Ramid movement to the scientific Intellectuality* and Social Doctrine of the ancient Synarchy, which will later determine the Constitution of a *People destined to safeguard the 50 Chapters containing this Intellectuality and this Social Doctrine.*

In the next chapter, we will return to Egypt, which Shalit (of the Hiksos) has just invaded.

We will closely follow the development of the neo-Ramid movement among orthodox Dorians, in lands governed by schismatic kings.

We will finally see *Moses masterfully seize the reins of the Order*, and call to him the Bodhonian Kelts, the old guard of the Synarchists, around a Royal University of God, *Is-ra-El*, contraction of *Iswara-EI*.

∞

CHAPTER XI
EGYPT - THE ORTHODOXES – MOSES

SCIENCE AND WISDOM ENCODED IN THE DIVINE VERB

Before continuing this expose, it is essential that the reader grasps the crucial import of the *Dorian Science*, which the Orthodoxes of Kaldea and Egypt wanted to save from the wreck of intellectual anarchy by producing testamentary legacy books. As this Science is partially contained in the *first 50 chapters of Moses*, it is of primary importance to be aware these books were *written in the sacerdotal manner* of the Orthodoxy of Kaldea and Egypt.

The Science of the Written Word had been elaborated by them, and before them, by the Sanctuaries of the Paradesa and India, up to its Principles, to the point of contact, to the chain of concordances and correspondences of the Language with what our quasi theologians call *the Verb* without fully understanding its profundity.

It is from this height of ancient Knowledge that the *written Word* was descending, like a Soul of social life, whenever a scholar of those times thought it necessary to bear witness to the sacerdotal and royal Mastery, by redefining a human Society around a Genic Book, suitable for a particular human environment, for any particular or general purpose.

It is in this spirit that we have seen Zoroaster write his lost but discoverable books.

It is in this depth of Science that we have seen Fo-Hi write the Y-Kings and Christna remodel the Vedas. It is in the same spirit, finally, that *Moses*, drawing from the double source of the encyclopedia of Kaldea and the hermetic libraries of Egypt and Ethiopia, will one day write the *Sepher(Thorah)*.

THE DIRE CONSEQUENCES OF LANGUAGE MISUSE

But just, as the physical faculty of secreting milk is extinguished for lack of practice in women whose mothers have not breastfed, in the same way after a small number of generations *the hyperphysical constitution of a human being can atrophy,* for lack of learning, not only the sciences, not only entire chains of realities and truths, but even the faculties of insighting and conceiving them, enjoying them and procreating them in the Intellectual Life of our Realm.

This is what happened to the Jews, and, consequently, to the whole of Christendom, and to the other exoteric communions, as the *ancient Science had to re-veil itself,* and to hide its Authority from the eyes of the persecuting political Power.

As long as the Synarchy of the Aries had lasted, that is to say until the thirty-second century BC, the scientific language was almost identical in the ideography of all Confederate Sanctuaries.

Hence verse 1 of chapter XI of Genesis, which we have already quoted. In the same chapter, we see that the division of Thoughts in regard with the Sex of the Principles, immediately engendered the division of Ideography across all the Sciences and all the applied Arts.

From then on, the Turanian and Aryas-Kushites schools opposed each other under the respective names of Kaldea and Akkad. Due to the schism, the *spoken languages, or feminine languages,* entered in the temples, and *phonetic empiricism gradually took precedence over scientific ideographism.*

VARIOUS REMEDIES TO LANGUAGE BLURS

Fo-Hi radically remediated this dire deviation from the underlying Source Language, the Savant Language.

But after him, without resorting to Fo-Hi's extreme algebraic ideographic reform, *Moses adopted without any change the traditional sacred language* of the Orthodox Sanctuaries of Egypt and Ethiopia; making use of it with genius.

What in fact was this language? The *language known today as Hebrew?* Not at all.

For a language to be constituted, it is necessary that a people live, united in *a Body of Nation,* bound by common institutions, enlightened by a special or specific intellectuality and teaching.

It is thus that a national Species unfolds through Life, a language in its image. Now, at that time there was no *Hebrew people per se*, but everywhere there were Bodhones Kelts, keeping a more or less clear memory of the ancient Arbitral Synarchy.

Everywhere, or almost everywhere, in order to escape the arbitrary administrative censuses, military conscription, land surveyors, they, as much as possible, shuttled back and forth, from one country to another, declaring themselves members of the ancient Empire, Kushites, peoples of free cities or neutral countries.

For the Egyptians, as for all other politically governed Peoples, they were the *Wanderers* par excellence, *the Bodhones, the Apurus*, both names meaning "without shelter", without fire or homeless: the Apurus of Africa today have the same origin.

But, outside and above these multitudes fiercely opposed to Politics and Arbitrariness, there were other classes of sedentary peoples who were exactly in the same state of mind.

Among those classes all the Orthodoxes of the Council of the Gods and of the Council of God were protesting, tacitly or openly, against the deviation implemented by the General Government or particular governments.

According to their degree of esoteric instruction only the members of the Council of God, could know, understand, and write the sacred ideographic language.

But the Bodhones spoke only vulgar dialects of all the centralized peoples, among whom they lived willingly or by force.

In Egypt, the vulgar and phonetic language was then Phoenician.

The *language of the temples was not spoken, reduced to ideographic principles*, as rigid as could be.

That original ancient language was the result of combinations of the Life and Intellectuality of the Black Race and the White Race.

The ideographism of that idiom was so much above the understanding of the people Moses will assemble, that its members will constantly forget its meanings and that *translators will always have to paraphrase* it into the current phonetic or vulgar language.

Until the establishment of Jewish royalty, the Initiates of the two first high Councils, Council of God and Council of the Gods, will have no greater concern than perpetual *study of that ideographic language.*

After the establishment of the kingship and its annihilation by the empire of Assyria, *Ezra-Esdras* will carry out for the Jews a reform analogous to that of Fo-Hi, by establishing a Corps of Literates, replacing the two first High Councils mutilated by the Kings.

Would the 50 chapters of the Sepher-Torah have been so difficult to understand and teach, if they had expressed ideas of a nature to be written in any phonetic tongue? Certainly not.

The ordinary student of our day can read Homer in Greek, Virgil in Latin, the Koran in Arabic, and analytic thoughts in all the spoken tongues of the world. The situation is quite different in regard with the written works emanating from the Dorian Order, as well as those connected to the universal synthetic Principles, at the level of *Pure intelligible Truths.*

This is why, when one read texts bequeathed by Moses to the Jews, says St. Paul, speaking of the uninitiated Jews, *"a veil blurs their comprehension".*

Now the blur is on the comprehension of the listener or the ignorant reader and does not apply to what *Moses* intended to make understood; for he would not have hermetically veiled his thought, *without leaving the means of unveiling it,* which was the way of Revelation in all antiquity.

LINGUISTIC PRINCIPLES OF THE DORIAN LEGACY

What is, then, the essence of this Dorian Order of Ancient Science, this blurred peak of human intellectuality and its ancient manifestation by ideography? Analogically, presented to a non-initiate an equation of astronomy, physics, mechanics, chemistry, will mean nothing although this person can read analytically, hear phonetically and rationally each isolated sign. A veil, too, will blur the comprehension of the non-initiate.

This is true of all the sacred legacies of the hierarchy of the Dorian Sciences and of Ideography, that is to say of the Symbolism by which they are manifested through the High Arts, all of which are only different facets, exterior forms of the same *universal Language*, reflection of the same Verb.

In vain, the modern archaeologists will dig the earth, the numismatists will stir the medals, the philologists will analyze the runic texts, cuneiform, protomedes, Zends, Kaldeans, Akkadians, Sanscrit, Hieroglyphic, Phoenician, Etruscan or Moisiac, still the veil will keep blurring the European Comprehension, preventing their minds from integrating these legacies as long as *the synthetic Spirit* is not internalized.

However, this ancient Synthesis holds us tight, as the dead holds the living, as the past holds the present, whether the latter knows it or not.

The two billion or so of human atoms that are continually renewing themselves on the Planet, like dust in the whirlwind of an invisible breath, has a *General Spirit* behind it, which moves it, carries it, and directs it. This Spirit has always communicated with visible Humanity by means of *spiritual imprints*, manifesting into social institutions.

The first of these forms is Religion, the Synthesis par excellence. This is why the Judeo-Christian Priesthoods who have been sleeping for so long on their crude translations of the sacred texts, will nonetheless overcome the nineteenth century as they overcame the preceding centuries, as well will they surpass the archaeologists, the philosophers and the exegetes, as they have previously overcome the encyclopedists and so many other illustrious naturalists.

SYNTHETIC SCIENCES VS ANALYTIC MODERN METHOD

In this century dominated by analytical studies, how can one illume the high value and the efficacy of the *ancient Synthesis*, of which our sacred books and our Judeo-Christian creeds are the perpetuation? Above all, it is through social cultural expressions that it manifests, and my 4 *"Missions"* books have no other purpose than to demonstrate that.

One of the most prevalent means for the Synthesis to manifest itself scientifically in the Universe and in the human Social Organism had been, as I said, *Qualitative Mathematics* and *Qualitative Morphology*. Hence the unfolding of the *Ideographic language*.

This is indeed the only method which makes it possible to maintain, while applying it, the *concordance of Science and Life, correspondence of the Intelligible Realm and the Sensorial Order*, of the Occult *invisible* reality and the *visible* Phenomenon, of the Universal and the Particular.

Lacking this method, one inevitably falls into fantasy adorned with the names of metaphysics, theology, etc., etc.

Our current sciences, whatever their development, scarcely allow us to awaken the Life of the synthetic Faculties of Intelligence.

Our modern sciences, being only nomenclatures of phenomena and sensorial effects, of which they still have to reveal, by means of Comparison, the correlations linking them, they still do not contain the tenth part of the corresponding series known to the ancient sciences. In truth, savant antiquity had explored *farther than the correlation of sensorial phenomena,* farther than the physical and chemical convertibility of forces, beyond the equivalence of archetypical symbols, of physical or hyperphysical forms.

The great initiation Mysteries opened the Intelligence on a whole scale of realities and truths even superior to those above mentioned.

It was then that, in possession of all its Faculties, imprinted by *the reflection of the Universe* itself, the Intelligence and the Soul of the human beings were perceiving *from top to bottom and from inside,* the realities that sensorial rationalism can only glimpse at from below upwards and from outside.

Once again, it is this descending method which constitutes

the Essence of Dorian Intellectuality, the characteristic qualities of its sciences and its legacies, as found in books or
ideographic monuments, whatever they may be.

I intend here to give the reader by direct examples, the feel,
the importance of this Degree of Intellectuality, when it manifests itself, as well as when it does not.

Bring together all the modern architects of Judeo-Christianity, all the sculptors, all the painters, and ask them for an
example of their own creation, a work as specific, in its category, as the Parthenon, the great Pyramid, the temples of
Philea, Abu-Sinbel, Dendera, Edfu, Karnac, Ellora in the
Decan, Copan in Guatemala, Nagkon-Ouat or Angkorom
(Angkor) in the Kingdom of Siam.

As in the Middle Ages, Synthetic Science was still radiating
from the depths of its former Eastern Affiliations, it has been
able to bestow Christianity with cathedrals, improperly called
Gothic; the total absence of this same Science today would
make it absolutely impossible to raise any equivalent testimony
fitting our time (1883 AD).

De facto, Architecture is par excellence the Synthesis of
the Visual Arts, and this Synthesis, or Special Ideography, cannot unfold without the Science that nurtures it.

Suppose, nevertheless, that all the modern artists were endeavoring at cooperating intellectually in order to endow
Judeo-Christendom with an auditorium as specific to our time
as the amphitheaters of Greece fitted their time.

Once this monument is built, fully respecting the Synthesis' Principles and the exact concordance between the relevant
Plastic Arts, gather all the poets, all the musicians, all the cho-
reographers, and add all the great thinkers of present time
Judeo-Christendom.

Then ask them to use this auditorium to host an expression
of a Synthesis of their respective Arts, to produce in the present, symbolically reflecting the actual Social State, the
equivalent of the sacred tragedies of Greece and India.

Having that well-built monument, you would not be able

to fill it with poetry, music, dramatic or tragic art, concordant to those Synthesis Principles. Let's move on to another order of proofs or experiment. Bring together all the modern erudite scientists of Judeo-Christianity and ask them to produce, not even a Cosmogony, let alone a Theogony, but a simple correlation of natural and physical sciences, or moral and political sciences at their level. They will produce nothing of true value.

Let's continue the same experiment in regard with a sequence of facts, which will affect you even more directly.

Bring together all the statesmen of present-day Europe, and ask them to organize in Europe alone, not even the ancient Peace of the Aries Empire and the Theocracy of the Lamb, but a simple reduction of armaments and military budgets, a simple outline of permanent arbitration as a substitute for war, and finally a beginning of a Social State common to the Judeo-Christian Nations.

They will only display cunning and force, using cannon shots and *financial extortions* more terrifying than ever.

2 TESTAMENTS: COMPENDIUM OF ETERNAL PRINCIPLES

Where then are to be found the Principles of the Scientific and Social Synthesis? In the *Sacred Books* and nowhere else.

All the forms of impotence we have just mentioned in Art, Science, Sociology, are also proofs of the *necessity of a revival of the Dorian Tradition.* Now neither *Providence* nor its intellectual representatives, who are, for the Judeo-Christians, *Moses and Jesus*, have certainly not let their heirs deprived of a potent Legacy.

However, in order for the promise of the Spirit encrypted in the words to be fulfilled, we must desire it and prove it by repositioning the persons in their proper social categories, into the three specific functional Powers, which are the topic of this book.

Why will Orpheus write an esoteric book on the sacred Verb, later quoted by the Fathers of the Church?

Why will Plato write an exoteric treatise on the property or the symbolism of names and words?

Why does Saint John, the favorite disciple, begin his Gospel with these words: "*In the Principle was the Verb, etc., etc ...?* Men of this quality speak and write only to act according to a sound Principle, and in view of a specific End.

Saint John will begin his Gospel recalling the first word of the Sepher of Moses, Berœshith, Arkê in Greek, *Principle* in English. It is not for nothing that he will revive all the Dorian Intellectuality of the Cycle of Ram, Abramids and Moses.

The books of Moses, from which Jesus draws social consequences, are, in fact, a monument of Dorian hermetism, where, by the force of Science, ideography merges with this universal Genie of the Word, which is called the Verb.

All of the preceding study had but one goal: make the reader understand the *importance of the Abramid movement*, in conformity with what Moses will explicit in his work.

In what follows, I wish to demonstrate that this movement carried within itself an indispensable and undeniable Intellectuality.

I will mention some examples soon. After having read them, the reader may ask: *How is it possible that three separate categories of truths and realities expressed by a single hierogram do not alter each other?*

I will answer this legitimate concern, by reminding that the first 50 Chapters of Moses, mainly the first 20, are founded on definite *several separate Principle layers*. Not only this way of writing does not mix their specific essences; but it is the only way that can make them intelligible.

HOW DO HUMANS PERCEIVE UNITY?

A *Principle is simple in itself.* It cannot be broken down by analysis; it is proven by synthesizing what is identical to it, meaning by analogy.

But the physiological human can conceive nothing simple without virtually decomposing it, as the prism of our atmosphere decomposes the white ray into multiple colors, the sound unit into multiple frequencies, etc., etc.

The human individuality is triple, and therefore the Ternary module is the only relative Unit that can be understood or refracted within a human being.

Being altogether instinctive, intellectual, moral, the human can perceive a fundamental unique Principle, through his own constitution, by condensing it to greatest simplicity and Unity, by force of virtue and science, which means initiation to wholeness, in other words reaching relative simplicity and Harmonic Unity. According to the method of the Divine or Dorian sciences, *Moses proceeded from top to bottom*, from the universal to the particular, from the intelligible to the intuitive, from occulted to the manifested.

But, in all their modes, the evolution of the Principles is mathematically the same, from Cycle to Cycle, be the Cycle the whole Universe or a single Solar System, the Hominal Reign of this Planet or the successive stages of the Planet itself.

HIEROGRAMS KAIN, ABEL, SETH: ESSENTIAL PRINCIPLES

I will now develop the example of *Kain/Abel, Seth*, before directing the path of the reader further behind the veil.

Kain, unveiled as a cosmogonic hierogram, represents the *Principle of Time* opposed to the Principle of the *Ethereal Space, Abel*.

Kain's/Abel's Father is the soulful Universe, inseparably united with its Capacity of ensoulment: *Adam-Eve*.

Their milieu is Plato's heavenly Earth, *Adamah*, the *Universal Substance*.

But what, in itself, is Kain? What is this Principle inherent to *Time-Kain,* which makes us *Time sensitive.?*

And in its Qualitative Unity, that is, in its Universality, in its living Essence, since it is about the living Universe, what is this Principle inherent to *Space-Abel* which *compresses Space* to produce something else that we can perceive as its contents.

Moses conceives Time as the Cause of Universal Centripetal Force. Time devours and transforms, and most certainly it is in itself of a powerful nature, whose positive knowledge would lead very far. Moses opposes it to the Ethereal Space, Cause of Universal Centrifugal Force.

Abel-Space, thus conceived, is a liberating and spiritual Principle par excellence.

But Moses is not a dualistic thinker, as attested by the presence of *Seth*, *third* son of Adam-Eve, born of the virtual overwhelming of Abel by Kain.

Seth, who plays an important role alongside his two symbolic brothers (Kain/Abel), represents Space weight, sidereal, double and six-fold, which is of great significance in Qualitative Mathematics. But these Principles are not material, for this is about the organicity of the Universe, or Cosmogony.

Let's now study the triple Cycle in which each of these hierograms exerts its action.

1-at the androgenic level, *Kain, Kronos*, will be identified as *the Universal Centralizer*, the *Crowned*.

Abel, overwhelmed, will represent the Decentralization.

Seth will represent local Life, establishing the ratio of the Center to the Circumference, and vice versa.

2-Let's go down one more degree, to anthropomorphism pure and simple.

At that level "Kain-Time" is figured as no more than a simple Romulus overwhelming the first Remus, therefore being the model for all the Khans, all the Khongs, all the Kaisers, all the Kings, all the Kaesars and all Monarchs.

These "Kains" subjugate Free Life, found Central Cities, subject the scattered Collectivities, tying them into Physical or Political Unity, by Force.

Instead of the Uræus (the Cobra symbol of sovereignty in ancient Egypt) symbol of the Orbs, they wear a crown of towers, symbol of the Urbs, the City. Always following the same principle in different versions, always opposed to the Principle of infinite renewal through Liberty.

Seth, here again, holding the middle position, participates in the *One Kain-centripetal* and the *Other Abel-centrifugal*, and it is through Seth that the conciliation is made possible between the Centralization Principle and its antagonistic Principle of Decentralization.

One will find these three sons of Adam explained

hieroglyphically in all the Cosmogonies of the Earth.

This does not mean that Moses plagiarized his predecessors, but it signals there is an *organic Constitution of the Cosmos*, and that at certain periods in the Life cycles of Humankind, the *corresponding Science must be updated, according to a renewed Synthesis fitting the Present and the Future.*

NOAH, SHEM. CHAM, JAPHET: NEW EARTH FOUDATION

Within the book of *Noah*, whose name symbolizes the Organic Principle of our Solar system, *Noah* and his three sons *Shem, Cham, Japhet*, manifest the primordial Quaternary, on another plane and in another realm.

On a different plane of reality Shem parallels Abel, and means Ethereal Space, radiant Spirit of our celestial Whirlwind within its Zodiacal Zone, precisely in that space the Egyptians called the Sky of *Akhimous-Sekous*.

Cham expresses Attraction, the Principle of Time proper to our Whirlwind, the Center of its Grand Cycle or Great Year.

Japhet expresses the Filled Space, with its sidereal and intersidereal Gravitation, its balanced organism, or its six-fold duality.

It corresponds to the Principle of *Akhimous-Urdu*.

In the medium sense between exoteric and esoteric, *Shem* represents Light itself, or rather the *Radiation of all intellectual, moral, physical light.*

Cham will be representing the concentration of *Heat. Japheth will represent Specification and Equilibrium* of all *Affinities*, local, elective and electrical, between a center and any circumference within the organic Whirlwind of our Solar System.

Finally, from the anthropomorphic point of view, *Shem* will represent an *enlightened man* or a yellow spiritual man; *Cham* will represent *man of Fire* or of the Equator; *Japheth* will represent a human with blue eyes bright like lightnings or just a *white human*.

KANAAN: CROSSROADS OF SYMBOLISM

Similarly, at the level of *Geogony, Kanaan* will symbolize, superlatively or intellectually, the *Principle of Aggregation*, the

Physical Morphology of the Globe and its four Reigns, as well as their dynamic relationship to their latent Heat. At the level of *Androgony, Kanaan* will be the *Principle of the Economy* of the Societies, in its relation to their intrinsic Energy. In the symbolism of everyday language, kanaan will designate no more than a mere merchant, a kanaanite.

This way of condensing thoughts through Science and Ideographic Art and illustrating the action of the Principles from the most Universal Realm to the most particular, from the most intellectual to the most sensorial, this magic of human language becoming the perfect prism of the divine Verb, is demonstrated without dilution of meaning through the 50 chapters of Moses.

It will therefore be understood, I hope, that a man of flesh and blood will be spoken of in such a book only as a symbol of the Principle it represents essentially, and in function of which he will act. Otherwise, it would be no longer a sacred book of the Doric Order, but a story more or less legendary, a tale for elementary school, written in phonetic, vulgar language.

But by the same token, all the theologians of the World might present the Holy Spirit in the guise of all subspecies of doves, in the ways their materialistic minds can fantasize, such a work would cease to be the scientific expression of Truth, and hence it would be without Life, without an Organic Power of Synthesis with respect to the human and natural sciences.

RENEWED SYMBOLISM OF ABRAHAM AND SARAH

In the previous chapter, I explained that the Dorian movement of the Abramids of Kaldea had as a feminine symbol a *scientific encyclopedia*, named *Sa-rai*, meaning sphere (Sa) mirror or ray (Rai), which later will be renamed *Sa-ra-h,* meaning ray, directing force of a Cycle.

This neo-Synthesis, which was found "beautiful" by the Initiate Orthodoxes of Egypt, surely was deeply upsetting the political Powers, be they schismatic, or having taken advantage of the schism to free themselves more or less from the Authority of the first two high Councils.

That's why we find in Genesis, Ch. XX, v. 16, these words addressed to Sarah by the king of kings Abi-Melech, whose name signifies Principle of military government: *"You will always wear a veil in front of those you meet with, and never forget that you have been my prisoner."* That is to say: *You Sarah are the Higher Truth, but you will not reveal yourself, for, otherwise, as you are the Highest Authority and I am only the Power that seized and subjugated you, lest you would go back to your higher rank in the Social Order and I would go back to my lower rank.*

Accustomed now to Dorian ideographism, the reader can be led further into some of its arcana.

Moses will give his written testimony, having in front of him this Kaldean encyclopedia and the innumerable sacred books of the Orthodoxes, then stored in the Egyptian and Ethiopian Sanctuaries.

Moses' nation, or at least the one that he will constitute, will be a *Royal University of God, Is-Ra-**El**, a sort of Great Pyramid in motion*, and all the new Social Order will be depicted in the same hierogrammatic style, one we must be careful not to materialize, if we want to really understand it.

The genealogies of the Principles expressed by hierograms are all written in the same spirit. Here are some proofs:

Abraham by *Agar*, produces *Ishmael*.

Ag-ar stands for *Central, Igneous Faculty of Earth*.

Is-ma-El, stands for *Principle of fluidic expansion*.

By *Sarah*, that is, by the *Sphere proportional to its Radius*, *Abraham* generates *Is-a-ac, meaning Principle of Aggregation at the Center*.

Finally, by *Ké-Thorah*, meaning *condensation of the Law, establishing the ratio of circumferential Action to Central Action*, he generates six Principles:

1 *Iam-Ran*, Multiple Puissance of Sound;

2 *Ick-San*, Divisible Puissance of the Light;

3 *Mad-An*, Static or Physical Divisibility;

4 *Mad-Ian*, Dynamic or Chemical Divisibility;

5 *Ies-Boch*, Silent Puissance of Void;

6 *Süe*, Undulation, Radiant State, Occultation or Destruction of Matter.

It is to be noted that all these Principles which enunciate so many levels of realities and sciences, emanate from the same Law, *Ke-thorah*, servant of Sarah, meaning *resultant of the Sphere-Radius.*

This law, which is essential to both Qualitative and Quantitative Mathematics, is commonly known as: π Pi= 3,1416…

We must not forget that, more than 2,000 years before this intellectual reform of the neo-Ramid Dorians, the Great Pyramid of Giseh had been built according to these Principles by the Ram Cycle Clerics.

That undeniable Quadrature of the Cercle (Pi) was indeed intended to perpetuate by its symbolic proportions the *Unity of the ancient Synthesis*, including its inner functions.

In Sanskrit, Pa-Rama, Py-Ramid, was symbolizing the Pontifical sovereignty of Ram

THE 12 TRIBES OF ISRAEL: SYMBOLS AND ARCHETYPES

Let's continue to lift the veil of Dorian Science some more:
Jacob-Israel has *Rebekah* for mother.
Reb-ek-kah means *igneous Movement, Center-Earth.*

She is the daughter of *Bàth-ou-El*, meaning Enveloping Space, Void or *Aether-God.*

Here are the sons of *Isa-ac*, meaning *Action of the Aggregation Center on the Angle* or *Central Point.*

I will limit myself to explicating the filiation of *Jacob, Ia-Kob,* meaning *Apparent Movement on the occult Center, Revolution on the Base, Modulation on the Tonic.* When simplified, this hierogram still means *to Subvert* and, by comparison, to *substitute, to supplant.*

I beg pardon for all my past, present, and future neologisms, but to such new ideas, though so ancient, equivalent words are missing in our languages.

From *Le-Ah*, meaning *Unitary League, Harmony of Transitions and Liaisons, Jacob* has six sons like Abraham had six sons from *Kethorah*;

1 *Ru-Ben*, Affiliated Seers;
2 *Sim-Eon*, Olfactives, Auditives, Fluidics of the Inner self;

3 *Lev-I*, Associated by Love or sympathy- within Iod, the male God, the Dorian Principle.

4 *Jud-Ah*, Males multipliers of the Center or the Principle, Decadarians of the Monad, Extenders of the Universal Angle;

5. *Is-sach-Ar*, Manifestation of the Expansion-Emigration of Fire;

6 *Zeb-Ulon*, Regulators of the Elemental Principle, of the primary Substance

Jacob's second fertile wife is *Rachel, the Ethereal Radiance*, and her sons are: 1-*Io-Seph*, Processor of reflected Light, the Magnetic Circuit, the Lunar Circumvolution.

2-*Ben-ya-min*, the Succession of days, Numeration from the Right side when facing the North Pole.

Bal-A, Rachel's servant, means the total Uplift of Unity, the Exaltation of the Universal Angle.

Her sons are *Dan*, the Triangle, the Judgment, the Zenith, and *Neph-Thali*, the Splendor of Glories, the Distribution of Grandeurs, and the Distribution of Trophies. Companion to Leah, *Zelphah*, consequence of the Harmonic League, means the *wide-open Cavern*, the *Opening of Profundity*, the *Opening of the Underside*, the *Voice of Silence*, the *Glow of Darkness*, the *Aspiration of the Void*. She is the Orb of the Shadow Cone of the Earth, she is this Queen of the Fright, who, nevertheless, will smile someday. *Zelphah* has two sons, like Rachel, her antithesis.

The first is *Gad*, meaning Entry and Invasion, the *Gate* and its *Outside projection*, the Strait and the Open Ocean, Gulf and the Engulfing.

The second son, *Asher*, meaning the *Threshold of the Mastery*, the Base of the Apotheosis, the Pedestal of the mastering Will, the Heavenly resurrection of the Victorious Soul over the Second Death, the Apotheotic entry into the Akasa. In the Mysteries of Eleusis and Isis, this resurrection was called the Winged Crown.

Interpreter of the Mysteries like all poets until the Christian era, Horace will still say, of this celestial effort of the Soul after the first death, this beautiful verse, speaking of Hercules: *Enisus arces attigit igneas. "His effort reached the Igneous Citadel."* Such is the profundity of the books of Moses and the Abramid Encyclopedia or Neo-Ramid, which they narrate.

2173 BC: THE ABRAMIDS ENTER EGYPT

Supported in Egypt by the Orthodoxes, consecrated in Salem by Melchizedek, condemned to remain underground by the political Power, we will see this intellectual and social movement, awaken with Jacob-Israel, master of substitution, and enter into action with Joseph, by enclosing Io or Isis.

The schism will, in fact, be encircled with such force that the Hyksos pastor Kings will be expelled, opening the way to Moses' manifestation.

The date of arrival of the Abramids in Egypt is known to be the year 2173 BC. It coincides with the invasion recounted by Manetho.

The terrible consequences of the personal empire of Assyria had disaffected all the Yonijas, from the Indus to Arabia. Their northward push drove them into Syria, and forced them, for fear of being caught between two fires, to seize Egypt and use it as shelter against the new empire.

The war was terrible, and a part of the male population of Egypt having been massacred, the other part was reduced to slavery.

The Hyksos, or Hirshuists of this invasion, consisted of all the working urban and rural classes of the Assyrian empire. Tired of mass levies, crushing taxes, unemployment and famine, arbitrariness and corruption, after having revolted, they had, as always, subjected themselves to the first dictator adventurer who had mustered an army as a foundation of his personal power.

THE REIGN OF SHALIT IN EGYPT

Shalit, also named Salatis or Saitis, was their Napoleon, he entered Memphis in triumph where he was crowned Pharaoh of divine right. But, fearing the Orthodoxes, he fortified himself against them in the eastern part of the Delta.

To flatter his Bodhones allies, he named Abaris the camp he had surrounded with enormous walls. It is from there that, for 19 years, he ruled the conquered Egypt.

His army was composed of many diverse ethnicities: Hykshos, Mentius, Satius, Arabs, Turanian Scythians, Kahettas (Hittites).

According to their origins, they were divided into different regiments, infantry, ballistic, cavalry, etc.

A sort of convention, or treaty extorted by force, had neutralized Thebes, ruled with a shadow of an Egyptian dynasty; and for nearly twenty years Shalit remained barricaded in the Delta against the claims of the Assyrian Caesarism of the far North, which the followers of the *Lama,* under the name of *Elamites,* vigorously attacked.

It is only much later that the fifth successor of the first pharaoh of the Hykshos united Egypt under his rule and took the name of Apapi II.

But the Theban Orthodoxy soon shook the yoke, and opposed him a seventeenth dynasty. The pastor kings required that there be only one regent in Thebes, the Hiq. The Theban Orthodoxes wanted a king, named *Souten.*

Thus a general war ensued. This time the three Councils met and launched an Egyptian uprising powerful enough to drive back the Yonijas/Hyksos to Memphis, and even expel them from Memphis which they stormed and took back.

Finally, the Orthodoxes did so well, that in 1703 BC, they uprooted out of the Abaris camp the schismatic conquerors, drove them up to Syria, and defeated them definitively at the battle of Sharouhen.

It was under the leadership of Amos, or Ahmes I, that the *ancient Synarchy proved once more its strength.*

This elected representative of the first two high Councils founded the eighteenth Dynasty.

The Pastors had adopted, as I have said, the writing glyphs, the arts, the religion of the vanquished, or at least the Trinitarianism symbolized in the name of Horus.

Joseph had been state minister under pharaoh Kamen.

Should we see in him a man simply bearing the name of Joseph or the representation of the advent of the Orthodox policy in the ministry?

There is no hesitation, and this name, which means the *Coiling of Io*, the *Suffocating of schism*, must leave no doubt about it.

Joseph is the symbolic son of Jacob-Israel, which name means in itself Revolution and Substitution, designating the return of the Royal University of God in lieu of the arbitrary powers.

He is supposedly sold as a slave to *Pedouphra*.

That last hierogram designates the *Sun Sign*, and this so-called *Pedouphra* character in fact was the *Ruler of the Satellites of the Sun.*

Joseph, who is none other than the Abramid Dorian Order, or its leader, at a certain stage of his action, while de facto forced to submit, in appearance, to the politics of the schismatics, nevertheless allied to the Trinitarian solar symbol.

This is why, his anthropomorphically explained hierogram, show *Joseph* marrying *Asnath*, priestess, daughter of a priest of On, Heliopolis, city of the Sanctuary of the Sun.

As the Hyksos invaders had taken over the land, the policy of the Abramids has been to return the lands to the Theban sovereignty, that is, to the second High Council, that of the Gods or the Laws. This was easy to do, for, like all political governments, the Pastor kings had been leading Egypt to ruin and starvation.

It has been reported the Orthodoxes used this flaw to their advantage, by delivering the seeding grains only if the Pastor kings agreed to pay to the Theban Councils a tax of twenty per cent on the harvests.

But if we reflect on the exception made in favor of the Priesthood, we cannot fail to see in this maneuver the game of an extremely tight political agenda, limited in its means and driven to use all possible means to arm themselves against the invader. There in Egypt, as everywhere, we see the Order of the Abramids work in agreement with the Council of God and the Council of the Gods.

HEBREW ABRAMIDS RESIDE IN THE LAND OF GOSHEN

When its policy had borne fruit under Ahmes, the Amos of the Greeks, the Dorian Kaldean Order demanded and obtained land in the Delta, named the *land of Goshen.* This new center of Orthodoxy, known under the hierogram *Jacob,* could not fail to become one of the focal points of attraction to the Dorians fleeing everywhere the new jurisdictions of political governments.

There, in Goshen, as at Karran, Kariath-Arba, as in the lands of Moab and Ammon, the inflexible Bodhones, temporarily mingled with the equally rebellious schismatics, coming from everywhere to form a large group; but the Egyptian people did not distinguish them from the Hyksos invaders, while on the contrary the members of the two High Councils recognized among that crowd the Abramids Bodhones as being affiliated to their own Theban Orthodoxy

This subtle difference between the "Apurus" affiliated to the Abramid Order (future Hebrews) and the collective Apurus explains the confusion in which historians have fallen.

The Egyptian priests, Manetho as well as the priests Strabo met with, even later Ammonius Sacchas (who gave the Christians the solar rites of the Communion), all those priests knew that Moses was one of them; and we have seen that the same confraternal assimilation is undeniable, with regard to the Abramids or Dorians who originated from Kaldea.

As for the few families, confined in the Land of Goshen around one of the convents of the Order, Manethon does not differentiate them from the Hyksos, neither does Josephus, historian of the Jews.

But their rallying around the Dorian Order of the Abramids, their long prepared mass levy when answering the call of Moses priest of Osiris, do not allow to see in them anything but *uncompromising Dorians,* whether confronting the schism of the Yonijas, or opposing the solar trinitarism of Christna, Mithras, Horus, or the triune Baal-Iswara-Linga.

There is no doubt those orthodox Bodhonian Kelts we are speaking of as *Apurus are the Hebrews*, with their communal hives ruled by their own arbiters, *and destined to become later the Beni-Israel*, the sons of the Royal University of the male God.

For 1,400 years these intractable people had already begun to give the world their great social teaching.

Though the ancient Synarchy gave up the front scene of history to Anarchy from above; that Anarchy could surreptitiously install everywhere the government of the Force over that of the ancient Law, the Arbitrary over Arbitration, Political Power over the intellectual Authority of universally agreed institutions, nevertheless the traditional Bodhonian Kelts temporarily *submitted only to raise up their heads quickly at the slightest opportunity*.

THE HEBREWS IN THE LAND OF GOSHEN

Their Kahals, or Communes, the election of their representative in the third Council by family fathers and mothers, the arbitration of all their differences by their own haqs or regents of the Council of Elders, such was, since the falling-out of the synarchic Authority, the minimum of social organization, to which they were reduced, and which, nevertheless, had saved them through all the general crises of Humanity, to the present day.

Their leaders or haqs having, thanks to the Abramids, their intelligent connections in the first two Councils of Egypt, claiming support from the ancient Law of Aries as members of the neo-Ramid movement, obtained special liberties in the Land of Goshen.

Those liberties singularly plead in favor of the social constitution of the ancient World, and, conversely, no government today would be smart enough or strong enough to concede similar liberties.

The famous ideal of *self-government* appears here, granted as soon as 1700 BC, to a small people no larger than one of our counties, although it was often confused with the former schismatic invaders by the many peoples of Egypt proper, the Nation which gave them hospitality.

Suppose the Alsatians-Lorrainers, the Poles of the Duchy of Posen, the Kingdom of Poland or Galicia, the Irish, were to demand such a favor: the political governments that dominate them could never muster enough intellectual and moral Authority, enough social foresight, to make such a concession.

The outcome would be certainly different, the day when the reconstitution of the three independent Powers would have raised the political governments out of their impotence, so onerous for all, so dangerous for them.

Let's focus now on that small piece of land laying between the Nile and the middle of the Suez Isthmus.

There, the soil fertility was remarkable.

There ran streams of milk and honey! will say later, with reproach, Dathan and Abiron rebelling against Moses, in the desert.

Disdained by the common people, appreciated by the civilized higher Egyptian classes, their families federated into clans or tribes, governed by their own *zakens*, one could easily *identify the ancient Aldea of the former Empire.*

They were connected with the State proper only by a Corps attached to the Second Council, that of the Scribes or Shoterim of Egypt. In the Land of Goshen most of the scribes belonged to the most educated of the Obérious (working class).

They were initiated to the Mysteries of the Temple of Ammon-Ra, that of the ancient Law; they collaborated with the haqs (judges) and zakens (elders) of the kahals (communes), in regard with the execution of the sacred Code: Conscription of men for the public works or for the army, collective taxes of the commune, to be paid in money, in wheat or in cattle, censuses, land cadaster, court of appeals, etc.

China, which has preserved intact part of the ancient Social Constitution, shows us still today, the very light weight the government applies on the governed, a tax of about two francs a year per man, when Wisdom and Science preside in their proper place. The only subjugation which excessively hampered the Hebrew communities of the Delta was the Public Works Department, to which each Nome was to provide laborers.

THE DEFENSE SYSTEM OF EGYPT

Since the rivalry between temples, followed by monarchical instability, the enrollment for public works had fallen from the hands of the first two Councils in the hands of kings, although architects, engineers, hydrographers, like all other savant Corps, were directly affiliated to the Sanctuaries.

In Egypt, the Pharaohs had organized militarily the work of the bridges and roads. It was thus that they had traced the strategic routes, commanding access to Syria by Mageddo, in front of Lebanon, and another artery, from Mageddo to Karkemish, supervising Assyria and Mesopotamia. Forts armed with a complete defense system formed a chain between Mageddo and Kadesh.

Such was the masterful obstacle that the traditional Orthodoxes had, through their kings, positioned to fend off the personal Powers, originally resulting from schism.

It was thanks to these defense works that Ramses I had restrained and tamed the resurgent league of the schismatics, from the Euphrates and from the Taurus mountains to the sea.

It is with the help of this powerful defense system that his father Séti I, in 1556 BC., had defeated, in Syria, the confederation of the Naturalists, of which Sapalel, king of the Khetes (Hittites), had become in turn the imperial chief. By Ramses on the Orontes, by Sethi at Kadesh, the Phoenician confederation, constantly conquered, was constantly reforming; under Motour, as under Sapalel, it was attacking strenuously the Egyptian garrisons of Gaza, Askalon, Mageddo, and Kadesh.

THE GREAT INFRASTRUCTURE WORKS OF EGYPT

During these brutal confrontations, other gigantic works required another contingent of laborers. They built a canal joining the Red Sea to the Nile, added artesian wells to increase soil fertility, opened a large commercial road, with military posts, for the caravans of Radasieh, vis-à-vis Edfou and the mines of Gold of Gib-el-Akaky.

Meanwhile, the Hypostyle Hall at Karnak was being repaired, the great temple of Abydos was enriched with new sculptural wonders, and the Valley of the Kings adorned with grandiose monuments.

Under Ramses II the intergovernmental anarchy continued to require from the pharaoh attentive energy everywhere.

Infiltrated by the separatists, by the Bodhones of Arabia, by Ethiopia, and by the Assyrian party, Sudan had torn up the treaties with Egypt.

On the other hand, the Asian and European Tourano-Phoenician coalition threatened the Nile Delta.

In this vast rebellious confederation which extended from the Caspian Sea to the Straits of Gibraltar, naturally participated the European Kelts of Thor, always ready for some piracy.

In Africa they swelled the ranks of their blue-eyed, blond-haired Libyan brothers, and incited the ancient Pelasgic colonies from Tripoli to Morocco.

Due to the breaking of the ancient International Law of Aries, the Mediterranean Sea was infested with Vasques, Ligures, Sardis, Achaeans, Cycladians, always ready to transform themselves into pirates, and bring much trouble to the last representatives of the ancient social Order, in Egypt, Crete, Etruria.

Such was the hostile circle that the politics of the Khetas (Hittites), from the borders of Asia Minor and of Northern Syria, tightly closed around Egypt, to stifle the mastery of the ancient Royalty of International Justice.

In the Land of Goshen, the repercussions of all these disorders were resulting in the form of chores for public works and enlistments in the armies of land and sea.

Ramses II first struck the league in Ethiopia.

Then, according to Herodotus and Strabo, he drove it

away, on the East, as far as the Indus, with a fleet of 400 sailing vessels with which he cleared the Red Sea and the Gulf of Oman, so bringing back all the coasts of the Red Sea under the control of Egypt; while in the West another army pursued, down to the center of Africa, the Libyans, Bodhones and Numidians.

Having thus struck the feet and wings of that league, the King of Justice kept their head in check, strengthening the garrisons of Syria, and leading two triumphant expeditions as far North as Beirut.

Having thus defeated the coalition of the feudal lords, the King of Justice used the period of peace to continue his defense work, from the year 1415 BC to the year 1401 BC, *shortly before the birth of Moses.*

PROTO HEBREWS AND PROTO ARABS

The Northern Apurus were quiet in the Land of Goshen, where they enjoyed their prosperity. Those of the far South of Egypt, the Arabs, were constantly agitating Sudan, Abyssinia, and Ethiopia. Turbulent, bellicose, nomadic, identifying themselves as Kushites, peoples of the former Arbitral Empire, to escape all national jurisdiction, they incessantly harassed the Viceroys of the Southern Nomes.

On the lookout for the faintest distant signal of war, marauding around the mines of precious metals, with their old friends the Blacks, they were always on the alert.

Their conduct had been the same vis-à-vis the Babylonian and Ninevite Caesars. In the past, in fact, they had obtained from Ram great prerogatives, and, therefore, had remained for a long time independent of any other arbitral jurisdiction except that of the Kousha of India.

But these times were long past; and now Egypt alone was making the last effort to slow the final collapse of the former Social State, which the Assyrian Caesarism had precipitated into the republicanism of an unbridled feudal anarchy.

This is why Ramses II, between Egypt and Arabia, set up a new fortress, Aanakhtou, or Pa-Ram-Ses, thus reminding the league of international anarchists that the ancient Pa-zi-Pa of the Paradesa still had a King of International Justice, *faithful to the Law of Ram, after 5,300 years, and despite 1,600 years of revolutions and wars.* These formidable labors were indispensable; but the populations suffered from it, in spite of the Wisdom of the Egyptian synarchy; and, as always, the malcontents, instead of revolting against the general causes of this particular evil, murmured against their own government.

WARRING KELTS, KHETAS, TURANIANS

At that time, *as Moses was just born*, Ramses II was still compelled to strike the league at its heart and head, besieging the main fortress of Khetas (Hittites).

After two hard battles, the Hydra was once again defeated, even if this enemy was to regain its forces, so requiring, for 15 years, perpetual waring actions from Ramses II.

The Kelts of Europe, faithful to the Zodiacal Law of the Taurus, continued to lend to the schismatics their belligerent hordes, their barbarian and turbulent mercenaries.

Allied for 1,600 years to the Ionians of Syria, to the Turanians of Asia, they had exchanged with them the worst superstitions: black magic, bloody sacrifices of animals and human beings.

Everywhere, they rushed on the peaceful Synarchies of Ram, Spain, Gaul, Etruria, Greece, Macedonia, Crimea, Phrygia, the coasts and the islands of the Mediterranean, in Africa, incapable to create or to build anything, unable to join forces for anything but destruction, then tearing each other apart, wherever they had struck the remnants of the ancient social Order.

Their Mediterranean confederations were united under a strange flag bearing the Taurus and the Red Dove; they were called *Toursha.*

Tour stands for none other than *Thor. Shaa* still designates in Arabic today the kind of cooing used for calling the flocks to the watering place.

In addition to hiding behind this powerful religious name,

Toursha, this mob of anarchists also had aspired to take over international jurisdiction. That is why they pompously called themselves *Shardan,* the *Free Power of Judgment,* which gave to one of their centers the name *Sardinia.*

For 15 years, this federal anarchy, at the head of which was King Motour, ally of Assyrian Caesarism, continued to attack Ramses II.

Motour died, and his brother Khéta-Sar returned to the alliance with Sethi, the Sethos from Etruria, and Ramses I.

The alliance was observed all the more loyally as the Pharaoh married the daughter of the king of the Khetas, and offered to his father-in-law a royal hospitality.

EGYPT DEFENDER OF ARBITRAL SOCIAL ORTHODOXY

If I have gone into such details, it is to keep my promise , step back down the course of historical events, and give the reader a genuine feeling regarding the colossal efforts made by Initiates and Rulers for supporting on Earth the ancient Public Law of Aries, the ancient Universal Theocracy of the Lamb, the precious fragments of the ancient Kingdom of God.

It is impossible not to see, through the expulsion of the schismatic Dynasts of Thanis, through the actions of the Orthodox Pharaohs since that time, the masterful implementation of a *return to the Wisdom and Science of the former General Government.*

Behind this plan which asserts itself in its very implementation, there is the ancient Synarchy, the ancient Social Science and its guardians, the Orthodox Dorians of the Council of God and the Council of the Gods.

Assembled in Egypt as if in their last stronghold, their aim was to disarm the Caesarean head of intergovernmental anarchy everywhere, by striking the absolute and arbitrary governments that exploited the universal disorder against the ancient arbitral governments.

After the Ninevite and Babylonian Caesars, it was the Syrian, Turanian and European confederations which the Orthodox Temples neutralized by means of kings of Justice who had been initiated in their sanctuaries, though conquest proper was never the goal, either of these temples or of these kings.

Such was, in these troubled times, the role of the Egyptian Synarchy: To limit intergovernmental anarchy, prevent arbitrary sovereignties, reduce the shocks of personal powers, counter the ensuing rebellions and the recourse to violence by criminal mobs overexcited by iniquitous kings and politician adventurers rising to the crown through feudal disorder, to block access to power by ambitious individuals without faith or law, without conscience or science.

But at this game, from century to century, the Pharaoh, the first Magistrate of the College of the Gods, however admirably intellectually educated by traditional Initiation, could not fail to emulate some aspects of arbitrary Caesarism, due to perpetual conflicts and state of war.

Not that these orthodox sovereigns were in any way on the par to the past and future tyrannical Caesars of Assyria or Rome, and all the subsequent swampy crowd of ignorant representatives of Anarchy crowned under the name of Monarchy.

Egypt never fell so low in the materialism of personal government, as long as its spirit thrived in its first two Synarchical high Councils, which were sustaining its healthy, strong religious and savant life. Its Priesthood, fortunately for Egypt, was not a simple school of basic morality, imposing submission to the multitudes, and leaving the rulers with no other control than their good pleasure and their ignorance: far from it.

Had it been so, Egypt, instead of lasting 18,000 years before Menes, and providing, since this Menes, nearly 40 royal dynasties, it would have lasted no more than peoples and Societies governed by ignorance, iniquity and waste, and not by Science, Justice and Economy. The secret of such longevity resides in the Authority of the whole savant Teaching Corps, and the submission of Power to this Authority, as well as the functions and responsibilities allocated through examinations and merit.

EGYPT: EDUCATION, INITIATION, GOVERNANCE

Far from being easier on the higher social classes, Initiation was on the contrary all the harder as the individuals ascended the degrees leading to greatest responsibilities.

When Jesus Christ will say how difficult it is to reach Supreme Knowledge, he will always emphasize that the simplicity of the heart and of the mind, is the fundamental condition for attaining Supreme Knowledge, as symbolized by little children.

But the individuals born near the throne are, by circumstance, so transformed, so much altered in their possible developments, that the attainment of ancient Wisdom was more difficult for them than for the sons and daughters of the lowest street beggars. That is why the first two High Councils taught the Royal Art as strictly as the Priestly Art, and rectified the ontology of the dynastic princes with formidable intellectual and moral calisthenics.

And if we see at times kings leave the throne with such rapidity, in Egypt, in India and elsewhere, it is because mediocrity or government deviation were not long tolerated by both the first High Councils, who preferred to subsidize at their own expense the more or less disorderly life of an idle prince, than to let him embody on the outside a sovereignty he did not possess within himself.

In Egypt, as in India, as in all the ancient Empire of Ram, local life, governed by the Third Council, was as free as possible.

But external circumstances had nonetheless convinced the Council of the Gods and the entire judiciary corps to allow the King of Justice to centralize a large number of functions in his hands. The same circumstances had also forced the Council of God to relinquish a large part of its Authority to the centralized powers of the First Magistrate.

As a result, among the traditional Orthodoxes, not only in the Land of Goshen, but also in all of Southern Egypt, there was a general uneasiness, a certain disillusionment, growing underneath an undeniable abundance and great prosperity.

Like his predecessors, Ramses II was forced to overburden the workers, the industry, the commerce, in short to be the center of a civilization overstrained in the extreme.

Egypt was busy to the utmost, and held the whole world under pressure, in war as in peace, for its trades absorbed the raw materials of three continents, of which the Phoenicians were the maritime transporters.

As in our modern capitals, large constructions had become a ruinous prerequisite of the public Economy.

The soldier returning to his Nome again became a workman, and it was indispensable to keep the mass of the workers busy; and what our politicians call "the building trade" fulfilled that purpose.

At Bubaste, Abydos, Memphis, they were building and re-building, and enhancing the ancient temples. At Luxor, the monument of Amen-Hotep III was completed. In Karnak, the triumphal pylon celebrating the victory of Kadesh was erected.

Speos of Ibsambul, temples of Gournah, Thanis, Ramesseum, obelisks, gigantic statues and monoliths, all was repaired, completed or newly erected in a feverish activity, un-stoppable without giving way to dangerous social unrest.

Outside the temples, the Pharaoh was hyperactive everywhere.

As supreme Magistrate, head of the Council of the Gods, head of the army, head of the savant Corps, always faithful to ancient tradition, great for his time, immense for ours, he was forced to carry on his shoulders a role of a frightening weight. Pharaoh under this weight, bent toward the gulf that attracts Power to its own ruination, inclining him to become increasingly personal.

However, when entering the temples, home of the traditional Priesthood, where the Authority of the Council of God sat empowered by all the lights of Wisdom and Science, the Pharaoh-King was no more than the first member of the Council of the Gods.

There he was restored to his true rank in the real hierarchy.

Both knees on the ground, bare headed, stripped of all weapons, he was piously accepting the chalice and the sacred bread offered to him by the High Priest. No insignia of commandment could be seen on his person.

Then, he heard other lessons than the usual tickling of disguised flatteries. Sitting in his stall at his true rank, he listened to the voice of the Prophets performing the sacred rites, evoking the living Soul of the Ancestors, dictating their teachings to their royal listener, correcting him for his past or present behaviors, if required. and predicting the future, if his answer to their questions was insufficient.

MOSES AND ORPHEUS STUDENTS AT THEBES

Within the lower grades of the Priesthood, dressed in white linen, wearing the ephod, a young priest of Osiris, small in size, with a profoundly gentle air, a forehead prominent like that of a ram, was sitting attentive, among the priests attached to the Royal House.

It was *Moses*, son of the first princess, daughter of the reigning Pharaoh.

Among the groups of Initiates who had converged from many countries to learn and take rank in the Council of the Gods, one could have noticed another man, also young, wearing long blond hair, which contrasted with the black hair of Moses.

This Nazarene of royal origin came from Thrace; his name was *Orpheus*, son of a priestess of Apollo. The ceremony ended with the royal offering, made according to the rites.

Wearing the Uraeus (Sacred cobra) and the ram-horned miter, as first Magistrate of the Council of the Gods, the Pharaoh, with a golden sickle, cut a sheaf of wheat which he offered through the hands of the Pontiff as a sacrifice to Isis.

Then, once the blessing was pronounced, the king would stand up and his squires would hand him his insignias and his military helmet.

At the door of the temple, he climbed back on his Keltic

shield, carried by twelve erpads, generals of his staff.

In front of him, 12 young Levites, on cushions embroidered with gold, held the royal insignias, the scepter of the arbiters, topped with the Aries head, the sword, the bow, the mace etc.

For a long time *Moses* studied among these Levites; we will see him again later within the sacred processions, carrying either the golden ark, or the tablets or the bread offerings, the chalices or the censer. In front, walked the royal orchestras, then followed innumerable choirs with their leaders waving their batons and marking the rhythm.

Then came the members of the King's House and of the Priests' Colleges, followed by the Great and Lesser Mysteries Initiates.

The magnificence of the garments was on a par with that of the ceremonies, beginning with the Pontiffs with their white tiara, their pectoral, their "theologal" resplendent with fiery symbolic stones, then followed by the dignitaries with the emblems of the Lamb, the Aries, the Lion, the Lily, the Bee, banners hanging from massive chains, admirably crafted.

Finally, the guilds closed the march, with their emblems and banners displayed. Under this pomp, the *Divinity of the Social State, Wisdom and Science* still manifested with a force and power incomprehensible to the modern minds.

However, the Orthodox Priesthood felt almost lonesome on Earth while defending, with weapons blunted by perpetual struggle in defense of the ancient Social God against the invasion of mediocrity, against politics, against despotism from above and from below, against the unleashed passions and screaming instincts hurtling around the magical circle of Egypt's borders.

Credulous people believed everything they fancied; for, apart from the first degree of professional instruction, apart from basic morality and the psychurgic rituals of the Cult of the Ancestors, nothing was imposed upon them, although all levels of knowledge was accessible to them, at will.

Erring as it does always in all times, the multitude was mistaking the signs for the things signified, the symbols for the Causes, the hieroglyphs for the cosmogonic Puissance, the princes for the Principles, the priests and the cult itself for the Religion and Truth.

But even among the most destitute people, moral and psychurgical teaching was excellent, although the symbols were not scientifically explained.

The lowest Initiate in the temples, the baptized and the eucharist, nurtured *precise notions*, though very rudimentary, *concerning visible and invisible Life.*

A *sacred scroll* containing a magnificent confession of faith was piously guarded by the adult until death, and still accompanied him to the *Life Beyond the Tomb*, which was admirably known, revered and supported by the Temples' priests.

ENJOY AN EGYPTIAN SACERDOTAL PROCESSION!

I promised myself to allow you to be spectator of a genuine sacerdotal procession.

Here comes the *Social God*, solemnly carried, *enclosed in the books of the Sacred Teaching.*

First walks the *Rector of Mathematicians.*

In front of him are carried the attributes of Music and the books of Hermes dealing with Quantitative and Qualitative Arithmology and Morphology, hymns to Gods composed arithmetically and geometrically according to the modes of their sphere of Cosmogonic Life, and to the rules of the Royal Life.

This component of Science has been the subject of one of the five books of Fo-Hi.

Then comes the *Horoscope, Grand Master of Genethliac Sciences.*

The clock and the palm precede him, as well as the books containing the Organic Cosmogony, the physiology of our Solar System, from both *a hyperphysical and physical* viewpoint.

Following him, the *Sacred Scribe, Grand Master of Hierogrammatic Science and Art*, the Symbolic Science in all its forms. The pen, the ruler, the inkwell are his emblems. His books reveal the *keys of hieroglyphs*, Cosmography, Geography, solar, lunar, and planetary Cycles, Chorography, Hydrography, instruments of physics and chemistry, the exact rules of sacred rites, the science of proper locations, Numbers, Weights and Measures, finally the aesthetics of ceremonies in all its kinds. The analogy with the Fo-Hi books is still here noticeable.

Then, the *great Master of Justice* marches on, with his symbols: the cubit representing Equality before the Law, the equity of the Law itself; the chalice or cup depicting the participation of the Council of the Gods in the great sacerdotal communion with the spiritual Life of the Universe, through Initiation to the integral Wisdom and Science. His books detail what the jurisconsults of Rome, inheritors of the Etruscan Synarchy, call the Science of divine and human things, that is to say the sacred and profane Law, the worship of the Gods, the sacrifices, the rule of judicial assemblies, etc.

Finally, *the Prophet* closes the march. The Levites bear his emblems: the golden ewer, the loaves of Communion. Like the Pontiff, he is the keeper of the ten sacerdotal books carried within the Holy Ark and reserved for the supreme Initiation. I will mention only four of these Sciences: Theurgy, Magic, Sacred Therapeutics, Alchemy. In Paris stands the statue of a high priest of Memphis, Phtah-Mer, which can be seen in the Louvre museum. On this statue are written these significant words: *"There was nothing veiled for him; and he was covering with a veil the essence of all that he had seen."* So will do *Moses* once priest of Osiris. Thus had to do the Dorian Order of the Abramids, obeying the Thorah or Law of the Taurus. Genesis, Ch. XX, v. 16: *"You will always have a veil in front of those with whom you will be "*

RULES OF INITIATION IN TEMPLES AND SANCTUARIES

Here is an excerpt from Zosimus, the Panopolitan, reproduced by Olympiodorus, and extremely significant, concerning the Sciences and applied Arts reserved for the priesthood, and particularly with regard to the *Agyropoeia and the Chrysopeia,* that is to say *the transmutation of base metals into silver and gold.*

"The whole kingdom of Egypt was sustained by these alchemical arts."

"It was only permissible for the highest priesthood to engage in it."

"Any priest who would comment on the hermetic writings of the ancients would have been outlawed."

"He possessed Science, but did not reveal it."

"It was a law among the Egyptians not to divulge anything on this subject, except to the sons of the Gods (High Initiates) and, when appropriate, to the Crown Prince."

Clement of Alexandria, according to many other authors, including Jamblique, confirms this information:

"The priests only disclosed their Mysteries to those Initiates whose exceptional virtue and wisdom were proved by examination and trial."

Such was the Law of Mysteries reinstated among the Orthodoxes, while resisting the consequences of Irshu's schism. Moreover, as a result of the Babylonian Empire, the political power of the schismatics incited a renewed enforcement of this measure of prudence, as we have seen about the Sarai meaning the Synthesis of Dorian Sciences saved by the Order of Abramids.

That is why we shall see Roman politics, criminal heir of the Assyrian governmental Iniquity, like the wretched Chinese autocrat who burned the Fo-Hi books and decimated the Corps of Literates, go on assaulting and drowning in blood the defenders of the ancient Synthesis and destroying in flames their sacred and savant books.

TOTAL DESTRUCTION OF BOOKS OF INTEGRAL SCIENCE

In Egypt, besides the 42 volumes of *Hermes* containing the Principles of this Synthesis and of this Social God, and carried in ceremonies, as we have just seen, there was, says Manetho, near 37,000 volumes detailing the Sacred Science.

This is why the anarchist Caesars, heirs of the anarchist Plebeians of the Senate of Rome, jealous of the ancient Authority, of which this wisdom and this science were the Spirit and the Soul, assaulted this sacred science enclosed in these sacred books.

The ill-famed Diocletian will launch his soldiers on Egypt, focusing on the members of the high Council of the Gods, on the Council of God, and, through heaps of corpses, will seize and throw in the fire the sacerdotal books.

Why?

Because that is where resided the Divine Source of Social Authority in Egypt and virtually the whole World, because the personal Power, challenged, knew it would never be able to enjoy fully the benefits of its crimes, nor to govern the Nations without Control, as long as a Sacred Ark contained the Wisdom and Science of which I speak.

Moreover, although deeply injured and bloodied by the Roman Beast, though exhausted by extortions and ransoms, Egypt never poor, was also never devoid of the force to resist iniquity by means of war, as long as a priest could study the Sacred Science and practice certain applied Arts in temples' laboratories.

NATURAL AND SACRED SCIENCES IN CLASSICAL EGYPT

I wanted to recreate in the mind of the reader the environment in which *Moses'* life was growing, at *this crucial moment in the life of the Human race*. The priesthood in which he grew up in Science and Wisdom knew that, for 1,600 years, the ancient Unity had been crumbling, in spite of all its indefatigable efforts, and the universal degeneration was thrusting Egypt itself in the storm of pure Politics.

The first two High Councils, with their ramifications throughout the whole World, saw everywhere brutal force eclipse the ancient Right, assert itself in the despotism of the rulers, in the revolts of the governed, in the worst barbarian slavery reinstated thanks to endless international wars replacing the former Arbitral Authority.

Throughout all the Orthodox sanctuaries of the world, representing all our current teaching fields and all those which are long lost, the Egyptian Sages and Savants devoted their ultimate efforts to maintain altars for the Truth, refuges for the Science, ramparts for the Civilization, asylums for Liberty, and for the Reign of the Social God, arks of Salvation riding the stormy waters of a deluge much more dangerous for Humanity than the terrors of the Oceans.

In Egypt, the constant war alert was not more appreciated by the three Councils than by the entire people, nor by the Hebrews of the Land of Goshen, who will lead towards the Wilderness a large multiethnic crowd of people.

The Egyptian organization was above all based on intellect and intelligence, and reluctant to use brute force, like all Social organization founded on the ancient Synarchy, China included.

THE ART OF WAR AND PEACE

"*One can go to war,*" say the old classical books of Chinese military art, "*however before resorting to this extreme, one must be absolutely certain to have the general Good of Humanity as a Principle, Universal Justice for Purpose, Equity for Rule.*

One must decide to attack the life of a collectivity of men only to preserve the life of a larger community; only the need to ensure public security may authorize the governing Will to disturb the tranquility of another part of this Unit.

The war on individuals can be motivated only by the general good of the Species.

Therefore, one must only want what is due, because it is due, to demand it only as it is due, by weighing the national motives themselves in the scales of the universal Right of Humanity.

It follows from this that only the most ineluctable necessity must bring the sword of the chief of the army out of the scabbard.

Now, if one wages war only out of necessity, and in the intellectual and moral conditions which I have just mentioned, one will like those very same adversaries against whom one fights.

One will know to stop in the middle of the most glorious conquests.

One will even have to forget one's own national interests in order to restore to all the peoples, both victorious and vanquished, all the conditions of the tranquility and the peace they enjoyed before the war."

A few centuries later, the same sentiments are expressed by

one of the greatest men of war in China, *Sun-Tzu*, chief of staff of the Celestial Empire:

"To wage war is bad thing in itself.

As long as Providence, present in human intelligence, can avoid war, there is never a need to start it.

Battles, whatever their outcome, are always fatal mostly for the winners.

Battles can be started only when one can no longer fight otherwise, meaning with the direct forces of the mind and conscience.

When a sovereign feels stirred by anger or revenge, he should refrain himself from drawing the sword, or mobilizing troops.

When a general feels the same sentiments, he should refrain from starting the battle.

For both are imbued by darkness, but it is serenity of the light that is needed for intelligence and conscience to illume their determinations and their enterprises with the blessings of Humanity and Divinity.

War is, to Peoples' interrelations, what acute malady is to the harmony of the organs of the body. One requires as much wisdom and science as the other.

In diseases, it is necessary to know the right moment for applying the remedies, the proper time necessary for them to start operating, the time when one can benefit from the effects of their action.

At war, one must know the time to start it, the time to press forward, to suspend it by an armistice, or terminate it with a treaty.

Not to make those distinctions, or, if one does, not to respect them, is to place oneself outside of real life, it is to want to lose everything, it is to have no Humanity. If you have Humanity, you will know, you will feel that every afflicted person deserves respect.

You will not add affliction to affliction, pain to pain, misfortune to misfortune.

In war, even in those facing you, you must not see enemies.

Conclude then what your feelings should be for your own people, for your soldiers, for your officers. "

I cannot resist the pleasure of quoting again one of those admirable passages of the moral instructions provided by the general staff school of the ancient Aries Empire, of which Fo-Hi himself has been a member.

Speaking of this ancient Empire, Fo-Hi says in his books:

"When necessity commanded the support of public Law by means of arms, great attention was given to ensure the war was short.

It ended quickly, for nobody had interest in extending its course. One fought without animosity, for one went to battle only to lend strength to the Law and the right Order of the whole Humanity.

Sometimes, whatever preparations had been made, however favorable the opportunity might be, one would dispense with fighting if, by persuasion or any other direct motive, kings or rebellious peoples could be enticed back into the fold of the Law.

This kind of victory was considered the most glorious, for it was direct, without the mediation of external arms, because it belonged to the realm of Justice, and was a triumph for Humanity.

That's how one used to behave before going to war.

There was a science and an art to prepare for war, to declare it, to begin it, to finish it, to conclude it, and consequently to put no passion in it.

Everything, on the contrary, was imbued with the Spirit we call Humanity."

WANING ANCIENT SCIENCE AND WISDOM

Such was, not only in China and Egypt, but throughout the ancient world, the Divine Teaching that the first two High Councils gave in regard to war.

So it took nothing less than all the political fatalities, unleashed by Irshu's schism, for India and Egypt to concede to the military power the large part that the new circumstances demanded.

The Pharaoh, International Arbiter, was in essence a King of Justice, a Melchizedek, the external leader of the College of the Gods or Magistrates, however the Army's Commander in Chief prevailed inside that College over Pharaoh.

The three Councils and the whole People were distressed by that situation, while complying with this inescapable necessity.

In the temples, in the depths of the Mysteries, the Orthodoxes still enjoyed the dazzling light of the past; but, in the outside world, they felt the empire of darkness was gaining every day more space.

They were pondering: How, in 1,600 years could have been so weakened the General Government of Wisdom, of Justice, of Universal Economy, the Synarchy, the common treasure of Humanity, which *Ram, a Genius associated with the Providence,* had received down from *Heaven* itself?

How to reclaim this Health, this Harmony, this Unity of the Spiritual body of the Human race?

Here, the hierograms engraved on the granite, on the porphyry, and on the basalt, are they not proof that the Reign of God exists, the reign that the people had manifested here below as a divine Kingdom, for 3,600 years?

What was, will be; but how, in how long a time?

Ram, the first Lama whose great Pyramid is the Astronomical and Geogonic symbol, the first Sovereign Pontiff whose Order missioned the ancient Menes to assist the government of Egypt in installing a Council of the Gods; did he not himself, before passing away*, promise to do in favor of Humanity, the giant effort, the immense sacrifice of detaching himself away from Blissful Life, away from the Temple of the Solar City and come back to Earth*, whenever needed, to experience anew the suffering in the womb of a woman and in the body of a wailing baby?

Such were the conversations of the Orthodoxes in the secrecy of the Sanctuaries; then, *they resorted to the Sacred Science, and the Ineffable was speaking to them.*

MOSES PREPARES HIS FUTURE MISSION

One may imagine *Moses* growing among these Sages, ascending with them the degrees of the Serapeum of Memphis, at the bottom of a majestic avenue lined with 600 sphinxes, visiting the colossal temples of Esneh, Denderah, Thebes, wandering in their shaded mazes and drinking abundantly the savant Light of initiations.

For a long time, having reached the higher degrees of Teachings, *Moses* belonged to the temple of Ammon-Ra.

From that fact, emerged the legend that he wore the horns of a Ram.

Often, after embracing past, present and future destinies of the Earth, his gaze left the vast Cycles to follow attentively what was happening in Syria and Kanaan and then came back to rest in the peaceful county of Goshen.

He felt attracted to these intractable, independent peoples.

These stiff-necked men and women, for whom any political power was foreign, any civil or administrative constraint a usurpation, arbitrariness an intolerable injustice; these peoples fascinated him.

In Egypt, as everywhere else, external necessities, weighing on the central Power, tended to definitively separate morality from politics, Religion from Law proper. There lies the most fatal morbid cause, the deadliest one that can disorganize any Government, either general or particular.

Christna had remedied to it in India, Zoroaster in Bactria, Fo-Hi in China, by absolutely submitting Politics to Morale, Power to Authority.

But the continual wars of the Assyrian Empire had crushed under its tyranny the corrective work of Zoroaster.

The same causes would have reached China, if it had not kept itself isolated from all contact with the great empires; and these same causes were compressing Egypt in a circle of wars that would surely lead to a fatal outcome.

That is why, in the temples crypts, while leafing through the hermetic encyclopedia, the Sarai of the Dorian Abramids, *Moses*, like the lion Sphinx, looked far into the Desert, and beyond, towards the towers of *Salem*, the city of Peace, the City faithful to the Law of the Kingdom of God.

That is why, looking towards the Land of Goshen, always he admired those obstinate, scorned, ignorant, stubborn, but still imbued with the Unitarianism of the ancient Cycle, not wanting to hear anything about separating Politics from Morality, Law from Faith, and strictly loyal to the Teaching and Arbitration of the Assembly of Fathers and Mothers, disdaining official controls, though bowing their heads respect-fully before their own *haqs* (judges)and *zakens (elders)*, hailing with piety any representative of Science and Wisdom.

Every day, *Moses*, priest of Osiris received and reviewed the reports of the scribes sent to tour the Delta.

No Egyptian Nome has people as punctilious as that little piece of land, none were more jealous of their rights, their local freedoms, none any more refractory to any abuse of power. There were endless quibbles, especially since the Egyptians themselves did not like the Apurus, who often dodged the chores, and then the central police ordered punishments, which the local officers translated into beatings.

The same independence, the same call to equality before the Law have always accompanied these Bodhones, while wandering from Western Europe to India, from India to North Africa.

This is why the young priest of Osiris sometimes went himself to control the reports of the scribes, and when he returned to his cell, he remained pensive for a long time, his vast forehead in his hands.

∞

CHAPTER XII
MOSES - ORPHEUS – THE EXODUS

ONE DAY, MOSES WAS ON AN INSPECTION TOUR.

The Priesthood still retained supervision of the services centralized in the hands of the King. The services of public works had for direct supervisors a large police body under the control of Pharaohs' House Military Guard, which included the famous legion of *Phra*. The police were limited to maintaining order among the workers of different ethnicities. The engineers and architects of the temples directed the works, and the sacred scribes were in charge of the administration proper.

Ground diggers, stonemasons, brickmakers, carpenters, blacksmiths, all the workers' corporations were enlisted in companies of two hundred men. A police captain headed each company of workers.

Labor issues were, then like today, a serious matter. Strikes existed as they do now, exploited by politicians from within and especially from outside.

As national exclusivism was less prevalent in these societies than in ours, all Races mingled in a State where the institutions still bore an impersonal character. But the establishment of pure politics in the Caesarean government of Assyria, in the republican federations of Syria and the Mediterranean, as well as in the direction of the Turanian peoples, the politicians were seizing the slightest opportunity to stir troubles in Egypt, India, Persia, Taurida of the Caucasus, Greece, Etruria.

TREATIES AND SETTLEMENTS CIRCA 2000 BC-1300 BC

Here are some of the trickeries used by the cunning foreign politicians: stir racial issues among workers, accentuate dissatisfaction in regard to the wages paid by the Egyptian State, provoke strikes and en masse emigrations to flood at once Egypt with foreign products once factories had been closed.

The settlement of these labor situations was one of the motivating factors of the wars supported by India, then by Egypt, and the peace treaties never neglected to give much attention to labor settlements.

These treaties were not, as nowadays (1884 CE), the work of a vain diplomacy, but the field of scholarly Corps specialized in the interrelations Worships to Worships, States to States, and Nations to Nations.

In the ancient Arbitral order, the ancient Synarchy, all these interrelations had been resolved through the most relevant scientific laws and carefully studied sacred Principles, but the Law of the Taurus had singularly modified the ancient Rama Order, known as the Law of Aries or Ammon in Egypt.

Nevertheless, since Ahmes, Egypt had reinstated the ancient Wisdom. Therefore, all *Egyptian wars were only intended to restore unceasingly the conditions of Peace* in the same Spirit expounded in the Chinese books written on this subject.

Treaties were the responsibility of the Priesthood, and the signing of the Peace included the following issues:

No conquest, independence of the vanquished, offensive and defensive alliance with the vanquished, neutrality of common land and sea routes, mutual protection of caravans, fleets, trade and industry, legal and economic courts of sacerdotal arbitrators, dismissal of emigrants free from all punishment, extradition of the criminals, except from the cities of refuge and religious purification.

These solemnly consecrated treaties were guaranteed by the Gods represented by the first two high Councils of the contracting countries. Thus Ramses I, Seti I, Ramses II, continued the program of their predecessors.

During war times, prisoners were not enslaved, as in the republics, but treated as free men, employed in the public works under the surveillance of the police. But Peace treaties leading necessarily to the liberation and exchange of captives, were reducing Egypt's own labor force, which would have been enough if strikes or emigration, at the instigations of the politics of other nations, did not diminish it.

Already under the leadership of Inachus and Cadmus,

important exoduses had taken place. Since Ramses II had married the daughter of Khétasar, king of the Khetians, Peace having returned, the lack of labor force had had to be filled. The Delta, like all the Nomes, had had to supply its contingent of workers, in proportion to the census that the Bodhones have always loathed.

HEBREWS DISCONTENT IS BUILDING UP

So, the hive of the small Hebrew Communes was more agitated than ever. Nothing was more unpleasant to a Hebrew worker than to leave his home, his kahal, to go and mix with strangers, to find himself led by another commander than his zaken.

For several months, it meant separation from family life, from aldea and tribe, the only lifestyle these people loved.

Once enlisted, in very small numbers in every company of two hundred men, they became the focus of all their Egyptian comrades. The bullying was going on, the revenge also, and the beating cane of the policeman was the ending conclusion.

As the exceptionally prosperous reign of Ramses II lasted 67 years, and the work there was incessant, brick and rubble became for the Land of Goshen an Apocalypse Beast of sort, and the agitation of the feelings was as momentous as the public works of Egypt. All the pyramids of this country soon weighed on the Hebrews' shoulders.

As much as the Apurus had taken pleasure in living in the Delta, as long as their family and communal habits had been unharmed, they were now disgusted at having to be submitted to harrowing administrative requirements, chores and official constraints, common to all the Egyptian people.

But what exasperated them above all was that they were not commanded by their own leaders.

Even today, the peoples whose free and wise social constitution carries the powerful stamp of the Ram Cycle, the divine mark of the Aries Synarchy, display the same repugnance to be directly ordered around by overseers not belonging to their clan or tribe.

Working far from their homeland, the Chinese associations obey as one man the voice of their own elected leader, if he is allowed to do so.

If so they are capable of absolute honesty, sobriety, unparalleled work, and nowhere else one can find such a level of intelligence, activity, and probity. But, under the direct command of a European, who cannot speak to their minds or souls in the language to which they are accustomed, the Chinese are like a ship without a captain, and their good will ceases absolutely.

The Hebrews battalions were behaving in such manner, whether working in the mines of Sinai, constructing strategic roads, laboring on canals, forts, temples, etc.

It does not mean the administration was neither wise nor prudent, nor that it did not faithfully distribute the foods, the clothes, the wages, or that the dwelling quarters were not safe. Far from it, Egypt was a model in this respect, as in many others, and from the scribe of the temple to the man in the cloak who was the official doctor, all the controls were very meticulous.

All these controls were reported as far up as the Council of God, even up to the Supreme Commission of this Council. The head of the latter was Kabagu, who was at the same time curator of the archives of the great library of Thebes.

UNFORTUNATE INCIDENT: MOSES KILLS AN EGYPTIAN

Moses was also an inspector, like his fellow Initiates, Hora, Meremapu, Anana, all sacred scribes.

During these inspection tours he would sometimes travel away from the nine savant priests attached to the person of the king, and from Sethi-Menephta, the son of Ramses II, as well from the royal princess, his adoptive or real mother.

We can see, in the report written in demotic language by the scribe Kanitzir to the attention of his superior Bakenptah, the Apurus, the Hebrews carrying stones under the command of the police captain Aménéman. The same document mentions the distribution of food to soldiers and recruits.

At that time, Egypt was endeavoring to connect Pelusium to Heliopolis by constructing a chain of forts and great strongholds, such as Ramses and Pachtum, near the freshwater canal which joined the Nile to the Red Sea, in the locations which are called today Wadi-Tumilat.

"During one of his inspection, Moses saw an Egyptian mistreat a Hebrew." Exodus, Ch. 11, v. 11. Religious Law made it a duty to defend the unjustly attacked man.

"In defending the Hebrew, Moses killed the Egyptian" Exodus, Ch. II, v. 12. The priest of Osiris was now confronted with the most redoubtable affair that could happen to him.

Under the Pastor Kings rule, he would have been easily vindicated; but under Ramses' judicial system, the ancient law had regained all its vigor. *"Moses buried the corpse in the sand"*: Exodus, Ch. II, v. 12. But the Hebrew he had saved, not recognizing him as one of his race, lacked gratitude.

The next day, indeed, wanting to stop two Apurus who were fighting, Moses heard them apostrophizing him in the following way: *"Are you our prince? Are you our judge? Do you want to kill us like the Egyptian of yesterday?"* (Exodus, Ch. II, v. 14);

With that disclosure, a denunciation could ensue, and a lawsuit begin. Moreover, Pharaoh, sensing the particular genius of *Moses*, feared that he might overpower his own son Sethi Ménephta.

REMNANTS OF RAM'S LAWS VS TAURUS KELTIC MORES

It is necessary here to remind the reader of the legal customs of that time. In all Societies of the Keltic Race, public reprisal did not belong to tribunals, but only to the next of kin of the victim. The next of kin turned into accuser like our prosecutors, and from then on he was registering as a *Goel*, meaning *blood avenger*.

Justice, represented by members of the Council of the Gods, remained absolutely neutral, purely arbitral, as it is still today in the countries where subsists the neo-Keltic custom, the Right of Odin.

The Council of the Gods merely demanded proof of the

crime or innocence and pronounced the sentence of condemnation or acquittal.

England has kept these arbitral habits. On the contrary, in this respect, the Napoleonic Code, the Roman Law, is a direct legacy of the Law of Taurus, the Babylonian schism, separation of Law proper from Religious Equity.

Once the unfavorable verdict pronounced, its execution belonged to the Goels. The convict was delivered to the parents of the victim, who required the application of the sentences, according to the mores, laws and rites of the country. The schism of Irshu, the despotism inaugurated by Ninus, the wars of conquest, unleashing the passions and instincts of Peoples and Races, had everywhere overshadowed the Science and Wisdom of Ram's laws.

As the crimes had multiplied, the penalties had been aggravated by the fact that politics complicated all social relations, on territories where orthodoxes and schismatics, vanquished and victors, conquered and conquerors, met each other at each step. Far from the regular courts, the retaliation corresponding to Lynch's law was applied frequently, leading to frightful abuses.

The first two High Councils, wherever they could, endeavored to mitigate, even far away from their temple, the reprisals among families and tribes which are still at play today.

In the Orthodox countries, like Egypt, the Council of the Gods retained an important prerogative: the conversion of the death sentence into exile.

For its part, the Council of God kept another equally solemn prerogative: the inviolability of the fugitive in the temples declared places of refuge.

Through the tragical dramas of Euripides, Sophocles, and Aeschylus, we can see how, in this so-called heroic period, the influence of the Assyrians, the Phoenicians, the Turanians, and the invasions of those schismatics in Europe, had overexcited the impulse for family retaliation. In *Furious Hercules*, c. 732; in *Oedipus at Colone*, c. 274; in the *Choephores*, c. 05; in *Electre*, c. 360, 388, 392.

Thus, the broad spirit of Ram, the universal right of Aries, no longer restrain the behaviors of the family, the commune, and the tribe. The general disorder is even the source of the later institution of the Ordalies, trial by ordeal. These old ordeals are voiced by the guards' coryphée in *Antigone*, a Sophocles' play.

"We offer to grab red irons from the flames,
To walk through burning pyres;
We take all the Gods to witness
That this crime was not committed or premeditated by us."

Thus was fading the Empire of Ram even in its Greek colonies, at the time when *Moses's classmate Orpheus* is about to leave Egypt to go to Thrace/Greece and reinstate the first two High Councils and the tribunal of the Amphictyons. It is to his movement, it is to his mission that Euripides refers in *Oreste*, from verse 511, speaking of the Orphic law, relative to the commutation of the death sentence into exile:

"In their wise equity, our ancestors wanted
That the man who had defiled his soul with a murder,
Could avoid avenging eyes focused on him,
And avoid retaliation by fleeing his country.

Eustatha of Constantinople, in his Commentaries on the *Iliad,* p. 609, reports that the murderer was to make the most of this forced absence *to be purified in a temple* and bring back a *certificate of rebirth.* Expiatory tests, both physical and moral, were severe. To endure them required an absolute desire to recover. Therefore, to this end, soul and body therapists had designed their rites and ceremonies with as much wisdom as science.

In Egypt those laws were enforced masterfully; and at that very time Orpheus was inspired by them.

MOSES FINDS REFUGE IN THE TEMPLE OF JETHRO

This is why *Moses* exiled himself in Upper Egypt, in the land of Midian (near the Nile's sources), in the vicinity of the Temple of which *Jethro* was the High Priest, the Raguel, Overseer of the Great God: Exodus, Ch. II, v. 18.

Exodus transcribed by Ezra, although based on ancient manuscripts, does not equal in depth the Orthodox Dorian revelation of Moses' fifty first chapters (Genesis), but it still contains important Mysteries-Revelations, retold in the Kaldean, Assyrian books, called M-Asshour, (the latter not to be mistaken with the second Massora).

Thus the story of the well, of the 7 daughters of the *Raguel,* coming to water the so-called flocks of their father, and the 7 so-called hostile pastors, allegorically represent certain mysteries of Initiation well-known by Kabbalists.

"Go, from the bottom of the pit, the Truth.". This verse shows that these ancient Mysteries have passed in our languages, although their ancient reality is no longer understood or explained. The name of *Moses* (Moïshe) himself means the *baptized,* and his Egyptian name before his purification was *Asarsiph.* (aSar=prince, Siph=wise, savant, purposeful).

I cannot reveal here to what realm of facts, cosmogonic and human, *baptism* was then connected; and we will not follow Moses walking down to the famous central well of the Pyramids, *seeking voluntary death,* in a tomb, the mundification (cleansing) by the water, the purification by fire, the vivification by air and by earth, finally the resurrection in the Living God by Aether or Akasa.

TRADITIONS OF PREVIOUS RACES AND CIVILIZATIONS

The country where *Moses* had taken refuge, the temple where he was going to receive his *supreme initiation* was predestined to transmit to him the oldest Traditions.

There was residing a college of Orthodox ramids Exodus., Ch. 2 v. 24-25. Its members were not of the Keltic race, nor did they belong to the Dorians of Kaldea like the Abramids; they were black skinned Ethiopians, of the same Race as the ancient masters of Asia and Africa before Ram.

This Race still exists today, mixed as the brown-skin Aryas. Their sacred Sciences and Traditions *went back to the first human cycles prior to that of the Aries*, although they had accepted the recasting of ancient Traditions, the Law marked by Aries, zodiacal hieroglyph. They were therefore Orthodoxes par excellence.

Ancient masters of Egypt to the Nile's sources, the men of this Race will still be its last defenders, and will consecrate, as Pharaoh, one of their own, under the significant name of *Tharaka*, third king of the twenty-fifth dynasty.

They will thus affirm until the year 670 BC, their absolute opposition to the schismatic Empire of Assyria; they will oppose to its tyrant Assar-Haddon, a prince of their own blood, bearing the same name as the ancient Kousha Tharak'hya, who had (4,580 years before) pushed away beyond the Indus the Prince Regent, Irshu, and his schismatic followers.

Among the books *quoted by Moses in his Sepher*, there are some that he studied in the temple of the Raguel: *Generations of Adam, Wars of IEVE, Judges, Prophecies,* etc.

There, Moses, who became the husband of Zipporah, daughter of the High Priest Jethro, prepared for many years all his intellectual work, all his social organization.

There Moses reached the last boundaries of Sciences and Sacred Arts.

Towards this little piece of land, a large number of Orthodoxes belonging to either the neo-Ramid or the Law of Ram proper, came on pilgrimage.

This place was also dear to the last remnants of the Red Race, as well as to the Bodhones Kelts faithful to the Traditions of the Dorians. Entire tribes of the latter rallied to Moses under the name of Massouas, before he made his move. although they do not belong to the Exodus of the Hebrews, they will play a great role in history by marching on to Egypt through the deserts and the Delta.

It would be improbable that apart from affiliating himself to the Abramids, *Moses*, in his symbolic genealogy, would not connect himself to the Cycle of Aries.

In fact, in the twenty-fifth verse of Veelleh-Shemoth (Exodus book), Moses said about himself that he was Ram's intellectual son: *"Now Am-Ram married Iokabed, of whom he had Aaron and Moses"*. Am-Ram is the son of the so-called *Levi*, which means the *"priesthood of all the Orthodox countries"*.

In original Egyptian, as in Hebrew and Arabic, *Am* means origin, genetic stock, family, mother, metropolis, rule.

In Arabic, this root still expresses the action of serving as a type and a model, of regulating and methodizing, of being or of having a principle or a cause.

MOSES IS HEIR OF AM-RAM AND IO-KA-BED

So, in the Am-Ram hierogram, Moses himself says hermetically to whom can understand it, that he is the heir of the theocratic and social *Tradition of Ram* by AM-Ram the father by the mother *Io-ka-bed*, that is to say by the sanctuary of *Io* or *Isis*.

The same root *AM* (as in Am-Ram) expresses in Coptic the Moon, in old Arabic the Sun; the Arabs properly are designated as *sons of the maid* (ouma) or *sons of the separate female Principle*, in reference to the rather injurious allegory coined by the Orthodoxes, because the Arabs had, during the Schism of Irshu, taken the side of those favoring the overthrow of the Male-Female conjoint attributes, such as the Turanians, Tatars and Mongols. Hence the lunar crescent on their pennants.

Here are the hierarchical elements of *Io-ka-bed*.

In Egyptian ideography, **Io** expresses, at the positive level *"the light"*, at the comparative level *"doctrine"*, at the superlative level *"manifested intelligence/spirit"*.

Ka, means positively *a place*, figuratively it means a *rally*, and at a pure intellectual level it means, a *condensation*, a *cohesive formation*. In Arabic, this sign *Ka* further indicates the action of gathering around oneself by a call, (call to prayer, war, riot, study).

Bed, the Keltic root of the word *bod*-hone, meaning *without a bed*, expresses literally a *bed*, figuratively an *isolation*, at the pure intellectual level it designates a *particular existence or specific individuality*.

It is therefore by the means of combination and synthesis of doctrines (*Io+Ka+Bed*) of which the temples of Isis were the teaching Institutions, that *Moses has rediscovered the Tradition of Ram*, and thus, as did the Abramid Order, he is following the rule, the pure Law of the Aries and the Lamb.

PRIESTS EVOKING MOSES' HISTORY AND DOCTRINE

Manetho has already shown *Moses* as an Orthodox, priest of Osiris, and we know that *Osiris* means *"the Intellectual Lord"*, and is the same as *Ammon-Ra, the Law of Aries*, the same as *Deva-Nahousha*, and *Dio-Nysos, "the Spirit of God"*, same as *Gian-Shyd*, same as *Ram*.

Let's listen here the Egyptian priests themselves recount the story of Moses, as they could tell it to strangers, especially to Romans. When Strabo visited Egypt with Ælius Gallus, who was its prefect, and with Athenodorus of Tarsus, Stoic philosopher, the priests of Egypt told him the following:

"A High priest of Osiris, Musaeus (Moses) was governing part of the southern country.

Dissenting with the external cult, Moses left the nome, with a crowd of followers who worshipped Divinity like him.

He professed that zoological symbolism kept the people in error about divine realities; that the andrological symbolism of Libyans and Greeks had the same inconvenience; that if the Living God manifests Himself throughout the entire Universe, it is a reason not to particularize him, by reducing Him to be only one of the partial forms of the Cosmos.

He was adding that one should limit oneself to worshiping the Ineffable in a sanctuary worthy of Him, surrounded by a consecrated territory, devoid of any representative image, any sign and any figurative attribute.

He recommended that well-chosen persons sleep at night in the Temple, to receive oneirocritical or other communications of interest to either the individual or the Society.

According to Moses, only the person of Wisdom and Righteousness alone merited that favor and was to be always ready to receive the benefit, and to be always worthy of being honored by the manifestation of the Supreme Will.

Nothing about Moses indicated intolerance.

His strength resided in God and the Sciences attached to God's worship.

His goal was: to find a neutral territory to establish a temple, a University of God.

He was promising to institute a Religion, a social Synthesis, without sacerdotal exaction, without imaginative fantasy under the pretext of revelation, without overload of formalism, without licentious practices. Moses gained great power over the public opinion of these regions.

So far, the foregoing refers to Moses *before the Exodus.*

Here is how the priests of Egypt who spoke to Strabo retold Moses' venture *after the Exodus:*

"A number of neighboring tribes came to enlarge the group of his followers. His Teachings and Promises enthused them, and he succeeded in creating a new State of relative importance.

His successors conformed to his precepts and walked straight in the ways of Justice and true Religion; but not for a long time. Soon this Society degenerated and went from ignorance to superstition and fanaticism."

This appreciation by the priests of Egypt is fair, measured and accurate; and they could say no more and no better, without exceeding their oaths of secrecy, to inquisitive foreigners, especially to Roman anarchists.

MOSES' TRUE PURPOSE AND MISSION

A continuator of the Abramids and Dorian Orthodoxes of the whole world, *Moses* did not intend only to establish a new Worship of the Supreme God, since, despite the schism and in the depths of Initiation, the true Religion, the true scientific and social Synthesis still existed in Egypt itself, as in Asia and Europe.

It does not really matter for the Sages of all times, whether individuals worship the Divinity in forms which, if exact, can only be the masterpiece of the Art and Genius manifesting integral Science, or whether they worship Divinity without a form.

This alternative way of worshiping Divinity though certainly possible, is more dangerous, because it allows a greater number of ignorant uninitiated individuals to inadequately materialize the Spirit and Soul, source-origin of our Universe's Life, by means of multiple random thought-forms or thought-words, while *only Wisdom and Science can truly reflect and manifest the Soul and Spirit of the Universe's Life.*

The members of the Council of God and the Council of the Gods had other aims, which took into account not only the individual, but also the collective Bodies that we *call Societies*, themselves *organs of Humanity.*

Thus thought Christna, Fo-Hi, Zoroaster, the Abramids, the Orthodox Egyptians, and finally Moses, himself a member of the Council of God, in Egypt.

That the Ram Cycle and its Law were in their memory is impossible to deny. That the Universal Law of this Cycle was broken by the schism of Irshu and all its political consequences, is also undeniable.

That the aim of all the Orthodoxes was to strive everywhere to remedy the public Evil and to bring back the renovation of the general Good, is what simple common sense suffices to assert.

At the Intellectual level, the *Science of the Principles*, which properly constitutes the hierarchy of Dorian knowledge, and corresponds to the first letter of the sacred name (Iod), this Science, the source of all possible Synthesis, was, either lost to the vulgar or condemned to remain veiled to the political Powers completely detached from all control and hostile to the ancient Authority.

In the Universal social Order, as long as at its own risk a People was not constituted around a purely Dorian University, it was impossible for the ancient Science to reinstate in the World the primacy of arbitral Authority over Power, and restore the healthy organism, national and international, of the Synarchy with its three arbitration Councils.

The Orthodoxes of the whole world knew all these things. We saw them recognizing themselves in Egypt, Syria and Kanaan, when the Abramids came there to expand their movement.

We have seen the fruits brought by this profound movement in Egypt itself, where it led to the expulsion of the schismatics by the Orthodoxes, and the enforcement of the ancient Mastery of International Justice by the Pharaohs, who, even in their initiation names, did not hesitate to link themselves to the Cycle of Ram, witness the *Ram-Ses*.

All these facts are connected together like a geometrical progression, and certainly they are not the result of chance.

Only one man of systemic genius capable of potent Synthesis, namely a Soul and Intelligence united with a cosmogonic Puissance, could push forward the intellectual and social program of the Orthodoxes, giving it broad universal views, and a nation as a defensive body, with its proper territory for sustenance, a Council of God and a Council of the Gods for Power.

Now, no one can doubt that *this was the goal of Moses*, because it is precisely thanks to the living leverage he has organized, that present Europe is beginning to manifest the universal Principle and the Goal that the Dorians of all times have assigned to the march of Humanity.

HUMANITY: A REFLECTION OF DIVINITY

I do not write here again for the basic theologians, nor for their pupils. Nor do I write for the "Atheological" iconoclasts, which are more dogmatic, more ignorant and even more elementary.

I write for those who, informed by the secondary and higher education of our Universities, see God as something other than a mere word, see in religions something other than clashing idols, see in Universal History other than a necrographic chronology without laws, without cause, without Principle and without Purpose. This is why I will recall here what was the Teaching that Moses received from his Egyptian and Ethiopian masters, not to mention the Encyclopedia of the Abramids, (Sarai) already explicated in the preceding chapter. It is the intellectual milieu that one must have present in mind to assess a man of the magnitude of Moses.

I know perfectly well that basic theologians avoid substantiating anything, making divine arbitrariness intervene at all times, as they fantasize it to be, and thus their fancy corners the human Spirit to pursue a double suicide: either rejecting the religious tradition, or abdicating its own power, according to the formula, *"Credo quia absurdum"*, *"I believe, because it's absurd."*

But among the theologians themselves, as in all the other categories of teachers, there are noble minds who suffer from such ignorance, and who feel its disastrous consequences.

I will not, therefore, be afraid to say, in front of them, that *Divinity acts within Humanity only through Humanity itself*, and that *Humanity, a reflection of the Divinity*, has, as supreme receptivity channel with the Divine: *Intelligence*, the Higher Attribute of the Human Soul.

HUMAN COMMUNICATION WITH DIVINITY IS A SCIENCE

Now, the *communication between Divinity and Humanity by Intelligence is Science and not otherwise.*

But the kind of Science focused on universal Cosmic and Divine Principles, is not accessible at whim.

It requires such an exercise of all the Faculties of the Soul, such an exercise of the physiological organism which is its support, that it is almost impossible for modern individuals to understand what the Ancients meant by achievement of Wisdom and Science; this achievement, here below on Earth, occurs by the *reintegration of Man in the Kingdom of God*, as the Roman poet Pindar has said, along with all the ancient Initiates.

Indeed, any piece of wood is not fit to be carved into a statue of Mercury, any kind of man cannot become an adept of Integral Science.

DEFINING GENIUS IN RELATION WITH PROVIDENCE

So, like today, Genius was rare, although less rare than today, because one had, if one willed it, access to all the relevant sources of information, all the means to reorient oneself and be re-formed in the image of God.

It is true that Genius escapes the usual boundaries,

disregards the pressures of all antecedence; *Genius* is, as its name indicates, the individualized generative force, the first Will which, similar to the divine powers of Cosmos, *creates and generates.*

In Genius, man is united directly with the Cosmogonic Puissance that originates him.

Times and milieus stimulate the manifestation of Genius, but do not explicate its Ontological reality, no more than do atavism, race, heredity or family.

Shakespeare, a Keltic born in misty England, has the creative Soul of an Oriental, the intellectual exuberant Life of a Hindu like Valmiki. Byron, born under the same misty climate, in a milieu and time when the most atrophying hypocritical "can't" was prevalent, nevertheless developed the free allure of a Hellene, the Soul of a Greek poet of the great classical epoch, the elegant lyricism of a Pindar, the strength of an Aeschylus, the sober and warm tone of a Sophocles.

To explain those facts by atavism or climate, and not by its true cause, *reincarnation,* is to explain nothing. It is through this mysterious gate that the unforeseen and the unknown come into play, and this entrance is basically only a return.

All, even the misfortune that Moses had to kill an Egyptian and to be forced to flee, seemed to repel him from Earth, send him back to the Unknown heights he was destined to manifest.

And so it is, always.

All the interrelated organs of sick Societies rally to oppose the therapist, as would a species against a kingdom, as would a flesh frenzied at the approach of a Spirit that will enliven or enlighten it. In vain: for, are the Times not propitious? Genius overcomes them; are the Milieus improper? he dominates them; is it about Race? he transforms it; is it about Family? he passes through one, and most often does not have one, for he is the Ancestor of all.

Among other humans as well as among his own family, he is the strange and the stranger, he is the Movement to Inertia, Light to Darkness, an Organic Force confronting the Social chaos, but having for mission, dead or alive, to enliven it, to coerce it to a more potent Life, and to re-imprint on its own forehead the mark of God, the triple tiara, the crown of light.

Scourge when he holds the sword, blessing when he carries the palm of Science and Wisdom, Genius is the Envoy for the punishment of the crimes or the reward of the virtues and the hope of the Peoples.

Now, if human dust on this Earth seems to be doing its own will, if it has the right and the relative liberty to oppose itself to its own happiness and to its own rebuilding into a divine Body, if, like the monster of Job's poem, it can unknowingly wallow in the Light rays and on all the gifts of Heaven, *there is, in the Cosmos, other Humanities to which the Universal Solidarity makes a duty to intervene when it is time.*

Ram, Christna, Fo-Hi, Zoroaster, Moses, Orpheus, are incontestable interventions of this divine Humanity: Providence.

MOSES POTENT AGENT OF DIVINE PROVIDENCE

Moses was one of the central forces under which the ruins of human institutions were opened either to collapse, or to whirlwind into rebuilding themselves.

But such Souls are fatal or providential Puissances: *Fatal,* when their own will does not subject them to their heavenly Principle, which they ignore; *Providential,* when it is given to them to orient themselves on a precise path of absolute Science and Wisdom, and from then on to act only according to an unerring Principle, with the appropriate means and with an unmistakable End Purpose.

Now, though weakened by Politics, the ancient temples were, par excellence, oriented by this *Providential Divine Principle,* which Europeans today can no longer recognize except after corporeal death.

To the potency of the Soul and Intelligence, to Genius in all possible orders, the temples offered all *the proofs, all the experiments, all the manifestations,* all the certainties which could endow their adepts with all the radiance of Science, Wisdom and Truth.

These Virtues were incorporated within Divinity itself and

infused the Initiate with some of their superlative Qualities. Consequently, it was demanded from the adept such an intense intellectual and moral exertion, such a degree of sacrifice, such an oblation of their own life, and if all were called, there were few who could achieve full initiation.

Moses was one of those Elects.

He climbed all the degrees of revelations, reached that summit of the Supreme Angle that the Sacerdotes designate as Universal, *the Divine Union*, image of the Unity of God, *manifesting on Earth as the great Social God.*

Physical *Natural Sciences* were, as I said, the first ones taught. They were the *Lesser Mysteries* of the Great Goddess, of the Eternal Feminine, of Isis, the wife of Osiris.

Human sciences came next, and, through the practice of the corresponding Arts, one would acquire the so-called heroic virtues. They were the Mysteries of Horus, Mithras or Hermes the Triple, Apollo the Great Mediator, and Psychurgy was the opening key. According to the value of the postulant, this initiation lasted more or less a long time, sometimes until death.

This degree of Initiation gave the postulant the title of *Son of Man*, the previous sciences having earned him the name of *Son of the Woman.*

The topic of the Third level of Initiation was *the Cosmogonic Sciences* and their applied Arts. This third level of Knowledge gave the title of *Son of the Great Goddess*, with rank in the Council of the Gods. Those three series encompassed the whole revelation of Isis, the *Physical and Hyperphysical Nature* of the triple EVE, to be re-associated with the I, Iod.

Finally, the fourth level in the hierarchy of Sciences and applied Arts, called the Divine Order proper, culminated in *Theogony* and through Theurgy attained the Supreme *Mystery of Unity.*

It was then that the new Epopte saw the last veils of Revelation fall down, and was reinstated in the Kingdom of God, having acquired the *Wisdom and the Divine Virtues*, with the title *of Son of God.*

The difficulty, the dangers of the ordeals increasing even

more as one climbed the quadruple hierarchy of revelations, very few postulants reached the third degree, a smaller number still reached the fourth, to sit on the Right or first letter of the divine name IEVE (Iod is the first letter of Ieve in Hebrew).

FOUR DISTINCT STEPS ON THE LADDER OF INITIATION

This division into four parts, into four series of Teachings, is presented by Pythagoras, who, after many years, reached them under the Greek names of *Parazkeyê*, Preparation, *Kathàrsis*, Purification, *Téléiotês*, Perfection, and finally *Epiphany*, or View from above. I know that this Spirit of Ancient Teaching and Science, will seem strange to theologians and to academics today; but it is not in my power to change the intellectual construct of those ancient times, which did not permit that *Truth* humans are capable of acquiring could be taught otherwise.

The first two High Councils *did not demand Faith* from anyone; but if they *provided* to individuals *the degree of Certitude* which their mental and moral strength allowed them to conquer, they nevertheless demanded from the mind power of every postulant all the guarantees necessary for their own development as well as for the Sanctity of the Living Truth, of which they, the Councils, had to defend the Existence in Humanity itself.

Never God in His Essence, nor in the Substance through which He manifests Himself, was lowered to the level of individual person, for that cannot be.

But the individual, according to the ascending force of his Spirit and his Soul, his Genius, and his Character, was informed that, providing he desired it, he would have to reach his own optimal level, and to rise, if he could, to the summit of Heaven, not solely in a verbal or imaginative way, but scientific and real.

WHAT ABOUT NATURAL PHYSICAL SCIENCES?

Not only all those sciences we know today were taught, up to those we do not know of yet, which were encompassing destruction of Matter proper, including the *transmutation* impossible without destructibility; was taught also the science of *superior homogeneous Substance* which sustains all other realities, this substance being itself a product of what the ancients called the *direct forces of the Soul of the World.*

WHAT ABOUT HUMAN SCIENCES?

Not only the physical, but *hyperphysical* constitution of the individual was demonstrated, from Anatomy to Physiology in its relations with the Life of the Cosmos, from Psychology to Psychurgy in its relations with the Soul of the World.

Was also scientifically demonstrated the existence of the Organic Soul, which, spiritualized by Intelligence while on Earth, is forming through expanded Science and Consciousness the Astral Body of Light which would raise the Soul away from Earth, as if carried on an ethereal chariot, will say Plato (the kabbalists will say: Merkabah).

This same positive demonstration was the foundation of the highly scholarly Cults of the Dead and of the glorified Souls, the mediator Angels being reinstated into Divinity.

Consider that the Ancients were far too positive and far too conscientious to practice a Cult of the Dead if they had not precisely known of the *Life Beyond the Grave and its different hierarchies;* and would they have raised altars to the Souls belonging to both heroic and divine hierarchies, if this worship had been useless to Humanity, and if Communion with these Souls had not been certain and experimentally proved.

WHAT ABOUT COSMOGONIC SCIENCES?

The living Universe, with its triple Life of Supreme Intelligence, Creative Soul, Generative Form, was studied and known up to the interconnective Unity of its total Organism; but I will not further lift Moses' veil.

FINALLY, WHAT ABOUT THE DIVINE SCIENCES PROPER?

The degrees which led up to the summit of those Sciences, to the supreme Union of the Soul with the pure Spirit through the Universe, were no less scientific than the preceding ones.

Tradition teaches that Moses and Orpheus climbed up all the steps of Initiation. Their very names were given to them in the temples, as was the custom.

Orpheus, Arpha, means *Savior, Moses,* means *saved by Water or Baptism;* for, surely, the story of the bitumen-coated basket must not be more literally understood than the so-called fish of Jonah, which is but one of the thousand forms of Ionah or Feminine Initiation. Like Moses, *Orpheus* offered to the Dorians of Thrace the worship of the organic or cosmogonic God, Masculine and Feminine at once:

Zeus arsen geneto, Zeus ambrotos epleto numphê.
Zeus is the divine Groom, Zeus is the Bride.

Obviously, the Creator God, presented in this indissoluble Union, points to orthodox neo-Ramism; this Zeus is very identical to IEVE, to Osiris-Isis, to Iswara-Pracriti, but *indivisibly united and not arbitrarily separated,* such as Irshu's schism had done.

ORPHEUS, MOSES: SAME SOURCE, DIFFERENT OUTCOME

The Cosmogonies of *Orpheus* and *Moses,* drawn from the same sources, also present the most striking analogies, even in the hierograms by which they characterize the Principles and Living Faculties of the Universe and of the Social State.

Their fundamental institutions themselves, the restoration of a Council of God, around a renewed universal Synthesis, and a Council of the Gods or lay Initiates, serving as magistrates or arbitrators in the Sanhedrinic Assemblies or Greek emphictyonic, were established on the same type as the ancient Synarchy.

Yet the religious and social work of these great men was as different as their individuality and the people they organized.

The Dorian *Orpheus* was divinely in love *with the Feminine Principle.*

He understood it with the enthusiasm of a genial artist; he felt it with a holy and irresistible adoration; he attested it in the Intellectual Life he impressed upon the sanctuaries of Hellas, and displayed it in a magical impulse, whence issued forth in a dazzling light all the divine forms of the Hyperphysical Universe, all the radiance of Beauty manifesting the Truth.

In contrast, *Moses*, shipwrecked of the social deluge launched by the Yonijas of Irshu, the man champion of the ancient Authority, standing up against the political Power, was a formidable *worshiper of the Male Principle*.

He understood that Principle with an admirable mental force, he felt it with a soul as deep as the tomb, rough as the desert; he testified to this in an intellectual and social masterwork, savant, pure, impenetrable and inextricable, indestructible like the Great Pyramid of Giseh.

Both Moses and Orpheus, drinking from the same sacred springs, saw there the same Goddess unveiled, the same Truth, but one in the Infinite, in its perfect Form, the other in the Absolute, in its incommunicable Essence.

So, reintegrating the angelic Genies, Orpheus revealed to Europe a doctrine of the Soul, Divine Beauty, EVE as Life in all its intellectual aspects; as for Moses, he revealed, to very few minds, the all-powerful Force of the resorbing absolute Being, in his Principle, all Life through Death.

If these two geniuses had been united in one, the Cycle of Ram would have been integrally renewed.

That did not happen, because the hunt for local symptoms was the only opportunity offered to them to cure the general political disease which assailed the terrestrial social body and opposed ones to the others its dissociated members

THE LEGACY OF ORPHEUS

Here is an overview of the works of *Orpheus*, all *esoteric*, and of which there remain only sketchy fragments:

Theogony, Symbolic Generation of Principles;

Cosmogony, Organic Constitution of the Universe;

The *Sacred Verb*, ideographic Grammar;

Mythology, Symbolic Aesthetics of Art, according to the Secret Science;

The *Mysteries*;

The *Oaths;*

Descent into *the Underworld,* Life after Death;

The three *Victories,* under Earth, in the Atmosphere, in Heaven;

The *Blessings;*

The *Veil and the Net of Souls;*

The *Corybantes,* Earth Mysteries;

Bacchus, Celestial Mysteries, or Mysteries of Pure Spirit;

Argonautics, the Great Hermetic Masterwork;

Argolic, the White or Dorian Tradition;

The Sphere, System of the Universe;

Astronomical books;

Books of the *12 Year Periods,* Modes or Cycles

Book of Changes, Chemistry and Alchemy;

Jupiter and Juno, Biology of Heaven and Earth;

Bacchus and Cybele, Spirit and Light, in their relationship with Substance and Matter;

Natural and magical botany;

Stones, natural and magical mineralogy;

Anemoscopy, Science of the Atmosphere;

Earthquakes.

There are still many books of Orpheus mentioned as lost, among others his magnificent *Reform of the Musical System,* as understood by the Ancients.

Orpheus gave back an intelligence and an organic soul to the turbulent and ferocious anarchy of the Kelts of Europe who, from the North, had assailed the Sanctuaries of the Colonies of Ram, Delphi among others.

To reach his goal, Orpheus spread honey on the golden cup containing the stern philter of sacred Wisdom and Science, he seized the Soul by the wings of Imagination.

Had it not been for this "honey", his fanciful and sanguinary compatriots would have rejected the divine cup and persecuted with all their Power the Authority presenting it to them, even more so if they had first tasted the bitterness of the remedy destined to correct their hateful passions and their brutal instincts.

Orpheus gave his life to accomplish a salutary reform, and he acted accordingly by ensnaring the Souls in the veil and in the golden net he had woven so cleverly.

He was, through the Art of Magic Science, the greatest wizard and the most accomplished civilizer that the Earth has ever known.

Through this divine man, like by a lyre well-tuned and touched by the fingers of Heaven, the Temples were purified, all their disagreements of doctrines dissolved, men and women came back to receive from the Mysteries a physical, moral and intellectual culture, that the barbarian vulgarity had profaned and distorted.

I know that the nineteenth century Boeotians (ignorant) and Philistines (hypocrite) have denied the very existence of Orpheus as they denied that of Moses.

But a coherent Social Corps does not create itself, neither does it surge from the mere will of enlightened individuals.

A Power of Specification is needed which determines it at the origin, and this Power is called the Religious or Synthetic Genius.

The Venus of Praxiteles supposes a sculptor, historical Greece proves the existence of Orpheus, like Israel, Christianity and Islam prove the existence of Moses, Jesus and Mohammed.

On the entire coast of Mediterranean Europe, the epoch Orpheus was to revive for 1,000 years, was the sunset and not the dawn of a civilization originated from India and Egypt.

A mixture of Keltic, Phoenician, Zend and Sanskrit, the so-called Greek language had already attained its peak of formation and perfection.

During those times, the power of the Lydians was, while declining, transmitting the trident (power of seafaring) to the Rhodians, themselves rivals of the Phoenicians of Sidon; and large sailing fleets passed between the bronze legs of the Apollo giant statue, which dominated the two docks of one of the ports of Rhodes.

Orpheus, a contemporary of Erechtheus, came to reconstruct an intellectual and social Synthesis among ferocious anarchists, certainly not naive barbarians. Descendants of formerly civilized nations, these peoples since long corrupted, then dis-associated, could no longer unite to defend themselves against the schismatic Kelts of Central Europe and Kourou, allies of Turanians and Caesars of Assyria.

Nevertheless, their temples still stored archives of Sciences, whose understanding and Synthesis was lost, but whose incontestable applications would do honor to present-day Europe. Today, Orpheus' spirit still inspires all manifestations of the Grand Art in Christendom, but in the form of a pale copy, without proper life, remaining weak until the Science of the Grand Art will be reconstituted.

This is the place to share an important Truth: it is not the artist who creates the Grand Art; the artist may be the one who analyses it, breaks it into elements of its divine associative harmony, but, more often it is the Grand Art that does create the artist. For the Grand Art to create the artist, the Science of Art must pre-exist, and that Science is included in *Religion, defined as Synthesis of all Sciences.*

This is why, without the Scientific Initiation of Orpheus (received in the Temple-Universities of Egypt), Greek Savant Art would never have existed, and would not have produced its multiple refractions in the intellectual and moral fields within social Christianity.

The radiance of this religious genius does not stop there.

That radiance will manifest in Christianism itself, from its beginning, in the Gospel of St. John.

THE LEGACY OF MOSES

But for now let's go back to Moses.

Moses was 60 years old when Ramses II died. But before, the reins of the Egyptian government had, from the hands of this king, passed into those of a Sovereign Pontiff.

The Ramses were Nazarenes, lay Initiates from the temples of Etruria.

In Egypt itself, as reported by Greek historians, the Ramses bore the name of Larthes, meaning in the Etruscan language *King of Justice*, the equivalent of the word Melchizedek in Hebrew.

When Ramses II had sufficiently secured the political and external peace of Egypt, he retired to private life, and placed at the head of the government his fourth son, Khamouas, Sovereign Pontiff.

According to the ancient law of Aries, the troops were dismissed once the war was over and the peace treaties were signed. The military general staffs then joined the other Savant Corps of the temples; the lower officers and the soldiers returned to their respective Nome, and were no longer drafted except to gymnastics schools, and several times a year, at certain festivals, they had to participate in great military maneuvers; as for the mercenaries they were fully dismissed or employed in public works, according to the mode of organization which we have described before.

Egypt, like China, like ancient India, ancient Iran, Greece and Italy of those times, absolutely did not favor the system of permanent armies, which was enforced by the Assyrian Caesarism under Asher-Ubalid, then under Bel-Nirari, then under Budil, who in turn took over the imperial throne of the Ionian federations, since the advent of Ramses II until the end of the reign of Menephtah I.

During this demobilization period the Assyrian politics unleashed the old leagues around Egypt, and even in Egypt, it stirred the revolution which *Moses* took advantage of for effecting his movement of escape.

Then, from the Delta to Ethiopia, turmoil resumed. The same was happening far away from Egypt; and the usual coalitions took advantage of the openings offered to them.

Khamouas died about 1,350 years before our era, and appointed to the throne his brother, Menephtah, the thirteenth son of Ramses II.

This sovereign was sixty years old when he took the Aries

scepter, and before he had readied his army for war, Egypt was invaded, to the north-west by Mermaiou, son of Deîd, king of a Kelto-Phoenician colony of a Libyan kingdom under the double regency of Tripoli and Tunis.

Meanwhile, in the north-east, there was a push of Akaians, (proto-Greeks) and the Assyrian Caesars, Budil, then Bel-Nirari I, intrigued as always, to submit to their suzerainty the Ionian confederations and Phoenician emporocracies of Asia Minor and of Syria, which Egypt, on the contrary and in accordance with the ancient Order, had to maintain in its jurisdiction, under penalty of death.

India, played only an indirect role in these disputes, firstly through its Sovereign Pontiff, and through its initiate Orders of military officers who -then under the name of Heraclids, ruled Lydia- had sent to Italy an expedition, or rather an immigration ordered by Tyrrhenius.

PLANNING OF THE EXODUS

It was while Menephtah filled its empty fortresses, gathered around the general staffs the regular corps of the Nômes, transferred from the public works of Thebes, Abydos, Memphis and the Delta, the working brigades of foreign mercenaries, that *Moses, supported by a whole formidable party of the Egyptian Priesthood*, made his famous emigration movement, famous enough not to insist upon it.

For a few years Ménephtah I was kept busy by the internal war, which he supported with the greatest energy, and which ended at the battle of Paarishaps with the bloody defeat he inflicted on Mermaiou.

The Abramids had their intelligence everywhere, in the Orthodox temples, in the palaces of kings, in the local debris of the ancient Councils. They were privy to Moses' project.

And Moses being ready for a long time, as well as his old master and his father-in-law Jethro with all his allies, the beginning of the action was decided, in *agreement with all the Dorians of the World* interested in the re-construction of a purely Dorian Synarchy.

Several millions of men of all races, of all classes, but whose core was formed by the Apurus of the Delta, whose general staff was formed by Dorians or Abramid Initiates, whose generals were priests of Osiris, whose general-in-chief was Moses and his master initiator, old Jethro, all this crowd of the Exodus started marching, and was carried to the Desert by a tremendous Spirit.

In the next chapter we shall see how, from the burning heights of Mount Sinai, this Spirit will mold that unruly crowd into an organic society

∞

CHAPTER XIII
SYNARCHIC CONSTITUTION OF ISRAEL -
COUNCIL OF GOD - COUNCIL OF THE GODS
COUNCIL OF THE ANCIENTS
MOSES' SCIENCE

INCOMPLETE CONSTITUTION OF ISRAEL

It is easy to understand, in Exodus as in Genesis, how much Moses opposed the political monarchy, in contrast with what the schism of Irshu had done.

Exodus, Ch. XVIII, v 16: *"The hand of the Lord will rise from His throne against Amalek and the Lord will wage war on him throughout the Cycles of all the Races.*

Obviously, this verse would have no real meaning if *Amalek* represented a mere man; in fact, that Amalek symbolizes the very Principle of the Military Power, crowned as absolute king, without submission to the Authority of the Teaching and Judicial Corps. It is therefore a Synarchy, a Social Government, in which impersonal Principles reign, that Moses will promote within the 50 Chapters of the Genesis book, a book which he wants to *transmit to future generations by means of a people* organized to be its guardian, watcher and keeper.

This synarchic Government has, as first highest institution, the High Council of God, or Priesthood, representing the integrality of the Teachings.

The second High Council of the Gods or Lay Initiates, is exercising the Judiciary, the Power proper.

Finally, in each tribe, the Council of Elders, exercises the local administration and small Magistracy.

This integral social body is structured by a scientific Constitution, reflecting, as a whole and in its details, the Duodecimal (12) System of the physical and hyperphysical Universe.

Such was then, more or less altered, the savant constitution of the Tyrians, the Trojans, the Greeks, the Etrurians, etc.

Then Jethro will journey to the Desert to complete with Moses his work of initiator, in accordance with the Order of Ram.

CONSTITUTION OF ISRAEL COMPLETED BY JETHRO

Until the arrival of Jethro, the institutions were incomplete, and confined to the Council of God and the twelve Councils of the Elders.

Exodus, Ch. XVIII, v. 7 "*As Moses had gone to meet his father-in-law, he bent down deeply before him.*"

Ibid., v. 12: "*And Jethro, Moses' father-in-law, made an offering of hosts to IEVE; and Aaron and all the elders of Israel came to break bread with him before IEVE.*"

Ibid., v. 13: "*The next day, Moses sat down to render justice to the people who came before him, from morning to evening.*"

Ibid., v. 17: "*You are not acting properly, replied Jethro.*"

Ibid., v. 19: "*Remember what I have to say to you, follow the advice that I have to give you, and IEVE will be with you. Give of your person only for all that concerns the Council of God, to express to "Him-God" the demands and needs of the people*".

Ibid., v. 20: "*And to teach the people the ceremonies, the manner of honoring IEVE, the method they must observe, and the rules of their actions*".

Ibid., v. 21: "*But choose from among all the people men that are tested as to their character, the strength of their soul, as to their fear of IEVE, as loving the Truth, as incorruptible, and give them Jurisdiction over 1000, 100, 50, and 10 men.*"

Ibid., v. 22: "*Let them be busy rendering justice to the people at all times.*"

Ibid., v. 23: "*If you do what I say to you, you will fulfill the Commandment of God, you will be able to actualize the Orders of His Kingdom; and all this people will return home peacefully.*"

Ibid., v. 24: "*Moses, having listened to his father-in-law, did what he had advised him.*"

In what precedes, the two Councils, the highest level, that of God and the third level, that of the Elders, indicated in verse 12, are complemented by the second level Power of the ancient social Trinity, known to the reader as the Council of the Gods.

This name is in too many passages of *W'eelle-Schemoth (Exodus* Ch. I, v1*)*, *W'ayera, W'ayedabber,* and I can't quote them all, but open any translated Bible, that of Lemaistre de Sacy (in French), for example, and you will find the following:

Exodus, Ch. XXII, v. 28: *"You will not speak badly of the Gods, that is, the Magistrates."*

Thus, the form of government instituted by Moses on the advice, on the order given him by his Initiator Jethro, in the name of IEVE, is indeed the *Synarchy*, that is to say *three Social Powers, none of which is political.*

Indeed, the Council of God formed by the Priesthood represents the Impersonal Authority of Science and Wisdom, as indicated by the words the High Priest wears on his chest: *Urim* and *Tumim, Science and Truth.*

This *mobile temple*, guarding the written and oral Dorian Science, delegates, by way of Exam and Selection, the Power of Justice to a Council of Lay Initiates, 70 in number, a number which we find in the Affiliation of Jacob, in the ancient Chinese University, and similarly, in the 70 affiliates Jesus Christ will send to the World.

Numbers, Ch. XI, v. 16: *"The Lord answered Moses: Assemble 70 men from among the Sages of Israel, whom you will know to be the most savant, and lead them to the entrance of the Tabernacle of the Covenant, where you will have them stay with you.*

Ibid., Ch. 17: *"I will come down there to speak to you; I will take from the Spirit that is in you, and I will inspire them."*

Ibid., Ch. 25: *"Then the Lord having descended into the cloud, spoke to Moses, took from the Spirit that was in him, and inspired it to these 70 men. The Spirit having thus rested in them, they began to be Prophets, and continued ever since."*

I believe these quotations suffice to prove to the reader the indestructible solidity upon which the present book rests, like the two that preceded it. (Missions of the Sovereigns – Missions of the Workers).

MOSES' TRINITARIAN CONSTITUTION OF ISRAEL

Once again, it is the Trinitarian Synarchy, the Social Government par excellence, that Moses reconstitutes, the true *first Temple* of Israel, a temple of *intelligence, of souls and human wills*, which will last 400 years before the erection of the stone temple in Jerusalem. That stone temple was but only the second, as Jesus knew very well, and in spite of the fact that the modern exegetes are claiming it to be the first.

The particular form which Moses gave to the worship, to the laws, to the details of the organization of his people, is not the main topic of this book, as it involves only secondarily the Social Sciences and the Universality of Humankind.

However, the basic *Archetype of Moses' Government* is of the deepest interest for our study.

To dare to reassert that *Archetype* as significantly reflecting the most *Celestial ancient Unit* of *Number, Weight, and Measure*, required the entire Authority of *Integral Wisdom and Science,* of which I have so often spoken. As we saw in the sacerdotal processions of Egypt, the Social God was present in this scientific form in the Sacred Book, for which the Golden Ark was built on the model of those of the Sanctuaries of Egypt.

THE ALCHEMISTS AARON, MIRYAM, MOSES.

Aaron, priest of Osiris like his brother Moses, had the same knowledge, for example: the demonstration of his mastery of Alchemy such as building the golden calf, that Moses hastened to dissolve with the famous *Alchaest;* for without the destruction of the golden calf, he would not have completed the demonstration of his full alchemical Mastery to the Egyptian Initiates present among those million peoples of the Exodus.

Such is the hidden meaning of the alleged worship of the golden calf by a people coming from a more civilized country than ours, and who would not have worshiped more than the moderns a stupid statue signifying nothing.

Tradition says that this Grand Masterwork was

accomplished by both Miryam, priestess of Isis, and Aaron, priest of Osiris, and this level of skills and knowledge was attained at the third degree of Sciences known as EVE / HVH.

We will now observe the Grand Art of Moses, corresponding to the fourth hierarchy, the first Letter on the Right side of the Holy Name I-EVE, in Hebrew EVE-I, (IEHOVA).

TECHNICAL ARTS APPLIED TO OPERATE THE ARK

I already explained that the Ark of the Testimony built to receive the *Fire Principle and the Book*, was built on the model of those existing in the Egyptian Sanctuaries.

On this subject we can compare chapter XXV of the *Exodus* with the *Book of the Dead* of the ancient Law of Ram, Ch. I, 1, 9, 10: *"I am the great Principle of the Work that rests in the Sacred Ark on the Support."*

The pure gold metal frame, which covers the interior and exterior of the Ark, as well as the rings and holding rods, are of great interest: *Exodus*, Ch. XXIV, v. 10, 11, 12. So are the two golden Cherubs of verses 18, 19 and 20.

But what is no less interesting is the *Orientation* of this Ark, in relation to *physical and hyperphysical Forces.*

Exodus, Ch. L, v. 19. *"And having brought the ark into the tabernacle, he hung the veil in front to fulfill the commandment of the Lord."*

Ibid., Ch. 20. *"And he set the table in the Tabernacle of Testimony, on the North side, out of the veil."*

Ibid., Ch. 22. *"And he put the candlestick in the Tabernacle of the Testimony, on the South side, opposite the table."*

Ibid., Ch. 28. *"He also laid the basin between the Tabernacle of Testimony and the altar, and filled it with water."*

Ibid., Ch. 29. *"Moses, Aaron, and his sons washed their hands and feet there, v. 30, before entering the Tabernacle of the Covenant and approaching the altar, as the Lord had commanded Moses."*

Ibid., Ch. 32. *"A cloud covered the Tabernacle of the Testimony, and it was filled with the glory of the Lord.*

Ibid., Ch. 33. *"And Moses could not enter into the tent of the Covenant, because the Cloud covered all, and the majesty of the Lord was bursting forth everywhere, everything being covered with this cloud.*

Ibid., Ch. 36. *"The Cloud of the Lord rested on the Tabernacle during the day, and the Flame appeared there during the night, the tribes of Israel seeing it from all the places of their encampment."*

I am following step by step the Theurgical Testimony of Moses, as all the Bibles translate it. It is about an Alliance with IEVE, it is about the *Psychurgical and Cosmogonic Union,* contracted by an Initiate and Initiator of the highest rank *with the Spirit and Soul of the Universe.* We will follow in this Tabernacle the leaders of the Council of God, among whom Miryam represents the head of the Women's College.

Once again, the Covenant is personally contracted with Moses.

Leviticus, Ch. XVI, v. 2: *"Tell your brother Aaron not to enter the Sanctuary behind the veil at all times, not to stand before the propitiatory which covers the Ark, lest he dies: for I will appear on the Oracle in the Clouds."*

Verse 4: *"Let him put on the linen tunic; that he covers what must be covered with a linen garment; that he girds himself with a linen belt; let him put on his head a tiara of linen: these clothes are healthy, and he will wear them all after having washed himself."*

Verse 12: *"Then he shall take hold of the censer which he will have filled with the coals of the Altar and seizing with his hand the fragrances which shall have been composed to be used as incense, he shall enter behind the veil in the Holy of Holies."*

Verse 13: *"That, when the fragrances are set on fire, their smoke and vapor shall spread over the Oracle above the Testimony, and Aaron shall not die."*

Verse 17: *"Let no man be in the Tabernacle, when the Pontiff enters the Holy of Holies."*

Numbers, Ch. IV, v. 19; *"Take heed that he does not touch the Holy of Holies, that he may live, lest he dies.*

Verse 20: *"Let no other persons surreptitiously look at the things that are in the Sanctuary before they are covered up; otherwise they will be death stricken "*

MIRYAM'S AND AARON'S REBELLION AGAINST MOSES

Numbers, Ch. XII: *"Miryam and Aaron spoke against Moses concerning his wife, who was Ethiopian."*

Verse 2: *"They said: Did the Lord speak only through Moses? Did he not talk to us like to him?"*

"The Lord heard them."

Verse 3: *"Moses was the sweetest of men."*

Verse 4: *"The Lord spoke immediately to Moses, Aaron and Miryam: Go, you three alone, to the Tabernacle of the covenant."*

"They went there."

Verse 5: *"The Lord descended in the pillar of the cloud, and standing at the door of the Tabernacle, He called Aaron and Miryam.*

"They came forward.

Verse 6: *"And He said unto them: If there be among you a Prophet of the Lord, I will appear to him through a vision, or I will speak to him through a dream."*

Verse 7: *"But it is not so with my servant Moses, my most faithful servant in my Temple."*

Verse 8: *"I speak to him from mouth to mouth, and he sees the Lord in full light, without enigmas, without symbols."*

Numbers, Ch. XII, v. 10: *"The cloud departed from the Tabernacle; and Miryam appeared immediately as white as snow as with leprosy."*

Verse 13: *"Then Moses cried out to the Lord and said to him: My God, heal her, I beseech you!"*

MOSES THE THEURGE

Every physicist, every sufficiently educated doctor will obviously recognize, in verse 10, the main symptom of *electro-leprosy.*

Electricity proper is there, but simply as an intermediary force present in our Atmosphere; *and there are, behind it, other forces,* enveloping what the Hindu call Akasa, itself veiling a *concentration of the Soul of the World* and of the pure Spirit, above this Tabernacle and on the Theurge Moses.

Moses would have been ineluctably devoured by

Lightning, if his soul and his mind had ceased for a single moment to be of the same essence as the Soul of the World and the Universal Spirit, with which he had conjoined himself through Wisdom and Science.

No more commentary is needed here, and all that is required is to let any Bible speak for us to see the Earthly Elements obey this Covenant and defend the intellectual and social work of the one whom IEVE had deemed worthy of his attention and love.

Among those elements, I will mention the *Fire-Principle*, which we find in all the ancient Dorian cults, from Etruria to Hebyreh.

UNSCIENTIFIC FAULTY PROCEDURE BRINGS DEATH

Leviticus, Ch. X, v. 1-10: *"Then Nadab and Abiu, sons of Aaron, put fire and incense upon it, and offered before the Lord a foreign fire, which had not been ordered to them."*

"Immediately, Fire came out of the Lord and devoured them, and they died before the Lord.

"And Moses said unto Aaron: Hear what the Lord said: I will be sanctified by those who know how and can approach me, and I will be glorified before all the people."Aaron, hearing this, kept silent, and Moses calling Misael and Elisaphan, son of Oziel, Aaron's uncle, said to them: Take your brothers off the sanctuary, and carry them out of the camp."

"They took them up, dead, as they were, clothed in their linen tunics, and carried them away, as they had been ordered.

"And Moses said to Aaron, and to Eleazar, and to Ithamar, Aaron's other sons:

"Beware, do not uncover your head and open your clothes, lest you die, and that the Lord's Fire does spread all over the people. Now, let your brothers, and all the house of Israel, lament the Fire that came from the Lord.

"As for you, do not go across the gates of the Tabernacle, for you will perish, because the oil of the holy anointing has been poured unto you."

I will not add one single bit of interpretation to the exposition of these terrible Mysteries.

I will limit myself to emphasizing verses 9 and 10 of the same chapter and the same book.

"The Lord also said to Aaron: You shall not, neither you, nor your sons, drink wine nor any kind of alcohol when you come into the Tabernacle of Testimony, lest you be punished with death, because it is an absolute prescription that must be transmitted to all your descendants. "You must have Science to discern between the holy and the profane."

PURPOSE AND MISSION OF ISRAEL AS A NATION

Until now the intellectual and moral forces of the Universe, the cosmogonic Principles, directly allied with Moses, operate within the Ark and in the Sanctuary of the theurgic Testimony of the Covenant (between Moses and the Lord).

We will see them exert their action elsewhere, with a Puissance of which Moses is the mediator, but which he does not order at will.

Let us be reminded what the Chinese Books say about war, as it will explain the extraordinary battle that is to follow.

The *purpose of Moses and Jethro* was not only *to constitute a nationality, but to institute it for certain universal purposes,* approved by the Intelligent Forces of the Cosmos and, as Moses says, by the God of the Spirits of all flesh, IOD, spouse of EVE. This is so true that the Lord tells him, at a certain moment, that he will give him, if necessary, another people greater, stronger, if needed.

MOSES LEADS A LARGE MULTI CULTURAL CROWD

To achieve his mission and to transmit through the Cycles to come the sealed book encrypting the Science of the Dorian Principles, Moses aggregated a massive crowd of Hebrews, Egyptians, Ethiopians, and others, about a tenth of whom represent 600,000 men fit for combat.

This crowd enthused and isolated in the Desert as on a fateful tripod, at the mercy of Moses, new Pygmalion breathing his Spirit on those people as a whole for this newly created nation, must be infused with the Soul of Trinitarian Synarchy, in the Forms as in the Essence of its institutions, or perish as a nation, drowning itself within the whole of Humankind from which it had been extracted.

It is a racehorse that Moses saddles and bridles, so that the invisible Spirit may ride it at full speed through the corpses of the Societies assailed by Anarchy.

If that horse resists, the terrible Force that controls it, squeezes it to the point of suffocating it; if it falls down, the Force pushes it up off the ground, planting spurs in its belly; if this race horse cannot bear this tremendous weight of a God, he will lie on the ground, and another sturdier stallion will be chosen.

But this people of 6,000,000 Orthodoxes was strong and worthy of the call that had been made to them.

ANARCHY ATTEMPTS A COUP AGAINST MOSES

That is why, for fear that it will perish entirely, a considerable party of rebels will have to be struck, as shown below.

Numbers, Ch. XIV, we can see democratic Anarchy, as always, attempting to give itself a purely political government, a Power without Authority.

Verse 3: "*Better we were rather dead in Egypt! Better we now die in this endless solitude!*"

"*God forbid we enter this land of Kanaan! We will perish by the sword, and our women and children will be taken prisoner! Is it not better we return to Egypt?*"

Verse 4: "*They therefore parleyed and said to each other: "Let's name a Chief and go back to Egypt!*"

Thus always opts democracy reduced to its own counsel, which was then that of the tribal elders; so it always ends up crowning its own anarchy by electing a Chief among themselves and choosing to return to the Land of Servitude.

In that same biblical chapter XIV, we can see the leaders of the first two High Councils driven to despair.

But the *invisible Puissances* are there.

"*As all the people casting an immense clamor wanted to stone them, the Glory of the Lord appeared on the Tabernacle of the Covenant for all the tribes of Israel to see."*

Then begins, between *Moses the Theurge and his Celestial Ally*, an admirable and mysterious argument, in which merciful Humanity speaks through the lips of Moses, mediating for his people, whom he shields with his supplications against the terrible thrust of the Supreme Will. What is the essence of this Will, concerning the Government of Israel? Synarchy, with its three arbitration councils. What is the opposition of the people to this Supreme Will? Political Anarchy, wishing to give itself by acclamations a Chief in its own image.

These tremendous teachings are similar to the *Genesis* text in regard to Nimrod, the verse quoted about Amalek, and concerning all that will be accomplished centuries later, when Israel and Judah will establish political kingship, despite the opposition of the first two High Councils, which will be drowned in blood. The revolt did not remain confined to the Third Council of the Elders. The first High Council itself rebelled strongly against its Master.

Moses, then a man of eighty years, apparently small, frail, stuttering, timid, had to carry the weight of his mission, of which only he knew the *Principle and the Final Purpose.*

Nothing is more tragic and more solemn in the History of the World than the situation of this High priest of Osiris and IEVE, having on this earth no direct force other than his Wisdom and Science, which had reinstated him above within the Kingdom of God, while still physically residing below.

Around Moses, in the first High Council as in the lowest, the revolt rises, and blows the sentiments of Anarchy through 6,000,000 souls, in this formidable arena in the Desert, between the armed Egypt on the rear and the hostile confederations of Syria in front.

The Lord had told him, Numbers, Ch. XIV, v. 12: *"Ah! I will chastise them; I will abandon them to the extermination by the common plague. As for you, I will make you leader of another people, greater, stronger than this one."*

At the prayer of the Theurge, his *celestial Ally* suspends this judgment.

Ibid., v. 20: *"I forgave them, in answer to your request."*

THE ARNARCHIC REVOLT SPREADS AND DEEPENS

Though, the revolt increases, the sacerdotal pride of the Orthodoxes of Egypt, the priests themselves, throw off their masks, and stand up as a single body in front of this old defenseless man.

Numbers, Ch. XVI, v. 1 to 50: *"Then Koreh the son of Isahar, the grandson of Caath, the great-grandson of Levi, and Dathan, and Abiron the son of Eliab, and Hon, son of Pheleth of the tribe of Reuben, started an insurrection against Moses with 250 men of the Beni-Israel, Principals of the Synagogue.*

"At the time of the Assemblies, they were called by name.

"And they rebelled against Moses and against Aaron, and said to them: just name all the people "Orthodox", and IEVE will be with them.

"Why do you want to rise above the Lord's people?

"Having heard that, Moses kissed the Earth.

"He said to Koreh and his troop: Tomorrow morning, I will reveal those whom the Lord chooses to be with Him.

"Let each one bring his censer, you, Koreh, and all your followers.

"Tomorrow, having brought burning coal, you shall offer incense before the Lord; and shall be holy he whom the Lord will have Himself chosen.

"You are up ranking yourselves a lot, children of Levi!

"And Moses sent for Dathan and Abiron the son of Eliab.

"We will not go, they replied. Suffice it for you to have taken us from a land where streams of milk and honey really flowed and brought us to kill us in the Desert! Do not augment our pain by your severe domination! Is this how you are keeping your promise! Is this the promised land flowing with streams of milk and honey? Are these the rich fields and abundant vineyards? And, besides, would you wish us blind? Surely we will not go.

"Moses, overwhelmed with indignation, said to IEVE: Do not take their sacrifices into account. You know that I have never accepted anything from them, that I have never done wrong to any of them.

"And he said to Koreh, You and your company, present yourself before the Lord, on the one side, and Aaron will present himself on the other side.

"Let each one of you hold his censer and add incense in it, offering to the Lord 250 censers.

"This was done in the presence of Moses and Aaron.

"All the people being gathered together, being at the entrance of the tabernacle, the Glory of the Lord appeared to all.

"The Lord spoke to Moses and Aaron: Separate yourself from this assembly, for I want to smite them all.

"And Moses and Aaron kissed the earth, and said: Most Powerful! God of the Spirits of all flesh! Will your indignation burst against all for the sin of one?

"The Lord said to Moses: Order all the people to depart from the tents of Koreh, Dathan, and Abiron.

"When the people had vacated all the environs of their tents, Dathan and Abiron going out stood before the entrance of their pavilions with their wives, their children, and all their troop.

"And Moses said: You are now going to acknowledge that it is the Lord who sent me to do all that you see, and that I did not invent it alone. If the Lord, by a new prodigy, opens up the earth and engulfs them and all that belongs to them, if still alive they fall into the infernal places, you will then know that they have blasphemed against the Lord.

"Moses had barely stopped talking, when the Earth rocked under their feet.

"It opened and devoured them, their tents and all that was theirs.

"Still alive, they went down to the infernal places.

"Earth covered them, Death effaced them from among the people.

"All Israel, who was there, forming the circle, fled under the cry of the dying, saying: the earth will engulf us too!

"At the same time, IEVE flashed the Fire, which devoured the 250 men who offered incense.

"The next day all the multitude of the Beni-Israel murmured against Moses and Aaron, saying: You have slain the people of the Lord!

"Sedition was reforming; the tumult was growing.

"Moses and Aaron then ran to the Tabernacle of the Covenant.

"As soon as they entered, the Cloud covered them and the Glory of the Lord appeared.

"The Lord said to Moses: Separate yourself from this multitude, that I may destroy them all at once.

"Moses and Aaron then prostrated themselves on the ground.

"And Moses said unto Aaron: Take thy censer, some fire from the Altar, and put the incense upon it, and run to the people, and intercede for them. The Fire surges from the throne of God, the scourge begins, it is already breaking out.

"Aaron obeyed, ran to the people, that the Fire was already burning, prayed for the people, offering incense.

"Standing among the dead and the living, he prayed for the people: the Fire stopped. "14,700 men perished, not to mention those who died in the sedition of Koreh. "Aaron returned to find Moses at the entrance of the Tabernacle of the Covenant, as death had stopped."

Or the foregoing is an abominable lie, or it is the expression of a historical fact. Let's look at those cases, starting with the last one. If it is the expression of a historical fact, as I believe it is, what does it mean?

In this terrible drama, the will of the Theurge, Moses' Ontology, is One with the Heavenly Kingdom and its Law.

In this Tabernacle is a *Testimony of Theurgic Alliance*, but between whom? Between IEVE and the people of Israel, as the seditious ones of the Council of God wanted to make believe? Not at all.

This *Alliance exists between IEVE and Moses personally*; but how? Through the Supreme Wisdom and the Supreme Science of Moses the Epopte, *personally reintegrated into the Kingdom of God through Initiation.*

AUTHORITY OF INTEGRAL WISDOM AND SCIENCE

What does want Providence, once invoked by Moses after he had attained the summit of Initiation through Integral Wisdom and Science?

Open the Book!

And it will answer you with all the History of Humankind:

Synarchy, with Specification of Authority, Power, Popular Will.

Authority belongs to the Sacerdotal Corps, that is to say, in the style of that time, to the totality of the Teaching Corps.

Consequently, *Authority belongs to Integral Science*, with its four hierarchies of knowledge, all subsumed into their Highest Principles and their core intelligible, spiritual Principle.

Consequently, *political Sciences must defer to Moral Sciences*, in intergovernmental relations, as well as in relations between the metropolis and its colonies: Do not do to others what you do not want done unto you.

The Power proper belongs to whom? As Authority belongs to the persons of integral Wisdom and Science, Power belongs to the persons of Justice.

How does Moses, how do all the Orthodoxes of the World, how does IEVE, how does the social God of the Universe and the Earth, Father and Mother of Spirits and Souls of all flesh, how do they understand the essence of Power and its exercise, and in which hands do they place its scepter?

Once again, it is to Justice this scepter must belong, and Justice is the first secular reflection of the sacerdotal Authority, meaning reflection of the totality of the Teaching.

The assembly of lays savant forming the College of the Gods manifests a second alliance with the entire Teaching Corps, in other words alliance with the High College of God.

They receive Initiation, and the civil Code is what it should be, the juridical reflection of the intellectual and moral Sciences, subsumed into their Principles and core Principle.

The ancient kings, up to Melchizedek, were Kings of Justice, and not kings of military Strength.

On this point as on many others, the Bible, even through its common translations, agrees with all the sacred Books of Humankind.

HOW DOES SYNARCHY FUNCTION?

Now, where does reside the legitimate field of action of the Popular Will, where does its legal power reside?

The legitimate field of the popular Will resides in the local economic administration; itself a reflection of the High Magistracy, it has legitimacy to form the small Magistracy pertaining to its immediate local interests; the Council of the Gods serves as its "Court of Appeals" and the Council of God serves as "Supreme Court".

How are the members of this third Council being recruited, where do they come from, how are they selected?

They are recruited from among each tribe, from each divisional district, they emanate from the moral local life, and it is the Morale principle which appoints them, through the conjoined voice of the hearths, where IEVE resides not only in the father, but also in the mother of the family.

Question: yes or no, is this the image of the essential Economy of the Ancient World and that of Moses' Synarchy in the Desert at the time of the direct Alliance between Moses and IEVE? Open the History book of the World, open the Bible. God and Moses will answer you, as, later, God and Samuel, and the History of the Ancient World will answer you also, by all the voices of China and Japan, where, since, from the hut of the peasant to the palace of the Emperor and the Mikado, the living source of this Economy is named Father and Mother, that is to say, I-EVE.

Now, if you have come so far in the reading of the book I am writing, and do not feel the living Truth stirring your soul and your breast with its divine warmth, what is the use of the teaching of the *History of the World?* What good is the Bible for you, if used conveniently to serve only your own willfulness and deviate from higher intellectual guidance and genuine moral-social life?

Am I inventing these things? Is not the life of the entire Humankind teaching them to you?

I am only re-positioning the Social Sciences on the altars of Humanity, where the Living God Himself has declared His Will to the Sages and Savants who have placed themselves in a state propitious to question Him with the same simplicity of heart and spirit displayed among the humblest humans, and the smallest among the children.

Now, to save from the anarchic onslaught a program so simple, so healthy, so true, it was then necessary that the highest divine *Science of Cosmogonic Principles be reconstituted*, in order to allow *future generations*, living in centuries *sufficiently enlightened* and prepared to re-establish everywhere *Unity in Knowledge and Life*.

That's why this Hermetic Book of 50 chapters was placed there, in this Ark of Alliance.

But, in the Universe as well as within Humankind, there are forces of dissociation, which must be anticipated, and, if necessary, combatted.

ALLIANCE OF MOSES WITH IEVE

That is why this theurgic Testimony of the Alliance between IEVE and Moses is present, shielding the Ark and the Book.

That is why Moses, this old man of eighty years, apparently weak, unarmed, without Power proper, founds his authority directly on this Theurgic Testimony, by which IÊVÊ, from the depth of an appropriate invisible Sanctuary, commands to certain laws and certain forces of the Earth, by activating Laws and Forces which belong only to the Cosmos and to Him-Her, the God-Nature.

Do we need other proofs? Let's open the Book.

From the Sinai Fires to the very heart of the Earth itself, we will see the planetary forces obey the Alliance of Moses the Theurge with IEVE, the Soul and Spirit creators of the Cosmos. Deuteronomy, Ch. V, v. 1 to 26; *Moses* speaks:

"The Lord enunciated His Commandments with a powerful voice, in front of you all on the mountain, surging from the core of the Fire.

"After you had seen the mountain all ablaze you sent to me the Judges of your tribes and your Elders and through them you said to me: The Lord Our God made us see His Splendor and His Greatness. We heard His Voice surging from the Fire.

"Are we going to die then, will we be devoured by this Great Fire? For if we are made to hear again the Voice of the Lord, our God, we surely will die.

"Because any human of flesh, made to hear again the voice of the living God, speaking from the center of the Fire, such as we have heard and seen, will they not surely die?

What is this Fire? Is it a physical fire, is it its Principle, not only Cosmogonic, but Theogonic and Theurgically invoked?

The translations give a glimpse of the immense scientific depth of this Mystery in Deuteronomy, Ch. IV, v. 36:

"From the Height of Heaven, He makes you hear His Voice to instruct you; He made you see his Fire, a terrible fire, and you have heard His words come out of the core of this Fire."

This Divine Fire, this Empyrean as it is called by Orpheus, that Fire known to all the ancient Orthodoxes, from the Ghiborim of the Hebyreh to the priests and Nazarenes of Etruria like Numa, this Fire, cited in the verse of Horace that I quoted in regard to certain Mysteries contained in the Abramid Encyclopedia, Moses tells us where this Fire comes from.

It comes from the Height of Heaven, it is the Fire pertaining to the male Principle or the pure Spirit, IOD, it is His Fire, and it has for *Athanor the Ark itself.*

Deuteronomy, Ch. XXXIII, verse. 1, 2:

"This is the blessing that Moses the Theurge gave to the children of Israel before his death. He said: The Lord came from the Sinai; He has risen upon you from Seir; He appeared on Mount Paran, and millions of Divine Beings appeared with Him; He carried at His Right the Law of Fire.

Therefore, that Fire is the Master of the Spiritual Puissances of the Cosmos, since millions of Celestial beings were with Him (verse 3), among whom all the ancient Orthodoxes. This Sovereign carried at his right the Law of Fire.

Now, in the hierogram of IÊVÊ, written in Egyptian from right to left, the right is the Iod, the Masculine Principle, the left being Hé-Vau-Hé, ÊVÈ, the Feminine Principle; and this sacred Name was ritually shouted in the course of Mysteries of

Ram, Dionysos, Bacchus: Iao-Hevauhe; and we find it again in the Y-King, even in the writings of Lao-tse.

Leviticus, Ch. X, v. 23, 24.

"And Moses and Aaron went into the Tabernacle of Testimony, and came out, and blessed the people. At the same time, the Glory of the Lord appeared to all the assembled people, and a fire from the Lord devoured the burnt offering and the fats that were on the Altar."

As for the action exerted on Moses himself by this Living Fire, about which he speaks, it is no less remarkable.

Exodus, Ch. XXX, v. 33, 34, 35.

When he had finished talking to them, he re-veiled his face.

When he was entering (the tabernacle) and speaking with IEVE, he would unveil himself until he exited.

When Moses was exiting, one could see his face radiating; though he would veil it again as soon as he had to speak to the people.

I do not want to keep on quoting the Bible, nor comment on it more than it is appropriate.

MOSES MIND-SOUL IN PERFECT UNION WITH IEVE

Such was the Puissance of ancient Wisdom and Science, when reaching the summit of the Dorian Initiation, as coincidentally, the Epopt was a man of genius, fully capable of manifesting Divinity in a just manner.

Suppose now that all of the foregoing, that all these biblical stories were fantasized at whim, much later, by Esdras, and not recounted from ancient manuscripts and the oral Tradition, bequeathed by Moses.

How is it possible to admit that within the blooming Babylonian civilization, among men as profoundly educated in natural, human, universal, divine knowledge, while the four hierarchies of Kaldean priests, of which Daniel was the Sovereign Pontiff, were fully functional, how would it be possible even to suppose that, in front of a College of the Gods, before 70 men, 70 Jewish Literates, Esdras could have made up such fantastic stories without being ridiculed and admonished?

My answer is therefore made, and it is indeed a historical fact, related in a more or less legendary way, more or less hermetic, in the Assyrian style; nevertheless, it is *with Theurgical facts* we are dealing with here.

Why is it these types of events will not be replicated after the death of Moses?

Because again, *the Alliance was personal between Moses and IEVE,* and I will attempt again to explain what it really means.

Moses acquired his Science and Wisdom in the temples of Egypt and Ethiopia. He recorded part of it in his Cosmogony, in his Androgony, as well as in the next three books.

These five books, written in Egyptian as Dorian priests wrote, compose what the translators have called *Genesis* and its fifty chapters.

4 STRATA OF MEANING WITHIN THE WORDS OF GENESIS

Yes or no, did the priests of the highest grade *handle the language* in a certain way particular to their innermost tradition? I think I have already proved it, but here are some more testimonials on this subject.

Here is first the testimony of the historian *Herodotus*, Book II, Ch. 36:

"The Greeks, he says, *write their letters and calculate from left to right; the Egyptians, on the contrary, from right to left.*

The Egyptians have two kinds of writings; one called sacred, the other demotic or vulgar"

Clement of Alexandria reveals even more, having no secrets to keep.

When he speaks of the forty-two books of Hermes, available to the priesthood only, he declares that ten of these books were called *hieratic,* and were exclusively studied by the temple's High Pontiff.

So much for the *hieratic* books proper; for there were others called *hieroglyphics,* which belonged to the domain of studies of the sacerdotal Scribe. Still other books were written in *symbols* whose studies were part of the School of Mathematics.

So there are three kinds of writings, not only correspond-ing to each type of literates, but also corresponding to the type of knowledge carried by each language: *the Hierogrammatic, the Hieroglyphic, the Symbolic.*

See, for the foregoing, Strom., Book VI, p. 633, 634.

All the ancient Universities also had a specific ideogra-phism unintelligible to the layman.

In Eusebius, Prep. evang., Book. IX, Ch. 9, Philo of Biblos reports that Sankoniathon, the Ionian, composed in an analytic language his Cosmogony with the assistance of certain mem-oirs which he found in the Temples, and which were written in Ammonian letters, unintelligible to the vulgar.

But we know that Ammon is the symbol of the Law of Aries, or Ram. So, the Ionian Sankoniathon had in his hands Dorian manuscripts, written in the manner of the Orthodox priests. But it was not enough to translate them into an analytic language, it was necessary to have the *scientific key* of their hier-ograms.

Is there still other proofs?

Diogenes Laertius, according to Thrasyllus, tells us that Democritus wrote two books, one of which dealt with the *sa-cred language* of the Babylonians, the other with the *hieratic language* of the Orthodox of Meroe. (Life of Democritus, segma XLIX, Book 9.)

Heliodore Book IV, confirms the preceding, concerning the Egyptians. Theodoret says the same thing about the Dorian temples of Greece.

Finally, the Egyptian Manetho, in Eusebius, edit. Scalig. Amsterdam., 1658, p. 6, states that he wrote his books from reading carvings on columns he discovered in the land of Siriad (Egypt). He adds that these columns were engraved by *Thoth,* that is to say by Initiates of the Teaching Corps, written in hi-eroglyphic characters, and formulated in *hierogrammatic sacred language.*

Libraries of granite, porphyry or basalt are found through-out the ancient Cycle, even among the Chinese.

All the expeditions of the savant Kings of Justice of the Cycle of Aries have sown those forms of carved libraries all over the World, from the farthest Orient to Gibraltar.

So *Moses,* priest of Osiris-Isis, of IEVE, that is to say, a Dorian Epopt of the temples of Egypt, *never separating the Male Principle from the Feminine Principle, nor the Sciences of the Intelligible Order from those of the Sensorial Order,* certainly conformed himself to the Law, of which he had received the supreme communications from the High Priest Jethro.

Here is the testimony of Moses himself:

"You will always be veiled". – in *Genesis,* quoted above; *Numbers,* Ch. XII, v. 8, cited above.

Finally, Saint Paul, instructed in the Oral Tradition, alludes very clearly to the veil cleverly extended by Moses on his thought. 2 Ep. to Corinth, Ch. III, v. 13:

"We do not do like Moses, who was veiling his face, marking that the children of Israel could not suffer the Light."

Verse 14: *"And so their minds remained materialized and darkened; for until this very day, when they read the Old Testament, this veil still remains on their heart, without being lifted."*

MOSES GAVE KEYS FOR DECRYPTING HIS TESTAMENT

I cannot fathom, however, that Moses would not have passed on an Initiation, an Oral Tradition, and we already observed he instituted a Council of the Gods on the express order of Jethro. However, once Moses gone, as the people adopted Ionian customs of the confederations of Asia Minor, they must have, with the passing of time, forgotten more and more the Dorian Principles which enabled the Interpretation of Moses' Books, and this happened for multiple reasons.

THE OCCULT CAN BE UNDERSTOOD BY SCIENCE

Common sense is sufficient to explain that, far removed from the academic source from which Moses' ideography originated, the savant Corps of Israel must necessarily have at first weakened, and then battled each other, either as partisan of literal interpretation, either as partisan of the spirit of Oral

Tradition, or as vague symbolists, wishing to reconcile the two extremes.

However, Dorian Science, in Egypt as in all ancient universities, was the topmost synthesis of all the Natural Sciences, organized in a *triple hierarchy of physical, human, and cosmic knowledge.*

That is why the ascending degrees of Egyptian Science and Initiation no longer existing in Judea, the Higher Principles of Moses' Cosmogony were no longer linked to their positive physical consequences through the descending Progression of all the other Sciences; and from then on, the scientific sense of Moses' writings became more and more veiled, indecipherable.

This is so true that it will take the favorable intellectual atmosphere of the University of Babylon *for Esdras to restore the text of Moses in Kaldaic characters,* and to provide a median meaning amalgamated with the literal one.

It remains for me now to prove that among the Sciences reserved for Initiation which Moses received, were those which I have quoted many times.

Much has been said and written about occult Sciences: some authors, in the last ten centuries, were without much understanding and propagated ridiculous ideas; others, more recently, targeted those fabricated ideas with their cheap irony and sarcasms.

The truth is that there are no occult Sciences, because what is *scientific ceases to be occult, and what is occult ceases to be so by becoming scientific.*

However, during many Cycles of Civilization before Ram's Cycle (circa 6600 BC, as of today about 8,750 years ago), and long after, Savants have deliberately occulted High Sciences because of their very import and the danger of revealing them, not only to the vulgar, but to any human being, even a leader, who was not absolutely inure to passionate motive. Among these Sciences and their corresponding applied Arts, here are some which were taught in the Mysteries: Theurgy, Astrology, Psychurgy, Alchemy.

Here I am evoking the Sciences as they were taught in the ancient Initiations and certainly not as they have become since the Middle Ages, in the hands of fools, charlatans, crooks and stupid fanatics of all kinds, to the exception of few eminent minds. It is to this class of charlatans that the Law emanating from the Initiates, in all antiquity, rendered verdicts requesting severe punishments as exposed in the civil Code of Moses.

During the Cycle of Ram, then in all its religious ramifications, the practice and even the search for these Sciences was formally forbidden outside the Assembly and the Control of the Savant Corps. The unfortunates who, for a personal gain, indulged themselves in clandestinely pursuing a more or less chimerical power, were often treated with too much rigor, and (I think) to denounce them would have been sufficient punishment.

Science, as it climbs to higher degrees, has more and more a *need for intellectual and moral guidance*, and it becomes more and more necessary to render it inaccessible to vice and error in all forms.

It is those souls of darkness, since the schism of Irshu and mainly among the Turanians, which have produced this infernal and ignorant reversal of purpose of the Magic Knowledge taught in the Sanctuaries, and it is that reversal which, under the name of black magic, has produced fully deserved Execration from Humankind and Anathemas from Religions.

SYNTHESIS OF SCIENCES, PHYSICAL AND SPIRITUAL

But let us return to the true secret Sciences of the Temples, whose Luminous Teachings were bestowed appropriately, and received humbly with a pure heart and with a love for Humanity and Divinity going so far as to sacrifice their own life.

My purpose here is not to defend these Sciences any more than to attack them. I am displaying the intellectual Genius of Antiquity, and everyone remains free to think what he wants of it; but I make use of this same freedom, confining myself to saying that *Religion was not then the fruit of ignorance, that it was on the contrary the Synthesis of all the Sciences*, ranging from the Physical Order to the Spiritual Order and vice versa.

It is because one knew, without any doubt, that from one end to the other of the Universe, *the Spirit is One, Nature is Homogeneous*, through the quadruple hierarchy of their living manifestations, I can assert that all the qualifying *aspect of Science and Life have been exactly known*, and that the quantitative aspect of the same Science and the same Life from top to bottom, had been validated.

That the four Sciences with their corresponding applied Arts mentioned above were taught and practiced in the temples, is reported by: *Hermes*, In Asclep., Ch. IX; *Jambl.*, Of Myst. Egypt., Ch. XXX; Maimon, Mor-Nevoch, § 2, Ch. X; Origen, Contr. Cels., Book. I; Synes, de Insomn., P. 134 et seq.; Niceph. Greg., Schol, in Synes. page 360 and following.

CONCLUSION

The Bible, the Gospels and the Fathers of the Church agreeing on this point, *Moses*, a Dorian Epopt, mastered these Sciences. Without these Sciences his Puissance would be scientifically inexplicable, and therefore doubtful. Given the religious Genius of antiquity, the graduated explanation of all the Mysteries of the Universe, from the physical Realm to the purely intelligible Realm, given the double ascending and descending aspect of universal Life, Universal and Integral Knowledge, therefore *the books and all the testimonies of Moses are Religiously true, because they were, and are still, Scientifically accurate.*

After having accomplished in the Wilderness his Social Mission, by constituting the social Synarchy around the Ark which contained his Intellectual Testament, after having transmitted orally the Theogonic Sciences which he had until then kept secret, and having given as well the necessary keys so that the most worthy disciples could decipher and understand the 50 chapters of his Hermetic Book, after having designated Joshua, his first Initiate, as his successor, *Moses retired in IEVE, at the age of 120.*

It should be noted that Joshua was a lay Initiate, not part of the Council of God, but a member of the Council of the Gods. He does not even belong to the tribe of Levi, that is to say to the official priesthood, but belongs to a tribe whose hierogrammatic name designates its Kaldean origin. *Numbers,* Ch. XIII, v. 9: "*Of the tribe of Ephraim, Oshea, "son of Nun."*

As always, in those times, Oshea *received a name of initiation, Joshua, Savior.* Here are the verses relating to *Joshua's supreme Initiation by his Initiator Moses*: Numbers, Ch. XXVII, v. 15 to 23:

"*And Moses answered to the Lord, "Let the God of the Spirits of all men choose a man who will watch over all this people.*

"*The Lord said to him, Take Joshua the son of Nun, this man in whom resides the Spirit of Wisdom, and lay your hands on him.*

"*Present him before Eleazar, High Priest, and before all the people.*

"*Give him your instructions concerning all the people, give him part of your glory, so that all the Assemblies of the children of Israel will listen to him and obey him.*

"*When something must be accomplished, the Hight Priest Eleazar will consult the Lord; and according to Eleazar's answer, Joshua will go out and walk first, followed by all the children of Israel, and the rest of the multitude."*

"*Moses did what the Lord commanded him and having called on Joshua he brought him before the High Priest Eleazar, and before the Plenary Assembly.*

"*He laid his hands on his head and told him what the Lord had commanded."*

In the verses above, the three social Powers of Synarchy are again being shown at work: Eleazar, head of the Council of God, represents the Authority of Teaching; Joshua, leader of the Council of the Gods, represents the Power of Justice, a secular reflection of Wisdom by Initiation. Finally, the people in plenary assembly, with the tribal elders at its head, represent the third Power, armed with its small local magistracy.

It is also to be noted that Moses, as Egyptian Epopt, withdraws from his position to let Joshua operate on his own, so that he Joshua may enter in direct and personal Alliance with the integral God of all the Dorian Orthodoxes of the World, while he, Moses, keeps veiling this God in his books so that it would be *only revealed to the entire Humankind, at the appropriate time.*

"Deuteronomy, Ch. XXI, v. 18: "*I will hide, I will cover My Face.*"

Before passing away, Moses predicted to his nation the coming of a Prophet as great as himself.

"Deuteronomy, Ch. XVIII, v. 15,16,18,19: "*The Lord your God will raise up a prophet like me, of your nation, and of your brethren: He will be heard by you, according to your request to the Lord your God, near Mount Horeb.*"

"*And the Lord said to me: All that this people has just said is right. I will raise from the midst of their brothers a Prophet like you. I will put My Words in his mouth, and he will tell them all that I will command him. If anyone does not want to hear the words that this Prophet will utter in My Name, it will be Me who will apply my own justice.*"

These verses announce the coming of a Prophet like Moses, one seeing the Lord face to face, reading without veil the Book of fifty chapters locked in the Ark (Genesis).

This Prophet rising from the Jewish nation will *be Jesus Christ, (Jehushua)* finding himself living in the same situation as Moses the Egyptian Epopt, a trinitarian Social Order composed by an official Priesthood, equivalent to the ancient Council of God (Sanhedrin), a Council of the Gods comprising the best scribes of the great Synagogue, and finally the Council of Elders issued from the tribe of Judah.

The other prophets, members of the two first High Councils, were instituted by Moses, either by way of the Nazareat *children's Initiation,* as in all the Orthodox Temples of the World at that time, or by way of *Initiation at mature age,* and Moses

designates differently these two kinds of Prophets, character-
izing each in a different way.

-First Level

Numbers, Ch. XII, v. 6 to 8: *"The Lord said to Aaron and to
Miryam: Listen: If there be a prophet of the Lord among you, I will appear
to him in vision, or I will speak to him in a dream."*

-Higher Level

*"But this is not so with my servant Moses, who is My faithful servant
par excellence in all my house, for I speak to him from mouth to mouth,
and he sees the Lord clearly and not in riddles and figures."*

It is undeniable that these two verses, extracted from Deuteronomy and from Numbers, are describing two kinds of
prophets; and it is also undeniable that the only one who, historically, must, in the course of time, satisfy the conditions
indicated in Deuteronomy, is Jesus Christ.

Moreover, Moses predicts only One prophet of this kind
will be rising in the future. In his last address, the divine old
man, from the top of the Abarim mountain, his eyes staring at
the land of Kanaan, tells his people words that the Babylonian
version may have altered, for lack of a precise memory; nonetheless that version still reports important verbatim.

In Chapter XXXII of Deuteronomy, the ancient Cycle, the
ancient Synarchy of Aries is still proposed as a model (at that
time 3,500 years ago).

Verse 7, for example, *"Take advice from <u>ancient ages</u>, consider
what happened in the <u>successive birth and life</u> of all Races."*

In chapter XXXIII of Deuteronomy, under the symbol of
the hierograms of the twelve tribes, Moses blessed all the Peoples of the World, all Israel, the *entire Royal University of God.*

Deuteronomy, Ch. XXXIV:

*"And Moses went up from the plain of Moab to mount Nebo, to the
top of Phasgah, facing Jericho; and the Lord showed him all the land of
Gilead to Dan, all Naphtali, and all the land of Ephraim and Manas-
seh, and all the land of Judah as far as the Western Sea, all the way to
the south, the extent of the country of Jericho, which is the city of Palm
trees, up to Ségor.*

"The Lord said to him, "This is the land I promised to Abram, to Isaac, and Jacob, saying to them, 'I will give this land to your posterity."You have seen this land with your eyes, but you will not enter it."

"Moses, the servant of the Lord, passed away in this very place in the land of Moab by the commandment of the Lord, who buried him in the valley of the land of Moab, facing Phogor. and no man until today has known the place where he was buried."

"He was a hundred and twenty when he passed away!! His sight was not weakened; his teeth were not loose".

The children of Israel wept for him in the plain of Moab for thirty days, at the end of which mourning ceased.

"No prophet had risen in Israel the like of Moses, to whom the Lord spoke face to face."

I wanted to let the Bible itself give reverence to this sovereign Epopt. All the ancient Initiates who have reached his rank have passed away, *without their bodies leaving any physical remains.* So with Pythagoras, Apollonius of Thyane, and Jesus Christ, we will see the same mysterious fact reoccur.

Henceforth, thanks to the superhuman effort of this great man, the *Principles of Organization of the Cosmos* and the Social State will be protected by a purely Dorian guard of honor.

In vain will the Politics feel the danger, in vain the Nineveh or Babylonian Caesarism which inaugurated with Ninus its own self-deification and apotheosis, in vain will it uproot from Kanaan these 12 tribes, in vain will it disperse away 10 of those tribes toward all corners of the World, such as they will become as untraceable as a grain of sand in the Ocean.

However, 2 tribes will remain in Kanaan, and that will suffice.

In vain will the Babylonian and Persian Caesarism weigh its strong arm on Judah and Benjamin, in vain the Macedonian Caesarism master will enter in the stone temple of Jerusalem.

The first 50 chapters of Moses' Books will be faithfully preserved, and that will also suffice.

In vain the Roman Empire, in its turn, will raise up the Law of Iniquity rejected by Moses under the name of Nimrod, the tiger; in vain will Dorianism and political Ionism use Judea as a battlefield; in vain will the stone temple of Jerusalem be destroyed forever by Caesarism perpetuating the usurpation of deification and apotheosis.

Jesus, as a man, will have given back to the entire Humankind the Social, Universal Spirit of the esotericism of Moses, and that also is enough. This divine man, this Son of God, may have been crucified as a criminal by the Romans, the deification and Apotheosis has been taken away from Nimrod, AMalek, the crowned Anarchy.

Thanks to Jesus, the schismatic temples will soon no longer be able to award this Deification and Apotheosis to the Western Nimrods, and finally it will be given back to the Highest Authority, it will, witnessed by dazzled minds and souls, be sent up to the Highest of the Heavens, which henceforth will never grant it to Powers on this Earth.

Such is the masterwork of the true theocrats issued from the Dorian Temples of the ancient Cycle, a work quite different, as we can see, from that of the Priesthoods swerved from their original Mission by their separation from the other Teaching Corps, and by their bending under the hand of personal Powers.

I ask the reader to recall the text of Moses on Nimrod, and to read page 56 of the Catechism for the use of all the Churches of the French Empire, Paris, printed by the Mame brothers. 1808, lesson VII.

Request. "Why are we bound to all these duties towards our Emperor?"

Reply. "It is because God who creates empires and distributes them according to his will, by awarding our emperor with gifts, either in peace or in war, has established him as our sovereign and as the minister of His Puissance and a reflection of His Image on Earth."

The outlined words are exactly the opposite of what Moses said and what Jesus will say in His cautious response to the insidious question of the Pharisians: *"Give to Caesar what is Caesar's, to God what is of God. "*

Now, if we take into account exactly what belongs to God in the Government of Humanity, what remains for Caesar?

Much remains, even more than when the arbitrary Caesar represents the crowning of pure Anarchy.

If he adheres to the Social Synarchy, that same head of State remains the true Crown, that of Melchizedek and all the former Kings of Justice of the Ram Cycle; he remains the real throne, that of the Council of the Gods; it remains to him to be the highest expression of the great Lay Magistracy, the glorious reflection of Wisdom and Science, the living incarnation of the Unity of Morality and Politics finally reconciled.

This is vaguely felt by kings and emperors worthy of the name; but, lacking initiation and often initiative, they do not know how to prepare themselves and society for the Kingdom of God. This is what instinctively feel in the simplicity of their hearts the multitudes for whom the monarchy still represents a Principle of Unity, for which it is a reflection of the God who reigns in Heaven, of Paternity and Maternity who govern each home on Earth.

So we must always remember this profound word of Jesus Christ: "*Forgive them, for they know not what they do.*"

And they do what they believe to be good, and that good is easy to realize, by placing Science in the Sanctuaries of Religion, by reconstituting Authority, by submitting to it, by building an Arbitral Synarchy.

That is why, as I retrace the history of the Theocrats taken out of the ruins of the ancient Cycle, to heal, locally or universally, the political diseases of the earthly social state, I uncover my head piously, and I pray and adore the same Wisdom, the same Science, the same heavenly God, the same Social God who lives among us, and is ready to reign here to insure the happiness of the whole of Humanity.

End of Tome
By Alexandre Saint-Yves d'Alveydre

DETAILED CHRONOLOGICAL SYNOPSIS

I-*12,900 to 11,500 years ago.* **The "Young Dryas Mini Ice Age" occurred swiftly and ended abruptly with cataclysmic floods.**

-When the north pole was struck with a giant meteorite/asteroid, human civilizations, evolving for 80,000 years, had attained a degree of social organization and intellectual potency yet not reached in the 21rst century.

II-*11,500 to 10,500 years ago*. **The period of Rebirth.**

-Scattered survivors gather in areas deemed safe, in mountains and valleys. Crucial scientific and technical knowledge almost obliterated, regression is prevalent. Rebirth progresses at different pace according to the presence or absence of "instructors", "helpers". Those Teachers were either humans still possessing useful knowledge, or celestial guides, some of them having tutored the development of previous civilizations.

III-*10,500 to 8,750 years ago*. **Hegemony of the Black Race known as the Gian Ben Gian Civilization.**

-Endowed with the legacy of prediluvian civilizations, 4 human races recreate new nations
1- The Black Race people, with the collaboration of the ancient Red Race people, are developing a worldwide civilization, with India as center, and many satellites on all continents, known as the Gian Ben Gian Alliance.

2-The Yellow Race nations grow actively, in isolation in China.

3-The White Race people having fled from the Nordic lands submerged by the flood are now surviving on the newly emerged lands of Northern Europe and dried lands from Poland to Ukraine. They are known as Ghiboreans, Keltoi, and Scythes.

4-Widely spread on Earth, a fourth "mysterious" race is an admixture of all other races with the Violet race, descendants of ADAM and EVE. Hebrew AM SEGULA literally means: the "violet people" figuratively means: the "liberated people", "free willed people". Modern Sapiens-Sapiens. They roam on Earth since 35,000 ago, along with other races.

IV-*9,150 to 8,750 years ago.* **The Kelts' peaceful migration**

-For 400 years, steady peaceful migration of Nordic Keltoi and Scythes, towards Crimean, Caspian, all Mediterranean settlements of the Gian Ben Gian. They are recorded as Kelt-Bodhones (Bedouin wandering Kelts).

-Later in time, about 5,500 years ago, some Keltic groups in Mesopotamia will be recorded as Akkadians (meaning "Unitatarians") living in harmonious symbiosis with Sumerians (means "Keepers of the Sum of Memories").

V-*8,750 to 5,500 years ago* **The Empire of Ram also known as the Empire of Kush.**

-This Empire is mentioned in Biblical Scriptures, in many Sacred texts in India, China and Iran. on Sumero-Akkadian tablets and reported on by ancient Egyptian Priests when speaking to Greek visitors.

-This Empire originated when a massive emigration of Male driven Nordic Kelts moved out of their lands to escape a certain death at the hands of domineering Druidesses sacrificing all male warriors.

-Ram (Rama) a Keltic High Priest-Savant formerly Initiated in the Temples-Universities of the Red and Black races, is taking the lead of this movement.

Identified as the Empire of the "Ram" (for strength) and of the "Lamb" (for peace) it will be organized into hierarchical communal societies for 3,500 years. It is perpetuated "in spirit" until today, thanks to Abram, Moses, Jesus and the Lamas in Asia, all connected to the "Ram" and the "Lamb", in one way or another.

VI-*5,500 to 4,900 years ago* **Social Upheavals and Wars, every-where: Wholeness and Unity are shattered.**

-*After 3,500 years* of social, scientific, spiritual evolution and law-ful peace among nations, tribes, clans, families and individuals, *Irshu*'s greed for personal power initiates a catastrophic interna-tional and social fragmentation.

This fragmentation within the unitarian principles involves the di-vide of all the indivisible polarities of life and the arbitrary prevalence of one polarity over the other. (Female-Male, Physical Nature-Hyperphysical Realms, etc.)

-The Wholeness of Universal hierarchical Principles is crushed, and personal arbitrary powers become pervasive all over Earth, destroying social constructs and internal, personal, cultural and national organic identities, all of them replaced by "political" identities.

-Naturalistic creeds are conjoined with Female predominance under the name of Ionian anarchical schism.

The wholeness of the "Universal promise" of humankind evolu-tion will be known as Dorian movement, or Orthodoxy.

VII-*5,250 to 4,250 years ago* **Great geniuses make great correc-tive reforms.**

-In time, many reformers will endeavor and succeed at eliminat-ing some of the harmful effects of the largest socio-cultural and spiritual divides ignited by *Irshu's* schism.

-*Christna*, 5,170 years ago, refocuses India on Spiritual and hy-pernatural Sciences.

-*Fo-Hi*, (4,970 years ago) with a large number of Initiates, travels from India and courageously takes necessary corrective measures in China.

-Later, *Zoroaster*, (4,470 years ago) in Iran, will preserve the balance and concordance of Natural and Hyperphysical Sciences.

-Under the impetus of these three great reformers, priests and scholars deem necessary to veil, the most "efficient" parts of Ram's Ancient Integral Science, and its potentially most "dangerous" applications.

-All fundamental aspects of the Ancient Science, physical and hyperphysical, natural and supernatural, are either concealed, encrypted in prediluvian languages, or presented under the appearance of symbols, metaphors, religious creeds and rituals.

VIII-*4,100 to 3,700 years ago* **Egypt is the living repository of Ram's Legacy**.

-Egypt (and its extensions in Africa, Europe and Mesopotamia) remain the stronghold protecting the Golden Thread of Ram's Orthodoxy and Universal Unity.

-It is the repository of the deepest memory of human history, including the sojourns on Earth of the "divine beings" who have presided over the physical and intellectual evolutions of the different Human Races, beginning one million years ago as "watchers", then 500,000 years as "tutors", and 50,000 years as "genetic enhancers".

-In Mesopotamia, the social milieu becomes unstable due to the warmongering of the personal arbitrary power of Ninus and Semiramis.

-Though, 3 major revival movements allow the historical thread to surface:

1-The Hammurabi dynasty based in Ur Kashdim, South of Babylon spreads all over the Middle East nations engraved steles promoting the legal codex reviving Ram's ancient Dorian legacy.

2- Na Ram-Sin creates the kingdom of Larsa, in the extreme south of the Tigris and Euphrates delta. The peoples of this kingdom will later emigrate to Anatolia, affecting the barbarian Hittites, then to Troy, from where their descendants, tutored by the Dorian Etruscans, will found Rome.

3-The Ramic Orthodox socio-religious movement of *Abram* emerges, moving first to Haran (South East of the Black Sea), then Kanaan, Salem and finally to Egypt.

IX-*Same period 4,100 to 3,700 years ago*. **Israel contracts a 400 years Alliance with the Orthodoxy of the Temples of Egypt, by Ab-Ram, Joseph, and Jacob-Israel.**

-The Orthodox Neo Ramid movement develops and vivifies itself by creating an alliance with Egypt, from the journey of Abram to Salem (meeting Melchizedek there), then to Thebes in Egypt (meeting the High Priests-Scientists, handing them the treasures of the Sumero Akkadian Ramid legacy), then Joseph (Io-seph) becomes a prominent minister of Egypt.

X-*3,700 to 3,350 years ago*. **Strengthening of Orthodoxy in most African Nations and all Mediterranean Societies**

-Long stay of the descendants of Jacob-Israel in Egypt, especially in the territory of Goshen (in the Pelusium branch of the Nile Delta).

3,450 years ago, two High Priests, Initiates at all levels of the Science of the Temple-University of Thebes, emerge: *Moses* and *Orpheus*. They undertake the mission to transmit the legacy of Ram, worldwide.

XI-*3,350 to 2,000 years ago*. **Orpheus and Moses.**

-*Orpheus* leaves Egypt with all his "Initiates-disciples" and settles in Thrace to overwhelm the Ionian dissent. He is the founder of the Greek culture and at the origin of a large network of sanctuaries, centers of Initiation to the Small and Great Mysteries, reuniting the Masculine and Feminine Universal Principles.

-*Moses* exits Egypt with 6,000,000 men and women, among them some carefully educated and prepared individuals.

These peoples are to settle as Israel and Judah, in the Land of Kanaan.

-This exodus will continue, from Kanaan, for several centuries in the four directions of the Earth, thus illustrating the "loss" of 10 of the 12 tribes of Israel.

-Ram's legacy alone, through the Orthodox Prophets, will preside over the Destiny of Israel and Judea. The golden thread of Ram's Orthodoxy will be broken when the "people" of Israel prefer the strong Power of a King over the sage Authority of the Judges, Prophets and the Assembly of Elders (in spite of the stark warnings of the Prophet Samuel).

XII-*2,000 years ago*. **Born in Bethlehem, Jesus is rising in Galilee.**

-The ancient Orthodoxy in Israel is enlivened and crowned by the incarnation of *Jehoshua, Jesus, the Christ*, the Redeemer. His actions, words, parables and resurrection initiate the worldwide bestowal of Judeo Christianity, clearly revealing the Golden Thread of the world history that eternally connects human peoples and the inhabitants of the heavenly kingdom.

-*Present time 2019 AD and onwards.*

-Today, the courageous holders of the *Golden Thread* must face and overcome the renascent schismatic divides: racial, religious, sexual, socio political, economic. Once victorious, they will resume unimpeded, their ascending journey, helped by the messengers and the celestial missionaries who always guide humans throughout the perpetual and metamorphic exodus leading toward the Divine finality which is their origin, their destiny and their destination.

By SIMHA SERAYA & ALBERT HALDANE, January 17, 2019

A Selection of Books Expanding on the Same Topic

Isha Schawaller de Lubicz

- Her-Bak: The Living Face of Ancient Egypt
- Her-Bak: Egyptian Initiate

Baird T. Spalding

- Life and Teaching of the Masters of the Far East

Antoine Fabre d'Olivet

- Hermeneutic Interpretation of the Origin of the Social State of Man and of the Destiny of the Adamic Race
- The Hebraic Tongue Restored: And the True Meaning of the Hebrew Words Re-Established and Proved by Their Radical Analysis

The Urantia Book

- The Urantia Book: Revealing the Mysteries of God, the Universe, World History, Jesus, and Ourselves

Simha Seraya & Albert Haldane

- The Sacred Ten: Moses'10 Commandments Deciphered
  Book 1 Quest for Immortality
  Book 2 Quantum Leap to Paradise
- Angel Signs - A Celestial Guide to The Powers of Your Own Guardian Angel

Plato, Socrates

- Timaeus
- Critias
- Cratylus

ABOUT THE TRANSLATORS-AUTHORS

SIMHA SERAYA, is a Graduate of Paris Sorbonne University, major in Psychology and Sociology. Fluent in English, French, Hebrew and Classical Arabic, she is also a long-time dedicated researcher and discoverer of the fundamental linguistic components and elements constitutive of all languages, ancient and modern. She lives, writes and paints in New York and South Florida.

Author of: Angel Signs (2002) The Sacred Ten, Moses Ten Commandments Decrypted (2011) The Golden Thread of World History (2019) Mission of the Jews – Translation (2019)

E-mail: archangel7997@gmail.com

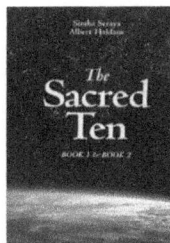

ALBERT HALDANE, is a published poet, author and philosopher. Continuing his classical education in ancient Greek and Latin, he graduated at Paris Sorbonne University, Master in Hellenistic and Renaissance Philosophy. Albert lives and writes in New York and South Florida.

Author of : Les Memoires du Future (1976) Alpha Song (1983) Angel Signs (2002) The Sacred Ten, Moses's Ten Commandments Decrypted (2011) The Golden Thread of World History (2019) Mission of the Jews – Translation (2019)

E-mail : archangel7997@gmail.com

*9 7 8 0 9 8 3 7 1 0 2 7 1 *